Middle School 3-1

중간고사 완벽대비

적중 100

영어 기출 문제집

중 **3**

금성 | 최인철

Best Collection

구성과 특징

교과서의 주요 학습 내용을 중심으로 학습 영역별 특성에 맞춰 단계별로 다양한 학습 기회를 제공하여
단원별 학습능력 평가는 물론 중간 및 기말고사 시험 등에 완벽하게 대비할 수 있도록 내용을 구성

Words & Expressions

Step1	Key Words 단원별 핵심 단어 설명 및 풀이 Key Expression 단원별 핵심 숙어 및 관용어 설명 Word Power 반대 또는 비슷한 뜻 단어 배우기 English Dictionary 영어로 배우는 영어 단어
Step2	실력평가 단원별 수시평가 대비 주관식, 객관식 문제풀이
Step3	서술형 대비 학업성취도 및 수행능력평가 대비 서술형 문제풀이

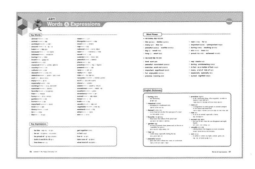

Conversation

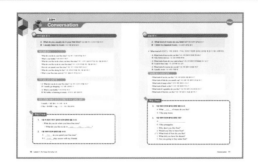

Step1	핵심 의사소통 소통에 필요한 주요 표현 방법 요약 핵심 Check 기본적인 표현 방법 및 활용능력 확인
Step2	대화문 익히기 교과서 대화문 심층 분석 및 확인
Step3	교과서 확인학습 빈칸 채우기를 통한 문장 완성 능력 확인
Step4	기본평가 시험대비 기초 학습 능력 평가
Step5	실력평가 단원별 수시평가 대비 주관식, 객관식 문제풀이
Step6	서술형 대비 학업성취도 및 수행능력평가 대비 서술형 문제풀이

Grammar

Step1	주요 문법 단원별 주요 문법 사항과 예문을 알기 쉽게 설명 핵심 Check 기본 문법사항에 대한 이해 여부 확인
Step2	기본평가 시험대비 기초 학습 능력 평가
Step3	실력평가 단원별 수시평가 대비 주관식, 객관식 문제풀이
Step4	서술형 대비 학업성취도 및 수행능력평가 대비 서술형 문제풀이

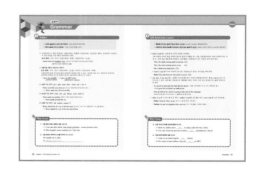

Reading

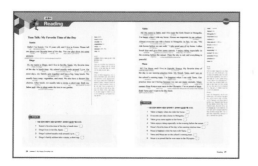

Step1	구문 분석 단원별로 제시된 문장에 대한 구문별 분석과 내용 설명 확인문제 문장에 대한 기본적인 이해와 인지능력 확인
Step2	확인학습A 빈칸 채우기를 통한 문장 완성 능력 확인
Step3	확인학습B 제시된 우리말을 영어로 완성하여 작문 능력 키우기
Step4	실력평가 단원별 수시평가 대비 주관식, 객관식 문제풀이
Step5	서술형 대비 학업성취도 및 수행능력평가 대비 서술형 문제풀이 교과서 구석구석 교과서에 나오는 기타 문장까지 완벽 학습

Composition

|영역별 핵심문제|

단어 및 어휘, 대화문, 문법, 독해 등 각 영역별 기출문제의
출제 유형을 분석하여 실전에 대비하고 연습할 수 있도록 문
제를 배열

|단원별 예상문제|

기출문제를 분석한 후 새로운 시험 출제 경향을 더하여 새롭
게 출제될 수 있는 문제를 포함하여 시험에 완벽하게 대비할
수 있도록 준비

|서술형 실전 및 창의사고력 문제|

학교 시험에서 점차 늘어나는 서술형 시험에 집중 대비하고
고득점을 취득하는데 만전을 기하기 위한 학습 코너

|단원별 모의고사|

영역별, 단계별 학습을 모두 마친 후 실전 연습을 위한
모의고사

교과서 파헤치기

- **단어Test1~3** 영어 단어 우리말 쓰기, 우리말을 영어 단어로 쓰기, 영영풀이에 해당하는 단어와 우리말 쓰기
- **대화문Test1~2** 대화문 빈칸 완성 및 전체 대화문 쓰기
- **본문Test1~5** 빈칸 완성, 우리말 쓰기, 문장 배열연습, 영어 작문하기 복습 등 단계별 반복 학습을 통해 교
  과서 지문에 대한 완벽한 습득
- **구석구석지문Test1~2** 지문 빈칸 완성 및 전문 영어로 쓰기

이책의 차례 **Contents**

Don't Judge a Book by Its Cover

🎤 의사소통 기능

- 동의나 이의 여부 묻기
  Don't you agree?
- 만족이나 불만족에 관해 묻기
  Are you satisfied with your group?

🎤 언어 형식

- 사역동사의 목적격보어 원형부정사
  Mrs. Choi would **let** me **change** my group.
- 동명사의 관용적 표현
  I **felt like crying** when I sat with my group members.

Words & Expressions

Key Words

- **advise**[ədváiz] 동 충고하다
- **agree**[əgrí] 동 동의하다
- **alone**[əlóun] 형 혼자 있는
- **anyway**[éniwèi] 부 어쨌든
- **board**[bɔːrd] 명 판, 칠판
- **boring**[bɔ́ːriŋ] 형 지루한
- **career**[kəríər] 명 직업, 이력
- **carefully**[kɛ́ərfəli] 부 조심스럽게
- **charge**[tʃɑːrdʒ] 명 요금, 책임
- **cheer**[tʃjər] 동 응원하다
- **classmate**[klǽsmeit] 명 학급 친구
- **concentrate**[kɑ́nsəntrèit] 동 집중하다
- **continue**[kəntínjuː] 동 계속하다
- **convince**[kənvíns] 동 납득시키다, 확신시키다
- **cover**[kʌ́vər] 명 덮개, (책이나 잡지의) 표지 동 다루다
- **culture**[kʌ́ltʃər] 명 문화
- **disagree**[dìsəgríː] 동 반대하다
- **edit**[édit] 동 편집하다
- **exciting**[iksáitiŋ] 형 흥미진진한
- **expert**[ékspəːrt] 명 전문가
- **grade**[greid] 명 성적
- **group**[gruːp] 명 집단
- **interest**[íntərəst] 명 관심
- **introduce**[ìntrədjús] 동 소개하다
- **judge**[dʒʌdʒ] 동 판단하다
- **look**[luk] 명 겉모습
- **lunch break** 점심시간
- **mean**[miːn] 동 의미하다
- **place**[pleis] 동 두다, 놓다
- **reason**[ríːzn] 명 이유
- **same**[seim] 형 같은
- **satisfied**[sǽtifàid] 형 만족한
- **scary**[skɛ́əri] 형 무서운
- **seem**[siːm] 동 ~인 것 같다
- **shy**[ʃai] 형 내성적인, 수줍어하는
- **soccer field** 축구장
- **strict**[strikt] 형 엄격한
- **surface**[sə́ːrfis] 명 표면
- **talkative**[tɔ́ːkətiv] 형 말이 많은
- **wonder**[wʌ́ndər] 동 궁금해 하다

Key Expressions

- **after a while** 잠시 뒤에
- **be in charge of ~** ~을 책임지다
- **be good at ~** ~을 잘하다
- **be over** 끝나다
- **check out** 확인하다
- **call out** 부르다
- **cannot help -ing** ~하지 않을 수 없다
- **come across** 우연히 마주치다, 우연히 찾아내다
- **do one's best** 최선을 다하다
- **feel like -ing** ~하고 싶은 기분이 들다
- **get to know** 알게 되다
- **go over** 검토하다
- **have ~ in common** ~을 공통으로 가지다
- **have one's nose in a book** 책벌레이다
- **judge a book by its cover** 겉모습으로 판단하다
- **make an announcement** 발표하다
- **turn into** ~으로 되다
- **too ~ to ...** 너무 ~해서 …할 수 없다
- **used to** ~하곤 했다
- **wish A the best of luck** A에게 행운을 빌다
- **Why not**? 왜 아니겠어?
- **worth -ing** ~할 가치가 있는

Word Power

※ 서로 비슷한 뜻을 가진 어휘
- [ ] **advise** 충고하다 – **consult** 충고하다
- [ ] **alone** 혼자 있는 – **isolate** 고립된
- [ ] **anyway** 어쨌든 – **anyhow** 어쨌든
- [ ] **boring** 지루한 – **dull** 지루한
- [ ] **career** 직업, 이력 – **job** 직업
- [ ] **cheer** 응원하다 – **encourage** 격려하다

- [ ] **concentrate** 집중하다 – **focus** 집중하다
- [ ] **continue** 계속하다 – **persist** 지속하다
- [ ] **exciting** 흥미진진한 – **interesting** 재미있는
- [ ] **reason** 이유 – **cause** 원인
- [ ] **expert** 전문가 – **specialist** 전문가
- [ ] **place** 두다, 놓다 – **put** 놓다

※ 서로 반대의 뜻을 가진 어휘
- [ ] **agree** 동의하다 ↔ **disagree** 반대하다
- [ ] **carefully** 조심스럽게 ↔ **carelessly** 부주의하게
- [ ] **exciting** 흥미진진한 ↔ **dull** 지루한
- [ ] **group** 집단 ↔ **individual** 개인
- [ ] **satisfied** 만족한 ↔ **dissatisfied** 불만족한

- [ ] **boring** 지루한 ↔ **exciting** 흥미진진한
- [ ] **cheer** 응원하다 ↔ **discourage** 낙심시키다
- [ ] **expert** 전문가 ↔ **amateur** 아마추어
- [ ] **reason** 이유 ↔ **result** 결과
- [ ] **shy** 내성적인 ↔ **outgoing** 외향적인

※ 동사 – 명사
- [ ] **advise** 충고하다 – **advice** 충고
- [ ] **concentrate** 집중하다 – **concentration** 집중

- [ ] **agree** 동의하다 – **agreement** 동의, 일치
- [ ] **convince** 확신시키다 – **conviction** 확신

English Dictionary

- [ ] **advise** 충고하다
  → to tell someone what you think they should do, especially when you know more than they do about something
  어떤 것에 대해 더 많이 알 때 다른 사람에게 무엇을 해야 할지 말해주다
- [ ] **agree** 동의하다
  → to have or express the same opinion about something as someone else
  무엇인가에 대해 다른 사람과 같은 의견을 가지거나 표현하다
- [ ] **alone** 혼자 있는
  → without any friends or people you know
  친구나 아는 사람이 없는
- [ ] **boring** 지루한
  → not interesting in any way
  조금도 재미가 없는
- [ ] **career** 직업, 이력
  → a job or profession that you have been trained for, and which you do for a long period of your life
  훈련을 받고, 생애의 오랜 기간 동안 해 온 일이나 직업
- [ ] **concentrate** 집중하다
  → to think very carefully about something that you are doing
  하고 있는 일에 대해 매우 신중하게 생각하다
- [ ] **convince** 확신시키다
  → to make someone feel certain that something is true
  어떤 것이 사실이라고 느끼도록 만들다
- [ ] **disagree** 반대하다
  → to have or express a different opinion from someone else
  어떤 다른 사람과 다른 의견을 가지거나 표현하다
- [ ] **introduce** 소개하다
  → tell them each other's names for the first time
  처음으로 서로의 이름을 말하다

[01~02] 다음 짝지어진 단어의 관계가 같도록 빈칸에 알맞은 단어를 고르시오.

01

| boring : dull = _____ : reason |

① advise
② career
③ crowd
④ cause
⑤ cheer

02 중요

| carefully : carelessly = _____ : strict |

① generous
② shy
③ cultural
④ convinced
⑤ considerate

03 다음 영영풀이에 해당하는 단어를 고르시오.

| to tell someone what you think they should do, especially when you know more than they do about something |

① destroy
② advise
③ take
④ agree
⑤ convince

04 중요 다음 대화의 빈칸에 들어갈 말로 적절한 것을 고르시오.

G: I think history is an interesting subject. Don't you agree?
B: I'm afraid I don't _____ with you. It's too hard for me.

① argue
② mean
③ place
④ know
⑤ agree

05 다음 문장의 빈칸에 들어가기에 가장 적절한 것은?

| Have you heard the phrase, "Never judge _____ by its cover"? |

① a car
② a house
③ a pot
④ a friend
⑤ a book

06 다음 중 밑줄 친 부분의 뜻풀이가 바르지 <u>않은</u> 것은?

① Don't you <u>agree</u> with me? (동의하다)
② She <u>won</u> first place in the contest. (수상했다)
③ I'm not happy with my <u>grade</u>. (학년)
④ I'm <u>satisfied</u> with the result. (만족하는)
⑤ He is fun and <u>talkative</u>. (수다스러운)

07 중요 다음 중 〈보기〉에 있는 단어를 사용하여 자연스러운 문장을 만들 수 <u>없는</u> 것은?

┤ 보기 ├
| expert create charge help |

① The project is to _____ a newspaper in groups.
② Lina will _____ Japanese culture.
③ Lina is an _____ on Japanese culture.
④ Jisu was in _____ of editing the whole newspaper.
⑤ I couldn't _____ thinking how unlucky I was.

01 다음 문장의 빈칸에 들어가기에 적절한 단어를 주어진 철자로 시작하여 쓰시오.

> Mrs. Choi, my social studies teacher, made an important _____.
> "You will create a newspaper in groups. Check out your new group members."

➡ a_____

02 다음 영영풀이에 해당하는 단어를 쓰시오. (주어진 철자로 시작할 것)

> to have or express the same opinion about something as someone else

➡ a_____

03 다음 대화의 빈칸에 들어가기에 적절한 단어를 주어진 철자로 시작하여 쓰시오.

> Ryan: Are you satisfied with your group?
> Jisu: Actually, I'm not. They seem so different from me. Don't you agree?
> Ryan: Well, on the surface they may seem different from you. But don't judge a book by its _____.
> Jisu: What do you mean by that?
> Ryan: I mean that you shouldn't judge people by their looks.

➡ c_____

04 다음 짝지어진 단어의 관계가 같도록 빈칸에 알맞은 단어를 쓰시오. (주어진 철자로 시작할 것)

> boring : dull = career : j_____

05 다음 우리말에 맞게 빈칸에 알맞은 말을 쓰시오. (주어진 철자가 있는 경우에는 주어진 철자로 시작할 것)

(1) 잠시 후에 내 이름이 불렸다.
➡ After a _____, my name was called.
(2) 나는 학급 친구들이 경기할 때 응원했다.
➡ I c_____ as my classmates played the games.
(3) 나는 최 선생님께 내가 친구들과 함께해야 한다고 확신을 심어 주었다.
➡ I c_____ Mrs. Choi that I should be with my friends.
(4) 나는 동아리 구성원들을 주의 깊게 살펴보았다.
➡ I c_____ watched my group members.

06 아래 문장의 빈칸에 다음 〈보기〉에 있는 단어를 넣어 자연스러운 문장을 만드시오.

> ┌ 보기 ┐
> came shy worth concentrate

(1) Don't you think it's _____ trying?
(2) I was too _____ to talk to anyone.
(3) It's harder to _____ when you sit at the back.
(4) I _____ across some amazing facts about them.

Conversation

1 동의나 이의 여부 묻기

Don't you agree? 동의하지 않으세요?

- 상대방에게 자신의 말에 대하여 동의를 구할 때 간단하게는 부가의문문을 덧붙여서 나타낼 수 있지만, 구체적인 영어 표현으로 'Don't you agree (with me)?'가 있다. '(제 생각에) 동의하지 않으세요?'의 의미로 'Don't you think so?'라고 할 수도 있다.

- 상대의 말에 동의할 때는 Yes/No의 응답을 할 수 있지만 좀 더 구체적으로 'I agree.' 'I don't agree.' 등을 사용할 수 있다. 동의하지 않는 것을 더 공손하게 표현할 때 'I'm afraid.'를 덧붙여 말할 수도 있다.

동의나 이의 여부 말하기

〈동의를 나타내는 표현〉
- I agree. 동의해
- Same here. 나도 마찬가지야.
- Me, too. 나도 마찬가지야.
- That's a neat/good/great idea. 좋은 생각이야.

〈이의를 제기하는 표현〉
- I don't agree. 저는 동의하지 않아요.
- I don't believe so. 그렇게 생각하지 않습니다.
- I don't think so. 그렇게 생각하지 않아요.
- I disagree with you. 저는 반대합니다.

핵심 Check

1. 다음 우리말과 일치하도록 빈칸에 알맞은 말을 쓰시오.

   > G: I think history is an interesting subject. Don't you _____?
   > 역사는 재미있는 과목이라고 생각해. 동의하지 않니?
   >
   > B: I'm _____ I don't agree with you. It's too hard for me.
   > 유감스럽게도 나는 네 의견에 동의하지 않아.
   >
   > G: Reading history comic books may make it easier.

2. 다음 주어진 대화를 적절한 순서로 배열하시오.

   > M: I'm too ugly and scary. Don't you think so?
   > (A) Of course, I'm happy with you.
   > (B) I don't think so. I think you are kind and sweet.
   > (C) Are you happy with me?
   >
   > ➡ _____

2 만족이나 불만족에 관하여 묻기

Are you satisfied with your group? 너는 네가 속한 모둠에 만족하니?

■ 상대방에게 '~에 만족하니?'의 의미로 'Are you happy with ~?' 'Are you satisfied with ~?'라고 물어볼 수 있다. '너는 ~가 어떠니?'라는 뜻으로 'How do you like ~?'라고 할 수도 있다.
  • Are you satisfied with your grade? 너는 너의 성적에 만족하니?
  • Are you happy with your group? 너는 너의 모둠에 만족하니?
  • How do you like your group? 너는 너의 모둠을 어떻게 생각하니?

■ 만족이나 불만족을 묻는 표현에 대한 대답은 'I'm satisfied with ~.', 'I'm happy with ~.'와 같이 '~에 만족한다.'에 해당하는 표현을 사용한다.

만족이나 불만족에 관하여 묻고 답하기

〈만족이나 불만족에 관해 묻는 표현〉
  • Are you satisfied with ~? ~에 만족하니?
  • How do you like ~? ~을 어떻게 생각하니?
  • Are you happy with ~? ~에 만족하니?
  • How do you find ~? ~을 어떻게 생각하니?

〈만족이나 불만족 물음에 답하는 표현〉
  • Yes, I am. I like it. 네, 좋아합니다.
  • It is/was really nice. 정말로 좋아요.
  • No, I'm not. I don't like it. 아뇨, 좋아하지 않아요.
  • Yes, I do. / No, I don't.

핵심 Check

3. 다음 우리말과 일치하도록 빈칸에 알맞은 말을 쓰시오.

> B: Are you _____ with your new partner? 너는 새로운 짝에 만족하니?
> G: Yes, I am.
> B: What do you like about him?
> G: He is fun and talkative.

4. 다음 주어진 문장을 자연스러운 대화가 되도록 배열하시오.

> B: Are you happy with your math teacher?
> (A) But his classes are easy to understand.
> (B) That's true, but he's sometimes too strict.
> (C) No, I'm not.

➡ _____

 Everyday English 1 – B

> G: What are you looking at?
> B: I'm looking at the school basketball game poster.
> G: Hmm... ❶Who do you think is the best basketball player in our school?
> B: I think Jihun is the best. Don't you agree?
> G: No, I don't agree. I think Minjae is the best player.
> B: Why do you think so?
> G: His class won the basketball game last year. Don't you remember?
> B: But ❷that was because Minjae's class had a lot of good basketball players.
> G: Anyway, we are lucky to have both of them in our class this year.
> B: Yes, we are. I think our class is going to win the basketball game this year.

G: 무엇을 보고 있니?
B: 학교 농구 경기 포스터를 보고 있어.
G: 음… 너는 우리 학교에서 누가 최고의 농구 선수라고 생각하니?
B: 나는 지훈이가 최고라고 생각해. 동의하지 않니?
G: 아니, 동의하지 않아. 나는 민재가 최고의 선수라고 생각해.
B: 왜 그렇게 생각해?
G: 그의 학급은 작년 농구 경기에서 우승했어. 기억 안 나니?
B: 그렇지만 그것은 민재네 반에 좋은 농구 선수들이 많았기 때문이었어.
G: 어쨌든, 우리는 올해 둘 다 우리 반에 있어서 다행이야.
B: 맞아. 나는 우리 반이 올해는 농구 경기에서 우승할 거라고 생각해.

❶ 'do you think'와 함께 쓰이는 의문사가 있는 간접의문문은 의문사를 문장의 앞에 써야 한다.
❷ 'that was because'는 앞에 소개한 사실에 대한 이유를 부연 설명하는 말이다.

Check(√) True or False

(1) Minjae and Jihun were both in the same class last year.   T ☐ F ☐

(2) The girl thinks Minjae is the best player in the school.   T ☐ F ☐

 Everyday English 2 – B

> *(Phone rings.)*
> G: Hello?
> B: Hi, Bora! It's me, Minsu!
> G: Minsu! Are you calling from France?
> B: Yes, I am.
> G: ❶How do you like your life in France?
> B: France is such a beautiful country, but I miss Korea.
> G: Are you happy with your new school?
> B: ❷Not so much. Everything is so different from Korea, so it's not easy for me.
> G: Do your classmates help you?
> B: Some of them do help me. They are really nice.
> G: Good for you. I wish you the best of luck.
> B: Thanks.

(전화벨이 울린다.)

G: 여보세요?
B: 안녕, 보라야! 나야, 민수!
G: 민수! 프랑스에서 전화하는 거니?
B: 응, 그래.
G: 프랑스에서의 생활은 어떠니?
B: 프랑스는 아주 아름다운 나라야. 그렇지만 한국이 그리워.
G: 새로운 학교는 마음에 드니?
B: 별로야. 모든 것이 한국과 너무 달라. 그래서 나에게는 쉽지 않아.
G: 네 학급 친구들은 너를 도와주니?
B: 그들 중 몇몇은 나를 도와줘. 그들은 정말 친절해.
G: 잘됐네. 너에게 행운을 빌어.
B: 고마워.

❶ 'How do you like ～?'는 '～는 어떠니?'라고 만족하는지를 물어보는 표현이다.
❷ 'Not so much.'는 '별로야.'라는 뜻이다.

Check(√) True or False

(3) Minsu is now in France.   T ☐ F ☐

(4) Minsu is happy with his new school.   T ☐ F ☐

Everyday English 1 A-1

G: I think history is an interesting subject. ❶ Don't you agree?

B: ❷I'm afraid I don't agree with you. It's too hard for me.

G: Reading history comic books may make it easier.

B: I think it would just be boring for me.

❶ Don't you agree?'는 'Don't you think so?'라고 할 수 있다.
❷ 'I'm afraid~'는 상대의 의견에 동의하지 않을 때 쓰는 말이다.

 Everyday English 1 A-2

G: I think soccer is the most popular sport in our class. Don't you agree?

B: ❶I agree. Many students play soccer during the lunch break.

G: And many students watch the soccer games at home, too.

B: You're right.

❶ 동의하는 의미의 'I agree.'는 'I think so.', 'Me, too.'라고 할 수 있다.

 Everyday English 2 A-1

B: ❶Are you satisfied with your new partner?

G: Yes, I am.

B: ❷What do you like about him?

G: He is fun and talkative.

❶ 'Are you satisfied with ~?'는 만족 여부를 묻는 말로 'Are you happy with ~?'라고 할 수도 있다.
❷ '그 사람의 무엇이 좋으니?'라는 의미로 상대방이 좋아하는 구체적인 면을 묻고 있다.

 Everyday English 2 A-2

B: ❶Are you happy with your math teacher?

G: ❷No, I'm not.

B: But his classes are easy to understand.

G: That's true, but he's sometimes too strict.

❶ 'Are you happy with your math teacher?'는 'Are you satisfied with your math teacher?'와 같은 의미이다.
❷ 상대의 질문한 만족하는 지의 여부에 대하여 만족하지 않는다는 의미의 대답이다.

 In Real Life

Ryan: Hey Jisu, who are your group members for the social studies project?

Jisu: Hi, Ryan. My group members are Lina, Inho, and Min.

Ryan: Are you satisfied with your group?

Jisu: Actually, I'm not. They seem so different from me. Don't you agree?

Ryan: Well, ❶on the surface they may seem different from you. But ❷don't judge a book by its cover.

Jisu: What do you mean by that?

Ryan: I mean that you shouldn't judge people by their looks. You may like your group members when you get to know them.

Jisu: Do you really think I can be friends with them?

Ryan: ❸Why not? There could be something special about them. Try to understand your group members first.

❶ 'on the surface'는 '표면적으로'라는 뜻이다.
❷ 'Don't judge a book by its cover.'는 '겉모습만으로는 판단하지 마라.'에 해당하는 관용어이다.
❸ 'Why not?'은 '왜 아니겠어?'라는 의미이다.

 Check Your Progress 1

B: Are you happy with your new seat?

G: No, I'm not. My seat is at the back of the classroom.

B: Why don't you want to sit at the back?

G: ❶It's harder to concentrate when you sit at the back. Don't you agree?

B: That's true, but I like sitting at the back.

G: Why?

B: When I sit at the front, ❷those who sit behind me can't see the board because I am too tall.

G: Oh, I understand.

❶ 'It is ... to ~'는 가주어, 진주어 구문이다.
❷ 'those who ~'는 '~하는 사람들'이라는 의미이다.

● 다음 우리말과 일치하도록 빈칸에 알맞은 말을 쓰시오.

Everyday English 1 A-2

G: I think _____ is an _____ subject. _____ you _____?

B: I'm _____ I don't _____ with you. It's _____ _____ for me.

G: _____ history _____ _____ may _____ it easier.

B: I think it _____ _____ be _____ for me.

Everyday English 1 A-2

G: I _____ soccer is the most _____ _____ in our class. _____ you _____?

B: I agree. Many students _____ _____ _____ the lunch break.

G: And many students _____ the soccer _____ at home, too.

B: You're right.

Everyday English 1 B

G: What are you _____ at?

B: I'm looking _____ the school _____ game _____.

G: Hmm... Who _____ _____ _____ is the _____ basketball _____ in our school?

B: I _____ Jihun is the best. _____ you _____?

G: No, I don't _____. I _____ Minjae is the _____ player.

B: _____ do you _____ _____?

G: His _____ _____ the basketball game last year. _____ you _____?

B: But that was _____ Minjae's _____ had a lot of _____ basketball _____.

G: _____, we are _____ to have _____ _____ _____ in our class this year.

B: Yes, we are. I think our _____ is going to _____ the basketball game _____ _____.

Everyday English 2 A-2

B: Are you _____ _____ your new partner?

G: Yes, I am.

B: _____ do you _____ about him?

G: He is _____ and _____.

Everyday English 2 B

(Phone rings.)

G: Hello?

B: Hi, Bora! _____ me, Minsu!

G: Minsu! _____ you _____ _____ France?

B: Yes, I am.

G: _____ do you _____ your _____ in France?

B: France is _____ _____ _____ country, but I miss Korea.

G: Are you _____ _____ your new school?

B: _____ _____ much. Everything is _____ _____ from Korea, so it's not _____ for me.

G: Do your _____ _____ you?

B: Some of them do _____ me. They are _____ _____.

G: Good for you. I _____ you the _____ of luck.

B: Thanks.

In Real Life

Ryan: Hey Jisu, _____ are your _____ _____ for the _____ studies project?

Jisu: Hi, Ryan. My group _____ are Lina, Inho, and Min.

Ryan: Are you _____ _____ your group?

Jisu: _____, I'm not. They _____ so _____ from me. Don't you agree?

Ryan: Well, _____ the _____ they may _____ _____ from you. But don't _____ a book _____ its _____.

Jisu: What do you _____ _____ that?

Ryan: I _____ that you _____ _____ people by their _____. You may _____ your group members when you _____ _____ _____ them.

Jisu: Do you _____ _____ I can be _____ _____ them?

Ryan: Why _____? There could be something _____ about them. _____ to _____ your group members first.

B: 너는 새로운 짝에 만족하니?

G: 응, 그래.

B: 그에 대해서 뭐가 좋아?

G: 그는 재미있고 말하기를 좋아해.

(전화벨이 울린다.)

G: 여보세요?

B: 안녕, 보라야! 나야, 민수!

G: 민수! 프랑스에서 전화하는 거니?

B: 응, 그래.

G: 프랑스에서의 생활은 어떠니?

B: 프랑스는 아주 아름다운 나라야, 그렇지만 한국이 그리워.

G: 새로운 학교는 마음에 드니?

B: 별로야. 모든 것이 한국과 너무 달라. 그래서 나에게는 쉽지 않아.

G: 네 학급 친구들은 너를 도와주니?

B: 그들 중 몇몇은 나를 도와줘. 그들은 정말 친절해.

G: 잘됐네. 너에게 행운을 빌어.

B: 고마워.

Ryan: 안녕, 지수야, 너의 사회 과제의 모둠 멤버가 누구니?

Jisu: 안녕, Ryan. 나의 모둠 구성원은 Lina, 인호, Min이야.

Ryan: 너는 너의 모둠에 만족하니?

Jisu: 사실은 아니야. 그들은 나와 너무 달라 보여. 동의하지 않니?

Ryan: 글쎄. 표면적으로는 그들은 너와 달라 보일지도 몰라. 하지만 표지만 보고 책을 판단하지 마.

Jisu: 그게 무슨 뜻이야?

Ryan: 내 말은 네가 사람을 겉모습으로 판단해서는 안 된다는 거야. 너는 너의 모둠 구성원들을 알게 되면 그들을 좋아할지도 모르잖아.

Jisu: 너는 정말로 내가 그들과 친구가 될 수 있다고 생각하니?

Ryan: 왜 안 되겠니? 그들에게는 특별한 것이 있을 수 있어. 먼저 너의 모둠 구성원들을 이해하려고 노력해 봐.

Conversation 시험대비 기본평가

[01~02] 다음 대화의 빈칸에 들어갈 말을 고르시오.

01

G: I think history is an interesting subject. Don't you agree?
B: I'm afraid I don't agree with you. It's too _____ for me.
G: Reading history comic books may make it easier.
B: I think it would just be boring for me.

① hard   ② interesting   ③ exciting

④ easy   ⑤ important

02

M: I'm too ugly and scary. Don't you think so?
W: I don't think so. I think you are kind and sweet.
M: Are you happy with me?
W: _____, I'm happy with you.

① No, not at all   ② So do I
③ You're welcome   ④ Of course
⑤ Don't mention it

[03~04] 다음 대화를 읽고 물음에 답하시오.

A: Were you (A)satisfy with sports day?
B: Yes, I was. I was able to make new friends on that day.
C: _____(B)_____ I think it was a great activity.
A: I think so too.

03 밑줄 친 (A)satisfy를 알맞은 형태로 고치시오.

➡ _____

04 빈칸 (B)에 들어갈 알맞은 말을 고르시오.

① Me too.   ② I don't know.   ③ Never mind.
④ Neither am I.   ⑤ How nice!

01 다음 대화의 빈칸에 들어갈 말을 고르시오.

> A: Hi, Bora, what are you doing?
> B: I was going over my report card.
> A: Are you _____ with your grades?
> B: Yes, I am. I got a good grade on my group project.

① scary   ② satisfied

③ worried   ④ convinced

⑤ sorry

02 다음 빈칸에 들어갈 말이 바르게 짝지어진 것은?

> B: Are you (A)_____ with your new partner?
> G: Yes, I am.
> B: (B)_____ do you like about him?
> G: He is fun and talkative.

	(A)	(B)
①	satisfied	When
②	happy	Which
③	relieved	Why
④	worried	How
⑤	satisfied	What

03 다음 대화의 빈칸에 들어갈 말을 고르시오.

> B: Are you happy with your new seat?
> G: No, I'm not. My seat is at the back of the classroom.
> B: Why don't you want to sit at the back?
> G: It's harder to concentrate when you sit at the back. Don't you agree?
> B: _____, but I like sitting at the back.

> G: Why?
> B: When I sit at the front, those who sit behind me can't see the board because I am too tall.

① That's true   ② It's difficult

③ I don't know   ④ Neither do I

⑤ I'm worried

서답형

04 다음 대화의 빈칸에 들어갈 말을 〈보기〉에서 골라 순서대로 배열하시오.

> G: What are you looking at?
> B: _____
> G: Hmm... Who do you think is the best basketball player in our school?
> B: _____
> A: No, I don't agree. I think Minjae is the best player.
> B: _____ .
> G: His class won the basketball game last year. Don't you remember?
> B: But that was because Minjae's class had a lot of good basketball players.
> G: _____
> B: Yes, we are. I think our class is going to win the basketball game this year.

> ┤ 보기 ├
> (A) Why do you think so?
> (B) I'm looking at the school basketball game poster.
> (C) Anyway, we are lucky to have both of them in our class this year.
> (D) I think Jihun is the best. Don't you agree?

➡ _____

[05~08] 다음 대화를 읽고 물음에 답하시오.

Ryan: Hey Jisu, who are your group members for the social studies project?

Jisu: Hi, Ryan. My group members are Lina, Inho, and Min.

Ryan: Are you (A)satisfied with your group?

Jisu: Actually, I'm not. They seem so different from me. Don't you agree?

Ryan: Well, on the surface they may seem different from you. (B)But don't judge a book by its cover.

Jisu: What do you mean (C)_____ that?

Ryan: I mean that you shouldn't judge people by their looks. You may like your group members when you get to know them.

Jisu: Do you really think I can be friends with them?

Ryan: Why not? There could be something special about them. Try to understand your group members first.

05 다음 중 밑줄 친 (A)와 바꿔 쓸 수 있는 것을 고르시오.

① sorry   ② happy
③ worried   ④ relieved
⑤ relaxed

서답형

06 위 대화에서 밑줄 친 (B)와 같은 의미로 쓰인 말을 한 문장으로 찾아 쓰시오.

➡ _____

07 빈칸 (C)에 들어갈 전치사는?

① for   ② in   ③ at   ④ for   ⑤ by

08 Which one of the following is NOT true according to the dialogue above.

① Jisu isn't satisfied with her group members.

② Ryan has a different idea than Jisu's idea.

③ Ryan wants Jisu to think again about her group members.

④ Ryan thinks that Jisu can be friends with her group members.

⑤ Jisu won't try to understand her group members.

[09~10] 다음 대화를 읽고 물음에 답하시오.

Tim: Were you satisfied with sports day?

Jack: Yes, I was. I was able to make new friends on that day.

Jane: (A)Me too. I think it was a great activity.

Tim: I think so too.

09 다음 중 밑줄 친 (A) 대신 쓸 수 있는 것은?

① You can't say that again.
② Neither was I.
③ Me, neither.
④ I agree.
⑤ I don't think so.

10 Which one of the following is TRUE according to the dialogue above?

① They are talking about sports day they will have.

② Tim wasn't satisfied with sports day.

③ Jack will make friends on sports day.

④ Jane is expecting sports day to be a great activity.

⑤ Tim thinks sports day was great.

[01~03] 다음 대화를 읽고 물음에 답하시오.

G: Hello?
B: Hi, Bora! ⓐIt's me, Minsu!
G: Minsu! Are you calling from France?
B: Yes, I am.
G: (A)너의 프랑스에서의 생활은 어떠니? (how, in)
B: France is such a beautiful country, but I ⓑ miss Korea.
G: Are you happy with your new school?
B: ⓒNot so much. Everything is so (B)_____ from Korea, so it's not easy for me.
G: Do your classmates help you?
B: Some of them do help me. They are ⓓ really rude.
G: Good for you. I ⓔwish you the best of luck.
B: Thanks.

01 (A)의 우리말에 어울리는 영어 문장을 주어진 단어를 넣어 완성하시오. (8 words)

➡ _____

02 빈칸 (B)에 알맞은 단어를 쓰시오.

➡ (B) _____

03 ⓐ~ⓔ 중에서 대화의 흐름상 어색한 것을 찾아 쓰고 적절한 것으로 바꾸어 쓰시오.

➡ _____

04 다음 대화의 빈칸에 들어가기에 적절한 단어를 쓰시오. (주어진 철자로 시작할 것)

G: I think history is an interesting subject. Don't you agree?
B: I'm _____ I don't agree with you. It's too hard for me.
G: Reading history comic books may make it easier.
B: I think it would just be boring for me.

➡ a_____

[05~06] 다음 대화를 읽고 물음에 답하시오.

Jisu: My group members are Lina, Inho, and Min.
Ryan: (A)너는 너의 모둠에 만족하니?
Jisu: Actually, I'm not. They seem so different from me. Don't you agree?
Ryan: Well, on (B)[they / different / the surface / may / you / seem / from]. But don't judge a book by its cover.

05 밑줄 친 (A)의 우리말을 영어로 쓰시오.

➡ _____

06 괄호 (B)에 주어진 어구를 적절하게 배열하시오.

➡ _____

Grammar

1 사역동사의 목적격보다 원형부정사

> • Mrs. Choi would **let** me **change** my group members.
> 최 선생님은 나에게 모둠원을 바꾸도록 해 주실 거야.
> • Dad **made** me **write** the diary. 아빠가 나에게 일기를 쓰도록 하셨다.
> • She **had** me **wash** the dishes. 그녀가 나에게 설거지 하도록 시켰다.

■ 사역동사는 '강제, 명령, 허락' 등의 의미를 나타내며, 'make, have, let' 등이 있다.

- Mom **made** me **do** my homework. 엄마는 나에게 숙제를 하라고 시켰다.
- Mrs. Smith **had** his son **wash** the dishes. Mrs. Smith는 그의 아들에게 설거지 하도록 시켰다.
- He **let** me **know** the truth. 그는 나에게 사실을 알려 주었다.

■ 5형식 문장(주어+동사+목적어+목적격보어)에서 사용되며, 목적격 보어로 원형부정사(동사원형)를 사용하며 '~하게 하다' 또는 '시키다'의 의미로 해석한다.

- This music **makes** me **feel** relaxed. 이 음악은 내가 편안하게 느끼도록 만들어 준다.
- I **had** the mechanic **repair** my bike. 나는 기술자가 내 자전거를 수리하도록 시켰다.
  * 준사역동사 help+목적어+목적격보어(원형부정사 또는 to부정사)
- He **helped** his mom **find[to find]** her car key. 그는 그의 엄마가 그녀의 자동차 열쇠를 찾도록 도왔다.
  * get+목적어+목적격보어(to+동사원형)
- I **got** him **to fix** my car. 나는 그가 내 차를 수리하게 했다.

■ 사역동사 뒤에 목적어와 목적격보어 관계가 능동일 때는 목적격보어에 원형부정사를 쓰며 수동일 때는 과거분사를 사용한다.

- I will **have** her **cut** my hair. 나는 그녀에게 나의 머리카락을 자르게 할 것이다. (능동)
- The teacher **makes** me **study** happily. 그 선생님은 내가 행복하게 공부하게 한다. (능동)
- Please **let** us **love** each other. 우리가 서로 사랑하게 해 주세요. (능동)
- I **had** my hair **cut**. 나는 머리를 잘랐다. (수동)
- She **had** her watch **stolen** a few weeks ago. 그녀는 몇 주 전에 시계를 도둑맞았다. (수동)
- You have to **get** it **finished** by seven in the evening. 너는 그것을 저녁 7시까지 끝내도록 해야 한다. (수동)
- We **get** our groceries **delivered**. 우리는 우리의 식료품을 배달시켰다. (수동)
  * let의 경우 수동의 관계일 때 '목적어+be+과거분사'를 쓴다.
- Jenny **let** the computer **be repaired**. Jenny는 컴퓨터를 수리 받았다.

핵심 Check

1. 괄호 안에서 알맞은 단어를 고르시오.

   (1) My parents will never let me (to go / go) to the party.

   (2) I will make my sister (do / to do) the dishes.

   (3) My English teacher had us (read / reading) many English books.

❷ 동명사의 관용적 표현

> • I **felt like crying** when I sat with my group members. 나는 그룹 멤버들과 앉았을 때 울고 싶었다.
> • Don't you think it**'s worth trying**? 그것은 시도해 볼 가치가 있지 않니?

■ 동명사와 함께 쓰이는 관용적인 표현들이 있다.
   (1) feel like -ing: ~하고 싶다
   • I **feel like** go**ing** on a trip. 나는 여행을 가고 싶다.
   (2) be worth -ing: ~할 가치가 있다
   • I think the audition **was worth** try**ing**. 나는 그 오디션은 볼 만할 가치가 있었다고 생각한다.
   (3) can't[couldn't] help -ing: ~하지 않을 수 없다[없었다] (= can't[couldn't] help but 동사원형)
   • I **couldn't help** feel**ing** sorry for him. 나는 그가 안쓰럽다고 느끼지 않을 수 없었다.
     = I **couldn't help but feel** sorry for him.
   • I **couldn't help** shar**ing** the chocolate with my brother. 나는 초콜릿을 내 남동생과 나누지 않을 수 없었다.
     = I **couldn't help but share** the chocolate with my brother.

■ 기타 동명사의 관용 표현
'look forward to -ing: ~하는 것을 고대하다[기대하다].', 'be busy -ing: ~하느라 바쁘다', 'be used to -ing: ~하는 데 익숙하다', 'spend+시간/돈+-ing: ~하는 데 (시간/돈)을 소비하다', 'It's no use -ing: ~해 봐야 소용없다', 'have trouble -ing', 'have difficulty -ing: ~하는 데 어려움이 있다', 'in -ing: ~할 때', 'on -ing: ~ 하자마자', 'need -ing: ~할 필요가 있다' 등
   • We're **looking forward to** hav**ing** a tea with you. 우리는 너와 차 마시기를 기대하고 있다.
   • They **are busy** mak**ing** plans for the work. 그들은 업무 계획을 짜느라 바쁘다.
   • She **is used to** study**ing** at night. 그녀는 밤에 공부하는 것에 익숙하다.
   • He s**pent three hours** play**ing** computer games. 그는 컴퓨터 게임을 하느라 세 시간을 썼다.
   • **It is no use** cry**ing** over spilt milk. 우유를 쏟고 울어봐야 소용없다.
   • I **have trouble** talk**ing** with him. 나는 그와 대화하는 것이 어렵다.
   • You may **have difficulty** do**ing** so. 그렇게 하는 데 어려움이 있을지도 몰라.
   • **In** try**ing** to protect the child, she put her own life in danger. 그 아이를 보호하려 애쓰다가, 그녀는 자신의 생명을 위험에 처하게 했다.
   • What was his reaction **on** see**ing** her? 그녀를 만나자마자 그의 반응은 어땠니?
   • Your house **needs** paint**ing**. 너의 집은 칠을 할 필요가 있다.
     = Your house **wants** paint**ing**. = Your house **needs**[**wants**] **to be** paint**ed**.

핵심 Check

2. 괄호 안에서 알맞은 단어를 고르시오.

   (1) I feel like (to go / going) for a walk tomorrow morning.

   (2) That book (is worth to buy / is worth buying).

   (3) I (couldn't help telling / couldn't help to tell) her the truth.

   (4) She spends too much time (watch / watching) TV.

01 다음 문장에서 어법상 <u>어색한</u> 부분을 바르게 고쳐 쓰시오.

(1) Her speech was worth listen to.

_____ ➡ _____

(2) She made her baby stopped crying.

_____ ➡ _____

(3) People couldn't help laugh at the dancing.

_____ ➡ _____

(4) My mother didn't let me to go traveling.

_____ ➡ _____

(5) My mom had the roof repair.

_____ ➡ _____

(6) All the students needs to get their homework do by tomorrow.

_____ ➡ _____

02 다음 중 어법상 바르지 <u>않은</u> 것은?

① She felt like eat cheese cake.
② The boy's glasses made him look smart.
③ These expensive jeans were worth buying.
④ He might not let him go.
⑤ I couldn't help looking at the boy.

03 다음 대화의 밑줄 친 부분 중에서 어법상 <u>잘못된</u> 곳을 고르시오.

> A: ①<u>Why</u> are you ②<u>doing</u> it?
> B: My father ③<u>makes</u> me ④<u>to do</u> ⑤<u>this work</u>.

04 다음 우리말에 맞게 주어진 어구를 알맞게 배열하시오.

(1) 어떤 학교들은 학생들이 교복을 입게 하지 않는다. (make, wear, school uniforms, some schools, students, don't)

➡ _____

(2) 우리는 바쁜 도시에 사는 것에 익숙해져 있다. (used to, we, are, in, a busy city, living)

➡ _____

서답형
01 다음 문장에서 어법상 **틀린** 부분을 찾아 바르게 고쳐 쓰시오.

He can't help but doing it.

_____ ➡ _____

02 다음 빈칸에 공통으로 들어갈 말로 알맞은 것은?

• She is _____ forward to seeing him.
• She couldn't help _____ up to the teacher.

① getting   ② seeing   ③ hearing
④ having   ⑤ looking

서답형
03 밑줄 친 부분을 어법에 맞게 고치시오.

(1) After lunch, she felt like <u>go</u> for a walk.
(2) The lake is worth <u>visit</u>.
(3) His mind was busy <u>make</u> plans for tomorrow.
(4) I'm used to <u>keep</u> a diary every day.
➡ (1) _____ (2) _____
    (3) _____ (4) _____

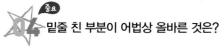
04 밑줄 친 부분이 어법상 올바른 것은?

① I think group projects aren't worth <u>to do</u>.
② They let us <u>learn</u> about working in groups.
③ I cannot help <u>to run</u> because I am late for school.
④ Let him <u>to go</u>!
⑤ I heard the bird <u>to sing</u>.

05 다음 괄호 안의 단어가 올바른 형태로 순서대로 바르게 짝지어진 것은?

• My parents will never let me (go) to the party.
• My English teacher had us (read) many English books.
• You can't help but (admire) her.

① go – read – admiring
② go – read – admire
③ go – to read – admire
④ to go – to read – admire
⑤ to go – to read – admiring

서답형
06 〈보기〉와 같이 다음 두 문장이 같은 의미를 갖도록 빈칸을 채우시오.

— 보기 —
I couldn't help but tell the truth.
= I couldn't help telling the truth.

(1) I couldn't help but feel sorry for my mother.
  = I _____ _____ _____ sorry for my mother.
(2) I couldn't help but agree with him
  = I _____ _____ _____ with him.

07 다음 빈칸에 알맞은 말이 순서대로 바르게 짝지어진 것은?

• Min _____ spend some time in Vietnam.
• Jisu had Lina _____ Japanese culture.

① is used to – introduce
② is used – to introduce
③ used to – introducing
④ used to – introduce
⑤ used to – to introduce

08 다음 중 어법상 어색한 것은?

① I had the boy in my school make Peter happy.
② I got it delivered.
③ My mom let me getting a dog.
④ He didn't let her sleep long.
⑤ He doesn't have his son answer him back.

09 다음 빈칸에 들어갈 말로 알맞은 것은?

> A: What do you think about the comic book?
> B: I think it _____.

① be used to read   ② be busy reading
③ is worth to read   ④ is worth reading
⑤ is used to reading

10 다음 밑줄 친 ⓐ, ⓑ를 어법상 알맞게 고친 것이 차례대로 짝지어진 것은?

> • I used ⓐplay football when I was a boy.
> • I am not used ⓑbe spoken to like that.

① play – to being   ② play – being
③ play – to being   ④ to play – to being
⑤ to play – being

11 다음 빈칸에 들어갈 말로 알맞은 것은?

> A: Jaemin, would you like to go to the movies after school?
> B: I'd love to, but I have to ask my dad first. He might not let _____.

① him go   ② me go
③ me to go   ④ him going
⑤ me going

12 다음 중 어법상 어색한 것을 모두 고르면?

① She doesn't let you to go.
② I think school uniforms are worth wearing.
③ He is used to using this computer.
④ They can't help to feel excited.
⑤ She makes me do the dishes.

13 다음 빈칸에 공통을 들어갈 단어는?

> • He _____ go fishing.
> • He is _____ using the machine.

① being used to   ② be used
③ being used   ④ be used to
⑤ used to

14 다음 중 어법상 옳은 것은?

① I helped him packing his suitcase.
② I helped him repair the car.
③ I helped my mom cleaning the house.
④ Could you help me moving this box?
⑤ Could you help me finding the car key?

15 다음 문장의 밑줄 친 동사와 같은 역할을 하는 것을 모두 고르시오.

> The teacher <u>made</u> my dream come true.

① The teacher <u>made</u> food for her students.
② I <u>made</u> him go there.
③ Dad <u>made</u> me wash my hands.
④ You <u>had</u> to wash your hands.
⑤ She <u>had</u> her husband do all the housework.

서답형

16 다음 각 문장에서 어법상 <u>어색한</u> 부분을 하나씩 찾아서 알맞게 고치시오.

(1) Let me to introduce myself.

　➡ ＿＿＿＿＿＿＿＿＿＿＿＿＿＿＿＿

(2) She let her friend using her camera.

　➡ ＿＿＿＿＿＿＿＿＿＿＿＿＿＿＿＿

(3) Dad had me to empty the trash can.

　➡ ＿＿＿＿＿＿＿＿＿＿＿＿＿＿＿＿

중요

17 다음 중 각 밑줄 친 부분의 쓰임이 주어진 문장의 밑줄 친 <u>had</u>와 같은 것은?

> My mom <u>had</u> me take you to your house.

① I <u>had</u> to take you to your house.
② I <u>had</u> my sister bring my umbrella.
③ I <u>had</u> dinner with my grandmother.
④ I <u>had</u> a great time yesterday.
⑤ I <u>had</u> something to give you.

서답형

18 다음 〈보기〉에 주어진 동사를 한 번씩만 사용하여 어법에 맞게 빈칸을 채우시오.

┌─── 보기 ├───
try, think, cry, spend, change
└──────────────

- I couldn't believe my ears. I didn't know anyone in that group. I felt like (A)＿＿＿＿＿ when I sat with my group members.
- Min was smart, but he always had his nose in a book. I couldn't help (B)＿＿＿＿＿ how unlucky I was.
- "Maybe she would let me (C)＿＿＿＿＿ the group," I thought.
- Min used to (D)＿＿＿＿＿ some time in Vietnam. He read a lot of history books and loved to talk about Vietnam and its history.
- Don't you think it's worth (E)＿＿＿＿＿?

19 Which of the following has the same usage as the underlined part below?

> Parents should <u>make</u> their children sit still during the concert.

① Security guards <u>make</u> regular patrols at night.
② The guard of the museum <u>let</u> Pedro take pictures of the sculpture.
③ <u>Add</u> an egg yolk to make the mixture bind.
④ Atoms of hydrogen are fused to <u>make</u> helium.
⑤ <u>Make</u> sure the ropes are securely fastened.

서답형

20 다음 괄호 안의 어휘들을 배열하여 우리말을 영작할 때, 다음 질문에 답하시오.

(1) 3번째와 6번째 단어를 쓰시오.

> 승무원들은 승객들에게 티켓을 보여 달라고 요청했다.
> (show, flight, attendants, passengers, tickets, had, the, their).

➡ ＿＿＿＿＿＿＿＿＿＿＿＿＿＿＿＿

(2) 3번째와 6번째 단어를 쓰시오.

> 엘리스의 부모님은 그녀가 혼자 이집트에 가는 것을 허락하셨다.
> (Alice's, her, to, parents, let, Egypt, go, herself, by)

➡ ＿＿＿＿＿＿＿＿＿＿＿＿＿＿＿＿

01 다음 각 문장의 괄호 안의 내용을 어법에 맞게 바꿔 쓰시오.

(1) I (felt like give up) the attempt.

　➡ _____

(2) These projects (are worth do).

　➡ _____

(3) May I (have the scarf wrap)?

　➡ _____

02 다음 괄호 안의 단어들을 바르게 배열하여 문장을 완성하시오. (단, 동사를 어법상 알맞은 형태로 변형할 것.)

(1) She _____ to their talk.
(could / listen / help)

(2) She _____ the first FIFA Women's World Cup in 1991 as well as the 1999 Women's World Cup. (the United States / win / help)

(3) Don't you think _____?
(is / worth / it / try)

03 괄호 안의 말을 활용하여 밑줄 친 우리말을 영어로 옮겨 쓰시오.

A: What are you doing?
B: I'm washing my dad's car.
A: Why are you doing it?
B: 아버지께서 내게 이 일을 시키셨어. (make, it, do)

➡ _____ .

04 다음 문장에서 어법상 어색한 부분을 찾아 바르게 고쳐 다시 쓰시오.

(1) I felt like to cry when I sat with my group members.

　➡ _____

(2) I couldn't help to think how unlucky I was.

　➡ _____

(3) She would let me to change the group.

　➡ _____

(4) It is no use to learn such a thing.

　➡ _____

(5) Do you have any difficulties to live with him?

　➡ _____

05 다음 그림과 우리말을 보고 알맞게 영작하시오.

I _____ on the right because I've lived in Britain for a long time.
(나는 오랫동안 영국에서 살았기 때문에 오른쪽에서 운전하는 것에 익숙하다.)

06 빈칸에 들어갈 말로 알맞은 것을 〈보기〉에서 고른 후 어법에 맞게 빈칸을 채우시오.

> ┤ 보기 ├
> have / clean / sit / help

(1) She made the children _____ up their own rooms.

(2) Would you _____ me go home alone?

(3) You should _____ the old woman cross the street.

(4) She lets her children _____ up late.

07 (1)~(3)의 문장을 (A)~(C)의 관용어 표현과 어울리는 것을 골라 알맞게 고쳐 쓰시오.

> (1) Alice is always using a computer because she is a game programmer.
> (2) Alice works till late at night these days.
> (3) Alice wants to take a rest.
> (A) be busy -ing
> (B) be used to -ing
> (C) look forward to -ing

➡ (1) _____
   (2) _____
   (3) _____

08 괄호 안의 어휘를 바르게 배열하여 문장을 완성하시오. (어법에 맞게 알맞은 형태로 변형할 것)

(1) I'll leave here tomorrow to travel abroad, so my brother _____
   _____ .
   (pack / my luggage / me / help)

(2) _____ , she put her own life in danger.
   (to, try, protect, in, the, child)

09 다음 우리말에 맞게 영작할 때, 빈칸에 알맞은 어휘를 〈보기〉에서 찾아, 어법에 맞게 활용하여 쓰시오.

> ┤ 보기 ├
> help – think, use to – read, use to – spend

(1) 나는 내가 운이 없다고 생각하지 않을 수 없었다.

➡ I couldn't _____ how unlucky I was.

(2) Min의 엄마는 베트남 사람이어서, Min은 베트남에서 약간의 시간을 보냈다.

➡ Min's mom was Vietnamese, and Min _____ some time in Vietnam.

(3) Lina는 일본 만화책을 읽는 데 익숙하다.

➡ Lina _____ Japanese comic books.

10 괄호 안의 어휘를 배열하여 우리말에 맞게 문장을 완성하시오.

> 이 프로젝트를 그만 두고 싶다고 생각한다면 그렇게 해라.
> = If you think _____ , do so.
> (felt / you / giving / this / like / project / up)

11 다음 우리말에 맞게 괄호 안에 주어진 단어를 알맞게 배열하시오.

> 그녀는 어려운 문제들을 푸는 데 익숙하다.
> (used to, she, solving, is, difficult problems)

➡ _____

Reading

교과서

How I Met My Best Friends

<u>Mrs. Choi, my social studies teacher</u>, made an important announcement.
'Mrs. Choi'와 'my social studies teacher'는 동격

"You will create a newspaper <u>in groups</u>. Check out your new group
그룹을 지어

members."

Mrs. Choi started <u>calling</u> out the names of the students in each group.
start는 동명사와 to부정사를 모두 목적어로 취할 수 있다.

After a while, <u>my name was called</u>.
능동태: Mrs. Choi called my name.

"Group 4, Jisu…"

"Who will be in my group?" I wondered.

Mrs. Choi continued, "Lina, Inho, and Min."

I couldn't believe my ears. I <u>didn't know anyone</u> in that group. I <u>felt</u>
= knew no one

<u>like crying</u> when I sat with my group members.
feel like –ing: ~하고 싶다

We didn't <u>have anything in common</u>. Lina was always drawing
have ~ in common : ~을 공통으로 가지다

something <u>by herself</u>. Inho never said anything, and his only <u>interest</u>
= alone   관심

seemed to be soccer.

announcement 발표
create 창조하다, 만들다
check out 확인하다
after a while 얼마 후에, 잠시 후
continue 계속하다
feel like –ing ~하고 싶다
sit with ~와 같이 앉다

📎 **확인문제**

● 다음 문장이 본문의 내용과 일치하면 T, 일치하지 <u>않으면</u> F를 쓰시오.

1 Mrs. Choi is a social studies teacher. ☐

2 All the students will create a newspaper alone. ☐

3 Jisu didn't know anyone in her group. ☐

4 Jisu cried when she sat with her group members. ☐

5 Lina was always drawing something alone. ☐

6 Inho always said something, and his only interest was soccer. ☐

Min was smart, but he always had his nose in a book. I couldn't help thinking how unlucky I was. I decided to convince Mrs. Choi
can't help -ing = can't help but+동사 원형 = can't but+동사 원형: '~하지 않을 수 없다'
that I should be with my friends.

"Maybe she would let me change the group," I thought.
= Perhaps   사역 동사 let+목적어+목적격보어(동사원형)
But before I could say anything, she gently placed her hand on my
= Mrs. Choi
shoulder.

"I know what you want, Jisu," she said, "but I'm sure you will get
간접의문문(의문사+주어+동사)   ~하게 되다
to like your group members. Don't you think it's worth trying?"
be worth -ing: ~할 만한 가치가 있다
I didn't really believe her, but I said, "Okay," and walked away.
= Mrs. Choi
The project wasn't easy from the start. We couldn't decide on the
처음부터   ...으로 정하다
topic for our newspaper. I felt like giving up on the project, so I asked
feel like -ing: ~하고 싶다
my friend Ryan for some advice.
advices(×)
"Try to understand your group members first," he said.
try to부정사: ~하려고 노력하다
So I carefully watched my group members. And I came across some
come across : ~을 우연히 발견하다
amazing facts about them. Lina read a lot of Japanese comic books,
= my group members   = many
so she was an expert on Japanese culture.

have one's nose in ~ ~에 열중하다
cannot help -ing ~하지 않을 수 없다
convince 설득하다
gently 부드럽게
get to ~하게 되다
be worth -ing ~할 가치가 있다
gently 부드럽게
place 놓다
come across 우연히 찾아내다
expert 전문가
spend (돈, 시간을) 보내다, 쓰다
culture 문화

📎 확인문제

● 다음 문장이 본문의 내용과 일치하면 T, 일치하지 않으면 F를 쓰시오.

1 Min was smart, but he was always reading a book. ☐

2 Jisu was sure she would get to like her group members. ☐

3 The project wasn't easy from the start. ☐

4 Ryan tried to understand the group members first. ☐

5 Jisu came across some amazing facts about her group members. ☐

6 Lina read a lot of Japanese comic books, but she wasn't interested in Japanese culture. ☐

Inho's Korean sounded a bit different, but that was because he lived in
_{Inho's Korean sounded a bit different}
Argentina when he was young. He knew a lot about Argentina and its
_{많이}
soccer. Min's mom was Vietnamese, and Min used to spend some time in
_{= Min's mom comes from Vietnam}   _{used to+동사 원형: 예전에 ~했다(과거의 상태 또는 예전에 했었던 규칙적인 습관을 나타냄.)}
Vietnam. He read a lot of history books and loved to talk about Vietnam
_{= talking}
and its history.

I thought of the perfect topic for our group. We decided to write about
_{decide는 to부정사를 목적어로 취하는 동사. to부정사의 명사적 용법}
world culture. I had Lina introduce Japanese culture.
_{사역동사 have+목적어+목적격보어(동사 원형)}
Inho wrote about Argentina and its soccer, and Min covered
Vietnamese culture and its history. I was in charge of editing the whole
_{전치사 of의 목적어(동명사)}
newspaper.

Our newspaper project was a great success. We received an A⁺, and
_{a success: '성공한 사람'이나 '사례'를 나타낼 때는 셀 수 있는 명사 취급}
my group members became my best friends.

I will end my story with this saying. Don't judge a book by its cover.
_{속담}   _{appearance를 비유한 말}
Read it. It might turn into your favorite book.

---

sound ~하게 들리다
a bit 조금
cover ~을 다루다
in charge of ~을 담당하는
edit 편집하다
success 성공
whole 전체의, 전부의
receive 받다
end 끝내다
judge 판단하다
turn into ~이 되다

📎 **확인문제**

• 다음 문장이 본문의 내용과 일치하면 T, 일치하지 않으면 F를 쓰시오.

1 Inho's Korean sounded a bit different. ☐

2 Min's mom lives in Vietnam now. ☐

3 Min loved talking about Vietnam and its history. ☐

4 Min thought of the perfect topic for their group. ☐

5 Inho wrote about Argentina and its soccer, and Min covered Vietnamese culture and

   its history. ☐

6 Inho was in charge of editing the whole newspaper. ☐

● 우리말을 참고하여 빈칸에 알맞은 말을 쓰시오.

1 _____ I Met My Best Friends

2 Mrs. Choi, my _____ _____ teacher, made an important _____.

3 "You will create a newspaper _____ _____.

4 _____ _____ your new group members."

5 Mrs. Choi started _____ _____ the names of the students in each group.

6 After a while, my name _____ _____.

7 "_____ 4, Jisu…"

8 "_____ _____ _____ in my group?" I wondered.

9 Mrs. Choi _____, "Lina, Inho, and Min."

10 I _____ _____ my ears.

11 I _____ _____ _____ in that group.

12 I _____ _____ _____ when I sat with my group members.

13 We didn't _____ anything _____ _____.

14 Lina _____ _____ _____ something by herself.

15 Inho never said anything, and _____ _____ _____ seemed to be soccer.

1 가장 좋은 친구들을 어떻게 만나게 되었나

2 사회 선생님인 최 선생님께서 중요한 발표를 했다.

3 "모둠별로 신문을 만들 겁니다.

4 새 모둠의 구성원을 확인하세요."

5 최 선생님은 각 모둠의 학생들 이름을 부르기 시작했다.

6 잠시 후, 내 이름이 불렸다.

7 "모둠 4, 지수…"

8 "내 모둠의 구성원들은 누굴까?" 나는 궁금했다.

9 최 선생님은 계속 말씀하셨다. "Lina, 인호, 그리고 Min."

10 나는 내 귀를 믿을 수 없었다.

11 나는 그 모둠에 아는 사람이 하나도 없었다.

12 모둠 구성원들과 함께 앉을 때 나는 울고 싶었다.

13 우리는 공통점이 하나도 없었다.

14 Lina는 항상 혼자서 무언가를 그리고 있었다.

15 인호는 아무 말도 하지 않았으며 그의 유일한 관심은 축구 같았다.

16 Min was smart, but he always _____ _____ _____ _____ _____ _____.

17 I _____ _____ _____ how unlucky I was.

18 I decided to convince Mrs. Choi that I _____ _____ _____ my friends.

19 "Maybe she would _____ _____ _____ the group," I thought.

20 But before I could say anything, she gently _____ her hand _____ my shoulder.

21 "I know _____ _____ _____, Jisu," she said, "but I'm sure you will _____ _____ _____ your group members.

22 Don't you think _____ _____ _____?"

23 I didn't really believe her, but I said, "Okay," and _____ _____.

24 The project wasn't easy _____ _____ _____.

25 We couldn't _____ _____ the topic for our newspaper.

26 I _____ _____ _____ up on the project, so I asked my friend Ryan for some advice.

27 "_____ _____ _____ your group members first," he said.

28 So I _____ _____ my group members.

29 And I _____ _____ some amazing facts about them.

30 Lina read a lot of Japanese comic books, so she was an _____ _____ Japanese culture.

---

16 Min은 영리했지만, 그는 항상 책만 보고 있었다.

17 나는 내가 참으로 불행하다는 생각을 하지 않을 수 없었다.

18 나는 내 친구들과 함께하겠다고 최 선생님을 설득하기로 했다.

19 "어쩌면 내가 모둠을 바꿀 수 있게 허락해 주실지 몰라." 나는 생각했다.

20 하지만 내가 말을 꺼내기도 전에, 선생님은 부드럽게 내 어깨에 손을 얹으셨다.

21 "네가 원하는 것이 뭔지 알아, 지수야." 선생님은 말했다. "하지만 네가 너의 모둠원들을 좋아하게 될 것이라고 확신해.

22 시도할 만한 가치가 있다고 생각하지 않니?"

23 나는 선생님의 말씀을 진짜로 믿진 않았지만, "네."라고 말하고 돌아섰다.

24 프로젝트는 처음부터 쉽지 않았다.

25 우리는 신문의 주제를 결정할 수 없었다.

26 나는 프로젝트를 포기하고 싶었고, 그래서 친구 Ryan에게 조언을 구했다.

27 "먼저 모둠 구성원들을 이해하려고 노력해 봐." 그는 말했다.

28 그래서 나는 모둠의 구성원들을 신중하게 살펴보았다.

29 그리고 그들에 관한 놀라운 사실들을 발견했다.

30 Lina는 일본의 만화책을 많이 읽었고, 그래서 일본 문화에 관해서는 전문가였다.

31 Inho's Korean sounded _____ _____ different, but that was _____ he lived in Argentina when he was young.

32 He knew _____ _____ about Argentina and its soccer.

33 Min's mom was _____, and Min _____ _____ _____ some time in Vietnam.

34 He read a lot of history books and loved _____ _____ _____ Vietnam and its history.

35 I _____ _____ the perfect topic for our group.

36 We decided _____ _____ about world culture.

37 I _____ _____ _____ Japanese culture.

38 Inho _____ _____ Argentina and its soccer, and Min _____ Vietnamese culture and its history.

39 I _____ _____ _____ _____ the whole newspaper.

40 Our newspaper project was _____ _____ _____.

41 We _____ _____ _____, and my group members became my best friends.

42 I will end my story _____ _____ _____.

43 Don't judge a book _____ _____.

44 _____ it.

45 It might _____ _____ your favorite book.

31 인호의 한국어 발음은 조금 다르게 들렸는데, 그 이유는 어렸을 때 아르헨티나에서 살았기 때문이었다.

32 그는 아르헨티나와 그 나라의 축구에 관해 많은 것을 알고 있었다.

33 Min의 엄마는 베트남 사람이었고, Min은 베트남에서 약간의 시간을 보냈다.

34 그는 많은 역사책을 읽었으며, 베트남과 그 역사에 관해 이야기하는 것을 좋아했다.

35 나는 우리 모둠을 위한 완벽한 주제를 생각해 냈다.

36 우리는 세계 문화에 관해 글을 쓰기로 했다.

37 나는 Lina가 일본 문화를 소개하도록 했다.

38 인호는 아르헨티나와 축구에 관해 썼고, Min은 베트남 문화와 역사를 다뤘다.

39 나는 신문 전체를 편집하는 역할을 맡았다.

40 우리의 신문 프로젝트는 대성공이었다.

41 우리는 A⁺를 받았고, 모둠 구성원들은 나의 가장 친한 친구가 되었다.

42 나는 이 말로 내 이야기를 끝내려고 한다.

43 책을 표지로 판단하지 마라.

44 그것을 읽어라.

45 그것은 네가 가장 좋아하는 책이 될 수도 있다.

● 우리말을 참고하여 본문을 영작하시오.

1 가장 좋은 친구들을 어떻게 만나게 되었나
➡ _____

2 사회 선생님인 최 선생님께서 중요한 발표를 했다.
➡ _____

3 "모둠별로 신문을 만들 겁니다.
➡ _____

4 새 모둠의 구성원을 확인하세요."
➡ _____

5 최 선생님은 각 모둠의 학생들 이름을 부르기 시작했다.
➡ _____

6 잠시 후, 내 이름이 불렸다.
➡ _____

7 "모둠 4, 지수…"
➡ _____

8 "내 모둠의 구성원들은 누굴까?" 나는 궁금했다.
➡ _____

9 최 선생님은 계속 말씀하셨다. "Lina, 인호, 그리고 Min."
➡ _____

10 나는 내 귀를 믿을 수 없었다.
➡ _____

11 나는 그 모둠에 아는 사람이 하나도 없었다.
➡ _____

12 모둠 구성원들과 함께 앉을 때 나는 울고 싶었다.
➡ _____

13 우리는 공통점이 하나도 없었다.
➡ _____

14 Lina는 항상 혼자서 무언가를 그리고 있었다.
➡ _____

15 인호는 아무 말도 하지 않았으며 그의 유일한 관심은 축구 같았다.
➡ _____

16 Min은 영리했지만, 그는 항상 책만 보고 있었다.
➡ _____

17 나는 내가 참으로 불행하다는 생각을 하지 않을 수 없었다.
➡ _____

18 나는 내 친구들과 함께하겠다고 최 선생님을 설득하기로 했다.
➡ _____

19 "어쩌면 내가 모둠을 바꿀 수 있게 허락해 주실지 몰라." 나는 생각했다.
➡ _____

20 하지만 내가 말을 꺼내기도 전에, 선생님은 부드럽게 내 어깨에 손을 얹으셨다.
➡ _____

21 "네가 원하는 것이 뭔지 알아, 지수야." 선생님은 말했다. "하지만 네가 너의 모둠원들을 좋아하게 될 것이라고 확신해.
➡ _____

22 시도할 만한 가치가 있다고 생각하지 않니?"
➡ _____

23 나는 선생님의 말씀을 진짜로 믿진 않았지만, "네."라고 말하고 돌아섰다.
➡ _____

24 프로젝트는 처음부터 쉽지 않았다.
➡ _____

25 우리는 신문의 주제를 결정할 수 없었다.
➡ _____

26 나는 프로젝트를 포기하고 싶었고, 그래서 친구 Ryan에게 조언을 구했다.
➡ _____

27 "먼저 모둠 구성원들을 이해하려고 노력해 봐." 그는 말했다.
➡ _____

28 그래서 나는 모둠의 구성원들을 신중하게 살펴보았다.
➡ _____

29 그리고 그들에 관한 놀라운 사실들을 발견했다.
➡ _____

30 Lina는 일본의 만화책을 많이 읽었고, 그래서 일본 문화에 관해서는 전문가였다.
➡ _____

31 인호의 한국어 발음은 조금 다르게 들렸는데, 그 이유는 어렸을 때 아르헨티나에서 살았기 때문이었다.
➡ _____
_____

32 그는 아르헨티나와 그 나라의 축구에 관해 많은 것을 알고 있었다.
➡ _____

33 Min의 엄마는 베트남 사람이었고, Min은 베트남에서 약간의 시간을 보냈다.
➡ _____

34 그는 많은 역사책을 읽었으며, 베트남과 그 역사에 관해 이야기하는 것을 좋아했다.
➡ _____

35 나는 우리 모둠을 위한 완벽한 주제를 생각해냈다.
➡ _____

36 우리는 세계 문화에 관해 글을 쓰기로 했다.
➡ _____

37 나는 Lina가 일본 문화를 소개하도록 했다.
➡ _____

38 인호는 아르헨티나와 축구에 관해 썼고, Min은 베트남 문화와 역사를 다뤘다.
➡ _____

39 나는 신문 전체를 편집하는 역할을 맡았다.
➡ _____

40 우리의 신문 프로젝트는 대성공이었다.
➡ _____

41 우리는 A⁺를 받았고, 모둠 구성원들은 나의 가장 친한 친구가 되었다.
➡ _____

42 나는 이 말로 내 이야기를 끝내려고 한다.
➡ _____

43 책을 표지로 판단하지 마라.
➡ _____

44 그것을 읽어라.
➡ _____

45 그것은 네가 가장 좋아하는 책이 될 수도 있다.
➡ _____

[01~03] 다음 글을 읽고 물음에 답하시오.

Mrs. Choi, my social studies teacher, made an important announcement.

"You will create a newspaper __ⓐ__ groups. Check out your new group members."

Mrs. Choi started (A)calling out the names of the students in each group. After a while, my name was called.

"Group 4, Jisu..."

"Who will be in my group?" I wondered.

Mrs. Choi continued, "Lina, Inho, and Min."

I couldn't believe my ears. I didn't know anyone in that group. I felt like crying when I sat __ⓑ__ my group members.

01 위 글의 빈칸 ⓐ와 ⓑ에 들어갈 전치사가 바르게 짝지어진 것은?

	ⓐ	ⓑ		ⓐ	ⓑ
①	with	for	②	in	with
③	in	for	④	with	to
⑤	to	with			

02 위 글의 밑줄 친 (A)calling과 문법적 쓰임이 같은 것을 모두 고르시오.

① I heard somebody calling me.

② I tried calling you several times

③ Thank you for calling me again.

④ May I ask who's calling, please?

⑤ Stop calling each other names.

03 According to the passage, which is NOT true?

① Mrs. Choi is Jisu's social studies teacher.

② Mrs. Choi started to call out the names of the group members.

③ Jisu belonged to Group 4.

④ Jisu couldn't believe her ears.

⑤ Jisu and Lina were close friends.

[04~06] 다음 글을 읽고 물음에 답하시오.

(A)We didn't have anything in common. Lina was always drawing something by herself. Inho never said anything, and his only ⓐinterest seemed to be soccer. Min was smart, but he always had his nose in a book. (①) I couldn't help thinking how unlucky I was. (②) I decided to convince Mrs. Choi that I should be with my friends. (③)

"Maybe she would let me change the group," I thought. (④)

"I know what you want, Jisu," she said, "but I'm sure you will get to like your group members. (⑤) Don't you think it's worth trying?"

I didn't really believe her, but I said, "Okay," and walked away.

04 위 글의 흐름으로 보아, 주어진 문장이 들어가기에 가장 적절한 곳은?

But before I could say anything, she gently placed her hand on my shoulder.

① ② ③ ④ ⑤

05 위 글의 밑줄 친 ⓐinterest와 같은 의미로 쓰인 것을 모두 고르시오.

① The money was repaid with interest.

② Do your parents take an interest in your friends?

③ Politics doesn't interest me.

④ It is to your own interest to keep silence.

⑤ He showed much interest in politics.

서답형

06 위 글의 밑줄 친 (A)를 다음과 같이 바꿔 쓸 때 빈칸에 들어갈 알맞은 한 단어를 철자 s로 시작하여 쓰시오.

➡ We didn't _____ anything.

[07~09] 다음 글을 읽고 물음에 답하시오.

The project wasn't easy from the start. We couldn't decide on the topic for our newspaper. I felt like giving up on the project, so I asked my friend Ryan for some advice.

"Try to understand your group members first," he said.

So I carefully watched my group members. And I came across some amazing facts about them. Lina read a lot of Japanese comic books, so she was an ⓐ on Japanese culture. Inho's Korean sounded a bit different, but that was because he lived in Argentina when he was young. He knew a lot about Argentina and its soccer. ⓑMin의 엄마는 베트남 사람이었고, Min은 베트남에서 약간의 시간을 보냈다. He read a lot of history books and loved to talk about Vietnam and its history.

서답형

07 주어진 영영풀이를 참고하여 빈칸 ⓐ에 철자 e로 시작하는 단어를 쓰시오.

a person who is very skilled at doing something or who knows a lot about a particular subject

➡ _____

서답형

08 위 글의 밑줄 친 ⓑ의 우리말에 맞게 주어진 어휘를 이용하여 13 단어로 영작하시오.

Vietnamese, used to, some

➡ _____

중요

09 Which question CANNOT be answered after reading the passage?

① How could Lina become a specialist on Japanese culture?
② Why did Inho's Korean sound a bit different?
③ Why did Inho live in Argentina when he was young?
④ About what did Inho know a lot?
⑤ What did Min love to talk about?

[10~12] 다음 글을 읽고 물음에 답하시오.

We didn't have anything in common. Lina was always drawing something (A)by herself. Inho never said anything, and his only interest seemed to be soccer. Min was smart, but he always had his nose in a book. (B)I couldn't help thinking how lucky I was. I decided to convince Mrs. Choi that I should be with my friends.

"Maybe she would let me change the group," I thought.

But before I could say anything, she gently placed her hand on my shoulder.

"I know ⓐ you want, Jisu," she said, "but I'm sure you will get to like your group members. Don't you think it's worth trying?"

I didn't really believe her, but I said, "Okay," and walked away.

10 위 글의 빈칸 ⓐ에 들어갈 알맞은 말을 고르시오.

① which ② if ③ what
④ that ⑤ whether

서답형

11 위 글의 밑줄 친 (A)by herself와 바꿔 쓸 수 있는 한 단어를 쓰시오.

➡ _____

서답형

12 위 글의 밑줄 친 (B)에서 흐름상 어색한 부분을 찾아 고치시오.

➡ _____

[13~16] 다음 글을 읽고 물음에 답하시오.

The project wasn't easy from the start. We couldn't decide on the topic for our newspaper. I felt like ⓐgiving up on the project, so I asked my friend Ryan for some advice.

"Try to understand your group members first," he said.

So I carefully watched my group members. And I came across ⓑsome amazing facts about them. Lina read a lot of Japanese comic books, so she was an expert on Japanese culture. Inho's Korean sounded a bit different, but that was because he lived in Argentina when he was young. He knew a lot about Argentina and its soccer. Min's mom was Vietnamese, and Min used to spend some time in Vietnam. He read a lot of history books and loved to talk about Vietnam and ⓒits history.

중요

13 위 글의 밑줄 친 ⓐgiving과 문법적 쓰임이 다른 것을 모두 고르시오.

① Giving her your advice was a good thing to do.
② Are you giving me a ticket?
③ I talked Mary into giving her sister a doll.
④ Love is giving others a help without hesitation.
⑤ He is giving us some apples.

서답형

14 위 글의 밑줄 친 ⓑ의 내용을 본문에서 찾아 우리말로 쓰시오.

➡ (1) Lina: _____

_____

(2) 인호: _____

_____

_____

(3) Min: _____

_____

서답형

15 위 글의 밑줄 친 ⓒits가 가리키는 것을 본문에서 찾아 쓰시오.

➡ _____

중요

16 위 글의 주제로 알맞은 것을 고르시오.

① the difficulty of the project
② how to decide on the topic for the newspaper
③ understanding group members first
④ how to become an expert on Japanese culture
⑤ various cultures of other countries

[17~19] 다음 글을 읽고 물음에 답하시오.

I thought of the perfect topic for our group. We decided to write about world culture. I had Lina introduce Japanese culture. Inho wrote about Argentina and its soccer, and Min covered Vietnamese culture and its history. I was in ⓐcharge of editing the whole newspaper.

Our newspaper project was a great success. We received an A⁺, and my group members became my best friends.

I will end my story with this saying. Don't judge a book by its cover. Read it. It might turn into your ⓑfavorite book.

17 위 글의 제목으로 알맞은 것을 고르시오.

① Judge Its Taste by How It Looks
② Not How It Looks But What It Says
③ Is Cooperation the Best Policy? Really?
④ What Matters Is How It Looks
⑤ All Is Not Gold That Glitters.

18 위 글의 밑줄 친 ⓐcharge와 같은 의미로 쓰인 것을 고르시오.

① Delivery is free of charge.
② Before use, you must charge the battery.
③ He couldn't charge Tom with a crime.
④ The city will be in your charge.
⑤ What did they charge for the repairs?

19 위 글의 밑줄 친 ⓑfavorite book이 비유하고 있는 것을 본문에서 찾아 쓰시오.

➡ _____

20 위 글의 빈칸 ⓐ에 cry를 알맞은 형태로 쓰시오.

➡ _____

21 위 글의 제목으로 알맞은 것을 고르시오.

① Meet Your Best Friends!
② How to Create a Newspaper in Groups
③ Check Out Your New Group Members!
④ Unbelievable! None of Them I Know!
⑤ Wow! Lina and I Belong to the Same Group!

22 위 글에서 알 수 있는 지수의 심경 변화로 가장 알맞은 것을 고르시오.

① satisfied → upset
② expectant → disappointed
③ bored → nervous
④ disappointed → hopeful
⑤ nervous → satisfied

[20~22] 다음 글을 읽고 물음에 답하시오.

Mrs. Choi, my social studies teacher, made an important announcement.

"You will create a newspaper in groups. Check out your new group members."

Mrs. Choi started calling out the names of the students in each group. After a while, my name was called.

"Group 4, Jisu..."

"Who will be in my group?" I wondered.

Mrs. Choi continued, "Lina, Inho, and Min."

I couldn't believe my ears. I didn't know anyone in that group. I felt like ___ⓐ___ when I sat with my group members.

[23~25] 다음 글을 읽고 물음에 답하시오.

We didn't have anything in common. Lina was always drawing something by herself. Inho never said anything, and his only interest seemed to be soccer. Min was smart, but he always had his nose in a book. I couldn't help thinking how unlucky I was. ⓐI decided convincing Mrs. Choi that I should be with my friends.

"Maybe she would let me change the group," I thought.

But before I could say anything, she gently placed her hand on my shoulder.

"I know what you want, Jisu," she said, "but I'm sure you will ⓑget to like your group members. Don't you think it's worth trying?"

I didn't really believe her, but I said, "Okay," and walked away.

23 위 글의 밑줄 친 ⓐ에서 어법상 **틀린** 부분을 찾아 고치시오.

➡ _____

24 위 글의 밑줄 친 ⓑget과 바꿔 쓸 수 있는 말을 <u>모두</u> 고르시오.

① come   ② continue
③ decide   ④ grow
⑤ become

25 Which question CANNOT be answered after reading the passage?

① Who was always drawing something alone?
② What did Inho's only interest seem to be?
③ Who liked reading in Jisu's group?
④ How did Mrs. Choi know what Jisu wanted?
⑤ What was Mrs. Choi sure?

[26~28] 다음 글을 읽고 물음에 답하시오.

I thought of the perfect topic for our group. We decided to write about world culture. I had Lina (A)[introduce / to introduce] Japanese culture. Inho wrote about Argentina and its soccer, and Min ⓐcovered Vietnamese culture and its history. I was in charge of (B)[editing / editting] the whole newspaper. Our newspaper project was (C)[great success / a great success]. We received an A⁺,

and my group members became my best friends. I will end my story with this saying. Don't ⓑ judge a book by its cover. Read it. It might turn into your favorite book. <I: Jisu>

26 위 글의 괄호 (A)~(C)에서 문맥이나 어법상 알맞은 낱말을 골라 쓰시오.

➡ (A)_____ (B)_____ (C)_____

27 위 글의 밑줄 친 ⓐcovered와 같은 의미로 쓰인 것을 고르시오.

① She covered her face with her hands.
② Snow covered the ground.
③ The lectures covered a lot of things.
④ By sunset we had covered thirty miles.
⑤ She covered a dish with the towel.

28 다음 지수의 말을 참조하여, 위 글의 밑줄 친 ⓑ에 대한 설명을 완성하시오.

Jisu: At first, I thought our group members had nothing in common. But now I'm glad I didn't convince Mrs. Choi to let me change my group.

At first, Jisu thought her group members had nothing in common, so she wanted to convince Mrs. Choi to let her change her group. That is, she judged a book (A)_____ _____ _____ and almost gave up (B)_____ _____.

[01~03] 다음 글을 읽고 물음에 답하시오.

I thought of the perfect topic for our group. We decided to write about world culture. ⓐ I had Lina introduce Japanese culture. Inho wrote about Argentina and its soccer, and Min covered Vietnamese culture and its history. I was in charge of editing the whole newspaper.

Our newspaper project was a great success. We received an A⁺, and my group members became my best friends.

I will end my story with this saying. Don't judge a book by its cover. Read it. It might turn into your favorite book.   <I: Jisu>

01 위 글의 밑줄 친 ⓐ를 다음과 같이 바꿔 쓸 때 빈칸에 들어갈 알맞은 말을 두 단어로 쓰시오.

➡ I got Lina _____ Japanese culture.

02 What did Jisu's group members decide to write about? Answer in English in a full sentence. (7 words)

➡ _____

03 위 글에서 지수의 모둠원들이 각각 맡은 역할을 우리말로 쓰시오.

➡ (1) Lina: _____
   (2) 인호: _____
   (3) Min: _____
   (4) 지수: _____

[04~06] 다음 글을 읽고 물음에 답하시오.

The project wasn't easy from the start. We couldn't decide on the topic for our newspaper. I felt like giving up on the project, so I asked my friend Ryan for some advice.

"Try to understand your group members first," he said.

So I carefully watched my group members. And I came across some amazing facts about ⓐ them. Lina read a lot of Japanese comic books, so she was an expert on Japanese culture. Inho's Korean sounded a bit different, but that was because he lived in Argentina when he was young. He knew a lot about Argentina and its soccer. Min's mom was Vietnamese, and Min used to spend some time in Vietnam. He read a lot of history books and loved to talk about Vietnam and its history.   <I: Jisu>

04 위 글의 밑줄 친 ⓐthem이 가리키는 것을 영어로 쓰시오.

➡ _____

05 Why did Inho's Korean sound a bit different? Fill in the blanks with suitable words.

Because he lived _____ _____ when he was young.

06 다음 빈칸 (A)와 (B)에 알맞은 단어를 넣어 Min에 대한 소개를 완성하시오.

Min's mom comes from (A)_____, and Min used to spend some time in Vietnam. He read many (B)_____ _____ and loved talking about Vietnam and Vietnamese history.

[07~10] 다음 글을 읽고 물음에 답하시오.

Mrs. Choi, my social studies teacher, made an important ___ⓐ___ .
"You will create a newspaper in groups. Check out your new group members."
ⓑ최 선생님은 각 모둠의 학생들 이름을 부르기 시작했다. After a while, my name was called.
"Group 4, Jisu..."
"Who will be in my group?" I wondered.
Mrs. Choi continued, "Lina, Inho, and Min."
I couldn't believe my ears. I didn't know anyone in ⓒthat group. I felt like crying when I sat with my group members.

07 위 글의 빈칸 ⓐ에 announce를 알맞은 형태로 쓰시오.

➡ _____

08 위 글의 밑줄 친 ⓑ의 우리말에 맞게 주어진 어휘를 알맞게 배열하시오.

> each group / calling out / of / Mrs. Choi / the students / in / started / the names

➡ _____
_____

09 위 글의 밑줄 친 ⓒthat group이 가리키는 것을 본문에서 찾아 쓰시오.

➡ _____

10 본문의 내용과 일치하도록 다음 빈칸 (A)와 (B)에 알맞은 단어를 쓰시오.

> When Jisu heard the names of the students in her group, she couldn't believe (A)____ ____ because she (B)____ ____ anyone in the group. She had a desire to cry when she sat with her group members.

[11~13] 다음 글을 읽고 물음에 답하시오.

We didn't have anything in common. Lina was always drawing something by herself. Inho never said anything, and his only interest seemed to be soccer. Min was smart, but ⓐhe always had his nose in a book. I couldn't help thinking how unlucky I was. I decided to convince Mrs. Choi that I should be with my friends.
"Maybe she would let me change the group," I thought.
But before I could say anything, she gently placed her hand on my shoulder.
"I know what you want, Jisu," she said, "but I'm sure you will get to like your group members. Don't you think ⓑit's worth trying?"
I didn't really believe her, but I said, "Okay," and walked away.

11 위 글의 밑줄 친 ⓐ를 다음과 같이 바꿔 쓸 때 아래 빈칸에 들어갈 알맞은 단어를 주어진 영영풀이를 참고하여 철자 b로 시작하여 쓰시오.

> someone who is very fond of reading

➡ he was a _____

12 위 글의 밑줄 친 ⓑ를 다음과 같이 바꿔 쓸 때 빈칸에 들어갈 알맞은 한 단어를 쓰시오.

➡ it's worth _____ to try

13 본문의 내용과 일치하도록 다음 빈칸 (A)와 (B)에 알맞은 단어를 쓰시오.

> Jisu thought her group members didn't have anything (A)____ ____, so she decided (B)____ ____ Mrs. Choi that she should be with her friends, but Mrs. Choi advised Jisu to try to get to like her group members.

Reading and Do

Inho's Korean sounded a bit different, but that was because he lived in
주어   2형식 감각동사(~처럼 들리다)+주격보어(형용사) / a bit은 형용사를 꾸며주는 부사구
Argentina when he was young. He knew a lot about Argentina and its soccer.
시간의 접속사
Min's mom was Vietnamese, and Min used to spend some time in Vietnam.
used to 동사원형: ~하곤 했다
He read a lot of history books and loved to talk about Vietnam and its history.
동사   등위접속사

해석

인호의 한국어 발음은 조금 다르게 들렸는데, 그 이유는 어렸을 때 아르헨티나에서 살았기 때문이었다. 그는 아르헨티나와 그 나라의 축구에 관해 많은 것을 알고 있었다. Min의 엄마는 베트남 사람이었고, Min은 베트남에서 약간의 시간을 보냈다. 그는 많은 역사책을 읽었으며, 베트남과 그 역사에 관해 이야기하는 것을 좋아했다.

After You Read B

Lina: I am an expert on Japanese culture because I read a lot of Japanese

comic books. I was in charge of writing about Japan.
전치사 of의 목적어(동명사)

Inho: My Korean may sound a bit different because I lived in Argentina when
sound+형용사: ~하게 들리다
I was young. I'm so glad our group received an A⁺ on our project.

Min: I always have my nose in a history book. Also, I know well about
have one's nose in a book: 책벌레이다
Vietnam because I spent some time there. So, I covered Vietnamese
= in Vietnam. cover: 다루다, 포함시키다
culture and its history.

Jisu: At first, I thought our group members had nothing in common. But now
have ~ in common = share: 공통점이 있다
I'm glad I didn't convince Mrs. Choi to let me change my group. I edited
convince+목적어+to부정사: 설득하다 사역 동사 let+목적어+목적격보어(동사 원형)
the whole newspaper.

Lina: 나는 일본의 만화책을 많이 읽었기 때문에 일본 문화에 관해서는 전문가이다. 나는 일본에 관해 글을 쓰는 역할을 맡았다.
인호: 나는 어렸을 때 아르헨티나에서 살았기 때문에 한국어 발음은 조금 다르게 들릴 수 있다. 나는 우리 모둠이 프로젝트에 대해 A⁺를 받아서 너무 기쁘다.
Min: 나는 항상 역사책만 본다. 또한 나는 베트남에서 약간의 시간을 보냈기 때문에 베트남에 대해서 잘 알고 있다. 그래서 나는 베트남 문화와 역사를 다뤘다.
지수: 처음에 나는 우리 모둠 구성원들이 공통점이 하나도 없다고 생각했다. 그러나 이제 나는 내 모둠을 바꿔 달라고 최 선생님을 설득하지 않은 것이 기쁘다. 나는 신문 전체를 편집했다.

구문해설 • **expert**: 전문가 • **in charge of**: ~을 담당하는 • **receive**: 받다 • **spend**: (돈, 시간을) 보내다, 쓰다 • **have ~ in common**: 공통점이 있다 • **convince**: 설득하다 • **edit**: 편집하다 • **whole**: 전부의

Check Your Progress 2

Are you satisfied with your school? Well, at the start of this year, I wasn't. I
be satisfied with ~에 만족하다   ~이 시작될 때
didn't know anyone in my class, and I was too shy to talk to anyone. So I was
too 형용사/부사 to부정사 : 너무 ~해서 …할 수 없다
always alone. But everything changed after sports day. On sports day, all of
특정한 날짜에는 전치사 on을 쓴다.
my class did our best to win the games. I'm not good at sports, but I did my
be good at : ~을 잘하다
best. I also cheered as my classmates played the games. When the day was
over, I was friends with my classmates. Now, I am very happy with my school
be happy with : ~에 만족하다 (= be satisfied with)
life.

너는 학교에 만족하니? 음, 올해 초에 나는 만족하지 않았어. 나는 반에 아는 사람이 없었고 나는 너무 내성적이어서 아무에게도 말을 걸지 못했어. 그래서 늘 혼자였어. 그러나 체육대회 이후에 모든 것이 바뀌었어. 체육대회 하는 날 우리 반 학생들은 모두 경기에 이기기 위하여 최선을 다했어. 나는 운동을 잘 못했지만 나는 최선을 다했어. 나는 우리 반 학생들이 경기할 때 응원을 했어. 그 날이 끝났을 때 나는 학급 친구들과 친구가 되었어. 이제는 나는 학교 생활에 매우 만족해.

구문해설 • **alone** 혼자 있는 **do one's best** 최선을 다하다 **be over** 끝나다

Words & Expressions

01 다음 중 밑줄 친 부분의 뜻풀이가 바르지 <u>않은</u> 것은?

① No, I don't <u>agree</u>. I think Minjae is the best player. (동의하다)
② His class won the basketball game last year. Don't you <u>remember</u>? (기억하다)
③ Anyway, we are <u>lucky</u> to have both of them in our class this year. (운 좋은)
④ I think our class is going to <u>win</u> the basketball game this year. (참가하다)
⑤ That's true, but he's sometimes too <u>strict</u>. (엄격한)

02 다음 영영풀이에 해당하는 단어를 고르시오.

a job or profession that you have been trained for, and which you do for a long period of your life

① career   ② culture   ③ grade
④ judge   ⑤ board

03 다음 밑줄 친 단어와 의미가 같은 단어를 고르시오.

I'm not good at sports, but I did my best. I also <u>cheered</u> as my classmates played the games.

① advised   ② consulted
③ continued   ④ introduced
⑤ encouraged

Conversation

04 다음 대화의 순서가 바르게 배열된 것을 고르시오.

B: Are you satisfied with your new partner?
(A) Yes, I am.
(B) He is fun and talkative.
(C) What do you like about him?

① (A) – (C) – (B)   ② (B) – (A) – (C)
③ (B) – (C) – (A)   ④ (C) – (A) – (B)
⑤ (C) – (B) – (A)

[05~07] 다음 대화를 읽고 물음에 답하시오.

B: Are you happy with your new seat?
G: No, I'm not. My seat is at the back of the classroom.
B: Why don't you want to sit at the back?
G: It's harder to concentrate when you sit at the back. Don't you agree?
B: That's true, but I (A)_____.
G: Why?
B: When I sit at the front, (B)<u>내 뒤에 앉은 사람들이 칠판을 볼 수 없다</u> because I am too tall.
G: Oh, I understand.

05 위 대화의 내용상 빈칸 (A)에 들어가기에 적절한 것은?

① don't like sitting at the back
② want to concentrate
③ like to sit at the front
④ want you to sit behind me
⑤ like sitting at the back

06 밑줄 친 (B)의 우리말에 해당하는 영어 표현으로 적절한 것은?

① those can't see the board which is behind me

② those who are behind the board can't see me

③ those who sit behind me can't see the board

④ those behind me sit at the board can't see

⑤ those who can't see me sit at the board

07 위 대화의 내용과 일치하지 않는 것은?

① The girl isn't happy with her new seat.

② The girl doesn't like to sit at the back of the classroom.

③ The boy didn't know why the girl doesn't like to sit at the back of the classroom.

④ The boy doesn't agree with the girl.

⑤ The boy chooses to sit at the back of the classroom.

[08~10] 다음 대화를 읽고 물음에 답하시오.

G: What are you looking at?

B: I'm looking at the school basketball game poster.

G: Hmm... (A)너는 우리 학교에서 누가 최고의 농구 선수라고 생각하니?

B: I think Jihun is the best. Don't you agree?

A: No, (B)I don't agree. I think Minjae is the best player.

B: Why do you think so?

G: His class (C)_____ the basketball game last year. Don't you remember?

B: But that was because Minjae's class had a lot of good basketball players.

G: Anyway, we are lucky to have both of them in our class this year.

B: Yes, we are. I think our class is going to win the basketball game this year.

08 밑줄 친 (A)의 우리말에 해당하는 영어 문장을 쓰시오.

➡ _____

09 밑줄 친 (B)와 바꿔 쓸 수 있는 것을 고르시오.

① I don't think so

② I like very much

③ That's true

④ That's right

⑤ You can say that again

10 빈칸 (C)에 들어갈 가장 알맞은 말을 고르시오.

① finished   ② won   ③ played

④ lost   ⑤ canceled

Grammar

11 다음 중 어법상 올바른 문장은?

① We're going to get air conditioning installed in our office.

② She got her purse stealing.

③ He got me study English harder.

④ I got my brother do the dishes.

⑤ They got their car to wash.

12 다음 중 어법상 올바른 문장은?

① I think the audition was worth to try.

② The movie was worth to watching.

③ Your food is worth waiting for.

④ I cannot help to leave the town.

⑤ We're looking forward to have a tea.

13 다음 빈칸에 알맞은 말이 바르게 짝지어진 것은?

> • Min is used to _____ the Korean language.
> • Lina felt like _____ a book.

① speaking – reading
② speaking – to read
③ speaking – read
④ speak – reading
⑤ speak – to read

14 다음 각 문장의 어휘를 활용하여 어법에 맞게 영작하시오.

(1) 그렇게 빨리 사 봤자 소용없어.
   (buy, use, is, no, it, that, early)
   ➡ _____

(2) 그녀는 요즘 잠을 잘 못자요.
   (have, she, sleep, trouble, days, these)
   ➡ _____

(3) 그는 그 진실을 밝혀내는 데 10년을 보냈다.
   (find, the, out, truth, spend, he, year, ten)
   ➡ _____

(4) 경찰을 보자마자, 그 소매치기는 도망치기 시작했다.
   (at, on, police, the, look, start, the, pickpocket, away, to, run)
   ➡ _____
   _____

(5) 길을 건너다가, 그는 그 사고를 당했다.
   (the, the, accident, meet, in, with, cross, street, he)
   ➡ _____

15 다음 밑줄 친 부분의 쓰임이 나머지와 다른 것은?

① They won't let him leave the country.
② He made me study French.
③ I had the painter paint my roof.
④ She made me happy.
⑤ The flight attendant had us stand in line.

16 다음 밑줄 친 부분의 어법이 어색한 것은? (2개)

① She is looking forward to travel to Europe.
② She is used to studying at night.
③ I couldn't help to feel sorry for him.
④ They are busy making plans for the work
⑤ I couldn't help but share the chocolate with my brother.

17 다음 그림을 보고 괄호 안의 단어를 활용해서 빈칸에 알맞게 채우시오.

(1)

➡ When the little prince saw a red rose, he didn't feel like _____ (pick) it up.

(2)

➡ It's worth _____ (travel) to Egypt to see pyramids.

[18~20] 다음 글을 읽고 물음에 답하시오.

We didn't have anything in common. Lina was ___ⓐ___ drawing something by herself. Inho never said anything, and his only interest seemed to be soccer. Min was smart, but he always had his nose in a book. I couldn't help thinking how unlucky I was. I decided to convince Mrs. Choi that I should be with my friends.

"Maybe she would let me change the group," I thought.

But before I could say anything, she gently placed her hand on my shoulder.

"I know what you want, Jisu," she said, "but ⓑI'm sure you will get to like your group members. Don't you think it's worth trying?"

I didn't really believe her, but I said, "Okay," and walked away.

18 과거진행형이 '습관'의 의미를 나타내도록 할 때, 위 글의 빈칸 ⓐ에 들어가기에 적절하지 <u>않은</u> 단어를 고르시오.

① constantly
② always
③ forever
④ immediately
⑤ continuously

19 위 글의 밑줄 친 ⓑ를 다음과 같이 바꿔 쓸 때 빈칸에 들어갈 알맞은 한 단어를 철자 c로 시작하여 쓰시오.

➡ it's _____ you will get to like your group members

20 위 글의 제목으로 알맞은 것을 고르시오.

① Unbelievable! Have Nothing in Common?
② Come on! It's Worth Trying!
③ Can It Be Possible to Have a Common Interest?
④ Really? Always Having His Nose in a Book?
⑤ How Lucky I Am!

[21~23] 다음 글을 읽고 물음에 답하시오.

The project wasn't easy from the start. We couldn't decide on the topic for our newspaper. I felt like giving up on the project, so I asked my friend Ryan for some advice.

"Try to understand your group members first," he said.

So I carefully watched my group members. And I came across some amazing facts about them. Lina read a lot of Japanese comic books, so she was an expert on Japanese culture. Inho's Korean sounded a bit different, but ⓐthat was because he lived in Argentina when he was young. He knew a lot about Argentina and its soccer. Min's mom was Vietnamese, and Min used to spend some time in Vietnam. He read ⓑa lot of history books and loved to talk about Vietnam and its history.   <I: Jisu>

21 위 글의 밑줄 친 ⓐthat이 가리키는 것을 본문에서 찾아 쓰시오.

➡ _____

22 위 글의 밑줄 친 ⓑa lot of와 바꿔 쓸 수 <u>없는</u> 말을 고르시오.

① lots of
② many
③ a great deal of
④ plenty of
⑤ a number of

23 According to the passage, which is NOT true?

① Jisu's group members couldn't decide on the topic for their newspaper.
② Jisu felt inclined to give up on the project.
③ Jisu asked her friend Ryan for some advice.
④ Ryan told Jisu to try to understand her group members first.
⑤ Ryan came across some amazing facts about Jisu's group members.

[24~25] 다음 글을 읽고 물음에 답하시오.

I thought of the perfect topic for our group. We decided to write about world culture. I had Lina introduce Japanese culture. Inho wrote about Argentina and its soccer, and Min covered Vietnamese culture and its history. ⓐ 나는 신문 전체를 편집하는 역할을 맡았다.

Our newspaper project was a great success. We received an A⁺, and my group members became my best friends.

I will end my story with this saying. Don't judge a book by its cover. Read it. It might turn into your favorite book.

24 위 글의 밑줄 친 ⓐ의 우리말에 맞게 주어진 어휘를 이용하여 9 단어로 영작하시오.

> in charge of

➡ _____

25 다음 빈칸에 들어갈 알맞은 말을 골라 위 글의 교훈을 완성하시오.

> You shouldn't prejudge the worth or value of something by its outward _____ alone.

① personality   ② quality
③ morality   ④ appearance
⑤ characteristic

[26~27] 다음 글을 읽고 물음에 답하시오.

Lina: I am ⓐan expert on Japanese culture because I read a lot of Japanese comic books. I was in charge of writing about Japan.

Inho: My Korean may sound a bit different because I lived in Argentina when I was young. I'm so glad our group received an A⁺ on our project.

Min: I always have my nose in a history book. Also, I know well about Vietnam because I spent some time there. So, I covered Vietnamese culture and its history.

Jisu: At first, I thought our group members had nothing in common. But now I'm glad I didn't convince Mrs. Choi to let me change my group. I edited the whole newspaper.

26 위 글의 밑줄 친 ⓐan expert와 바꿔 쓸 수 없는 말을 모두 고르시오.

① a specialist   ② an explorer
③ an authority   ④ a professor
⑤ an amateur

27 위 글을 읽고 알 수 없는 것을 고르시오.

① Why is Lina an expert on Japanese culture?
② Where did Inho live when he was young?
③ Why does Min always have his nose in a history book?
④ What did Min cover?
⑤ Who edited the whole newspaper?

01 다음 짝지어진 단어의 관계가 같도록 빈칸에 알맞은 단어를 고르시오.

> agree : disagree = cause : _____

① game ② advice
③ result ④ reason
⑤ idea

02 다음 중 밑줄 친 부분의 뜻풀이가 바르지 <u>않은</u> 것은?

① Lina introduced Japanese <u>culture</u>. (문화)
② Jisu was in charge of editing the <u>whole</u> newspaper. (전체의)
③ Jisu's group got a B on their newspaper <u>project</u>. (과제)
④ We didn't have anything in <u>common</u>. (공통)
⑤ Inho never said anything, and his only <u>interest</u> seemed to be soccer. (목표)

03 다음 대화의 빈칸에 들어갈 말로 적절한 것을 고르시오.

> A: Were you satisfied with sports day?
> B: Yes, I was. I was able to make new friends on that day.
> C: Me, too. I think it was a _____ activity.
> A: I think so too.

① busy ② boring ③ gloomy
④ cheap ⑤ great

04 다음 영영풀이에 해당하는 단어를 고르시오.

> without any friends or people you know

① alone ② worried
③ satisfied ④ scary
⑤ boring

05 다음 중 〈보기〉에 있는 단어를 사용하여 자연스러운 문장을 만들 수 <u>없는</u> 것은?

> ┤ 보기 ├
> herself nose scary convince

① I'm too ugly and _____. Don't you think so?
② Lina was always drawing something by _____.
③ I decided to _____ Mrs. Choi that I should be with my friends.
④ Min was smart, but he always had his _____ in a book.
⑤ She gently _____ her hand on my shoulder.

06 다음 대화의 순서가 바르게 배열된 것을 고르시오.

> (A) Well, I don't agree with you. I think Jina would be the best. She won first place in the school singing contest last year.
> (B) I think Suji would be the best singer in our class. Don't you agree with me?
> (C) Who do you tink would be the best singer in our class?

① (A) – (C) – (B) ② (B) – (A) – (C)
③ (B) – (C) – (A) ④ (C) – (A) – (B)
⑤ (C) – (B) – (A)

[07~10] 다음 대화를 읽고 물음에 답하시오.

(Phone rings.)

G: Hello?

B: Hi, Bora! It's me, Minsu!

G: Minsu! Are you calling from France?

B: (가)_____

G: How do you like your life in France?

B: France is such a beautiful country, but I miss Korea.

G: Are you happy with your new school?

B: Not so much. Everything is so (A)_____ from Korea, so it's not easy for me.

G: Do your classmates help you?

B: Some of them do help me. They are really nice.

G: Good for you. (B)행운을 빌게.

B: Thanks.

출제율 95%

07 빈칸 (가)에 들어갈 가장 알맞은 말을 고르시오.

① Yes, I do.　　② Yes, I am.
③ No, I wasn't.　④ Yes, I have.
⑤ No, I'm not.

출제율 90%

08 빈칸 (A)에 알맞은 말을 고르시오.

① familiar　　② exciting
③ bright　　　④ interesting
⑤ different

출제율 100%

09 Which one of the following is NOT true according to the dialogue above?

① Bora is calling Minsu from France.
② Minsu thinks France is a beautiful country.
③ Some classmates are helping Minsu.
④ Minus isn't happy with his new school life.
⑤ For Minsu, everything is different from Korea.

출제율 90%

10 밑줄 친 (B)의 우리말에 해당하는 영어를 쓰시오. (wish, luck, best를 포함할 것) (7 words)

➡ _____

출제율 100%

11 다음 중 밑줄 친 단어의 우리말 의미가 바르지 않은 것은?

① She made me work out. (~하게 시켰다)
② Please let me go. (~하도록 허락하다)
③ I had him open the door. (~하게 시켰다)
④ I helped my grandmother move her bag. (~하게 도왔다)
⑤ The news made me sad. (~하게 시켰다)

출제율 95%

12 다음 문장을 괄호 안에 주어진 어휘를 활용하여 영작하시오.

(1) 그들은 나에게 뉴스를 말하지 않을 수 없었다. (couldn't, tell, help, the news) (7 words)

➡ _____

(2) 나는 하루종일 자고 싶다. (feel, sleep, all day long) (7 words)

➡ _____

(3) 나는 아침에 산책하는 것에 익숙하다. (used, take a walk) (10 words)

➡ _____

(4) 그는 바닥에 눕자마자 잠들었다. (lie, fall asleep, on) (8 words)

➡ _____

(5) 그들은 직업을 얻는 데 어려움을 겪었다. (difficulty, get, jobs) (5 words)

➡ _____

(6) 이 차는 고칠 필요가 있다. (need, repair) (4 words)

➡ _____

(7) 나는 그 미팅에 참석할 것을 기대하고 있다. (forward, attend, meeting) (7 words)

➡ _____

13 주어진 단어를 활용하여 다음 우리말을 여섯 단어로 이루어진 한 문장의 영어로 쓰시오.

> 너의 음식은 기다릴 만한 가치가 있다. (worth / wait)

➡ _____

[14~15] 다음 글을 읽고 물음에 답하시오.

Mrs. Choi, my social studies teacher, made an important announcement.

"You will create a newspaper in groups. Check out your new group members."

Mrs. Choi started calling out the names of the students in each group. After a while, ⓐ my name was called.

"Group 4, Jisu..."

"Who will be in my group?" I wondered.

Mrs. Choi continued, "Lina, Inho, and Min."

I couldn't believe my ears. I didn't know anyone in that group. I felt like crying when I sat with my group members.

14 위 글의 밑줄 친 ⓐ를 능동태로 고치시오.

➡ _____

15 Which question CANNOT be answered after reading the passage?

① What subject does Mrs. Choi teach?
② What did Mrs. Choi announce?
③ Which group did Jisu belong to?
④ Did Jisu know her group members well?
⑤ How did Jisu's group members feel when they heard the announcement?

[16~17] 다음 글을 읽고 물음에 답하시오.

We didn't have anything in common. Lina was always drawing something by herself. Inho never said anything, and his only interest seemed to be soccer. Min was smart, but he always had his nose in a book. ⓐ나는 내가 참으로 불행하다는 생각을 하지 않을 수 없었다. I decided to convince Mrs. Choi that I should be with my friends.

"ⓑMaybe she would let me change the group," I thought.

But before I could say anything, she gently placed her hand on my shoulder.

"I know what you want, Jisu," she said, "but I'm sure you will get to like your group members. Don't you think it's worth trying?"

I didn't really believe her, but I said, "Okay," and walked away.

16 위 글의 밑줄 친 ⓐ의 우리말에 맞게 한 단어를 보충하여, 주어진 어휘를 알맞게 배열하시오.

> was / how / thinking / I / unlucky / I / couldn't

➡ _____

17 위 글의 밑줄 친 ⓑ를 다음과 같이 바꿔 쓸 때 빈칸에 들어갈 알맞은 말을 두 단어로 쓰시오.

➡ Maybe she would allow me _____ _____ the group

[18~20] 다음 글을 읽고 물음에 답하시오.

The project wasn't easy from the start. We couldn't decide ⓐ the topic for our newspaper. I felt like giving up on the project, so I asked my friend Ryan ⓑ some advice.

"Try to understand your group members first," he said.

So I carefully watched my group members. And I ⓒcame across some amazing facts about them. Lina read a lot of Japanese comic books, so she was an expert on Japanese culture. Inho's Korean sounded a bit different, but that was because he lived in Argentina when he was young. He knew a lot about Argentina and its soccer. Min's mom was Vietnamese, and Min used to spend some time in Vietnam. He read a lot of history books and loved to talk about Vietnam and its history.

출제율 95%

18 위 글의 빈칸 ⓐ와 ⓑ에 들어갈 전치사가 바르게 짝지어진 것은?

	ⓐ	ⓑ		ⓐ	ⓑ
①	for	– of	②	on	– of
③	in	– for	④	for	– to
⑤	on	– for			

출제율 90%

19 위 글의 밑줄 친 ⓒcame across와 바꿔 쓸 수 없는 말을 모두 고르시오.

① ran into　　② bumped into

③ took up　　④ ran across

⑤ ran through

출제율 100%

20 다음 중 위 글에 대한 이해가 바르지 못한 사람을 고르시오.

① 희준: 그들의 프로젝트는 처음에는 어렵지 않았어.

② 경민: Lina가 일본 문화에 관해 전문가가 된 것은 일본의 만화책을 많이 읽었기 때문이야.

③ 정희: 인호는 어렸을 때 아르헨티나에서 살았기 때문에 한국어 발음이 조금 다르게 들려.

④ 동수: 그런데 그는 아르헨티나와 그 나라의 축구에 관해 많은 것을 알고 있어.

⑤ 윤지: Min은 베트남과 그 역사에 관해 이야기하는 것을 좋아해.

[21~22] 다음 글을 읽고 물음에 답하시오.

I thought of the perfect topic for our group. We decided to write about world culture. I had Lina introduce Japanese culture. Inho wrote about Argentina and its soccer, and Min covered Vietnamese culture and its history. I was in charge of editing the whole newspaper.

(①) Our newspaper project was a great success. (②) We received an A⁺, and my group members became my best friends.

(③) Don't judge a book by its cover. (④) Read it. (⑤) It might turn into your favorite book.　　　　　　　　　　＜I: Jisu＞

출제율 95%

21 위 글의 흐름으로 보아, 주어진 문장이 들어가기에 가장 적절한 곳은?

> I will end my story with this saying.

①　　　②　　　③　　　④　　　⑤

출제율 100%

22 According to the passage, which is NOT true?

① Jisu thought of the perfect topic for her group.

② Lina had Jisu introduce Japanese culture.

③ Jisu was in charge of editing the whole newspaper.

④ The newspaper project of Jisu's group was a great success.

⑤ Jisu's group received an A⁺, and her group members became her best friends.

[01~02] 다음 대화를 읽고 물음에 답하시오.

A: Hi, Bora, what are you doing?
B: I was going over my report card.
A: (A)너는 네 점수에 만족하니? (satisfied)
B: Yes, I am. I got a good grade on my group project.
A: Really? What was it about?
B: We made a movie about the beautiful islands of Korea. It wasn't easy, but is was fun.
A: Do you like group projects?
B: Yes, I do. I think we can learn from each other. (B)_____
A: Well, I don't. I think it's not easy working with others.

01 (A)에 주어진 우리말에 어울리는 영어 문장을 쓰시오. (주어진 단어를 반드시 포함할 것)

➡ _____

02 위 대화의 내용으로 보아, 빈칸 (B)에 들어가기에 적절한 말을 쓰시오. (don't을 포함할 것, 3 words)

➡ _____

[03~04] 다음 대화를 읽고 물음에 답하시오.

B: Do you know Lionel Messi?
G: Yes, I do. He is known for his speed and control of the ball.
B: That's right. (A)그는 공을 다루는 데 익숙해.
G: During this summer vacation, I'm going to travel Spain. To watch him playing, I'll buy soccer tickets.
B: It sounds great!

03 주어진 단어를 활용하여 밑줄 친 우리말 (A)를 영어로 쓰시오.

(handle / ball) (7 words)

➡ _____

04 위 대화의 내용에 맞게 빈칸에 알맞은 말을 쓰시오.

The girl will travel Spain during this summer vacation, and she _____. (forward를 사용할 것.)

05 다음 상황을 읽고 빈칸에 알맞은 말을 쓰시오. 한 칸에 하나의 단어만 쓰시오.

In 1498, Europeans arrived in India. Men from Portugal came to India, and by 1858, India became part of the British Empire. Around 1920, a lawyer named Gandhi began to tell people that they should fight for their country.
Teacher: Do you think Gandhi _____ _____ _____ for his country?

[06~08] 다음 글을 읽고 물음에 답하시오.

ⓐWe didn't have anything in common. Lina was always drawing something by herself. Inho never said anything, and his only interest seemed to be soccer. Min was smart, but he always had his nose in a book. ⓑI couldn't help thinking how unlucky I was. I decided to convince Mrs. Choi that I should be with my friends.

"Maybe she would let me change the group," I thought.

But before I could say anything, she gently placed her hand on my shoulder.

"I know what you want, Jisu," she said, "but I'm sure you will get to like your group members. ⓒ그것은 시도할 만한 가치가 있다고 생각하지 않니?"

I didn't really believe her, but I said, "Okay," and walked away.

06 다음 각각의 학생들의 특징을 우리말로 써서, 지수가 ⓐ처럼 말한 이유를 설명하시오.

➡ (1) Lina: _____
   (2) 인호: _____
          _____
   (3) Min: _____

07 위 글의 밑줄 친 ⓑ를 다음과 같이 바꿔 쓸 때 빈칸에 들어갈 알맞은 말을 각각 두 단어로 쓰시오.

➡ (1) I couldn't _____
   (2) I couldn't _____ think
   (3) I had no choice but _____

08 위 글의 밑줄 친 ⓒ의 우리말에 맞게 주어진 어휘를 이용하여 6 단어로 영작하시오.

worth

➡ _____

[09~11] 다음 글을 읽고 물음에 답하시오.

The project wasn't easy from the start. We couldn't decide on the topic for our newspaper. I felt like giving up on the project, so I asked my friend Ryan for some (A)[advice / advices].

"Try to understand your group members first," he said.

So I carefully watched my group members. And I came across some (B)[amazing / amazed] facts about them. Lina read a lot of Japanese comic books, so she was an expert on Japanese culture. Inho's Korean (C)[sounded / sounded like] a bit different, but that was because he lived in Argentina when he was young. He knew a lot about Argentina and its soccer. Min's mom was Vietnamese, and Min used to spend some time in Vietnam. He read a lot of history books and loved to talk about Vietnam and its history.

09 위 글의 괄호 (A)~(C)에서 문맥이나 어법상 알맞은 낱말을 골라 쓰시오.

➡ (A)_____ (B)_____ (C)_____

10 Why did Jisu carefully watch her group members? Fill in the blanks with suitable words.

Because she wanted to understand her _____ _____ first.

11 다음 빈칸에 알맞은 단어를 넣어 Lina에 대한 소개를 완성하시오.

Lina was an expert on _____ _____ because she read many Japanese comic books.

창의사고력 서술형 문제

01 다음 내용을 바탕으로 일기의 빈칸을 채우시오. (사역동사와 동명사를 활용할 것.)

Circumstance
• In social studies class • Teacher had us make a newspaper
Main Idea
• Don't judge a book by its cover.
Supporting Detail 1 – about Lina
• read a lot of Japanese comic books • an expert on Japanese culture
Supporting Detail 2 – about Inho
• lived in Argentina • know a lot about Argentina and its soccer
Supporting Detail 3 – about Min
• his mom was Vietnamese • read a lot of history books and loved to talk about Vietnam and its history

Our teacher had us (A)_____ a newspaper in groups. When I checked my group members, I felt (B)_____ because we didn't have anything in common. I couldn't (C)_____ how unlucky I was. We couldn't decide on the topic of our newspaper. I (D)_____ up on the project, so I tried to understand my group members first. Lina read a lot of Japanese comic books, so she is (E)_____ Japanese culture. Inho lived in Argentina when he was young and he knew a lot about Argentina and its soccer. He also likes to play soccer, so he is busy (F)_____ soccer every day after school. Min's mom was Vietnamese, and Min used to (G)_____ some time in Vietnam. He read a lot of history books and loved to talk about Vietnam and its history. We decided to write about world culture. Our newspaper project was a great success. I will end my story with this saying. (H)_____.

02 다음 내용을 바탕으로 모둠 활동에 관한 자신의 의견을 나타내는 문장을 쓰시오.

I think group projects are worth doing. They let us learn about working in groups.
Three reasons why I think group projects are good:
• They let us learn from each other.
• They let us make new friends.
• They let us learn to work with others.

Teachers usually have us do group projects because they think they're good for us.
And I agree with them for three reasons.
(A)_____, we can learn (B)_____.
Second, we can make (C)_____.
Third, we can learn (D)_____.
In conclusion, I think group projects are worth (E)_____.

단원별 모의고사

01 다음 영영풀이에 해당하는 단어를 고르시오.

> to have or express a different opinion from someone else

① disagree ② advise
③ edit ④ cheer
⑤ continue

02 다음 주어진 단어를 이용해 빈칸을 완성하시오.

> B: Are you satisfied with your new partner?
> G: Yes, I am.
> B: What do you like about him?
> G: He is fun and _____ .

➡ _____ (talk)

03 다음 우리말에 맞게, 주어진 첫 글자로 시작하는 알맞은 말을 빈칸에 쓰시오.

(1) 우리는 공통점이 아무것도 없었다.
  ➡ We didn't have anything in c_____ .
(2) 나는 우리 모둠을 위하여 완벽한 주제를 생각해 내었다.
  ➡ I thought of the p_____ topic for our group.
(3) 우리는 세계의 문화에 관하여 쓰기로 결정하였다.
  ➡ We decided to write about world c_____ .
(4) 나는 그들에 관하여 놀라운 사실들을 발견하였다.
  ➡ I came across some a_____ facts about them.

04 다음 중 〈보기〉에 있는 단어를 사용하여 자연스러운 문장을 만드시오.

> ┤ 보기 ├
> crying while announcement carefully

(1) Mrs. Choi, my social studies teacher, made an important _____ .
(2) After a _____ , my name was called.
(3) I felt like _____ when I sat with my group members.
(4) So I _____ watched my group members.

[05~07] 다음 대화를 읽고 물음에 답하시오.

> G: I think history is an interesting subject. Don't you (A)_____ ?
> B: I'm afraid I don't agree with you. It's too hard for me.
> G: (B)역사 만화책을 읽는 것이 역사를 쉽게 해줄 수 있어. (may / reading / make / history comic books / easier / it).
> B: I think it would just be boring for me.

05 빈칸 (A)에 들어갈 알맞은 말을 고르시오.

① charge ② agree ③ cheer
④ convince ⑤ judge

06 밑줄 친 (B)의 우리말을 주어진 단어를 배열하여 영어로 쓰시오.

➡ _____

07 Which one of the following is NOT true according to the dialogue above?

① The girl thinks history is an interesting subject.

② The boy doesn't like history.

③ The girl wants to introduce an interesting way of studying history.

④ The boy thinks that history is too hard for him.

⑤ The topic of this dialogue is how to read history comic books.

[08~10] 다음 대화를 읽고 물음에 답하시오.

> G: What are you looking at?
>
> B: I'm looking at the school basketball game poster. (ⓐ)
>
> G: Hmm... (A)_____ do you think is the best basketball player in our school?
>
> B: I think Jihun is the best. (ⓑ)
>
> A: No, I don't agree. I think Minjae is the best player.
>
> B: Why do you think so? (ⓒ)
>
> G: His class won the basketball game last year. Don't you remember? (ⓓ)
>
> B: But that was because Minjae's class had a lot of good basketball players.
>
> G: Anyway, we are lucky to have both of them in our class this year. (ⓔ)
>
> B: Yes, we are. I think our class is going to win the basketball game this year.

08 빈칸 (A)에 들어가기에 적절한 의문사는?

① What　　② Who

③ Which　　④ Why

⑤ Whose

09 ⓐ~ⓔ 중 주어진 문장이 들어갈 곳은?

> Don't you agree?

① ⓐ　　② ⓑ　　③ ⓒ　　④ ⓓ　　⑤ ⓔ

10 위 대화의 내용과 일치하지 않는 것은?

① The boy is looking at the school basketball game poster.

② The boy thinks Jihun is the best basketball player in his school.

③ The girl thinks Minjae is the best player in her school.

④ Jihun's class won the basketball game last year.

⑤ Minjae's class had many good basketball players last year.

11 우리말과 일치하도록 괄호 안의 어구를 바르게 배열하시오.

(1) 그녀는 미국이 첫 번째 FIFA 여성 월드컵에서 이기도록 도왔다.

(the United States, helped, the first, win, she, FIFA Women's World Cup)

➡ _____

_____

(2) 나는 내일 아침에 산책을 하고 싶다.

(I, for, like, feel, going, a walk, tomorrow, morning)

➡ _____

12 다음 주어진 문장과 같은 뜻이 되도록 영작하시오.

> I need to clean my room.

➡ _____

_____

13 다음 중 어색한 문장을 골라 바르게 고치시오.

① I think the audition was worth trying.
② I feel like to go on a trip.
③ I couldn't help but feel sorry for him.
④ I'm used to editing articles.
⑤ I'm busy cleaning my room.

➡ _____

14 다음 밑줄 친 동사의 쓰임이 나머지와 다른 것은?

① It will make you feel dizzy.
② Chloe had my cat climb up the desk.
③ The custom officer had him open his suitcase.
④ Please make a fire here.
⑤ I made him clean the windows.

15 우리말과 일치하도록 괄호 안의 어구를 바르게 배열하시오.

(1) 나는 지금 점심을 먹고 싶지 않다.
   (I, feel, don't, like, lunch, having, now)
   ➡ _____

(2) Lisa는 어떤 차가운 것을 마시고 싶지 않았다.
   (Lisa, like, feel, didn't, something, drinking, cold)
   ➡ _____

(3) 나는 그가 버스 타는 것을 보았다.
   (him, get, saw, I, on, bus, the)
   ➡ _____

(4) 그는 수화를 통해 우리에게 그의 계획을 이해시켰다.
   (he, us, his plan, the sign language, understand, made, through)
   ➡ _____

(5) 그녀는 선풍기 바람에 그녀의 머리를 말렸다.
   (let, the breeze, blow, she, from, her, dry, hair, an electric fan)
   ➡ _____

[16~17] 다음 글을 읽고 물음에 답하시오.

Mrs. Choi, my social studies teacher, made an important announcement.

"You will create a newspaper in groups. Check out your new group members."

Mrs. Choi started calling out the names of the students in each group. After a while, my name was called.

"Group 4, Jisu..."

"Who will be in my group?" I wondered.

Mrs. Choi continued, "Lina, Inho, and Min."

I couldn't believe my ears. I didn't know anyone in that group. I felt ⓐlike crying when I sat with my group members.

16 위 글의 밑줄 친 ⓐlike와 문법적 쓰임이 다른 것을 고르시오.

① She was like a daughter to me.
② It looks like rain.
③ You should do it like this.
④ Would you like a drink?
⑤ Students were angry at being treated like children.

17 다음 문장에서 위 글의 내용과 다른 부분을 찾아서 고치시오.

Mrs. Choi called out the names of the students who would create a newspaper alone.

➡ _____

[18~20] 다음 글을 읽고 물음에 답하시오.

ⓐWe didn't have anything in common. Lina was always drawing something by herself. Inho never said anything, and his only interest seemed to be soccer. Min was smart, but he always had his nose in a book. I couldn't help thinking how unlucky I was. I decided to convince Mrs. Choi that I should be with my friends. "Maybe she would let me change the group," I thought.

But before I could say anything, she gently placed her hand on my shoulder.

"I know what you want, Jisu," she said, "but I'm sure you will get to like your group members. Don't you think it's worth trying?" I didn't really believe ⓑ<u>her</u>, but I said, "Okay," and walked away.

18 위 글의 밑줄 친 ⓐ에 어울리는 속담으로 가장 알맞은 것을 고르시오.

① Too many cooks spoil the broth.
② So many men, so many minds.
③ A friend in need is a friend indeed.
④ Two heads are better than one.
⑤ Birds of a feather flock together.

19 위 글의 밑줄 친 ⓑher가 가리키는 것을 본문에서 찾아 쓰시오.

➡ _____

20 According to the passage, which is NOT true?

① Jisu's group members had nothing in common.
② Lina was always drawing something alone.
③ Min always had his nose in a book.
④ Jisu didn't think how unlucky she was.
⑤ Jisu was not allowed to change the group.

[21~23] 다음 글을 읽고 물음에 답하시오.

The project wasn't easy (A)<u>from</u> the start. (①) We couldn't decide on the topic (B)<u>for</u> our newspaper. (②) I felt like giving up (C)<u>to</u> the project, so I asked my friend Ryan for some advice. (③)

So I carefully watched my group members. (④) And I came across some amazing facts (D)<u>about</u> them. (⑤) Lina read a lot of Japanese comic books, so she was an expert (E)<u>on</u> Japanese culture. ⓐ<u>Inho's Korean sounded a bit different, but that was why he lived in Argentina when he was young.</u> He knew a lot about Argentina and its soccer. Min's mom was Vietnamese, and Min used to spend some time in Vietnam. He read a lot of history books and loved to talk about Vietnam and its history.

21 위 글의 흐름으로 보아, 주어진 문장이 들어가기에 가장 적절한 곳은?

> "Try to understand your group members first," he said.

①   ②   ③   ④   ⑤

22 위 글의 밑줄 친 (A)~(E)에서 전치사의 쓰임이 적절하지 <u>않은</u> 것을 찾아 알맞게 고치시오.

➡ _____

23 위 글의 밑줄 친 ⓐ에서 어법상 틀린 부분을 찾아 고치시오.

➡ _____

Lesson 2

Waste Not, Want Not

의사소통 기능

- 충고하기

  If I were you, I'd pull the plug out.
- 방법 묻기

  Do you know how to save energy in other ways?

언어 형식

- the 비교급 ~, the 비교급 …

  The more ideas we share, **the more** energy we can save!

- 부정사의 의미상의 주어

  It is essential **for all students to use** fewer resources at school.

Words & Expressions

Key Words

- **add** [æd] 동 더하다
- **additional** [ədíʃənl] 형 추가적인
- **alone** [əlóun] 형 혼자 있는
- **already** [ɔːlrédi] 부 이미, 벌써
- **amount** [əmáunt] 명 양
- **bubble wrap** 비닐 포장재
- **character** [kǽriktər] 명 글자, 성격
- **charge** [tʃɑːrdʒ] 동 충전하다
- **check** [tʃek] 동 확인하다
- **Chinese character** 한자
- **concentrate** [kánsəntrèit] 동 집중하다
- **conference** [kánfərəns] 명 회의, 발표회
- **consider** [kənsídər] 동 고려하다
- **cool** [kuːl] 동 식히다
- **environmental** [invàiərənméntl] 형 환경의
- **escape** [iskéip] 동 벗어나다, 탈출하다
- **essential** [isénʃəl] 형 필수적인
- **exercise** [éksərsàiz] 동 운동하다
- **experiment** [ikspérəmənt] 명 실험
- **fix** [fiks] 동 고치다
- **forest** [fɔ́ːrist] 명 숲
- **grocery** [gróusəri] 명 식료품
- **heat** [hiːt] 동 데우다 명 열
- **information** [ìnfərméiʃən] 명 정보
- **leave** [liːv] 동 남겨두다, 떠나다
- **meal** [miːl] 명 식사
- **nervous** [nɔ́ːrvəs] 형 불안한
- **normally** [nɔ́ːrməli] 부 보통
- **pay** [pei] 동 지불하다
- **plant** [plænt] 명 식물
- **pot** [pɑt] 명 화분
- **press** [pres] 동 누르다
- **prevent** [privént] 동 가로막다, 방해하다
- **price** [prais] 명 가격
- **reduce** [ridjúːs] 동 줄이다
- **refrigerator** [rifrídʒərèitər] 명 냉장고
- **regularly** [régjulərli] 부 규칙적으로
- **resource** [ríːsɔːrs] 명 자원
- **rooftop** [rúftɑp] 명 옥상
- **save** [seiv] 동 절약하다, 아끼다
- **space** [speis] 명 공간, 우주
- **spend** [spend] 동 보내다
- **spring** [spriŋ] 명 옹달샘
- **thickness** [θíknis] 명 두께
- **truth** [truːθ] 명 사실, 진실
- **unique** [juːníːk] 형 독특한
- **waste** [weist] 명 낭비
- **whole** [houl] 형 전체의

Key Expressions

- **as often as possible** 될 수 있는 한 자주
- **based on ~** ~을 바탕으로
- **be good at ~** ~을 잘하다
- **be in danger** 위험에 처하다
- **be worth -ing** ~할 가치가 있다
- **brush off** 털어내다
- **by oneself** 혼자서
- **come up with** ~을 생각해 내다
- **full of** ~로 가득 찬
- **go shopping** 쇼핑하러 가다
- **had better ~** ~하는 편이 낫다
- **have no choice** 선택의 여지가 없다
- **keep -ing** ~하기를 계속하다
- **not ~ at all** 결코 ~ 아닌
- **pick up** 집어 들다
- **prevent A from -ing** A가 ~하지 못하게 하다
- **pull out** ~을 뽑다
- **put on** ~을 붙이다
- **standby power** 대기 전력
- **stay up** 잠을 자지 않고 깨어 있다
- **stick to ~** ~에 달라붙다
- **the same as ~** ~와 같은
- **turn off** ~을 끄다
- **with the lights on** 불이 켜진 채로

Word Power

※ 서로 비슷한 뜻을 가진 어휘

□ **add** 더하다 – **sum** 합을 내다
□ **additional** 추가적인 – **extra** 추가적인
□ **alone** 혼자 있는 – **isolated** 고립된
□ **whole** 전체의 – **entire** 전체의
□ **character** 글자 – **letter** 문자
□ **unique** 독특한 – **unusual** 흔치 않은
□ **concentrate** 집중하다 – **focus** 집중하다

□ **consider** 고려하다 – **think** 생각하다
□ **essential** 필수적인 – **basic** 기본적인
□ **prevent** 가로막다 – **stop** 가로막다
□ **fix** 고치다 – **repair** 수리하다
□ **conference** 회의 – **meeting** 회의
□ **nervous** 불안한 – **unstable** 불안한
□ **price** 가격 – **cost** 비용

※ 서로 반대의 뜻을 가진 어휘

□ **add** 더하다 ↔ **subtract** 빼다
□ **cool** 식히다 ↔ **heat** 데우다
□ **nervous** 불안한 ↔ **calm** 차분한
□ **prevent** 가로막다 ↔ **allow** 허용하다

□ **spend** 쓰다, 보내다 ↔ **save** 저축하다
□ **essential** 필수적인 ↔ **optional** 선택적인
□ **whole** 전체의 ↔ **partial** 부분적인
□ **unique** 독특한 ↔ **ordinary** 평범한

※ 동사 – 명사

□ **add** 더하다 – **addition** 더하기
□ **consider** 고려하다 – **consideration** 고려
□ **prevent** 가로막다 – **prevention** 예방, 방지

□ **concentrate** 집중하다 – **concentration** 집중
□ **pay** 지불하다 – **payment** 지불
□ **reduce** 줄이다 – **reduction** 축소, 감소

English Dictionary

□ **essential** 필수적인
→ extremely important and necessary
대단히 중요하고 필요한

□ **resource** 자원
→ something such as useful land, or minerals such as oil or coal
유용한 토지나 석유와 석탄같은 광물질 같은 것

□ **add** 더하다
→ to put something with something else
어떤 것에 다른 어떤 것을 놓다

□ **alone** 혼자 있는
→ without any friends or people you know
친구 또는 아는 사람이 없는

□ **fix** 고치다
→ to repair something that is broken or not working properly
고장 났거나 제대로 작동하지 않는 것을 수리하다

□ **leave** 떠나다
→ to go away from a place or a person
어떤 장소나 사람으로부터 멀어지다

□ **nervous** 불안한
→ worried or frightened about something
무엇인가에 대해 걱정하거나 겁먹은

□ **pay** 지불하다
→ to give someone money for something you buy
구입한 물건에 대해 돈을 주다

□ **rooftop** 옥상
→ the upper surface of a roof 지붕의 위쪽 면

□ **waste** 낭비
→ not to be used in a way that is effective, useful, or sensible
효과 거나 쓸모 있거나 유용한 방식으로 사용되지 않는 것

□ **concentrate** 집중하다
→ to think very carefully about something that you are doing 하고 있는 일에 매우 신중하게 생각하다

□ **check** 확인하다
→ to do something in order to find out whether something really is correct, true, or in good condition
어떤 것이 올바르거나 사실이거나 또는 상태가 좋은지 알아내려고 무엇인가를 하다

□ **information** 정보
→ facts or details that tell you something about a situation, person, event etc
상황, 사람, 사건 등에 관하여 무엇인가를 알게 해주는 사실이나 상세한 사항

□ **consider** 고려하다
→ to think about something carefully, especially before making a choice or decision 선택하거나 결정을 하기 전에 신중하게 무엇인가에 대하여 생각하다

[01~02] 다음 짝지어진 단어의 관계가 같도록 빈칸에 알맞은 단어를 고르시오.

01

| add : sum = _____ : isolated |

① nervous   ② alone
③ worried   ④ depressed
⑤ popular

02 중요

| charge : discharge = _____ : heat |

① cool   ② save
③ prevent   ④ check
⑤ consider

03 다음 영영풀이에 해당하는 단어를 고르시오.

| extremely important and necessary |

① careful   ② leave
③ normal   ④ essential
⑤ experimental

04 서답형 다음 〈보기〉에 있는 단어를 사용하여 자연스러운 문장을 만드시오.

┌─ 보기 ─┐
decide   experiment   waste   save
└─────┘

(1) So how can we _____ energy?
(2) They help students not to _____ water.
(3) We did an _____ last winter.
(4) We will _____ to make a garden on the rooftop of the school.

05 중요 다음 대화의 빈칸에 들어갈 말로 적절한 것을 고르시오.

> **B:** You look worried. What's the problem?
> **G:** I lost my brother's watch. He loves the watch so much.
> **B:** If I were you, I'd tell him the _____.
> **G:** I guess I have no choice.

① information   ② advice
③ meal   ④ charge
⑤ truth

06 다음 밑줄 친 단어와 의미가 같은 단어를 고르시오.

> First, you should consider the price of a new refrigerator.

① exercise   ② amount
③ character   ④ cost
⑤ pot

07 중요 다음 중 밑줄 친 부분의 뜻풀이가 바르지 않은 것은?

① This is because we are wasting a lot of energy. (낭비하는)
② I was surprised to see some empty classrooms with the lights on. (불이 켜진)
③ We found that bubble wrap can help to save energy. (아끼다)
④ Three different environmental clubs are here to share their activities. (공유하다)
⑤ So we have designed some resource saving stickers. (자원)

[01~02] 다음 빈칸에 공통으로 들어가기에 적절한 단어를 쓰시오.

01

- Did you stay _____ late last night?
- It's very clever of you to come _____ with such great ideas!

02

- I think he doesn't understand your idea _____ all.
- I don't think I'll be any good _____ tennis, but I'll give it a try.

03 아래 문장의 빈칸에 〈보기〉에 있는 단어를 넣어 자연스러운 문장을 만드시오.

┌─ 보기 ─┐

electricity   order   energy   choose

(1) Just check all the food you want and press the _____ button.

(2) Do you know how to _____ a good refrigerator?

(3) They tell us which light should be turned on, so that we can waste less _____.

(4) A lot of _____ is used to heat and cool our school.

04 다음 짝지어진 단어의 관계가 같도록 빈칸에 알맞은 말을 쓰시오. (주어진 철자로 시작할 것)

spend : save = n_____ : calm

05 다음 주어진 단어를 이용해 빈칸을 완성하시오.

The boiler will need to use an _____ 2% of gas or oil to heat your house.

➡ _____ (add)

06 다음 우리말에 맞게 빈칸에 알맞은 말을 쓰시오. (주어진 철자가 있는 경우에는 주어진 철자로 시작할 것)

(1) 우리는 지구가 위험에 빠졌다는 사실을 모두 알고 있다.

➡ We all know that the Earth is in _____.

(2) 마지막으로 교실을 떠나는 학생이 불을 꺼야 한다.

➡ The last student who l_____ the classroom should turn off the lights.

(3) 두 교실에서의 온도는 16℃이었다.

➡ The _____ was 16℃ in both classrooms.

(4) 우리는 여름에 건물을 냉방하기 위하여 사용하는 에너지를 아낄 수 있다.

➡ We can save some of the energy we use to _____ the buildings in the summer.

Conversation

교과서

1 충고하기

If I were you, I'd pull the plug out. 만약 내가 너라면, 나는 플러그를 뽑을 것이다.

- 곤란한 일이나 어려운 일을 당한 사람에게 적절한 방법을 알려주거나 도움이 되는 충고를 할 때 "만약 내가 너라면, 나는 ~할 텐데."의 의미로 "If I were you, I would ~."의 표현을 사용한다. "~하는 편이 더 낫다"의 의미로 "You had better ~"도 충고하는 의미로 쓰인다. "You had better ~"는 줄여서 "You'd better ~"라고 하고, 주로 부모님이나 선생님처럼 더 권위가 있는 사람이 긴급한 상황이나 충고가 필요한 상황에서 쓴다. 친구 사이에 충고를 하는 경우에는 "You should ~."를 더 많이 쓴다.

- 어려운 일을 당해서 "어떻게 해야 할까요?"의 의미로 상대에게 충고를 요청할 때는 "What should I do?"라고 하거나 "What can I do?"라고 한다. 그 외에도 충고를 구하는 말은 "Can[Could] you give me some tips?", "What would you advise me to do?" 등이 있다.

충고하기

• If I were you, I'd ~ .	만약 내가 너라면, 나는 ~할 텐데.
• If I were in your shoes, I'd ~.	만약 내가 네 입장이라면, 나는 ~할 텐데.
• You had better ~.	너는 ~하는 편이 더 낫다.
• Why don't you ~?	~하는 것이 어떠니?
• You should be careful about ~.	너는 ~에 대하여 조심해야 해.
• Make sure that you ~.	반드시 ~하도록 해라.

충고 구하기

- What should I do?
- What do you think I should do?
- What would you advise me to do?
- What can I do?
- What would you do if you were in my shoes?

핵심 Check

1. 다음 대화의 빈칸에 들어가기에 적절한 말을 고르시오.

> B: You look worried. What's the problem?
> G: I lost my brother's watch. He loves the watch so much.
> B: _____, I'd tell him the truth.
> G: I guess I have no choice.

① If it were not for you ② If I were you ③ You had better
④ Though you should worry ⑤ Because I know it

2 방법 묻기

Do you know how to save energy in other ways? 다른 방법들로 어떻게 에너지를 절약하는지 아니?

- 문제를 해결하는 방법을 상대방에게 물어볼 때는 "어떻게 ~하는지 압니까?"의 의미로 "Do you know how to ~?", "Do you know how 주어+동사 ~?"를 사용한다. 동사 know 대신 tell, show 등을 사용하여 "Would you tell me how to ~?", "Would you show me how ~?"라고 할 수도 있다.

- "Can you explain how to ~?", "Can you explain how 주어+동사 ~?"라고 방법을 물어보기도 하지만, 좀 더 공손하게 표현할 때는 would, could를 사용하여 "Would you explain how to ~?", "Could you explain how ~?"라고 한다.

- 상대방에게 구체적으로 문제 해결에 대하여 질문하는 경우에는 "해결하다"의 의미를 가지는 동사 "solve"를 사용하여 "How can I solve this problem?"이라고 할 수도 있다.

방법을 묻는 표현

- How can I solve this problem? 어떻게 이 문제를 해결할까요?
- Can you explain how this machine works? 어떻게 이 기계가 작동하는지 설명해 줄래?
- Can you show me how to use the copy machine? 복사기 사용 방법 좀 알려 줄래?
- Would you tell me how to ~? ~하는 방법 좀 말해주시겠습니까?

핵심 Check

2. 다음 대화의 빈칸에 들어갈 말을 고르시오.

> G: This restaurant is famous for its fresh and delicious food.
> B: Great. But do you know _____ this restaurant?
> G: Just pick up what you want. You can pay at the end.
> B: Oh, I see. Thanks.

① what to pay ② where to find ③ when to order
④ how to use ⑤ how to pay

3. 다음 우리말과 일치하도록 주어진 어구를 이용하여 빈칸에 알맞은 말을 쓰시오.

> A: _____? (how / do / know / use / you / to / this washing machine)
> (어떻게 이 세탁기를 사용하는지 아니?)
> B: Sure. You need to put 8 coins in first, and then press the start button. (물론. 먼저 동전 8개를 넣고, 시작 버튼을 눌러.)

Everyday English 1 B

W: Jihu, what are you holding? ❶It looks like a bag full of fruit!

B: Yes, I went to a grocery store.

W: Let me see. Why did you buy the apples?

B: I just bought them because they were really cheap.

W: We already have a bag of apples at home! It's such a waste of money!

B: Oh, I didn't know that.

W: ❷If I were you, I'd check what I have first before I go shopping.

B: Yes, you're right.

W: And then I'd make a shopping list based on that information.

B: Okay, I'll do that next time, Mom.

W: 지후야, 무엇을 들고 있니? 마치 과일로 가득 찬 가방 같은데!

B: 네, 식료품점에 갔었어요.

W: 어디 보자. 사과를 왜 샀니?

B: 사과가 정말 싸서 그냥 샀어요.

W: 집에 이미 사과 한 봉지가 있어! 이건 정말 돈 낭비야!

B: 오, 그건 몰랐어요.

W: 내가 너라면 쇼핑을 가기 전에 무엇이 있는지 먼저 확인할 거야.

B: 네, 엄마 말씀이 맞아요.

W: 그리고 나서 그 정보를 바탕으로 쇼핑 리스트를 만들 거야.

B: 알겠어요. 다음에는 그렇게 할게요, 엄마.

❶ look like ~ = ~처럼 보이다
❷ 'If I were you, I'd ~'는 상대에게 충고하는 의미로 '내가 너라면, ~할 것이다'에 해당한다.

Check(√) True or False

(1) The boy bought apples because there weren't any apples at home.　　T ☐ F ☐

(2) The woman advised the boy to make a shopping list.　　T ☐ F ☐

In Real Life

Inho: Lina, you are not charging your phone. If I were you, I'd pull the plug out.

Lina: Why? I'll use the charger later. Leave it that way.

Inho: But you are wasting electricity.

Lina: It's only a little bit.

Inho: Actually, if we add up a year's standby power, it is the same as the amount of electricity we normally use for a month.

Lina: Oh, I didn't know that.

Inho: Yeah, there are a lot of ❶things like that which we waste without knowing in our daily lives.

Lina: Do you know how to save energy ❷in other ways?

Inho: I hear that there's going to be an energy-saving conference at school next week.

Lina: Maybe we should go together!

인호: Lina야, 내 전화기를 충전하고 있지 않잖아. 내가 너라면 플러그를 뽑을 거야.

Lina: 왜? 나중에 충전기를 쓸 거야. 그렇게 놔둬.

인호: 하지만 너는 전기를 낭비하고 있는 거야.

Lina: 조금밖에 안 되잖아.

인호: 실제로 만약 우리가 1년의 대기 전력을 합하면 보통 한 달 동안 쓰는 전기량과 같아.

Lina: 오, 그건 몰랐어.

인호: 그래, 그렇게 우리가 일상생활에서 모르는 사이에 낭비하는 것들이 많이 있어.

Lina: 에너지를 절약하는 다른 방법들을 아니?

인호: 다음 주에 학교에서 에너지 절약 회의가 있을 거라고 들었어.

Lina: 그럼 같이 가야겠구나!

❶ 'things like that which ~'는 선행사 things를 수식하는 관계대명사 which를 사용하였다. 'like that'은 삽입된 부사구이다.
❷ in other ways = 다른 방식들로

Check(√) True or False

(3) Lina is not charging her phone at the moment.　　T ☐ F ☐

(4) There will be a conference for the environment next week.　　T ☐ F ☐

Everyday English 1 A-2(1)

B: You ❶look worried. What's the problem?
G: I lost my brother's watch. He loves the watch so much.
B: If I were you, I'd tell him the truth.
G: I guess I ❷have no choice.

❶ look worried 걱정스러워 보이다 ❷ have no choice 선택의 여지가 없다

Everyday English 1 A-2(2)

G: Oh, it's ❶too hard for me to concentrate in class.
B: Did you ❷stay up late last night?
G: Yeah, I just couldn't sleep well last night.
B: If I were you, I'd get some fresh air before the next class starts.

❶ too ~ for A to ... = A가 …하기에 너무 ~하다 ❷ stay up late 밤늦게까지 자지 않다

Everyday English 2 A-2(1)

B: I ❶keep getting this kind of message again and again.
G: I had the same problem with my computer.
B: Oh, then, do you know ❷how to fix this?
G: You need to download a program.

❶ keep ~ing = 계속 ~하다
❷ how to fix = 어떻게 수리하는지 (의문사+to부정사 = 의문사+주어+should 동사원형 ~)

Everyday English 2 A-2(2)

G: This restaurant ❶is famous for its fresh and delicious food.
B: Great. But do you know how to use this restaurant?
G: Just pick up ❷what you want. You can pay at the end.
B: Oh, I see. Thanks.

❶ be famous for ~ = ~로 유명하다
❷ what은 선행사를 포함하는 관계대명사로 '~하는 것'이라고 해석한다. 'what you want = 네가 원하는 것'

Everyday English 2 B

M: Do you know how to choose a good refrigerator? First, you should consider the price of a new refrigerator. ❶How much can you spend on your refrigerator? The question leaves a few options for you. Next, you should think of its size. You might think that larger ones are better. But if it's too big, you will waste space and energy. ❷Try to choose the right size for you. ❸The last thing you have to consider is how much energy it uses. When you look at the refrigerator, there is a sticker. Choose a refrigerator with a greener sticker as it uses less energy.

❶ spend (돈) on A = A에 (돈)을 쓰다
❷ try to ~ = ~하려고 애쓰다 (try -ing = 시험 삼아 ~해 보다)
❸ the last thing you have to consider = 마지막으로 네가 고려할 것 / 목적격 관계대명사 생략

Check Your Progress 1

G: Do you know how to ❶be good at Chinese characters?
B: Oh, did you start to learn them?
G: Yeah, I heard that learning them is really helpful. But it is ❷too hard to remember all the characters.
B: If I were you, I'd try to understand ❸how each character is made first.
G: What do you mean?
B: For example, look at this character. A human is standing next to a tree.
G: Oh, I see. Now I can easily remember ❹what the character looks like.
B: Then how do you feel when you're next to a tree?
G: Maybe I feel like I am resting.
B: Now you have the meaning of the character, too.

❶ be good at ~ = ~을 잘하다
❷ too ~ to ... = ~하기에는 너무 …하다, 너무 ~해서 …할 수 없다
❸ 동사 understand의 목적어로 쓰인 간접의문문이다.
❹ looks like의 목적어로 how가 아니라 what을 써야 한다.

● 다음 우리말과 일치하도록 빈칸에 알맞은 말을 쓰시오.

Everday English 1 A-2(1)

B: You _____ worried. What's the _____?

G: I _____ my brother's _____. He _____ the watch so _____.

B: If I _____ you, I'd tell him the _____.

G: I _____ I have no _____.

Everday English 1 A-2(2)

G: Oh, it's too _____ for me to _____ in class.

B: Did you _____ up late last night?

G: Yeah, I just couldn't _____ well last night.

B: _____ I _____ you, I'd _____ some _____ air before the next class _____.

Everday English 1 - B

W: Jihu, _____ are you _____? It looks _____ a bag _____ of fruit!

B: Yes, I _____ to a _____ store.

W: _____ me see. Why did you _____ the apples?

B: I just _____ them _____ they were really _____.

W: We _____ have a bag of _____ at home! It's _____ a waste of _____!

B: Oh, I didn't know that.

W: _____ I _____ you, I'd _____ what I have _____ before I go _____.

B: Yes, you're right.

W: And then I'd _____ a shopping list _____ on that _____.

B: Okay, I'll _____ that next time, Mom.

Everday English 2 A-2(1)

B: I keep _____ this kind of _____ again and again.

G: I _____ the same problem with my computer.

B: Oh, then, do you know _____ _____ this?

G: You need to _____ a program.

해석

B: 걱정 있어 보여. 무슨 일 있니?

G: 내 동생 시계를 잃어버렸어. 그는 그 시계를 무척 좋아하는데.

B: 내가 너라면 그에게 사실대로 말하겠어.

G: 선택의 여지가 없는 것 같아.

G: 아, 나는 수업 시간에 집중하기가 너무 어려워.

B: 어젯밤에 늦게까지 안 잤니?

G: 응, 어젯밤에 잠을 잘 못 잤어.

B: 내가 너라면 다음 수업이 시작하기 전에 맑은 공기를 좀 마실 거야.

W: 지후야, 무엇을 들고 있니? 마치 과일로 가득 찬 가방 같은데!

B: 네, 식료품점에 갔었어요.

W: 어디 보자. 사과를 왜 샀니?

B: 사과가 정말 싸서 그냥 샀어요.

W: 집에 이미 사과 한 봉지가 있어! 이건 정말 돈 낭비야!

B: 오, 그건 몰랐어요.

W: 내가 너라면 쇼핑을 가기 전에 무엇이 있는지 먼저 확인할 거야.

B: 네, 엄마 말씀이 맞아요.

W: 그러고 나서 그 정보를 바탕으로 쇼핑 리스트를 만들 거야.

B: 알겠어요, 다음에는 그렇게 할게요, 엄마.

B: 나는 계속해서 이런 종류의 메시지를 받고 있어.

G: 내 컴퓨터에도 같은 문제가 있었어.

B: 오, 그럼, 이것을 고치는 법을 아니?

G: 어떤 프로그램을 내려받아야 해.

Everday English 2 B

M: Do you know _____ to _____ a good _____? First, you should _____ the price of a new refrigerator. How much can you _____ on your refrigerator? The question _____ a few options for you. Next, you should _____ _____ its size. You might think that _____ ones are better. But if it's _____ big, you will _____ space and _____. Try to choose the _____ size for you. The last thing you have to _____ is _____ _____ energy it uses. When you _____ at the refrigerator, there is a sticker. Choose a refrigerator with a greener _____ as it _____ _____ energy.

In Real Life

Inho: Lina, you are not _____ your phone. If I were you, I'd _____ the plug out.

Lina: Why? I'll use the _____ later. _____ it that way.

Inho: But you are _____ electricity.

Lina: It's only a little bit.

Inho: _____, if we _____ up a year's _____ power, it is the same as the _____ of electricity we _____ use for a month.

Lina: Oh, I didn't know that.

Inho: Yeah, there are a lot of _____ like that _____ we waste _____ _____ in our daily lives.

Lina: Do you know _____ to _____ energy in other _____?

Inho: I hear that there's going to be an energy-saving _____ at school next week.

Lina: Maybe we should go together!

Check Your Progress 1

G: Do you know how to be _____ _____ Chinese _____?

B: Oh, did you _____ to learn them?

G: Yeah, I _____ that learning them is really _____. But it is _____ hard to _____ all the characters.

B: If I were you, I'd try to _____ how each _____ is made first.

G: What do you _____?

B: For example, look at this _____. A human is _____ next to a tree.

G: Oh, I see. Now I can easily _____ what the character _____ like.

해석

M: 여러분은 좋은 냉장고를 선택하는 방법을 알고 계시나요? 우선, 새 냉장고의 가격을 고려해야 합니다. 냉장고에 얼마나 쓸 수 있나요? 그 질문은 여러분에게 몇 가지 선택지를 남겨 줍니다. 다음으로, 냉장고의 크기를 생각해야 합니다. 더 큰 것이 더 좋다고 생각할지도 모릅니다. 하지만 너무 크면 공간과 에너지를 낭비하게 될 것입니다. 여러분에게 맞는 사이즈를 고르도록 하세요. 마지막으로 고려해야 할 것은 그것이 얼마나 많은 에너지를 사용하는지 고려해야 합니다. 냉장고를 보면 스티커가 붙어 있습니다. 에너지를 적게 쓰기 때문에 녹색 스티커가 붙은 냉장고를 선택하세요.

인호: Lina야, 내 전화기를 충전하고 있지 않잖아. 내가 너라면 플러그를 뽑을 거야.

Lina: 왜? 나중에 충전기를 쓸 거야. 그렇게 놔둬.

인호: 하지만 너는 전기를 낭비하고 있는 거야.

Lina: 조금밖에 안 되잖아.

인호: 실제로 만약 우리가 1년의 대기 전력을 합하면 보통 한 달 동안 쓰는 전기량과 같아.

Lina: 오, 그건 몰랐어.

인호: 그래, 그렇게 우리가 일상생활에서 모르는 사이에 낭비하는 것들이 많이 있어.

Lina: 에너지를 절약하는 다른 방법들을 아니?

인호: 다음 주에 학교에서 에너지 절약 회의가 있을 거라고 들었어.

Lina: 그럼 같이 가야겠구나!

G: 너는 어떻게 하면 한자를 잘하는지 아니?

B: 오, 너는 그것들을 배우기 시작했니?

G: 응, 그것들을 배우는 게 정말 도움이 된다고 들었어. 하지만 모든 글자를 기억하는 게 너무 힘들어.

B: 내가 너라면 먼저 각 글자가 어떻게 만들어졌는지 이해하려고 할 거야.

G: 무슨 말이니?

B: 예를 들면, 이 글자를 봐. 사람이 나무 옆에 서 있잖아.

G: 아, 알겠다. 이제 그 글자가 어떻게 생겼는지 쉽게 기억할 수 있어.

[01~02] 다음 대화의 빈칸에 들어갈 말을 고르시오.

01

> G: Oh, it's too hard for me to _____ in class.
> B: Did you stay up late last night?
> G: Yeah, I just couldn't sleep well last night.
> B: If I were you, I'd get some fresh air before the next class starts.

① add   ② charge   ③ check
④ concentrate   ⑤ consider

02

> B: I keep getting this kind of message again and again.
> G: I had the same problem with my computer.
> B: Oh, then, do you know _____ fix this?
> G: You need to download a program.

① what to   ② where to   ③ how to
④ whom to   ⑤ which to

[03~04] 다음 대화를 읽고 물음에 답하시오.

> B: Do you know how to use this machine? (A)
> G: Touch the screen. (B) Then you can see the menu. (C)
> B: Oh, right. (D)
> G: Just check all the food you want and press the order button. (E)

03 (A)~(E) 중에서 다음 문장이 들어가기에 가장 적절한 곳은?

> What's next?

① A   ② B   ③ C   ④ D   ⑤ E

04 위 대화의 내용과 일치하지 않는 것은?

① The boy explains how to use the machine
② They can order food with the machine.
③ First the boy will touch the screen.
④ After selecting, the boy will press the order button.
⑤ Before seeing the menu, the boy should tough the screen.

01 다음 대화의 순서가 바르게 배열된 것을 고르시오.

> B: I think we should save electricity at home.
> (A) Also, pulling out the plug of the computer or the TV will be helpful.
> (B) Do you know how to save electricity at home?
> (C) We can save electricity by turning off the computer and the TV.

① (A) – (C) – (B)   ② (B) – (A) – (C)
③ (B) – (C) – (A)   ④ (C) – (A) – (B)
⑤ (C) – (B) – (A)

[02~04] 다음 대화를 읽고 물음에 답하시오.

> G: Minjae, is this plant yours?
> B: Yeah, it was my last year's birthday gift from my sister.
> G: It seems that it has grown a lot.
> B: Oh, do you think so?
> G: Yeah. If I were you, I'd (A)_____ to a larger pot.
> B: Hmm... I didn't know that I have to change its pot.
> G: If you change the pot, the plant will grow better.
> B: But I don't know how to do it. Do you know (B)_____ it to another pot?
> G: Sure. I've done that a lot of times. I can teach you how to do it now if you want.
> B: That's great!

 02 위 대화의 빈칸 (A)에 들어갈 말로 알맞은 것은?

① change the plant   ② clear the pot
③ move the plant   ④ buy a new pot
⑤ remove from the plant

03 빈칸 (B)에 들어가기에 적절한 것은?

① where to plant   ② which to change
③ what to buy   ④ when to do
⑤ how to move

04 위 대화의 내용과 일치하지 않는 것은?

① The plant was Minjae's birthday gift from the girl.
② The girl knows how to change the pot.
③ The boy asks the girl how to change the pot.
④ The boy didn't know that he had to change the pot.
⑤ The plant will grow better in a larger pot.

05 다음 빈칸에 들어갈 말이 순서대로 바르게 짝지어진 것은?

> Inho: Lina, you are not charging your phone. If I were you, I'd pull the plug (A)_____.
> Lina: Why? I'll use the charger later. Leave it that way.
> Inho: But you are (B)_____ electricity.
> Lina: It's only a little bit.
> Inho: Actually, if we (C)_____ up a year's standby power, it is the same as the amount of electricity we normally use for a month.
> Lina: Oh, I didn't know that.

	(A)	(B)	(C)
①	out	wasting	use
②	out	saving	add
③	in	using	use
④	in	saving	add
⑤	out	wasting	add

[06~08] 다음 대화를 읽고 물음에 답하시오.

Inho: Lina, you are not charging your phone.
(A) If I were you, I'd pull the plug out.

Lina: Why? I'll ①use the charger later. (B)

Inho: But you are wasting electricity.

Lina: It's only a little bit. (C)

Inho: Actually, if we add up a year's standby power, it is ②the same as the amount of electricity we normally use for a month. (D)

Lina: Oh, I didn't know that. (E)

Inho: Yeah, there are a lot of things like that ③which we waste without knowing in our daily lives.

Lina: Do you know ④how to save energy in other ways?

Inho: I hear that there ⑤are going to be an energy-saving conference at school next week.

Lina: Maybe we should go together!

06 (A)~(E) 중에서 다음 문장이 들어가기에 가장 적절한 곳은?

> Leave it that way.

① (A) ② (B) ③ (C) ④ (D) ⑤ (E)

07 ⓐ~ⓔ 중에서 어법상 어색한 것은?

① ⓐ ② ⓑ ③ ⓒ ④ ⓓ ⑤ ⓔ

08 Which one CANNOT be answered from the dialogue above?

① Will Lina pull the plug out?
② How much electricity can be saved by pulling out the plug?
③ How can we save energy in other ways?
④ When will the conference be?
⑤ Where is the conference going to be?

[09~11] 다음 대화를 읽고 물음에 답하시오.

M: Do you know ⓐhow to choose a good refrigerator? First, you should consider the (A)_____ of a new refrigerator. How much can you spend on your refrigerator? The question ⓑleaves a few options for you. Next, you should think of its (B)_____. You might think that ⓒlarger ones are better. But if it's too big, you will ⓓsave space and energy. Try to choose the right size for you. The last thing you have to ⓔconsider is how much energy it uses. When you look at the refrigerator, there is a sticker. Choose a refrigerator with a greener sticker as it uses less energy.

서답형
09 빈칸 (A)와 (B)에 들어가기에 적절한 단어를 각각 쓰시오.

➡ (A) _____ (B) _____

10 ⓐ~ⓔ 중에서 내용상 어색한 것은?

① ⓐ ② ⓑ ③ ⓒ ④ ⓓ ⑤ ⓔ

11 다음 중 위 대화의 내용과 일치하지 않는 것은?

① There are a few options for a good refrigerator.
② You should consider the price for a new refrigerator.
③ The larger the refrigerator is, the better it is.
④ You should consider the energy the refrigerator spends.
⑤ A refrigerator with a green sticker uses less energy.

[01~03] 다음 대화를 읽고 물음에 답하시오.

> Inho: Lina, you are not charging your phone. If I ⓐwere you, I'd (A)_____ the plug out.
>
> Lina: Why? I'll use the charger later. Leave it ⓑthat way.
>
> Inho: But you are wasting electricity.
>
> Lina: It's only ⓒa little bit.
>
> Inho: Actually, if we add up a year's standby power, (가)그것은 보통 우리가 한 달 동안 쓰는 전기의 양과 같다.(the same as / electricity / normally use)
>
> Lina: Oh, I didn't know that.
>
> Inho: Yeah, there are a lot of things like that ⓓwhat we waste without knowing in our daily lives.
>
> Lina: Do you know how to (B)_____ energy in other ways?
>
> Inho: I hear that there's ⓔgoing to be an energy-saving conference at school next week.
>
> Lina: Maybe we should go together!

01 내용상 빈칸 (A), (B)에 들어가기에 적절한 한 단어를 쓰시오.

➡ (A) _____ (B) _____

02 ⓐ~ⓔ 중에서 어법이 어색한 것을 찾아 번호를 쓰고 올바르게 고치시오.

➡ _____

03 주어진 단어를 포함하여 밑줄 친 우리말 (가)를 영작하시오. (15 words)

➡ _____
_____

04 다음 대화의 문맥상 또는 어법상 어색한 것을 찾아 고치시오.

> W: Jihu, what are you holding? It looks like a bag full of fruit!
>
> B: Yes, I went to a grocery store.
>
> W: Let me see. Why did you buy the apples?
>
> B: I just bought them because they were really cheap.
>
> W: We already have a bag of apples at home! It's such a waste of money!
>
> B: Oh, I knew that.
>
> W: If I were you, I'd check what I have first before I go shopping.
>
> B: Yes, you're right.

➡ _____

05 다음 대화의 빈칸에 적절한 단어를 쓰시오.

> A: Do you know how to _____ the medicine?
>
> B: Sure. You need to take it three times a day before you have your meals.

06 우리말과 일치하도록 주어진 단어를 배열하여 문장을 만드시오.

> G: Oh, 내가 수업 시간에 집중하기가 너무 어려워. (it's / for / hard / too / in class)
>
> B: Did you stay up late last night?
>
> G: Yeah, I just couldn't sleep well last night.
>
> B: If I were you, I'd get some fresh air before the next class starts.

➡ _____

Grammar

1 the 비교급 ~, the 비교급 …

> **The more** ideas we share, **the more** energy we can save.
> 우리가 아이디어를 더 많이 공유할수록 우리는 더 많은 에너지를 아낄 수 있다.

- 형태: the 비교급 (주어+동사), the 비교급 (주어+동사)

  의미: ~하면 할수록 더 …

- 비교급을 사용하는 관용적 표현 중에 '~하면 할수록 더 …하다'의 의미로 'the 비교급 (주어+동사), the 비교급 (주어+동사)'의 구문이 있다. 이는 두 가지의 비례하는 증가나 감소를 보여줄 때 사용하는 표현이다..
  - **The less** you spend, **the more** you save. 네가 덜 쓸수록 너는 더 많이 저축한다.
  - **The sooner** they go, **the better** it is. 그들이 빨리 가면 빨리 갈수록 더 좋다.

- 'the 비교급 ~, the 비교급'의 구문에서 비교급의 형용사나 부사를 주어 앞에 쓴다. 만약 목적어 또는 보어의 명사구 일부분인 형용사를 비교급으로 하여 이 구문을 만들면 그 명사구 전체를 주어 앞으로 이동해야 한다.
  - **The more** you give, **the more** you receive. 네가 많이 줄수록 너는 더 많이 받는다.
  - **The more difficult** the test is, **the harder** students should study. 시험이 어려울수록, 학생들은 더 열심히 공부해야 한다.

    cf. **The more** the test is **difficult**, the harder students should study. (✕)
      (difficult의 비교급은 more difficult이다.)
  - **The more** money you spend, **the less** money you save. 네가 돈을 많이 쓰면 쓸수록 너는 더 적은 돈을 저축한다.

    cf. The more you spend money, the less you save money. (✕)

핵심 Check

1. 다음 주어진 문장에서 적절한 것을 고르시오.

   (1) The (little / less) I see him, the more I like him.

   (2) The (many / more) he reads, the less he understands.

   (3) The (old / older) we grow, the (wise / wiser) we become.

2. 다음 주어진 단어를 적절하게 배열하여 자연스러운 문장을 만드시오.

   (1) (you, it, climb, gets, the higher, the colder)

   ➡ _____

   (2) (the car, it, is, is, to drive, dangerous, the faster, the more)

   ➡ _____

② 부정사의 의미상 주어

It is essential **for all students to use** fewer resources at school.
모든 학생이 학교에서 더 적은 자원을 사용하는 것이 필수적이다.

■ 형태: It ~ for A to …
의미: A가 …하는 것은 ~하다

■ 부정사의 행위자를 '부정사의 의미상 주어'라고 한다. 부정사의 의미상의 주어는 to부정사 앞에 'for+목적격'의 형태로 사용한다. 보통 'It ~ for A to동사원형'의 형태가 되며 It을 가주어, 'for A'를 의미상의 주어, 'to+동사원형'을 진주어라고 한다.
  • **It** is strange **for her to be** so late for class. 그녀가 수업에 그렇게 늦는 것이 이상하다.
  • **It** is impossible **for us to finish** the job in time. 우리가 그 일을 제때 끝내는 것은 불가능하다.

■ 부정사의 의미상의 행위자가 주어, 목적어 등으로 이미 문장에 언급이 되어 있는 경우를 제외하고, 부정사의 의미상의 주어가 필요할 때는 to부정사 앞에 'for+목적격' 형태로 쓰지만, 사람의 성격이나 상태를 나타내는 표현 다음에는 'of+목적격'을 쓴다.
  • I would like **him to come** on time. (문장의 목적어가 부정사의 의미상의 주어이다.) 나는 그가 제시간에 오기를 원한다.
  • **It** is very clever **of you to come** up with such great ideas! 네가 그렇게 좋은 아이디어를 생각해 내는 것을 보니 매우 영리하구나!

■ 사람의 성격이나 상태를 나타내는 형용사: kind, nice, wise, clever, honest, polite, thoughtful, careful, bad, foolish, silly, careless 등
  • **It** is kind **of you to show** me the way. 나에게 길을 알려주시다니 당신은 친절하십니다.
    = You are kind to show me the way.

핵심 Check

3. 괄호 안의 말을 올바르게 배열하여 문장을 완성하시오.

(1) It is _____.
    (important, to get up, early, for Jake)

(2) It is _____.
    (of you, for me, very kind, to carry the bag)

(3) It is _____.
    (to come up with, of him, very clever, such a good idea)

(4) It is _____.
    (to wear their helmet, for the cyclists, when riding the bike, necessary)

Grammar 시험대비 기본평가

01 다음 빈칸에 들어갈 말로 알맞은 것은?

> The _____ one grows, the greater one's worries are.

① rich   ② richest   ③ great

④ richer   ⑤ greatest

02 다음 우리말을 영어로 바르게 옮긴 것은?

> 당신이 더 많은 책을 읽으면 읽을수록, 당신은 더 많은 것을 알게 된다.

① The more books you read, the more things you will know.

② The more you read books, the much you will know things.

③ The many books you read, the many things you will know.

④ The many you read books, the many you will know things.

⑤ The more books you read, you will know the many things.

03 다음 문장의 밑줄 친 It과 쓰임이 같은 것은?

> It is difficult for Ann to ride a bike.

① It becomes hotter every year.

② It has been snowing since last Sunday.

③ It's a student environmental organization.

④ It's important to use public transportation.

⑤ It'll save much energy.

04 다음 중 주어진 문장에 들어갈 말과 같은 것은?

> It is lazy _____ Jack to sleep until noon.

① It was foolish _____ me to lose my key.

② It is easy _____ Jenny to repair a camera.

③ It is important _____ you to keep promises.

④ It was difficult _____ Ann to ride a bike.

⑤ It is dangerous _____ him to drive in this snow.

01 다음 중 어법상 <u>어색한</u> 것은?

① It's nice of you to say so.
② It's hard for me to make friends.
③ It's necessary for us to help them.
④ It's difficult of a child to sit still for a long time.
⑤ It's important for teachers to speak loudly.

서답형
02 다음 주어진 문장을 〈보기〉와 같이 바꿔 쓰시오.

┤ 보기 ├

As you become kinder, your friends will like you more.
➡ <u>The kinder you become, the more your friends will like you.</u>

(1) As you study harder, you will get a better grade.
(2) As you exercise more, you will become healthier.
(3) As we plant more trees, we will have more fresh air.
(4) As the weather becomes hotter, you should drink more water.

(1) _____

_____

(2) _____

_____

(3) _____

_____

(4) _____

_____

03 다음 중 어법상 올바른 문장은?

① It's hard of me to do it all alone.
② It is kind for her to lend me her camera.
③ It is exciting of me to play basketball.
④ It was wise of him to save money for his future.
⑤ It is safe of Janet to wear a helmet when riding a bicycle.

04 다음 우리말의 뜻과 같도록 주어진 단어들을 바르게 배열할 때 여섯 번째로 오는 것은?

우리가 더 높이 올라갈수록 더 추워진다.
(the / gets / colder / the / climb / we / it / higher)

① it ② we ③ gets
④ climb ⑤ colder

05 다음 중 밑줄 친 부분이 어법상 올바른 것은?

① It is very kind <u>of you</u> to say that.
② It is difficult <u>of us</u> to move this chair.
③ It is not easy <u>of me</u> to speak English.
④ It is very nice <u>for you</u> to wash the dishes.
⑤ Is it necessary <u>for his</u> to leave a little early today?

서답형
06 다음 우리말과 의미가 같도록 주어진 어구를 배열할 때 네 번째로 오는 것은?

너의 형이 너에게 크게 소리를 지르는 것은 당연하다.
(natural / to / it / at you / your brother / is / shout out loudly / for).

➡ _____

07 다음 중 빈칸에 들어갈 말이 나머지와 <u>다른</u> 것은?

① It is dangerous _____ the kids to go there.

② It is boring _____ me to watch action movies.

③ It was silly _____ me to believe your promise.

④ It is difficult _____ me to write letters in English.

⑤ It was not easy _____ me to get some exercise regularly.

08 Which is grammatically CORRECT?

① The hoter you get, the more you sweat.

② As the weather is warmer, I feel the much better.

③ The more expensive a course is, better its taste is.

④ The more advice we are given, the harder it is to decide.

⑤ As we study the harder, we find ourselves more ignorant.

09 다음 중 어법상 어색한 문장은?

① The more we have, the much we want.

② The higher we go up, the colder it becomes.

③ The older you get, the wiser you will become.

④ The more you smile, the more people will like you.

⑤ The more we get together, the happier we'll be.

10 다음 문장의 의미가 자연스럽도록 빈칸에 들어갈 말로 알맞은 것은?

> The more people you meet, _____ .

① the sooner can we leave

② the sooner we can leave

③ the happier was the party

④ the more things can you learn

⑤ the more things you can learn

서답형

11 다음 〈보기〉와 같이 주어진 문장을 바꾸어 다시 쓰시오.

┤ 보기 ├
• She will repair the radio.
• It is easy.
➡ <u>It is easy for her to repair the radio.</u>

(1) • He will take care of the cat.
   • It is difficult.
   ➡ _____

(2) • She will buy an umbrella.
   • It is necessary.
   ➡ _____

(3) • She helped the old lady.
   • It was kind.
   ➡ _____

12 다음 중 빈칸에 들어갈 말이 나머지와 <u>다른</u> 것은?

① It is hard _____ them to win the game.

② It is necessary _____ her to lose weight.

③ It is rude _____ him to ask such questions.

④ It's not safe _____ us to play outside at night.

⑤ Is it okay _____ Mike to go there early today?

13 다음 중 어법상 올바른 문장은?

① The rich we are, the happier we'll be.
② The older you get, the wise you will become.
③ The more you smile, the many people will like you.
④ The more you love, the more will you be loved.
⑤ The earlier you start the day, the better it will be.

14 다음 우리말을 영어로 바르게 옮긴 것은?

> 상황이 어려울수록, 나는 그것을 더 즐기게 된다.

① The hard the situation will be, I will enjoy it more.
② The harder the situation will be , more I will enjoy it.
③ As the situation is harder, I enjoy it the more.
④ As the situation is the harder, I enjoy it more.
⑤ The harder the situation is, the more I enjoy it.

15 다음 중 빈칸에 들어갈 말이 나머지와 <u>다른</u> 것은?

① It's very generous _____ you to say so.
② It's difficult _____ us to move chairs in an hour.
③ Is it okay _____ me to leave the room a little early?
④ It is impossible _____ him to climb the tall tree.
⑤ It is important _____ him to listen to others.

16 Which is grammatically CORRECT?

① The tall you get, the farther you can see.
② As the weather gets colder, I wear a more thick jacket.
③ The more you have, you want the more.
④ The more help you give, the more satisfied you will be.
⑤ As you study more hard, you can answer more questions.

17 다음 중 (A)~(E)의 빈칸에 들어갈 말로 바르게 짝지어진 것은?

> (A) It was hard _____ me to watch the boring game.
> (B) It was careless _____ me to take the wrong bus.
> (C) It's easy _____ me to remember phone numbers.
> (D) It might be difficult _____ Tom to share his toys with other kids.
> (E) _____ get up early is important.

	(A)	(B)	(C)	(D)	(E)
①	of	of	for	of	To
②	of	for	of	of	For
③	for	for	of	for	For
④	for	of	for	of	To
⑤	for	of	for	for	To

18 다음 중 어법상 <u>어색한</u> 문장은?

① The harder you practice, the easier it is to learn a new language.
② The more the teacher talked, the less she understood.
③ The longer it takes, the worse it gets.
④ The faster you drive, the sooner you'll get there.
⑤ The more you practice, the more early you will become a professional baseball player.

01 다음 문장의 괄호 안에 주어진 단어를 지시대로 고쳐 문장을 다시 쓰시오.

(1) It's difficult (we) to swim in the river.
(의미상의 주어)

➡ _____

(2) It's kind (you) to hold the bag for me.
(의미상의 주어)

➡ _____

02 다음 우리말과 같은 뜻이 되도록 "the+비교급~, the+비교급…" 구문을 써서 바꿔 쓰시오.

(1) 날씨가 좋을수록 공원에서 사람을 더 많이 볼 수 있다.

When the weather is better, we can find more people in the park.

➡ _____
_____

(2) 과일이 신선할수록 더 맛있다.

When the fruit is fresher, it tastes better.

➡ _____

(3) 그녀는 나이가 들수록 더 현명해졌다.

As she grew older, she became wiser.

➡ _____

03 다음 〈보기〉와 같이 주어진 문장을 다시 쓰시오.

┤ 보기 ├
• You should finish it by noon.
• It is necessary.
→ It is necessary for you to finish it by noon.

She was late for work. It was strange.

➡ _____

04 다음 문장 (A), (B)에서 어법상 잘못된 부분을 찾아 바르게 고치시오.

(A) The cheaper the apples are, the most apples you'll buy.
(B) It's not easy of him to finish the report today.

(A) _____ ➡ _____
(B) _____ ➡ _____

05 다음 〈보기〉에서 알맞은 단어를 골라 자연스러운 문장이 되도록 빈칸을 완성하시오. (단, 주어진 단어는 중복으로 사용할 수 있으며, 필요시 변형할 것)

┤ 보기 ├
high, healthy, more, far, good

(1) The _____ you study, the _____ grade you get.

(2) The _____ a bird flies, the _____ it can see.

(3) The _____ you exercise, the _____ you get.

06 다음 괄호 안에서 필요한 단어만 골라 우리말 의미에 맞도록 영작하시오.

(1) 우리가 이 의자를 옮기는 것은 어렵지 않다.

➡ It isn't difficult _____.
(move, for, to, this, chair, of, us)

(2) 네가 창문을 연 것은 조심성이 없었다.

➡ It was careless _____.
(the, window, open, of, to, for, you)

07 다음 우리말의 의미에 맞게 〈보기〉의 두 문장을 'It'으로 시작하는 한 문장으로 연결하시오. (kind와 help를 반드시 사용할 것)

> 길 잃은 소년이 엄마를 찾도록 도와주다니 Tom은 아주 친절했다.

┤ 보기 ├
- A lost boy was crying on the street.
- Tom helped him to find his mother.

➡ _____

_____

08 다음 우리말과 의미가 같도록 주어진 단어를 사용하여 〈조건〉에 맞게 문장을 완성하시오.

┤ 조건 ├
'the 비교급, the 비교급'을 사용하여 어법에 맞는 완전한 영어 문장을 쓸 것

(1) 나이를 먹어갈수록, 우리는 더 현명해진다.
(old, wise)

➡ _____

(2) 비가 심하게 올수록, 사람들은 더 빨리 걷는다.
(heavily, fast)

➡ _____

_____

09 다음 우리말과 의미가 같도록 〈조건〉에 맞게 빈칸을 완성하시오.

┤ 조건 ├
- 주어와 동사를 갖춘 완전한 문장으로 쓸 것
- 한 칸에 한 단어씩 쓸 것
- 주어진 단어(It)로 문장을 시작할 것

> Mary가 그 제안을 거절한 것은 현명했다.
> (refuse, suggestion)
>
> ➡ It _____ _____ _____
>
> _____ _____ _____ _____.

10 다음 주어진 〈조건〉에 맞게 우리말을 영작하시오.

┤ 조건 ├
1. 'The+비교급+주어+동사, the+비교급+주어+동사' 구문을 사용할 것
2. 우리말에 맞게 영작하되 시제에 유의할 것

> 날씨가 따뜻해지면 따뜻해질수록, 나는 기분이 더 좋다. (get)
>
> ➡ _____
>
> _____

11 다음 주어진 우리말과 같은 뜻이 되도록 주어진 단어를 순서대로 배열하시오.

> 그들이 매일 운동을 계속하는 것은 어렵다.
> (hard, for, to, keep, exercising, them, is)
>
> ➡ It _____ every day.

➡ _____

Reading

Energy-Saving Conference

Welcome to the Energy-Saving Conference. The Earth is in danger.

The air is getting dirtier every day. More and more animals are dying.
get+비교급: 점점 더 ~해지다   비교급 and 비교급: 점점 더 ~한

This is because we are wasting a lot of energy. So how can we save
why(×)

energy? Three different environmental clubs are here to share their
to부정사의 부사적 용법(목적),

activities. The more ideas we share, the more energy we can save!
The 비교급+주어+동사, the 비교급+주어+동사: 더 ~할수록 더 …하다 = As we share more ideas, we can save more energy!

Jimin: Hello, friends. A few months ago, I was surprised to see some
to부정사의 부사적 용법(감정의 원인)

empty classrooms with the lights on. That's not right at all. It
불을 켜 놓은 채

is essential for all students to use fewer resources at school. So
It … for ~ to부정사: It: 가주어, for ~: 의미상의 주어, to부정사: 진주어

we have designed some resource saving stickers and put them

on the switches. They tell us which light should be turned on, so

that we can waste less electricity. They also tell the last student
so that 주어 can 동사: 그래서 ~할 수 있다   tell A to B: A에게 B하라고 말하다

who leaves the classroom to turn off the lights. We also put some
주격 관계대명사

stickers on the mirrors in the restrooms. They help students not to
'not'을 to부정사의 앞에 두어 부정을 표현

waste water. The more stickers we put up, the more resources we
The 비교급+주어+동사, the 비교급+주어+동사: 더 ~할수록, 더 …하다

can save at school.

be in danger 위험에 처하다
essential 필수적인
switch 스위치
turn on/off ~을 켜다/끄다
put up ~을 붙이다

확인문제

● 다음 문장이 본문의 내용과 일치하면 T, 일치하지 <u>않으면</u> F를 쓰시오.

1   The Earth is in danger. ☐

2   The more ideas we share, the more energy we can waste! ☐

3   A few months ago, Jimin was surprised to see some empty classrooms with the
    lights on. ☐

4   Some teachers have designed source saving stickers and put them on the switches.
    ☐

5   Resource saving stickers tell us which light should be turned on, so that we can
    waste less electricity. ☐

Dongsu: Hi, everyone. A lot of energy is used to heat and cool our
셀 수 없는 명사로 단수 취급   에너지는 '사용되는' 것이기 때문에 수동태
school. It is important for students to reduce the amount of
가주어   의미상의 주어   진주어
energy we use. We did an experiment last winter and found
find-found-found
that bubble wrap can help to save energy. Look at this chart.
= save
   In Classroom A we put bubble wrap on the windows and in
Classroom B we didn't. When we turned off the heater, the
'didn't' 다음에 'put bubble wrap on the windows'가 생략
temperature was 16 ℃ in both classrooms. Sixty minutes later, the
= An hour later
temperature in Classroom B went down to 7 ℃. But it was 9 ℃ in
Classroom A! We learned that bubble wrap only lets a little heat
let+목적어+목적격 보어(동사 원형)
escape from the building. So we started putting bubble wrap on
= to put
the school windows. This will also prevent heat from getting into
prevent A from B: A를 B로부터 막다. A가 B하는 것을 막다
the classroom in the summer. The more bubble wrap we put on the
The 비교급+주어+동사.
windows, the cooler our summer will become!
the 비교급+주어+동사: 더 ~할수록, 더 …하다

experiment 실험
bubble wrap 뽁뽁이
temperature 온도
escape 도망치다
prevent ~을 막다

확인문제

● 다음 문장이 본문의 내용과 일치하면 T, 일치하지 않으면 F를 쓰시오.

1 Dongsu's club members did an experiment last winter and found that bubble wrap can help to save energy. ☐

2 In Classroom A they didn't put bubble wrap on the windows and in Classroom B they did. ☐

3 When they turned off the heater, the temperature was 16 ℃ in both classrooms. ☐

4 Sixteen minutes later, the temperature in Classroom B went down to 7 ℃. ☐

5 Bubble wrap only lets a little heat escape from the building. ☐

6 The more bubble wrap we put on the windows, the hotter our summer will become! ☐

Minwoo: Hello, friends. We decided to make a garden on the rooftop of the
making(X)

school to save energy. Only a few people know how it works. It's
to부정사의 부사적 용법(목적)   간접의문문 어순: 의문사+주어+동사. work: 작용하다, 작동하다

just like bubble wrap. It prevents heat from getting in and out of

the buildings. So when we have rooftop gardens on our buildings,

we can save some of the energy we use to cool the buildings in
'the energy'와 'we' 사이에 목적격 관계대명사 'which(혹은 that)'가 생략된 문장   to부정사의 부사적 용법(목적)

the summer. Also, the fresh air from the rooftop garden helps to

cool the whole city. So it is necessary for us students to make more
가주어   의미상의 주어   to부정사의 명사적 용법(진주어)

rooftop gardens at our school! The more beautiful our rooftops
The 비교급+주어+동사

become, the less energy our school will use!
the 비교급+주어+동사: 더 ~할수록, 더 …하다

MC: It's very clever of you to come up with such great ideas!
사람의 성품이나 성질을 나타내는 형용사(wise. kind. careful. nice. stupid 등)가 있으면 의미상의 주어는 'of+목적격'으로 나타낸다.

These are all worth trying at school or at home. Thank you for your
be worth –ing = It is worth while to부정사: ~할 가치가 있다

unique ideas and activities!

rooftop 옥상
unique 독특한

 확인문제

- 다음 문장이 본문의 내용과 일치하면 T, 일치하지 않으면 F를 쓰시오.

1 Minwoo's club members decided to make a garden on the rooftop of the school to
   save energy. ☐

2 Many people know how a garden on the rooftop of the school works. ☐

3 A garden on the rooftop of the school prevents heat from getting in and out of the
   buildings. ☐

4 When we have rooftop gardens on our buildings, we can waste some of the energy
   we use to cool the buildings in the summer. ☐

5 The fresh air from the rooftop garden helps to cool the whole city. ☐

6 The more beautiful our rooftops become, the more energy our school will use! ☐

● 우리말을 참고하여 빈칸에 알맞은 말을 쓰시오.

1   _____ Conference

2   Welcome to the _____ Conference.

3   The Earth _____ _____ _____.

4   The air is _____ _____ every day.

5   _____ _____ _____ animals are dying.

6   This is _____ we are wasting a lot of energy.

7   So _____ can we _____ _____?

8   Three different environmental clubs are here _____ _____ their activities.

9   _____ _____ _____ we share, _____ _____ _____ we can save!

10 Jimin: Hello, friends.

11 A few months ago, I was surprised to see some empty classrooms _____ _____ _____ _____.

12 That's _____ right _____ _____.

13 It is essential _____ all students _____ _____ fewer resources at school.

14 So we have designed some _____ _____ _____ and put them on the switches.

---

1   에너지 절약 회의

2   에너지 절약 회의에 오신 것을 환영합니다.

3   지구는 지금 위험에 처해 있습니다.

4   공기는 매일 더러워지고 있습니다.

5   점점 더 많은 동물이 죽어가고 있습니다.

6   이것은 우리가 많은 에너지를 낭비하고 있기 때문입니다.

7   그렇다면 우리는 어떻게 에너지를 절약할 수 있을까요?

8   세 개의 다른 환경 동아리들이 그들의 활동을 공유하기 위해 여기에 있습니다.

9   우리가 더 많은 아이디어를 공유할수록, 우리는 더 많은 에너지를 절약할 수 있습니다!

10 지민: 친구들, 안녕하세요.

11 몇 달 전에, 저는 전등이 켜진 몇 개의 빈 교실을 보고 놀랐습니다.

12 그것은 전혀 옳지 않습니다.

13 모든 학생이 학교에서 더 적은 자원을 사용하는 것이 필수적입니다.

14 그래서 우리는 몇 장의 자원 절약 스티커를 디자인해서 스위치에 붙였습니다.

15 They tell us which light should _____ _____ _____, _____ _____ we can waste less electricity.

16 They also tell the _____ student who leaves the classroom _____ _____ _____ the lights.

17 We also _____ _____ _____ _____ the mirrors in the restrooms.

18 They help students _____ _____ _____ water.

19 _____ _____ _____ we put up, _____ _____ _____ we can save at school.

20 Dongsu: Hi, everyone.

21 A lot of energy _____ _____ to heat and cool our school.

22 _____ is important _____ students _____ _____ the amount of energy we use.

23 We _____ _____ _____ last winter and found that bubble wrap can _____ _____ _____ energy.

24 _____ _____ this chart.

25 In Classroom A we _____ bubble wrap _____ the windows and in Classroom B we didn't.

26 When we _____ _____ the heater, the temperature was 16 ℃ in both classrooms.

27 Sixty minutes later, the temperature in Classroom B _____ _____ _____ 7 ℃.

28 But _____ was 9 ℃ in Classroom A!

29 We learned that bubble wrap only lets a little heat _____ _____ the building.

15 그것들은 어떤 전등이 켜질 것인지 알려 줘서, 우리는 전기를 덜 낭비할 수 있습니다.

16 그것들은 또한 교실을 떠나는 마지막 학생이 전등을 꺼야 한다고 알려 줍니다.

17 우리는 또한 화장실에 있는 거울에도 몇 장의 스티커를 붙였습니다.

18 그것들은 학생들이 물을 낭비하지 않도록 도와줍니다.

19 우리가 더 많은 스티커들을 붙일수록, 학교에서 더 많은 자원을 절약할 수 있습니다.

20 동수: 모두 안녕하세요.

21 많은 에너지가 우리 학교의 난방과 냉방을 위해 사용됩니다.

22 우리가 사용하는 에너지양을 학생들이 줄이는 것이 중요합니다.

23 우리는 지난겨울 실험을 해서 뽁뽁이가 에너지를 절약하는 데에 도움이 된다는 것을 발견했습니다.

24 이 도표를 보세요.

25 우리는 교실 A에는 창문에 뽁뽁이를 붙였고 교실 B에는 붙이지 않았습니다.

26 우리가 히터를 껐을 때, 두 교실 온도는 모두 16℃였습니다.

27 60분 뒤, 교실 B의 온도는 7℃로 내려갔습니다.

28 하지만 교실 A는 9℃였어요!

29 우리는 뽁뽁이가 오직 적은 양의 열만 건물에서 빠져나가게 한다는 것을 알았습니다.

30 So we started _____ bubble wrap _____ the school windows.

31 This will also _____ heat _____ _____ into the classroom in the summer.

32 _____ _____ _____ _____ we put on the windows, _____ _____ our summer will become!

33 Minwoo: Hello, friends.

34 We decided _____ _____ a garden _____ _____ _____ of the school to save energy.

35 _____ _____ _____ people know _____ _____.

36 _____ _____ _____ bubble wrap.

37 It _____ heat _____ getting _____ _____ the buildings.

38 So when we have rooftop gardens on our buildings, we can save some of the energy _____ _____ _____ _____ the buildings in the summer.

39 Also, the fresh air from the rooftop garden _____ _____ the whole city.

40 So it _____ necessary _____ us students _____ _____ more rooftop gardens at our school!

41 _____ _____ _____ our rooftops become, _____ _____ _____ our school will use!

42 MC: It's very clever _____ you to _____ such great ideas!

43 These are all _____ _____ at school or at home.

44 Thank you for your _____ ideas and activities!

---

30 그래서 우리는 학교 창문에 뽁뽁이를 붙이기 시작했습니다.

31 이것이 여름에 열이 교실로 들어오는 것 또한 막아 줄 것입니다.

32 우리가 창문에 더 많은 뽁뽁이를 붙일수록, 우리의 여름도 더 시원해질 거예요!

33 민우: 안녕하세요, 친구들.

34 우리는 에너지를 절약하기 위해 학교 옥상에 정원을 만들기로 했습니다.

35 오직 몇몇 사람들만이 그것이 어떻게 작용하는지 알고 있습니다.

36 그것은 마치 뽁뽁이와 같습니다.

37 그것은 열기가 건물 안팎으로 드나드는 것을 막습니다.

38 그래서 건물에 옥상정원을 가지고 있으면, 우리는 여름에 건물을 식히기 위해 사용하는 에너지 일부를 절약할 수 있습니다.

39 또한, 옥상정원에서 나오는 신선한 공기는 도시 전체를 식히는 것을 도와줍니다.

40 그래서 우리 학생들이 우리 학교에 더 많은 옥상정원을 만드는 것이 필요합니다!

41 우리의 옥상이 더 아름다워질수록, 우리 학교는 에너지를 덜 사용하게 될 겁니다!

42 진행자: 이런 멋진 아이디어를 떠올리다니 여러분은 아주 똑똑하군요!

43 학교나 집에서 모두 해볼 만한 것들 입니다.

44 여러분의 고유한 아이디어와 활동에 감사합니다!

• 우리말을 참고하여 본문을 영작하시오.

1 에너지 절약 회의
➡ _____

2 에너지 절약 회의에 오신 것을 환영합니다.
➡ _____

3 지구는 지금 위험에 처해 있습니다.
➡ _____

4 공기는 매일 더러워지고 있습니다.
➡ _____

5 점점 더 많은 동물이 죽어가고 있습니다.
➡ _____

6 이것은 우리가 많은 에너지를 낭비하고 있기 때문입니다.
➡ _____

7 그렇다면 우리는 어떻게 에너지를 절약할 수 있을까요?
➡ _____

8 세 개의 다른 환경 동아리들이 그들의 활동을 공유하기 위해 여기에 있습니다.
➡ _____

9 우리가 더 많은 아이디어를 공유할수록, 우리는 더 많은 에너지를 절약할 수 있습니다!
➡ _____

10 지민: 친구들, 안녕하세요.
➡ _____

11 몇 달 전에, 저는 전등이 켜진 몇 개의 빈 교실을 보고 놀랐습니다.
➡ _____

12 그것은 전혀 옳지 않습니다.
➡ _____

13 모든 학생이 학교에서 더 적은 자원을 사용하는 것이 필수적입니다.
➡ _____

14 그래서 우리는 몇 장의 자원 절약 스티커를 디자인해서 스위치에 붙였습니다.
➡ _____

15 그것들은 어떤 전등이 켜질 것인지 알려 줘서, 우리는 전기를 덜 낭비할 수 있습니다.
➡ _____

16 그것들은 또한 교실을 떠나는 마지막 학생이 전등을 꺼야 한다고 알려 줍니다.
➡ _____

17 우리는 또한 화장실에 있는 거울에도 몇 장의 스티커를 붙였습니다.
➡ _____

18 그것들은 학생들이 물을 낭비하지 않도록 도와줍니다.
➡ _____

19 우리가 더 많은 스티커들을 붙일수록, 학교에서 더 많은 자원을 절약할 수 있습니다.
➡ _____

20 동수: 모두 안녕하세요.
➡ _____

21 많은 에너지가 우리 학교의 난방과 냉방을 위해 사용됩니다.
➡ _____

22 우리가 사용하는 에너지양을 학생들이 줄이는 것이 중요합니다.
➡ _____

23 우리는 지난겨울 실험을 해서 뽁뽁이가 에너지를 절약하는 데에 도움이 된다는 것을 발견했습니다.
➡ _____

24 이 도표를 보세요.
➡ _____

25 우리는 교실 A에는 창문에 뽁뽁이를 붙였고 교실 B에는 붙이지 않았습니다.
➡ _____

26 우리가 히터를 껐을 때, 두 교실 온도는 모두 16℃였습니다.
➡ _____

27 60분 뒤, 교실 B의 온도는 7℃로 내려갔습니다.
➡ _____

28 하지만 교실 A는 9℃였어요!
➡ _____

29 우리는 뽁뽁이가 오직 적은 양의 열만 건물에서 빠져나가게 한다는 것을 알았습니다.
➡ _____

30 그래서 우리는 학교 창문에 뽁뽁이를 붙이기 시작했습니다.
➡ _____

31 이것이 여름에 열이 교실로 들어오는 것 또한 막아 줄 것입니다.
➡ _____

32 우리가 창문에 더 많은 뽁뽁이를 붙일수록, 우리의 여름도 더 시원해질 거예요!
➡ _____

33 민우: 안녕하세요, 친구들.
➡ _____

34 우리는 에너지를 절약하기 위해 학교 옥상에 정원을 만들기로 했습니다.
➡ _____

35 오직 몇몇 사람들만이 그것이 어떻게 작용하는지 알고 있습니다.
➡ _____

36 그것은 마치 뽁뽁이와 같습니다.
➡ _____

37 그것은 열기가 건물 안팎으로 드나드는 것을 막습니다.
➡ _____

38 그래서 건물에 옥상정원을 가지고 있으면, 우리는 여름에 건물을 식히기 위해 사용하는 에너지 일부를 절약할 수 있습니다.
➡ _____
_____

39 또한, 옥상정원에서 나오는 신선한 공기는 도시 전체를 식히는 것을 도와줍니다.
➡ _____

40 그래서 우리 학생들이 우리 학교에 더 많은 옥상정원을 만드는 것이 필요합니다!
➡ _____

41 우리의 옥상이 더 아름다워질수록, 우리 학교는 에너지를 덜 사용하게 될 겁니다!
➡ _____

42 진행자: 이런 멋진 아이디어를 떠올리다니 여러분은 아주 똑똑하군요!
➡ _____

43 학교나 집에서 모두 해볼 만한 것들입니다.
➡ _____

44 여러분의 고유한 아이디어와 활동에 감사합니다!
➡ _____

[01~03] 다음 글을 읽고 물음에 답하시오.

Welcome to the Energy-Saving Conference. The Earth is ⓐ danger. The air is getting dirtier every day. More and more animals are dying. This is because ⓑwe are wasting a lot of energy. So how can we save energy? Three different environmental clubs are here to share their activities. The more ideas we share, the more energy we can save!

서답형

01 위 글의 빈칸 ⓐ에 들어갈 알맞은 전치사를 쓰시오.

➡ _____

서답형

02 위 글의 밑줄 친 ⓑ로 인해 나타나게 된 결과 두 가지를 본문에서 찾아 쓰시오.

➡ (1) _____
　 (2) _____

03 위 글의 뒤에 올 내용으로 가장 알맞은 것을 고르시오.

① the introduction of the various species of plants and animals
② the way to save endangered animals
③ the way to reduce global warming
④ the introduction of the activities of three different environmental clubs
⑤ the way to preserve the resources of the earth

[04~06] 다음 글을 읽고 물음에 답하시오.

Dongsu: Hi, everyone. A lot of energy is used to heat and cool our school. It is important ⓐ students to reduce the amount of energy we use. We did an experiment last winter and found that bubble wrap can help to save energy. Look at this chart.

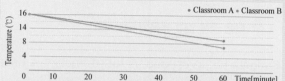

In Classroom A we put bubble wrap on the windows and in Classroom B we didn't. When we turned off the heater, the temperature was 16 ℃ in both classrooms. Sixty minutes later, the temperature in Classroom B went down to 7 ℃. But it was 9 ℃ in Classroom A! We learned that bubble wrap only lets a little heat escape from the building. So we started putting bubble wrap on the school windows. This will also prevent heat ⓑ getting into the classroom in the summer. ⓒMore bubble wrap we put on the windows, cooler our summer will become!

중요

04 위 글의 빈칸 ⓐ와 ⓑ에 들어갈 전치사가 바르게 짝지어진 것은?

ⓐ　ⓑ	ⓐ　ⓑ
① for – to	② of – in
③ in – to	④ for – from
⑤ of – from	

서답형

05 위 글의 밑줄 친 ⓒ에서 어법상 틀린 부분을 찾아 고치시오. (두 군데)

➡ _____

서답형
06 다음 문장에서 위 글의 내용과 <u>다른</u> 부분을 찾아서 고치시오.

> Sixty minutes later, the temperature in Classroom A was two degrees lower than that in Classroom B.

➡ _____

[07~09] 다음 글을 읽고 물음에 답하시오.

Dongsu: Hi, everyone. A lot of energy is used to heat and cool our school. ⓐ<u>It</u> is important for students to reduce the amount of energy we use. We did an experiment last winter and found that bubble wrap can help to save energy. Look at this chart.

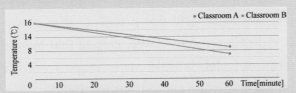

In Classroom A we put bubble wrap on the windows and in Classroom B we didn't. When we turned off the heater, the temperature was 16 ℃ in both classrooms. Sixty minutes later, the temperature in Classroom B went down to 7 ℃. But it was 9 ℃ in Classroom A! ⓑ <u>We learned that bubble wrap only lets much heat escape from the building.</u> So we started putting bubble wrap on the school windows. This will also prevent heat from getting into the classroom in the summer. The more bubble wrap we put on the windows, the cooler our summer will become!

서답형
07 위 글의 밑줄 친 ⓑ에서 흐름상 어색한 부분을 찾아 고치시오.

➡ _____

08 위 글의 밑줄 친 ⓐ<u>It</u>과 문법적 쓰임이 같은 것을 고르시오.

① <u>It</u>'s ten past twelve.
② <u>It</u>'s no use shouting.
③ Start a new file and put this letter in <u>it</u>.
④ I found <u>it</u> impossible to get there in time.
⑤ I had a good time of <u>it</u>.

중요
09 위 글의 제목으로 알맞은 것을 고르시오.

① A Lot of Energy Used in Our School
② The Importance of Reducing the Amount of Energy
③ An Experiment Conducted Last Year
④ How to Read a Chart Well
⑤ Want to Save Energy? How about Using Bubble Wrap?

[10~12] 다음 글을 읽고 물음에 답하시오.

Jimin: Hello, friends. A few months ago, I was surprised to see some empty classrooms with the lights on. ⓐ<u>That</u>'s not right at all. It is essential for all students to use fewer resources at school. So we have designed some resource saving stickers and put them on the switches. They tell us which light should be turned on, so that we can ⓑ <u>waste</u> less electricity. They also tell the last student who leaves the classroom to turn off the lights. We also put some stickers on the mirrors in the restrooms. They help students not to waste water. The more stickers we put up, the more resources we can save at school.

서답형
10 위 글의 밑줄 친 ⓐ<u>That</u>이 가리키는 것을 우리말로 쓰시오.

➡ _____

11 위 글의 밑줄 친 ⓑwaste와 같은 의미로 쓰인 것을 고르시오.

① We must handle the <u>waste</u> products properly.
② Disease and hunger <u>waste</u> people.
③ Why do you <u>waste</u> money on clothes you don't need?
④ It is a mere <u>waste</u> of labor to do such a thing.
⑤ Let's cultivate the <u>waste</u> land.

12 중요

According to the passage, which is NOT true?

① Jimin was surprised to see some empty classrooms with the lights on a few months ago.
② Jimin thinks it is essential that all students should use fewer resources at school.
③ Jimin's club members have designed some resource saving stickers and put them on the switches.
④ Jimin's club members tell their classmates which light should be turned on, so that they can waste less electricity.
⑤ Jimin's club members also put some stickers on the mirrors in the restrooms.

[13~15] 다음 글을 읽고 물음에 답하시오.

> **Minwoo:** Hello, friends. We decided to make a garden on the rooftop of the school to save energy. Only a few people know how it works. It's just like bubble wrap. It prevents heat from getting in and out of the buildings. So when we have rooftop gardens on our buildings, we can save some of the energy we use to cool the buildings in the summer. Also, the fresh air from the rooftop garden helps to cool the whole city. So it is necessary (A)[for us / of us] students to make more rooftop gardens at our school! The more beautiful our rooftops become, the (B)[less / more] energy our school will use!
>
> **MC:** It's very clever (C)[for you / of you] to come up with such great ideas! ⓐThese are all worth trying at school or at home. Thank you for your unique ideas and activities!

서답형

13 위 글의 괄호 (A)~(C)에서 문맥이나 어법상 알맞은 낱말을 골라 쓰시오.

➡ (A)_____ (B)_____ (C)_____

14 위 글의 밑줄 친 ⓐ를 다음과 같이 바꿔 쓸 때 빈칸에 들어갈 알맞은 말을 두 단어로 쓰시오.

➡ It is worth while _____ _____ all of these at school or at home.

15 중요

위 글의 주제로 알맞은 것을 고르시오.

① the preference for the rooftop of the school
② making a garden on the rooftop of the school to save energy
③ the similar mechanism of bubble wrap and the rooftop of the school
④ putting bubble wrap on the school windows to save energy
⑤ making a garden on the rooftop of the school to enjoy nature

[16~18] 다음 글을 읽고 물음에 답하시오.

Jimin: Hello, friends. A few months ago, I was surprised to see some empty classrooms with the lights on. That's not right ⓐat all. (①) It is essential for all students to use fewer resources at school. (②) They tell us which light should be turned on, so that we can waste less electricity. (③) They also tell the last student who leaves the classroom to turn off the lights. (④) We also put some stickers on the mirrors in the restrooms. (⑤) They help students not to waste water. ⓑ우리가 더 많은 스티커들을 붙일수록, 학교에서 더 많은 자원을 절약할 수 있습니다.

16 위 글의 흐름으로 보아, 주어진 문장이 들어가기에 가장 적절한 곳은?

So we have designed some resource saving stickers and put them on the switches.

①   ②   ③   ④   ⑤

서답형
17 위 글의 밑줄 친 ⓐat all과 바꿔 쓸 수 있는 말을 쓰시오. (3 단어)

➡ _____

서답형
18 위 글의 밑줄 친 ⓑ의 우리말에 맞게 주어진 어휘를 알맞게 배열하시오.

at school / put up / more stickers / we / the / can / we / more resources / save / the / ,

➡ _____

_____

[19~21] 다음 글을 읽고 물음에 답하시오.

Dongsu: Hi, everyone. A lot of energy is used to heat and cool our school. It is important for

students to reduce the amount of energy we use. We did an experiment last winter and found that bubble wrap can help to save energy. Look at this chart.

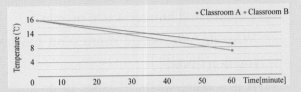

In Classroom A we put bubble wrap on the windows and in Classroom B we didn't. When we turned off the heater, the temperature was ⓐ16 ℃ in both classrooms. Sixty minutes later, the temperature in Classroom B went down to ⓑ7 ℃. But it was ⓒ9 ℃ in Classroom A! We learned that bubble wrap only lets a little heat escape from the building. So we started putting bubble wrap on the school windows. ⓓThis will also prevent heat from getting into the classroom in the summer. The more bubble wrap we put on the windows, the cooler our summer will become!   <We: Dongsu's club members>

19 위 글을 읽고 알 수 없는 것을 고르시오.

① In which Classroom did Dongsu's club members put bubble wrap, in Classroom A or in Classroom B?

② What does the red line in the chart show?

③ When Dongsu's club members turned off the heater, what was the temperature in both classrooms?

④ Two hours later, what was the temperature in Classroom B expected to be?

⑤ Is putting bubble wrap on the school windows helpful for saving energy?

20 위 글의 밑줄 친 ⓐ~ⓒ를 영어로 읽는 법을 쓰시오.

➡ ⓐ _____

　 ⓑ _____

　 ⓒ _____

21 위 글의 밑줄 친 ⓓThis가 가리키는 것을 본문에서 찾아 쓰시오.

➡ _____

[22~25] 다음 글을 읽고 물음에 답하시오.

> **Minwoo:** Hello, friends. We decided to make a garden on the rooftop of the school to save energy. Only a few people know how it ⓐ <u>works</u>. It's just like bubble wrap. It prevents heat from getting in and out of the buildings. So when we have rooftop gardens on our buildings, we can save some of the energy we use to cool the buildings in the summer. Also, the fresh air from the rooftop garden helps to cool the whole city. So it is necessary for us students to make more rooftop gardens at our school! The more beautiful our rooftops become, the less energy our school will use!
>
> 　MC: It's very clever of you to come up with such great ideas! ⓑ<u>이것들은 모두 학교나 집에서 해볼 만한 것들입니다.</u> Thank you for your unique ideas and activities!

22 위 글의 밑줄 친 ⓐworks와 같은 의미로 쓰인 것을 고르시오.

① This machine <u>works</u> by turning a handle.
② She bought complete <u>works</u> of Tolstoy.
③ I'm interested in the <u>works</u> of a watch.
④ He often <u>works</u> very long hours.
⑤ They started engineering <u>works</u>.

23 위 글의 밑줄 친 ⓑ의 우리말에 맞게 주어진 어휘를 이용하여 10 단어로 영작하시오. (10 words)

```
these, all, trying
```

➡ _____

24 위 글의 제목으로 알맞은 것을 고르시오.

① The Similarity between Bubble Wrap and a Garden on the Rooftop
② The Basic Principle of Saving Energy
③ A Garden on the Rooftop, a Beautiful Way to Save Energy
④ The Efficiency of a Garden on the Rooftop in Landscaping
⑤ The Effect of a Garden on the Rooftop on Academic Achievement

25 다음 중 위 글에 대한 이해를 올바르게 하지 <u>못한</u> 사람을 고르시오.

① 경숙: 학교 옥상정원이 어떻게 작용하는지를 아는 사람은 많지 않다.
② 상훈: 학교 옥상정원은 마치 뽁뽁이와 같이 열기가 건물 안팎으로 드나드는 것을 막아준다.
③ 민지: 건물에 옥상정원이 있으면, 여름에 건물을 식히기 위해 사용하는 에너지 일부를 절약할 수 있다.
④ 은성: 옥상정원에서 나오는 신선한 공기로 도시 전체를 식히는 것을 돕는 것은 불가능하다.
⑤ 태훈: 학교 옥상정원이 더 아름다워질수록, 학교는 에너지를 덜 사용하게 될 것이다.

[01~03] 다음 글을 읽고 물음에 답하시오.

> Minwoo: Hello, friends. We decided to make a garden on the rooftop of the school to save energy. Only a few people know how it works. It's just like bubble wrap. It prevents heat from getting in and out of the buildings. So when we have rooftop gardens on our buildings, we can save some of the energy we use to cool the buildings in the summer. Also, the fresh air from the rooftop garden helps to cool the whole city. So it is necessary for us students to make more rooftop gardens at our school! The more beautiful our rooftops become, the less energy our school will use!
>
> MC: ⓐIt's very clever of you to come up with such great ideas! These are all worth trying at school or at home. Thank you for your unique ideas and activities!

01 위 글의 밑줄 친 ⓐ를 다음과 같이 바꿔 쓸 때 빈칸에 들어갈 알맞은 말을 두 단어로 쓰시오.

➡ _____ very clever to come up with such great ideas!

02 다음 글에서 위 글의 내용과 다른 부분을 찾아서 고치시오.

> A lot of people know how a garden on the rooftop of the school works. It's just like bubble wrap. It prevents heat from getting in and out of the buildings.

➡ _____

03 Why is it necessary for us students to make more rooftop gardens at our school? Fill in the blanks (A) and (B) with suitable words.

> (1) Because we can save some of the energy we use (A)_____ _____ the buildings in the summer when we have rooftop gardens on our buildings.
> (2) Because (B)_____ _____ _____ from the rooftop garden helps to cool the whole city.

[04~05] 다음 글을 읽고 물음에 답하시오.

> Jimin: Hello, friends. A few months ago, I was surprised to see some empty classrooms ⓐ전등이 켜진. That's not right at all. It is essential for all students to use fewer resources at school. So we have designed some resource saving stickers and put them on the switches. They tell us which light should be turned on, so that we can waste (A)[more / less] electricity. They also tell the last student who leaves the classroom to turn (B)[on / off] the lights. We also put some stickers on the mirrors in the restrooms. They help students not to waste water. The more stickers we put up, the (C)[more / fewer] resources we can save at school.

04 위 글의 밑줄 친 ⓐ의 우리말에 맞게 주어진 어휘를 이용하여 4 단어로 영작하시오.

with

➡ _____

05 위 글의 괄호 (A)~(C)에서 문맥상 알맞은 낱말을 골라 쓰시오.

➡ (A) _____ (B) _____ (C) _____

[06~07] 다음 글을 읽고 물음에 답하시오.

Dongsu: Hi, everyone. A lot of energy is used to heat and cool our school. It is important for students to reduce the amount of energy we use. We did an experiment last winter and found that bubble wrap can help to save energy. Look at this chart.

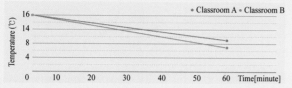

In Classroom A we put bubble wrap on the windows and in Classroom B we didn't. When we turned off the heater, the temperature was 16 ℃ in both classrooms. Sixty minutes later, the temperature in Classroom B went down to 7 ℃. But it was 9 ℃ in Classroom A! ⓐWe learned that bubble wrap only lets a little heat to escape from the building. So we started putting bubble wrap on the school windows. This will also prevent heat from getting into the classroom in the summer. The more bubble wrap we put on the windows, the cooler our summer will become!

06 What does the difference between the red line and the blue line of the chart mean? Fill in the blanks (A) and (B) with suitable words.

> It means that the temperature in (A)_____ _____ with bubble wrap on its windows went down less than that in (B)_____ _____ without bubble wrap.

07 위 글의 밑줄 친 ⓐ에서 어법상 틀린 부분을 찾아 고치시오.

➡ _____

[08~09] 다음 글을 읽고 물음에 답하시오.

Minwoo: Hello, friends. We decided to make a garden on the rooftop of the school to save energy. Only a few people know how it works. It's just like bubble wrap. It prevents heat from getting in and out of the buildings. So when we have rooftop gardens on our buildings, we can save some of the energy we use to cool the buildings in the summer. ⓐAlso, the fresh air from the rooftop garden helps to cool the whole city. So it is necessary for us students to make more rooftop gardens at our school! The more beautiful our rooftops become, the less energy our school will use!

MC: It's very clever of you to come up with such great ideas! These are all worth trying at school or at home. Thank you for your unique ideas and activities!

08 위 글의 밑줄 친 문장 ⓐ에서 생략할 수 있는 부분을 생략하고 문장을 다시 쓰시오.

➡ _____

_____

09 주어진 영영풀이에 해당하는 숙어를 본문에서 찾아 쓰시오. (3 단어)

> to think of an idea, an answer to a question or a solution to a problem

➡ _____

Communication Activity

A: Do you know how to save water?
"의문사+to부정사 – 어떻게 아끼는지"

B: Of course I do. If we use a cup when we brush our teeth, we can save
"do"는 대동사로 "know how to save water"를 대신하고 있다.　　　　양치질하다
water.

A: That's a great idea. How about oil?
　　　　　　　　　How about ~? = ~에 대해서는 어떠니?
　Do you know how to save oil?

C: We can save oil by … .

해석

A: 어떻게 물을 아끼는지 아니?

B: 물론이지. 양치질할 때 컵을 사용하면 물을 아낄 수 있어.

A: 좋은 생각이야. 기름은 어때?

　기름은 어떻게 아끼는지 아니?

C: 우리는 기름을 …해서 아낄 수 있어.

Before You Read A

1. I try to reuse glass or plastic bottles.
　try+to부정사: ~하려고 노력하다

2. I use the stairs when I go to the second floor.

3. I pull the plug out when I am not using my computer.
　　　　　　　　　　　　　　　　현재분사

4. I walk to school. (Or I bike to school.)
　　= I go to school on foot.

5. I turn off the light when it is bright.

6. I use used paper when I study.
　　　사용된, 헌

7. I open the door of the refrigerator only when it is necessary.

8. I try to shorten the time for taking a shower.
　　　　　　　　　　　take a shower: 샤워하다

1. 나는 유리나 플라스틱 병들을 재활용하려고 노력한다.
2. 나는 2층에 갈 때 계단을 사용한다.
3. 나는 컴퓨터를 사용하지 않을 때 플러그를 뽑는다.
4. 나는 학교에 걸어간다. (혹은 나는 학교에 자전거를 타고 간다.)
5. 나는 환할 때 불을 끈다.
6. 나는 공부할 때 헌 종이를 사용한다.
7. 나는 필요할 때만 냉장고 문을 연다.
8. 나는 샤워하는 시간을 줄이려고 노력한다.

구문해설 ・reuse: 재활용하다　・refrigerator: 냉장고　・shorten: 줄이다

After You Read

This chart shows how the temperature changed in Classroom A and in Classroom B. In Classroom A the students put bubble wrap on the windows
put A on ~: ~에 A를 설치하다
and in Classroom B they didn't. When the heater was turned off, the
be turned off: 꺼지다
temperatures were the (same / different) in both classrooms. Sixty minutes (before / later), the temperature in Classroom B went (up / down) to 7 ℃. But the temperature in Classroom A was (higher / lower) than that in Classroom B.
that = the temperature
It was 9 ℃. This is because bubble wrap only lets (a little / much) heat escape from the building.

이 도표는 교실 A와 B에서 온도가 어떻게 변했는지를 보여준다. 교실 A에서는 학생들이 창문에 뽁뽁이를 붙였고, 교실 B에서는 붙이지 않았다. 난방기가 꺼졌을 때, 온도가 양쪽 방에서 같았다. 60분 뒤에 교실 B의 온도는 7도로 내려갔다. 그러나 교실 A의 온도는 교실 B의 온도보다 높았다. 온도는 9도였다. 이것은 뽁뽁이가 아주 작은 열만 건물에서 빠져나갈 수 있도록 했기 때문이다.

01 다음 빈칸에 들어가기에 적절한 단어를 고르시오.

> Do you know how to read this Chinese
> _____?

① amount   ② exercise   ③ charge

④ experiment   ⑤ character

02 다음 영영풀이에 해당하는 단어를 고르시오.

> something such as useful land, or minerals
> such as oil or coal

① environment   ② information

③ grocery   ④ resource

⑤ rooftop

03 다음 두 문장에 공통으로 알맞은 것을 고르시오.

> • I don't like to sleep _____ the lights on.
> • I think you can come up _____ the answer
> to that if you really think about it.

① about   ② by   ③ for

④ with   ⑤ on

04 다음 밑줄 친 단어와 같은 의미로, 대신 쓸 수 있는 것은?

> This door can <u>prevent</u> rain water from
> running into the house.

① return   ② flow   ③ stop

④ take   ⑤ make

[05~06] 다음 우리말과 일치하도록 빈칸에 알맞은 말을 쓰시오.

05

> B: You look worried. What's the problem?
> G: I lost my brother's watch. He loves the
> watch so much.
> B: _____
> (내가 너라면, 그에게 사실대로 말하겠어.)
> G: I guess I have no choice.

06

> G: This restaurant is famous for its fresh
> and delicious food.
> B: Great. But _____
> _____? (이 식당을 어떻게 사
> 용하는지 아니?)
> G: Just pick up what you want. You can
> pay at the end.
> B: Oh, I see. Thanks.

07 짝지어진 대화가 <u>어색한</u> 것을 고르시오.

① A: I fought with my best friend. What
  should I do?

  B: If I were you, I'd tell him I am sorry first.

② A: You look worried. What's the problem?

  B: I broke my father's vase. He loves it
  so much.

③ A: Oh, it's too hard for me to concentrate
  in class.

  B: Did you stay up late last night?

④ A: Do you know how to take the medicine?

  B: I don't know. You need to take it three
  times a day before you have your meals.

⑤ A: The talent show last night was really great.

  B: Yeah. By the way, did you decide on
  the afternoon program?

[08~10] 다음 대화를 읽고 물음에 답하시오.

W: Jihu, (A)_____ are you holding? It looks like a bag full of fruit!

B: Yes, I went to a grocery store. (ⓐ)

W: Let me see. (ⓑ)

B: I just bought them because they were really cheap. (ⓒ)

W: We already have a bag of apples at home! It's such a waste of money!

B: Oh, I didn't know that. (ⓓ)

W: If I were you, I'd check (B)_____ I have first before I go shopping.

B: Yes, you're right. (ⓔ)

W: And then I'd make a shopping list based on that information.

B: Okay, I'll do that next time, Mom.

08 ⓐ~ⓔ 중 주어진 문장이 들어갈 곳은?

> Why did you buy the apples?

① ⓐ　　② ⓑ　　③ ⓒ　　④ ⓓ　　⑤ ⓔ

09 빈칸 (A), (B)에 공통으로 들어가기에 알맞은 말을 고르시오.

① what
② where
③ when
④ why
⑤ how

10 Which one CANNOT be answered from the dialogue above?

① What is Jihu holding?
② Why did Jihu buy the apples?
③ Where did Jihu go?
④ How were the apples that Jihu bought?
⑤ What will Jihu make before going shopping?

[11~13] 다음 대화를 읽고 물음에 답하시오.

Inho: Lina, you are not charging your phone. (A)만약 네가 너라면 나는 플러그를 뽑을 거야.

Lina: Why? I'll use the charger later. Leave it that way.

Inho: But you are wasting electricity.

Lina: It's only (B)_____.

Inho: Actually, if we add up a year's standby power, it is the same as the amount of electricity we normally use for a month.

Lina: Oh, I didn't know that.

Inho: Yeah, there are a lot of things like that which we waste without knowing in our daily lives.

Lina: Do you know how to save energy in other ways?

Inho: I hear that there's going to be an energy-saving conference at school next week.

Lina: Maybe we should go together!

11 밑줄 친 (A)의 우리말을 영작하시오.
(pull 포함, 축약하지 않고 10단어)

➡ _____

12 대화의 내용으로 보아 빈칸 (B)에 들어가기에 적절한 것은?

① quite a lot
② a little bit
③ just a few
④ a lot of
⑤ quite an amount of

13 위 대화의 내용과 일치하지 않는 것은?

① Inho found that Lina wasn't charging her phone.
② Lina thought that she didn't waste much electricity.
③ Lina didn't know how much it will be if we add up a year's standby power.

④ There are a lot of things that we waste without knowing.

⑤ Lina doesn't want to go to an energy-saving conference.

Grammar

14 다음 중 밑줄 친 부분이 어법상 <u>어색한</u> 것은?

① It would be easy <u>for Mike</u> to solve this problem.

② It is stupid <u>for you</u> to believe what she said.

③ It is kind <u>of you</u> to help the people in need.

④ It is so nice <u>of him</u> to lend me those books.

⑤ It is important <u>for you</u> to solve math problems every day.

15 다음 우리말과 같은 의미가 되도록 주어진 어구를 바르게 배열하여 문장을 완성하시오.

네가 많이 사랑할수록, 너는 더 많이 사랑받을 것이다.
(you / love / will / the more / you / the more / be loved)

➡ _____

16 다음 우리말을 바르게 영작한 것은?

강에서 수영하는 것은 위험하다.

① It's dangerous to swim in the river.

② It's dangerous that to swim in the river.

③ To swim in the river it's dangerous.

④ That's dangerous to swim in the river.

⑤ That's dangerous that swim in the river.

17 Which of the following is appropriate for the blank?

As I eat more sweets, I feel happier.
= The more sweets I eat, _____.

① the happier

② happier I feel

③ the happiest I feel

④ the happier I feel

⑤ the more happier I feel

18 다음 중 어법상 <u>어색한</u> 것은?

① It was difficult for her to read the book.

② It is dangerous for you to go out alone.

③ Is it interesting to visit different places?

④ It is very kind for you to say so.

⑤ It was not easy for him to carry the boxes.

19 다음 우리말을 영어로 바르게 옮긴 것은?

나이가 들면 들수록 그는 더 현명해진다.

① The old he gets, the wise he becomes.

② He gets the older, he becomes the wiser.

③ Because he gets older, he becomes wiser.

④ The older he gets, the wiser he becomes.

⑤ The older gets he, the wiser becomes he.

20 다음 〈보기〉와 같이 괄호 안의 주어진 단어를 사용하여 문장을 바꾸어 쓰시오.

┤ 보기 ├
• The mountain isn't high.
• We can climb up to the top of it.
➡ <u>It is easy for us to climb up to the top of the mountain.</u> (easy)

• The problem wasn't very difficult to solve.
• Sam could solve it.

➡ _____ (easy)

Reading

[21~22] 다음 글을 읽고 물음에 답하시오.

Welcome to the Energy-Saving Conference. The Earth is in danger. The air is getting dirtier every day. More and more animals are dying. (A)This is why we are wasting a lot of energy. So how can we save energy? Three different environmental clubs are here to share their activities. The more ideas we ⓐ_____, the more energy we can ⓑ_____!

21 위 글의 빈칸 ⓐ와 ⓑ에 들어갈 말로 알맞은 것을 고르시오.

① need – waste
② share – save
③ need – use
④ share – waste
⑤ refuse – save

22 위 글의 밑줄 친 (A)에서 어법상 틀린 부분을 찾아 고치시오.

➡ _____

[23~24] 다음 글을 읽고 물음에 답하시오.

Jimin: Hello, friends. A few months ago, I was surprised to see some empty classrooms with the lights on. That's not right at all. It is essential for all students to use (A)[fewer / more] resources at school. So we have designed some resource saving stickers and put them on the switches. They tell us which light should be turned on, so that we can waste less electricity. They also tell the (B)[first / last] student who leaves the classroom to turn off the lights. We also put some stickers on the mirrors in the restrooms. They help students not to waste water. The (C)[more / fewer] stickers we put up, the more resources we can save at school.   <We: Jimin's club members>

23 위 글의 괄호 (A)~(C)에서 문맥상 알맞은 낱말을 골라 쓰시오.

➡ (A)_____ (B)_____ (C)_____

24 Which question CANNOT be answered after reading the passage?

① Why was Jimin surprised a few months ago?
② Why have Jimin's club members designed some resource saving stickers?
③ Where have Jimin's club members put the resource saving stickers?
④ What do some stickers on the mirrors in the restrooms help students not to do?
⑤ How many resource saving stickers did Jimin's club members put in all?

[25~27] 다음 글을 읽고 물음에 답하시오.

Dongsu: Hi, everyone. ⓐA lot of energy is used to heat and cool our school. It is important for students to reduce the amount of energy we use. We did an experiment last winter and found that bubble wrap can help to save energy. Look at this chart.

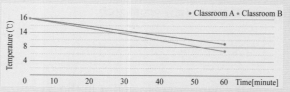

In Classroom A we put bubble wrap on the windows and in Classroom B we didn't. When we turned off the heater, the temperature was 16 ℃ in both classrooms. (①) Sixty minutes later, the temperature in Classroom B went down to 7 ℃. (②) But it was 9 ℃ in Classroom A! (③) We learned that bubble wrap only lets a little heat escape from the building. (④) This will also prevent heat from getting into the classroom in the summer. (⑤) The more bubble wrap we put on the windows, the cooler our summer will become!

<We: Dongsu's club members>

25 위 글의 밑줄 친 ⓐ를 능동태로 고치시오.

➡ _____

26 위 글의 흐름으로 보아, 주어진 문장이 들어가기에 가장 적절한 곳은?

So we started putting bubble wrap on the school windows.

①   ②   ③   ④   ⑤

27 According to the passage, which is NOT true?

① Dongsu's club members put bubble wrap on the windows in Classroom A.

② Dongsu's club members didn't put bubble wrap on the windows in Classroom B.

③ When Dongsu's club members turned off the heater, the temperature was 16 ℃ in both classrooms.

④ An hour later, the temperature in Classroom B went down more than that in Classroom A.

⑤ Dongsu's club members learned that bubble wrap only lets a little heat escape from the building in the summer.

[28~29] 다음 글을 읽고 물음에 답하시오.

W: There is a simple way to save some of the gas or oil that is used to heat your house. ⓐ It is cleaning the boiler. When you use a boiler for a long time, a lot of black dust will stick to the inside of the boiler. This black dust prevents gas or oil from heating your house. When the thickness of this dust is 1 mm, the boiler will need to use an additional 2 % of gas or oil to heat your house. If the thickness is 1.5 mm, you will waste 4 % more energy. When the thickness is 3 mm, an additional 8 % of gas or oil will be wasted! So you should clean the boiler as often as possible.

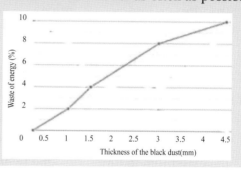

28 위 글의 밑줄 친 ⓐIt이 가리키는 것을 본문에서 찾아 쓰시오.

➡ _____

_____

29 According to the passage, which is NOT true?

① When you use a boiler for a long time, a lot of black dust will stick to the inside of the boiler.

② This black dust keeps gas or oil from heating your house.

③ When the thickness of this dust is 1 mm, the boiler will need to use an additional 2 % of gas or oil to heat your house.

④ If the thickness is 2 mm, you will waste 4 % more energy.

⑤ When the thickness of this dust is 3 mm, an additional 8 % of gas or oil will be wasted.

01 짝지어진 단어의 관계가 같도록 빈칸에 알맞은 말을 쓰시오.

출제율 90%

> add : addition = concentrate : _____

02 다음 빈칸에 들어갈 말로 적절한 것은?

출제율 95%

> The hotel was really popular in summer because of its open-air _____ restaurant.

① charge
② resource
③ rooftop
④ price
⑤ plant

03 다음 빈칸에 공통으로 들어가기에 적절한 것은?

출제율 90%

> • They also tell the last student who leaves the classroom to turn _____ the lights.
> • Take the black net out of the air conditioner and brush _____ the dust on it.

① about
② off
③ on
④ with
⑤ to

04 다음 제시된 단어로 자연스러운 문장을 만들 수 <u>없는</u> 것은?

출제율 100%

> ┌─ 보기 ┐
> heat pick prevent come

① She bent down to _____ up her glove.
② A lot of energy is used to _____ and cool our school.
③ This will _____ heat from getting into the classroom.
④ If you are not charging your phone, _____ the plug out.
⑤ It's very clever of you to _____ up with such great ideas!

[05~07] 다음 대화를 읽고 물음에 답하시오.

> G: Do you know how to be good at Chinese characters?
> B: Oh, did you start to learn them?
> G: Yeah, ⓐI heard that learning them is really helpful. But (가)모든 글자를 기억하는 것은 너무 어려워.
> B: If I were you, ⓑI'd try to understand how each character is made first.
> G: What do you mean?
> B: For example, look at this character. A human is standing next to a tree.
> G: Oh, I see. Now I can easily remember ⓒwhat does the character look like.
> B: Then how do you feel ⓓwhen you're next to a tree?
> G: Maybe ⓔI feel like I am resting.
> B: Now you have the meaning of the character, too.

05 밑줄 친 (가)의 우리말을 영어로 적절하게 옮긴 것은?

출제율 90%

① to remember is too hard all the characters
② all the characters are to remember hardly
③ it is too hard to remember all the characters
④ it is too remember all the characters too hard
⑤ it is too hard all the characters to remember

06 밑줄 친 ⓐ~ⓔ 중에서 <u>어색한</u> 것을 적절하게 고친 것은?

출제율 95%

① ⓐI heard that learning them is really helpless.
② ⓑI'd try to understand how is each character made first.
③ ⓒwhat the character looks like.
④ ⓓwhen are you next to a tree
⑤ ⓔI feel like to be resting.

07 Which one of the following is NOT true according to the dialogue above?

① The girl didn't start to learn Chinese characters.

② The girl heard that learning Chinese characters is helpful.

③ The boy told the girl to understand how each character is made.

④ The boy showed the girl how to understand Chinese characters.

⑤ The girl understood what the boy said.

[08~10] 다음 대화를 읽고 물음에 답하시오.

> G: Minjae, is this plant ⓐyours?
>
> B: Yeah, it was my last year's birthday gift from my sister.
>
> G: It seems ⓑthat it has grown a lot.
>
> B: Oh, do you think so?
>
> G: Yeah. If I ⓒam you, I'd move the plant to a larger pot.
>
> B: Hmm… I ⓓdidn't know that I have to change its pot.
>
> G: If you ⓔchange the pot, the plant will grow better.
>
> B: But I don't know how to do it. Do you know how to (A)move it to another pot?
>
> G: Sure. I've done that a lot of times. I can teach you how to do it now if you want.
>
> B: That's great!

출제율 95%

08 밑줄 친 ⓐ~ⓔ 중에서 어법상 어색한 것은?

① ⓐ ② ⓑ ③ ⓒ ④ ⓓ ⑤ ⓔ

출제율 90%

09 의미상 밑줄 친 (A)에 해당하는 것은?

① has grown a lot

② do you think so

③ change its pot

④ know how to do it

⑤ have done it a lot of times

출제율 100%

10 Which one CANNOT be answered from the dialogue above?

① What did Minjae get from his sister for his birthday?

② What does the girl think about the plant?

③ What's the advice that the girl is giving?

④ What kind of pot will the girl use?

⑤ What will the girl teach to Minjae?

출제율 85%

11 다음 중 〈보기〉의 밑줄 친 it과 쓰임이 같은 것은?

> ┌─ 보기 ┐
>
> <u>It</u> is necessary for us to study hard.

① <u>It</u> will be getting dark soon.

② <u>It</u> takes about 5 minutes by bus.

③ <u>It</u> isn't far from here to your school.

④ <u>It</u> is difficult for me to solve this problem.

⑤ <u>It</u> will be snowy and windy tomorrow.

출제율 95%

12 다음 빈칸 (A), (B)에 들어갈 말로 바르게 연결된 것은?

> (A)_____ we learn English, (B)_____ it will be.

	(A)	(B)
①	The much	the interesting
②	The more	the interesting
③	More	more interesting
④	The more	the more interesting
⑤	More	the more interesting

출제율 90%

13 다음 중 어법상 어색한 것은?

① It is kind for you to help me with my homework.

② To eat healthy food is very important.

③ It won't be easy for you to solve this.

④ It will be possible for you to leave early.

⑤ It was hard for me to finish the English homework.

출제율 85%

14 다음 문장을 〈보기〉와 같이 'The+비교급, the+비교급'을 이용하여 다시 쓰시오.

┌─ 보기 ┤
As you study harder, you will learn more.
➡ The harder you study, the more you will learn.
└─

As we got closer to the fire, we felt warmer.
➡ _____ _____ we got to the fire, _____ _____ we felt.

출제율 100%

15 다음 중 어법상 옳은 것은?

① It is easy for her speaking Chinese.

② It is important of him to pass the exam.

③ It is hard for me to solve this problem.

④ It's foolish for you to act like that.

⑤ It is impossible for his to finish the work.

[16~18] 다음 글을 읽고 물음에 답하시오.

Dongsu: Hi, everyone. A lot of energy is used to heat and cool our school. ⓐ학생들이 우리가 사용하는 에너지의 양을 줄이는 것이 중요합니다. We did an experiment last winter and found that bubble wrap can help to save energy. Look at this chart.

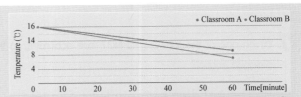

In Classroom A we put bubble wrap on the windows and in Classroom B we didn't. When we turned off the heater, the temperature was 16 ℃ in both classrooms. Sixty minutes later, the temperature in Classroom B went down to 7 ℃. But it was 9 ℃ in Classroom A! We learned that bubble wrap only lets a little heat escape from the building. So we started putting bubble wrap on the school windows. This will also ⓑprevent heat from getting into the classroom in the summer. The more bubble wrap we put on the windows, the cooler our summer will become!

<We: Dongsu's club members>

출제율 90%

16 위 글의 밑줄 친 ⓐ의 우리말에 맞게 13 단어로 영작하시오. (It ... for ~ to부정사 구문을 사용하시오.)

➡ _____

_____

출제율 100%

17 위 글의 밑줄 친 ⓑprevent와 바꿔 쓸 수 있는 말을 모두 고르시오.

① keep   ② protect   ③ stop
④ allow   ⑤ reduce

출제율 95%

18 본문의 내용과 일치하도록 다음 빈칸 (A)와 (B)에 알맞은 단어를 쓰시오.

In the experiment done by Dongsu's club members last winter, it was found that putting (A)_____ _____on the school windows is helpful for (B)_____ energy.

[19~20] 다음 글을 읽고 물음에 답하시오.

Minwoo: Hello, friends. We decided to make a garden on the rooftop of the school ⓐto save energy. Only a few people know how it works. (①) It's just like bubble wrap. (②) It prevents heat from getting in and out of the buildings. (③) Also, the fresh air from the rooftop garden helps to cool the whole city. (④) So it is necessary for us students to make more rooftop gardens at our school! (⑤) The more beautiful our rooftops become, the less energy our school will use!

출제율 100%

19 위 글의 흐름으로 보아, 주어진 문장이 들어가기에 가장 적절한 곳은?

> So when we have rooftop gardens on our buildings, we can save some of the energy we use to cool the buildings in the summer.

① ② ③ ④ ⑤

출제율 90%

20 위 글의 밑줄 친 ⓐto save와 to부정사의 용법이 다른 것을 모두 고르시오.

① It is not easy to save energy.
② This machine is efficient enough to save energy.
③ Tell me some ways to save energy.
④ He invented this machine to save energy.
⑤ We were happy to save energy.

[21~23] Minsu가 작성한 자원 절약 습관을 나타내는 다음 표를 읽고 물음에 답하시오.

		A	B	C
1	I try to reuse glass or plastic bottles.		✓	
2	I use the stairs when I go to the second floor.			✓
3	I pull the plug out when I am not using my computer.		✓	
4	I walk to school. (Or I bike to school.)		✓	
5	I turn off the light when it is bright.			✓
6	I use used paper when I study.			✓
7	I open the door of the refrigerator only when it is necessary.			✓
8	I try to shorten the time for taking a shower.		✓	

※ A: never(0), B: sometimes(1), C: always(2)

Total:

0~5: You're in trouble. You're wasting a lot of resources!

6~12: Not good enough. Try harder to save resources.

13~16: Excellent! You're very good at saving resources. Keep up the good work!

출제율 90%

21 Add up the scores. What is Minsu's score?

➡ _____

출제율 95%

22 Is Minsu "excellent" in saving resources?

➡ _____

출제율 90%

23 What advice can you give to Minsu?

➡ _____

[01~02] 다음 대화를 읽고 물음에 답하시오.

W: Jihu, what are you holding? It looks like a bag full (A)_____ fruit!

B: Yes, I went to a grocery store.

W: Let me see. Why did you buy the apples?

B: I just bought them because they were really cheap.

W: We already have a bag of apples at home! It's such a waste (B)_____ money!

B: Oh, I didn't know that.

W: If I were you, (가)나는 쇼핑을 가기 전에 무엇을 가지고 있는지 먼저 점검을 할 것이다. (check, before)

B: Yes, you're right.

W: And then I'd make a shopping list based (C)_____ that information.

B: Okay, I'll do that next time, Mom.

01 위 대화의 빈칸 (A), (B), (C)에 들어가기에 적절한 단어를 보기에서 찾아 쓰시오. (중복사용 가능)

┤ 보기 ├
with to of in on out

➡ (A)_____ (B)_____ (C)_____

02 밑줄 친 (가)에 해당하는 우리말을 주어진 단어를 포함해서 영어로 옮기시오.

➡ I'd _____.

03 다음 우리말과 의미가 같도록 〈조건〉에 맞게 영작하시오.

네가 경험을 통해 배우는 것이 중요하다. (experience)

┤ 조건 ├
• 괄호 안에 주어진 단어를 사용하시오.
• 가주어 'It'을 사용하시오.
• 의미상의 주어를 포함시켜 문장을 만드시오.

➡ _____

04 다음 문장의 의미에 맞게 〈조건〉에 주어진 표현을 활용하여 알맞은 문장을 완성하시오.

┤ 조건 ├
1. [the + 비교급]의 표현을 사용하여 문장을 완성할 것.
2. [our rooftops, become, less, beautiful, the]를 활용하고, 필요한 단어를 추가할 것.
3. 위에 제시된 단어는 필요한 경우 문맥에 맞게 변형하여 사용할 것.

우리 학교 옥상이 아름다워질수록 우리 학교는 더 적은 에너지를 쓸 것이다.

➡ _____
_____

[05~07] 다음 글을 읽고 물음에 답하시오.

Dongsu: Hi, everyone. A lot of energy is used to heat and cool our school. It is important for students to (A)[increase / reduce] the amount of energy we use. We did an experiment last winter and found that bubble wrap can help to save energy. Look at this chart.

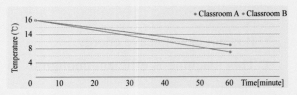

In Classroom A we put bubble wrap on the windows and in Classroom B we didn't. When we turned off the heater, the temperature was 16 ℃ in both classrooms. Sixty minutes later, the temperature in Classroom B went down to 7 ℃. But it was 9 ℃ in Classroom A! We learned that bubble wrap only lets a little heat (B)[enter / escape] from the building. So we started putting bubble wrap on the school windows. ⓐ이것이 여름에 열이 교실로 들어오는 것 또한 막아 줄 것입니다. The more bubble wrap we put on the windows, the (C)[cooler / hotter] our summer will become! <We: Dongsu's club members>

05 위 글의 괄호 (A)~(C)에서 문맥상 알맞은 낱말을 골라 쓰시오.

➡ (A)_____ (B)_____ (C)_____

06 위 글의 밑줄 친 ⓐ의 우리말에 맞게 한 단어를 보충하여, 주어진 어휘를 알맞게 배열하시오.

> This / the classroom / also / getting / prevent / in the summer / into / will / heat

➡ _____

_____

07 본문의 내용과 일치하도록 다음 빈칸 (A)~(D)에 알맞은 단어를 쓰시오.

> The chart shows how the (A)_____ in Classroom A and B changes as time passes. The (B)_____ line shows the change of the temperature in Classroom A over time and the (C)_____ line shows that in Classroom B. Though the temperature

was the same (D)_____ ℃ in both classrooms when Dongsu's club members started to check it, the temperature in Classroom B went down more than that in Classroom A as time passed.

[08~09] 다음 글을 읽고 물음에 답하시오.

> Minwoo: Hello, friends. We decided to make a garden on the rooftop of the school to save energy. Only a few people know how ⓐit works. ⓑIt's just like bubble wrap. It prevents heat from getting in and out of the buildings. So when we have rooftop gardens on our buildings, we can save some of the energy we use to cool the buildings in the summer. Also, the fresh air from the rooftop garden helps to cool the whole city. So it is necessary for us students to make more rooftop gardens at our school! ⓒThe more beautiful our rooftops become, the less energy our school will use!

08 위 글의 밑줄 친 ⓐit과 ⓑIt이 공통으로 가리키는 것을 본문에서 찾아 쓰시오.

➡ _____

09 위 글의 밑줄 친 ⓒ를 다음과 같이 바꿔 쓸 때 빈칸 (A)와 (B)에 들어갈 알맞은 말을 각각 두 단어로 쓰시오.

> As our rooftops become (A)_____ _____, our school will use (B)_____ _____!

01 다음 괄호 안에서 알맞은 낱말을 고르시오.

1. You'd better not (save / waste) energy.
2. These days, we're facing (environmental / natural) problems, like trash mountains.
3. I want to live in a house with a beautiful (garden / forest).
4. I need a (clever / stupid) partner to solve this problem together.
5. Jessica was kind enough to (save / share) her umbrella with her friends when it rained.
6. Why do you want to enter the (empty / dirty) classroom? There is no one there to meet!

02 다음 내용을 바탕으로 도표를 설명하는 문장을 쓰시오.

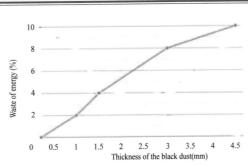

- The chart shows how the waste of the energy changes as the black dust inside the boiler gets thicker.
- When the thickness of this dust is 1 mm, the boiler will need to use an additional 2 % of gas or oil to heat your house.
- If the thickness is 1.5 mm, you waste 4 % more gas or oil.
- When the thickness is 3 mm, an additional 8 % of gas or oil will be wasted.
- When the thickness is 4.5 mm, 10 % more gas or oil will be wasted.

There is a simple way to save some of the gas or oil that is used to heat your house. It is cleaning the boiler. When you use a boiler for a long time, a lot of (A)_____ will stick to the inside of the boiler. This black dust prevents gas or oil from heating your house. When the (B)_____ of this dust is (C)_____ mm, the boiler will need to use an additional 2 % of gas or oil to heat your house. If the thickness is (D)_____ mm, you will waste 4 % more energy. When the thickness is (E)_____ mm, an additional 8 % of gas or oil will be wasted. When the thickness is (F)_____ mm, 10% more gas or oil will be wasted! So you should clean the boiler as often as possible.

단원별 모의고사

01 다음 짝지어진 단어의 관계가 같도록 빈칸에 알맞은 말을 쓰시오.

> pay : payment = consider : _____

02 다음 빈칸에 들어가기에 적절한 것은?

> A: I lost too much weight. What should I do?
> B: If I were you, I'd exercise _____.

① regularly
② hardly
③ anxiously
④ rarely
⑤ extremely

03 다음 영영풀이에 해당하는 단어를 고르시오.

> the upper surface of a roof

① yard
② rooftop
③ experiment
④ conference
⑤ character

04 다음 문장의 빈칸에 알맞은 것을 〈보기〉에서 찾아 쓰시오.

> ┌ 보기 ┐
> resources   bubble
> experiment   conference

(1) We put _____ wrap on the school windows to save energy.
(2) I hear that there's going to be an energy-saving _____ at school next week.
(3) The stickers can help save _____ like electricity and water.
(4) He wasn't satisfied with the result of the _____.

[05~07] 다음 대화를 읽고 물음에 답하시오.

> B: Do you know how to clean the air conditioner? I haven't done it by myself.
> G: Yes. (A)_____
> B: Why?
> G: It can be dangerous if you don't do that.
> B: Oh, I see. Now I've pulled the plug out. What's next?
> G: Take the black net out of the air conditioner and brush off the dust on it.
> B: Wow, there is a lot of dust.
> G: Yeah, I know. Then, clean the net with water.
> B: Cleaning an air conditioner isn't that easy.
> G: Yes, but if I were you, I'd clean the air conditioner often. (B)그것은 전기가 낭비되는 것을 막는 데 도움을 준다.

05 위 대화의 내용으로 보아 빈칸 (A)에 들어가기에 적절한 것은?

① Turn on the switch first.
② Open the windows.
③ Close the door, please.
④ Pull the plug out first.
⑤ Wash the filter.

06 밑줄 친 (B)의 우리말을 영어로 옮기시오. (주어진 단어 포함)

➡ _____

(prevent) (7 words)

07 Which one CANNOT be answered from the dialogue above?

① Does the girl know how to clean the air conditioner?
② Why do you pull the plug out first?
③ What do you do after pulling out the plug?
④ Why do you clean the air conditioner?
⑤ How often should you clean the air conditioner?

[08~10] 다음 대화를 읽고 물음에 답하시오.

> Inho: Lina, you are not charging your phone. (A)If I were you, I'd pull the plug out.
>
> Lina: Why? I'll use the charger later. Leave it that way.
>
> Inho: But you are wasting electricity.
>
> Lina: It's only a little bit.
>
> Inho: Actually, if we add up a year's standby power, it is the same as the amount of electricity we normally use for a month.
>
> Lina: Oh, I didn't know that.
>
> Inho: Yeah, there are a lot of things like that (B) which we waste without knowing in our daily lives.
>
> Lina: Do you know how to save energy in other ways?
>
> Inho: I hear that there's going to be an energy-saving conference at school next week.
>
> Lina: Maybe we should go together!

08 밑줄 친 (A)가 의도하는 것은?

① to ask ways
② to appreciate
③ to express satisfaction
④ to give advice
⑤ to make an apology

09 다음 중 밑줄 친 (B)와 쓰임이 같은 것은?

① Which bag is better of the two?
② He found the house which he wanted to visit.
③ He told me which of the jackets he wanted to buy at the store.
④ He showed me which way to go at the corner.
⑤ She asked me which car I liked better.

10 다음 중 위 대화의 내용과 일치하지 않는 것은?

① Inho thinks that we should pull the plug out when not using.
② Lina wanted to pull the plug out when Inho found it.
③ Lina didn't know how much electricity she was wasting.
④ Inho knows how to save electricity.
⑤ They will be at the energy-saving conference next week.

11 다음 빈칸에 들어갈 말로 알맞은 것은?

> The more carefully you write, _____ mistakes you will make.

① the less　　② the fewer
③ the easier　　④ the more
⑤ the better

12 다음 중 어법상 어색한 것은?

① It is kind of you to help her.
② It is important for you to eat healthy food.
③ It will be easy for you to move the table.
④ It will be possible for you to get up early.
⑤ It was good of you to finish the English homework early.

13 다음 두 문장의 의미가 같도록 빈칸에 알맞은 말을 쓰시오.

> As we share more ideas, we can save more energy!
>
> ➡ The _____ _____ we share, the _____ _____ we can save!

14 우리말과 일치하도록 괄호 안의 말을 바르게 배열하여 문장을 완성하시오.

> 어린아이들이 많은 책을 읽는 것은 도움이 된다.
> (children, books, a lot of, helpful, to, for, read)

➡ It is _____.

[15~17] 다음 글을 읽고 물음에 답하시오.

Jimin: Hello, friends. A few months ago, I was surprised to see some empty classrooms with the lights on. That's not right at all. It is essential for all students to use fewer resources at school. So we have designed some resource saving stickers and put ⓐthem on the switches. ⓑThey tell us which light should be turned on, so that we can waste less electricity. ⓒThey also tell the last student who leaves the classroom to turn off the lights. We also put some stickers on the mirrors in the restrooms. ⓓThey help students not to waste water. The more stickers we put up, the more resources we can save at school.

15 위 글의 주제로 알맞은 것을 고르시오.

① the wasteful habit of students
② the way to recycle the waste at school
③ the difficulty of saving energy at school
④ to save resources at school by putting up resource saving stickers
⑤ the difficulty of designing resource saving stickers

16 위 글의 밑줄 친 ⓐ~ⓓ가 공통으로 가리키는 것을 본문에서 찾아 쓰시오.

➡ _____

17 How can some resource saving stickers on the switches help to waste less electricity? Fill in the blanks (A) and (B) with suitable words.

> (1) By telling the students (A)_____ _____ should be turned on.
> (2) By telling the last student who leaves the classroom to (B)_____ _____ the lights.

[18~19] 다음 글을 읽고 물음에 답하시오.

Dongsu: Hi, everyone. A lot of energy is used to heat and cool our school. It is important for students ⓐto reduce the amount of energy we use. We did an experiment last winter and found that bubble wrap can help to save energy. Look at this chart.

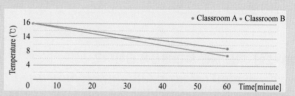

In Classroom A we put bubble wrap on the windows and in Classroom B we didn't. When we turned off the heater, the temperature was 16 ℃ in both classrooms. Sixty minutes later, the temperature in Classroom B went down to 7 ℃. But it was 9 ℃ in Classroom A! We learned that bubble wrap only lets a little heat escape from the building. So we started putting bubble wrap on the school windows. This will also prevent heat from getting into the classroom in the summer. The more bubble wrap we put on the windows, the cooler our summer will become!

18 위 글의 밑줄 친 ⓐto reduce와 to부정사의 용법이 같은 것을 모두 고르시오.

① It is necessary to reduce energy consumption.

② I don't know how to reduce energy consumption.

③ There are many ways to reduce energy consumption.

④ It is time for you to reduce energy consumption.

⑤ They tried to reduce energy consumption.

19 How can bubble wrap on the windows help to save energy? Fill in the blanks (A) and (B) with suitable words.

> In winter, bubble wrap on the windows only lets a little heat (A)_____ _____ the building and in summer it also prevents heat from (B)_____ _____the building. So, we can say that bubble wrap can help to save energy.

[20~22] 다음 글을 읽고 물음에 답하시오.

Minwoo: Hello, friends. We decided to make a garden on the rooftop of the school to save energy. ⓐ오직 몇몇 사람들만이 그것이 어떻게 작용하는지 알고 있습니다. It's just like bubble wrap. It prevents heat from getting in and out of the buildings. So when we have rooftop gardens on our buildings, we can save some of the energy we use to cool the buildings in the summer. Also, the fresh air from the rooftop garden helps to cool the whole city. So it is necessary for us students to make more rooftop gardens at our school! The more beautiful our rooftops become, the less energy our school will use!

<We: Minwoo's club members>

20 위 글의 밑줄 친 ⓐ의 우리말에 맞게 주어진 어휘를 알맞게 배열하시오.

> how / only / people / it / know / works / a few

➡ _____

21 What are the two advantages of a rooftop garden? Answer in English in a full sentence.

➡ (1) _____
    _____
   (2) _____
    _____

22 According to the passage, which is NOT true?

① Minwoo's club members decided to make a garden on the rooftop of the school to save energy.

② A garden on the rooftop of the school is just like bubble wrap.

③ When there are rooftop gardens on the buildings, it is possible to save some of the energy we use to cool the buildings in the summer.

④ It is necessary that students should make more school gardens.

⑤ Minwoo thought that the more beautiful the rooftop of his school became, the less energy his school would use.

All You Need Is Love

🎙 의사소통 기능

- 도움 제안하기
  Can I give you a hand?
  Let me give you a hand.
- 바람, 소원, 요망 표현하기
  I wish I could get better faster.

🎙 언어 형식

- not only A but also B
  Eunchong **not only** is still alive **but also** got first place in his first triathlon.

- I whish 가정법 과거
  I wish I could run with you.

Words & Expressions

Key Words

- **abroad**[əbrɔ́ːd] 부 해외에, 해외로
- **achievement**[ətʃíːvmənt] 명 성취, 달성
- **alive**[əláiv] 형 살아 있는
- **although**[ɔːlðóu] 접 (비록) ~이긴 하지만
- **appear**[əpíər] 동 나타나다
- **blame**[bleim] 동 ~을 탓하다
- **borrow**[bárou] 동 빌리다
- **bravely**[bréivli] 부 용감하게
- **bright**[brait] 형 밝은, 발랄한
- **century**[séntʃəri] 명 100년, 세기
- **challenge**[tʃǽlindʒ] 명 도전 동 도전하다
- **cheer**[tʃiər] 동 응원하다
- **colorful**[kʌ́lərfəl] 형 다채로운, 화려한
- **comfortably**[kʌ́mfərtəbli] 부 편안하게
- **courage**[kə́ːridʒ] 명 용기
- **cycle**[sáikl] 동 자전거를 타다
- **dark**[dɑːrk] 형 어두운
- **depressed**[diprést] 형 (기분이) 우울한
- **depression**[dipréʃən] 명 우울함
- **disability**[dìsəbíləti] 명 (신체적, 정신적) 장애
- **disease**[dizíːz] 명 질병
- **endure**[indjúər] 동 참다, 견디다
- **excellent**[éksələnt] 형 탁월한
- **face**[feis] 동 직면하다
- **factor**[fǽktər] 명 요인
- **hardship**[há:rdʃip] 명 어려움, 곤란
- **hide**[haid] 동 숨다, 숨기다
- **imagine**[imǽdʒin] 동 상상하다
- **instead**[instéd] 부 대신에
- **journey**[dʒə́ːrni] 명 여행, 여정
- **leg**[leg] 명 다리
- **meaningful**[míːniŋfəl] 형 의미 있는
- **overcome**[óuvərkəm] 동 극복하다
- **participant**[pɑːrtísəpənt] 명 참가자
- **planet**[plǽnit] 명 행성, 지구
- **present**[préznt] 명 선물
- **receive**[risíːv] 동 받다
- **recommendation**[rèkəməndéiʃən] 명 추천
- **relationship**[riléiʃənʃip] 명 관계
- **research**[risə́ːrtʃ] 명 조사
- **rest**[rest] 명 휴식 동 쉬다
- **result**[rizʌ́lt] 명 결과
- **scenery**[síːnəri] 명 경치
- **since**[sins] 전 ~부터[이후]
- **skin**[skin] 명 피부
- **support**[səpɔ́ːrt] 동 지지하다
- **survival**[sərváivəl] 명 생존
- **talent**[tǽlənt] 명 재능
- **thankful**[θǽŋkfəl] 형 감사하는
- **tiredness**[táiərdnis] 명 피곤함
- **touched**[tʌtʃt] 형 감동한
- **treat**[triːt] 동 (특정 태도로) 대하다, 취급하다
- **triathlon**[traiǽθlən] 명 철인 레이스
- **view**[vjuː] 명 경관, 전망
- **wheelchair**[wiltʃer] 명 휠체어
- **whether**[hwéðər] 접 ~인지 아닌지

Key Expressions

- **A as well as B** B 뿐만 아니라 A도
- **be good at** ~을 잘하다
- **be in the habit of** ~하는 습관이 있다
- **be interested in** ~에 관심이 있다
- **be lost** 길을 잃다
- **be proud of** ~을 자랑스러워하다
- **by the way** 그런데
- **do some research** 조사하다
- **get through** 통과하다, 연락이 닿다
- **give a hand** 도움을 주다
- **give up** 포기하다
- **in need of help** 도움이 필요한
- **look after** ~을 돌보다
- **look for** ~을 찾다
- **look forward to** ~을 기대하다
- **make way for** ~에 길을 내주다
- **not ~ anymore** 더 이상 ~가 아닌
- **not only ~ A but also B** A 뿐만 아니라 B도
- **participate in** ~에 참가하다
- **stand by** 곁을 지키다, 대기하다
- **take care of** ~을 돌보다
- **with all of one's heart** 진심으로
- **thanks to** ~ 덕분에
- **would like to** ~하고 싶다

Word Power

※ 서로 비슷한 뜻을 가진 어휘

☐ **abroad** 해외에 – **overseas** 해외에
☐ **bravely** 용감하게 – **boldly** 대담하게
☐ **disease** 질병 – **sickness** 질병
☐ **excellent** 탁월한 – **outstanding** 뛰어난
☐ **journey** 여행, 여정 – **travel** 여행
☐ **research** 조사 – **investigation** 조사
☐ **achievement** 성취, 달성 – **accomplishment** 성취

☐ **blame** ~을 탓하다 – **criticize** 비난하다
☐ **cheer** 응원하다 – **encourage** 용기를 불어넣다
☐ **endure** 참다, 견디다 – **tolerate** 참다, 견디다
☐ **hide** 숨다, 숨기다 – **conceal** 감추다
☐ **touched** 감동한 – **moved** 감동받은
☐ **participate in** 참가하다 – **take part in** 참가하다

※ 서로 반대의 뜻을 가진 어휘

☐ **alive** 살아 있는 ↔ **dead** 죽은
☐ **borrow** 빌리다 ↔ **lend** 빌려주다
☐ **courage** 용기 ↔ **cowardice** 비겁
☐ **thankful** 감사하는 ↔ **ungrateful** 은혜를 모르는

☐ **appear** 나타나다 ↔ **disappear** 사라지다
☐ **bravely** 용감하게 ↔ **timidly** 소심하게
☐ **face** 직면하다 ↔ **avoid** 피하다
☐ **meaningful** 의미 있는 ↔ **meaningless** 의미 없는

※ 동사 – 명사

☐ **achieve** 이루다 – **achievement** 성취, 달성
☐ **depress** 우울하게 하다 – **depression** 우울함
☐ **participate** 참가하다 – **participation** 참가
☐ **survive** 생존하다 – **survival** 생존

☐ **appear** 나타나다 – **appearance** 등장
☐ **endure** 참다, 견디다 – **endurance** 인내
☐ **recommend** 추천하다 – **recommendation** 추천

※ 명사 – 형용사

☐ **color** 색깔 – **colorful** 다채로운
☐ **depression** 우울함 – **depressed** 우울한
☐ **meaning** 의미 – **meaningful** 의미 있는

☐ **courage** 용기 – **courageous** 용감한
☐ **excellence** 우월함 – **excellent** 탁월한

English Dictionary

☐ **abroad** 해외에, 해외로
→ in or to a foreign country
외국에 또는 외국으로

☐ **alive** 살아 있는
→ still living and not dead
여전히 살아 있고 죽지 않은

☐ **century** 100년, 세기
→ a period of 100 years
100년의 기간

☐ **disability** (신체적, 정신적) 장애
→ a physical or mental condition that makes it difficult for someone to use a part of their body properly
신체의 일부를 제대로 사용하기 어렵게 만드는 신체적 또는 정신적 상태

☐ **hardship** 어려움, 곤란
→ something that makes life difficult or unpleasant

삶을 어렵게 하거나 불쾌하게 만드는 것

☐ **overcome** 극복하다
→ to successfully control a feeling or problem that prevents you from achieving something
무엇을 성취하지 못하게 하는 감정이나 문제를 성공적으로 조절하다

☐ **participant** 참가자
→ someone who is taking part in an activity or event
활동이나 행사에 참가하고 있는 사람

☐ **planet** 행성, 지구
→ a very large round object in space that moves around the Sun or another star
태양이나 다른 별 둘레를 도는 우주에 있는 매우 큰 둥근 물체

☐ **triathlon** 철인 레이스
→ a sports competition in which competitors run, swim, and cycle long distances
참가자가 먼 거리를 달리고, 수영하고, 자전거를 타는 스포츠 대회

[01~02] 다음 짝지어진 단어의 관계가 같도록 빈칸에 알맞은 단어를 고르시오.

01

| blame : criticize = _____ : overseas |

① abroad
② journey
③ survival
④ instead
⑤ lately

02

| alive : dead = appear : _____ |

① cool
② overcome
③ receive
④ imagine
⑤ disappear

03 다음 영영풀이에 해당하는 단어를 고르시오.

a very large round object in space that moves around the Sun or another star

① treat
② tiredness
③ cycle
④ planet
⑤ experiment

서답형

04 다음 중 〈보기〉에 있는 단어를 사용하여 자연스러운 문장을 만드시오.

┌ 보기 ┐
appeared   achievement   courage
relationship

(1) I have a very close _____ with my brother.
(2) My _____ surprised everyone.
(3) When smoke _____ in the sky, I could hear the fire alarm.
(4) I don't have the _____ to travel alone.

05 다음 대화의 빈칸에 들어갈 말로 적절한 것을 고르시오.

B: Excuse me. I'm afraid I'm lost. Could you _____ me a hand?
W: Sure.
B: I want to buy a shirt. Can you tell me where the nearest shop is?
W: Sure. Go straight and turn left. The shop is next to the fruit store.
B: Thank you very much.

① give
② borrow
③ imagine
④ blame
⑤ hide

06 다음 밑줄 친 부분과 의미가 같은 것은?

He participated in the dance competition.

① gave up
② was interested
③ brought out
④ took part
⑤ paid attention

07 다음 중 밑줄 친 부분의 뜻풀이가 바르지 않은 것은?

① I talk to my friends when I am depressed. (기분이 우울한)
② I like to think in a positive way. (긍정적인)
③ What is the result of today's soccer match? (결과)
④ Thanks to my friend, I could find my wallet. (덕분에)
⑤ Disability can happen to anyone. (질병)

[01~02] 다음 빈칸에 공통으로 들어가기에 적절한 단어를 쓰시오.

01 중요

> • Let me _____ you a hand with washing the dishes.
> • He chose to _____ up the plan.

02

> • She is in the habit _____ sitting up late.
> • She must be very proud _____ herself.

03 아래 문장의 빈칸에 다음 〈보기〉에 있는 단어를 넣어 자연스러운 문장을 만드시오.

> ┌─ 보기 ─┐
> research hardships factor participants

(1) Diligence is a key _____ for a successful life.

(2) Most of the _____ help people mature.

(3) There are more _____ this year than last year.

(4) Have you done some _____ about Korea?

04 다음 짝지어진 단어의 관계가 같도록 빈칸에 알맞은 말을 쓰시오. (주어진 철자로 시작할 것.)

> meaning : meaningful
> = excellence : _____

05 다음 주어진 단어를 이용해 빈칸을 완성하시오.

> I asked the professor to write a letter of _____ for me.

➡ _____ (recommend)

06 난이도 다음 우리말에 맞게 빈칸에 알맞은 말을 쓰시오. (주어진 철자가 있는 경우에는 주어진 철자로 시작할 것.)

(1) 너는 20년 후의 네 생활을 상상할 수 있니?
  ➡ Can you _____ your life in 20 years?

(2) 도와드리지 못해 죄송합니다. 대신 제 동생이 도와드릴 겁니다.
  ➡ I'm sorry I can't help you. _____, my sister will help you.

(3) 나는 너의 개가 아직 살아 있다는 소식을 들으니 기쁘다.
  ➡ I am happy to hear that your dog is still _____.

(4) N Seoul 타워에 가면 서울 경관을 볼 수 있어.
  ➡ If you go to N Seoul Tower, you can see the _____ of Seoul.

07 중요 다음 영어 설명에 해당하는 단어를 주어진 철자로 시작하여 쓰시오.

> a sports competition in which competitors run, swim, and cycle long distances

➡ t_____

Conversation

① 도움 제안하기

> **Can I give you a hand?** 도와 드릴까요? / **Let me give you a hand.** 제가 도와드리겠습니다.

■ 일반적으로 도움을 제안하는 표현은 help(도움을 주다), give a hand(도움을 주다) 등을 사용한다. 도움을 제공하고자 할 때는 "Can I give you a hand?" 또는 "May I help you?", "How may I help you?", "Do you need any help?"라고 물어볼 수 있다. "give ~ a hand"는 "~를 돕다"라는 의미의 관용적 표현이다.

■ 상대방의 상황을 보고 도움을 제안할 때 "Do you want me to ~?"(제가 ~해 드리기를 원하세요?)라고 물어보거나 "Let me help you with ~."(내가 너에게 ~하도록 도와줄게.)와 같은 표현을 쓸 수 있다. 반대로 도와달라는 표현은 "Can you help me with ~?"(~ 좀 도와주시겠어요?)이다.

도움 제안하기 표현

- Can I give you a hand?
- May/Can I help you?
- What can I do for you?
- Let me help you/give you a hand.
- How may I help you?
- Do you need any help?

도움 제안에 대답하는 표현

- 승낙 · Yes, please. · Sure. · Thank you. · Of course.
- 거절 · No, thank you. · Thank you, but ~. · It's okay.

도움 요청하기 표현

- Can/Could you help me with ~?
- Can/Would you do me a favor?
- Please help me.
- Would/Could you give me a hand?

핵심 Check

1. 다음 대화의 빈칸에 들어가기에 적절하지 <u>않은</u> 것을 고르시오.

> B: Excuse me, I have lost something.
> W: What have you lost? _____
> B: Thank you. I have lost my smartphone.

① Let me give you a hand.　② Let me help you.
③ Can I give you a hand?　④ Do you need any help?
⑤ Could you help me?

2 **바람, 소원, 요망 표현하기**

> **I wish I could get better faster.** 빨리 건강이 회복이 되면 좋을 텐데.

■ 소망이나 바람을 나타낼 때 사용하는 표현 "I wish I could~"는 "I wish+가정법 과거"의 형태를 사용하여 "내가 ~할 수 있다면 좋을 텐데."라는 뜻이다. 뒤에 나오는 가정법 과거는 동사의 과거형으로 나타내고, be동사는 주로 were를 쓴다. 이 표현은 할 수 있으면 좋겠지만 실제로 당장은 할 수 없는 현재의 일에 대하여, 그 사실과 반대가 되는 말하는 사람의 소원을 나타내는 문장이다.

■ 앞으로 일어날 일이나 하고 싶은 일에 대한 기대를 표현할 때는 "~을 기대한다."의 의미로 "looking forward to ~."나 "I look forward to ~."의 표현을 사용한다. 여기서 to는 전치사이므로 뒤에 명사나 동명사가 와야 한다. "빨리 ~하고 싶다, ~을 너무 하고 싶다."의 뜻으로 "I can't wait for ~." "I am dying to ~." "I'm expecting to ~."이라고 하기도 한다.

■ 강한 소원, 기대를 나타낼 때는 "기대하다"는 의미의 expect를 써서 "I'm expecting to 동사원형 ~"이라고 하거나 "열망하다"는 의미의 동사 long을 써서 "I'm longing to+동사원형 ~", "I'm longing for+명사"라고 하거나 형용사 eager(열망하는)를 써서 "I'm eager to+동사원형 ~", "I'm eager for+명사"의 형태로 나타내기도 한다.

바람, 소원, 요망을 나타내는 표현

- I wish 주어+과거 동사 ~. ~할 수 있으면 좋을 텐데.
- I hope to ~. ~하기를 희망한다.
- I'm looking forward to -ing ~ ~하기를 기대한다.
- I am longing to 동사원형 ~. ~하기를 열망한다.
- I want to ~. ~하기를 원한다.
- I'd like to ~. ~하고 싶다.
- I am expecting to 동사원형 ~. ~하기를 기대한다.
- I am eager to 동사원형 ~. ~하기를 간절히 원한다.

핵심 Check

2. 다음 대화의 빈칸에 들어가기에 적절한 말을 고르시오.

> G: _____
> M: Why?
> G: Look at these amazing pictures of planets. I want to see them with my own eyes, not from a book.
> M: I'm glad you are interested in space. Let's continue reading this book.

① I want to meet him today.
② I hope to see the picture.
③ I am looking forward to visiting you.
④ I wish I could visit space.
⑤ I am reading a book.

Everday English 1 B

W: Excuse me, I'm looking for a birthday present for my son.

M: Oh, ❶can I give you a hand?

W: Yes, please. My son is 15 years old. Do you have any recommendations?

M: ❷What about this colorful jacket? It is very popular.

W: ❸It looks fine, but my son doesn't like colorful clothes.

M: What about this green colored jacket?

W: It is very pretty. Do you have it in a large size?

M: Yes, there is a large one here!

W: Thank you. I'll take it.

W: 실례합니다만, 아들 생일 선물을 찾고 있는데요.

M: 아, 제가 도와드릴까요?

W: 네, 제 아들은 15살이에요. 추천해 주실 만한 것이 있나요?

M: 이 컬러풀한 재킷은 어떠세요? 아주 인기가 많아요.

W: 괜찮아 보이지만 제 아들은 컬러풀한 옷을 좋아하지 않아요.

M: 이 녹색 재킷은 어떠세요?

W: 아주 예쁘군요. 라지(L) 사이즈로 있나요?

M: 네, 여기 라지(L) 사이즈가 있어요!

W: 고맙습니다. 그걸로 살게요.

❶ "can I give you a hand?"는 "도와드릴까요?"라는 의미로 도움을 제안하는 표현이다.
❷ "What about ~?"는 상대방의 의견을 묻거나 제안하는 표현이다.
❸ "~해 보이다"의 의미인 동사 "look"은 형용사 보어가 와야 한다.

Check(√) True or False

(1) The woman's son is 15 years old.　　　　　　　　　　　　T ☐ F ☐

(2) The son of the woman likes colorful clothes.　　　　　　　T ☐ F ☐

In Real Life

Ryan: How do you feel? Can I give you a hand, Mom?

Mom: Yes. ❶Can you please get me some medicine?

Ryan: Of course. ❷I will also get you some water to drink.

Mom: Thank you. I wish I could get better faster.

Ryan: I hope you can, too. By the way, I'm sorry Mom.

Mom: What do you mean?

Ryan: When I was sick, you looked after me with all of your heart. But back then I didn't even say a word of thanks.

Mom: Oh, it's okay.

Ryan: I really want to thank you for your love.

Ryan: 좀 어떠세요? 제가 도와드릴까요, 엄마?

Mom: 그래. 약을 좀 가져다줄 수 있니?

Ryan: 물론이죠. 마실 물도 좀 가져다 드릴게요.

Mom: 고맙구나. 내가 더 빨리 나아지면 좋을 텐데.

Ryan: 저도 그러길 바라요. 그런데 죄송해요, 엄마.

Mom: 무슨 말이니?

Ryan: 제가 아팠을 때 엄마는 온 마음을 다해 저를 돌봐 주셨잖아요. 하지만 그때 저는 감사하다는 말 한마디도 하지 않았어요.

Mom: 오, 괜찮다.

Ryan: 엄마의 사랑에 정말 감사드리고 싶어요.

❶ 동사 get은 간접목적어(me)와 직접목적어(some medicine)가 있는 4형식 문장 구조를 만들고 있다.
❷ "some water to drink"에 사용된 "to drink"는 water를 수식하는 형용사적 용법의 부정사이다.

Check(√) True or False

(3) Ryan's mom is sick in bed.　　　　　　　　　　　　　　T ☐ F ☐

(4) Ryan said thank you to his mother when he was sick.　　　T ☐ F ☐

Everday English 1 A-1

B: Excuse me. ❶I'm afraid I'm lost. Could you give me a hand?

W: Sure.

B: I want to buy a shirt. ❷Can you tell me where the nearest shop is?

W: Sure. Go straight and turn left. The shop is next to the fruit store.

B: Thank you very much.

❶ "I'm afraid ～."는 걱정, 염려 등을 나타낼 때 덧붙이는 말이다.
❷ "where the nearest shop is"는 간접의문문으로 tell의 직접목적어이다.

 Everday English 1 A-2

B: Excuse me, ❶I have lost something.

W: What have you lost? Let me give you a hand.

B: Thank you. I have lost my smartphone.

W: Is this black smartphone yours?

B: No, mine is red.

❶ 현재완료 "have lost"는 결과를 나타내는 용법이다.

 Everday English 1 C

A: I have lost my brother. ❶I don't know what to do.

B: Can I give you a hand?

A: Yes, please.

B: ❷What does your brother look like?

A: He is short and has brown hair.

B: What is he wearing?

A: He is wearing a white shirt and blue jeans.

B: Oh, I see. I have found him.

❶ "what to do"는 "의문사+to부정사"의 형태로 "의문사+주어+동사～"로 고쳐 쓸 수 있다.
❷ "look like"의 목적어로 how가 아니라, 의문대명사 what이 있어야 한다.

 Everday English 2 A-1

G: ❶I wish I could visit space.

M: Why?

G: Look at these amazing pictures of planets. ❷I want to see them with my own eyes, not from a book.

M: I'm glad you are interested in space. Let's continue reading this book.

❶ "I wish+가정법 과거"의 문장은 소원을 나타내는 표현이다.
❷ "소유격+own"은 "～ 자신의"라는 뜻으로 own은 소유의 의미를 강조한다.

 Everday English A-2

G: Dad! Look at this beautiful scenery. I wish I could live here.

M: It's amazing, isn't it? ❶Standing on the top of this mountain makes me feel good.

G: ❷I'm so sad that we have to walk down soon.

M: Don't be sad. You can enjoy this view again next week!

❶ "Standing on the top of this mountain"은 문장의 주어로 쓰인 동명사구이다.
❷ "so+형용사+that+주어+동사"의 문장으로 "～하게 되어서 너무 ～하다"의 의미이다.

 Everday English 2 B

M: About 10 years ago, ❶I was hit by a car while I was riding a bicycle at night. I lost my left leg and ❷stayed in the hospital for six months. I was depressed and couldn't find a reason to live. However, my parents supported me and took care of me with their love. ❸ Thanks to them, I was able to overcome the situation. By doing so, I found out that life can be meaningful to everybody. Now, I'm a wheelchair basketball player and every year I ❹run a campaign for people in need of help. During each campaign, I give a speech about the importance of positive thinking. Some people seem to be in the habit of negative thinking. I wish my speech would help them think more positively.

❶ "was hit"은 수동태로 차에 치인 것을 나타낸다.
❷ 접속사 and 뒤에 나오는 stayed는 lost와 병렬 관계이다.
❸ thanks to ～ = ～ 덕택에
❹ run a campaign for ～ = ～을 위한 (모금, 선거 등의) 운동을 하다

다음 우리말과 일치하도록 빈칸에 알맞은 말을 쓰시오.

Everday English 1 A-1

B: _____ me. I'm _____ I'm lost. _____ you _____ me a _____?

W: Sure.

B: I _____ to buy a _____. Can you _____ me _____ the nearest shop is?

W: Sure. Go _____ and turn _____. The shop is _____ to the fruit _____.

B: Thank you very _____.

Everday English 1 A-2

B: _____ me, I have _____ something.

W: What _____ you lost? Let me _____ you a _____.

B: Thank you. I _____ lost my _____.

W: _____ this black _____ yours?

B: No, _____ is red.

Everday English 1 B

W: Excuse me, I'm _____ for a birthday _____ for my son.

M: Oh, _____ I give you a _____?

W: Yes, please. My _____ is 15 _____ old. Do you _____ any _____?

M: What _____ this colorful _____? It is very _____.

W: It looks _____, but my son doesn't like _____ clothes.

M: _____ about this _____ colored _____?

W: It is very _____. Do you have it in a _____ size?

M: Yes, there is a large _____ here!

W: Thank you. I'll _____ it.

Everday English 1 C

A: I have _____ my brother. I don't _____ _____ to do.

B: _____ I give you a _____?

A: Yes, please.

B: What _____ your brother _____ like?

A: He _____ short and _____ brown hair.

B: 실례합니다. 제가 길을 잃은 것 같아요. 도와주실 수 있을까요?
W: 물론이지.
B: 셔츠를 사고 싶은데요. 가장 가까운 상점이 어디에 있는지 알려 주실래요?
W: 물론이지. 곧장 가다가 왼쪽으로 돌아. 과일 가게 옆에 그 상점이 있어.
B: 정말 고맙습니다.

B: 실례합니다. 제가 뭘 잃어버렸어요.
W: 무엇을 잃어버렸니? 내가 도와줄게.
B: 고맙습니다. 제 스마트폰을 잃어버렸어요.
W: 이 검정색 스마트폰이 네 거니?
B: 아니요, 제 것은 빨간색이에요.

W: 실례합니다만, 아들 생일 선물을 찾고 있는데요.
M: 아, 제가 도와드릴까요?
W: 네, 제 아들은 15살이에요. 추천해 주실 만한 것이 있나요?
M: 이 컬러풀한 재킷은 어떠세요? 아주 인기가 많아요.
W: 괜찮아 보이지만 제 아들은 컬러풀한 옷을 좋아하지 않아요.
M: 이 녹색 재킷은 어떠세요?
W: 아주 예쁘군요. 라지(L) 사이즈로 있나요?
M: 네, 여기 라지(L) 사이즈가 있어요!
W: 고맙습니다. 그걸로 살게요.

A: 내 남동생을 잃어버렸어. 어떻게 하면 좋을지 모르겠어.
B: 내가 도와줄까?
A: 그래.
B: 네 남동생은 어떻게 생겼니?
A: 그는 키가 작고 갈색 머리를 하고 있어.

B: What is he _____?

A: He is wearing a white _____ and blue _____.

B: Oh, I _____. I have _____ him.

Everday English 2 A-1

G: I wish I could visit _____.

M: _____?

G: Look at _____ _____ pictures of _____. I want to see them with my _____ eyes, not _____ a book.

M: I'm _____ you are _____ in space. Let's _____ reading this _____.

Everday English 2 B

M: About 10 _____ ago, I was _____ by a car _____ I was _____ a bicycle at night. I _____ my left leg and _____ in the hospital _____ six months. I was _____ and couldn't _____ a reason to _____. However, my parents _____ me and _____ care of me _____ their love. Thanks to them, I was _____ to _____ the situation. _____ doing so, I found _____ that life can be _____ to everybody. Now, I'm a _____ basketball _____ and every year I _____ a campaign for people _____ need of _____. During each _____, I give a _____ about the _____ of _____ thinking. Some people _____ to be in the _____ of _____ thinking. I _____ my speech would _____ them think more _____.

In Real Life

Ryan: _____ do you feel? Can I _____ you a _____, Mom?

Mom: Yes. Can you _____ get me some _____?

Ryan: Of course. I will also _____ you some _____ to drink.

Mom: Thank you. I wish I could _____ _____ faster.

Ryan: I _____ you can, too. By the _____, I'm _____ Mom.

Mom: What do you _____?

Ryan: When I was _____, you _____ _____ me with all of your _____. But _____ then I didn't even _____ a word of _____.

Mom: Oh, it's _____.

Ryan: I really _____ to _____ you for your love.

해석

B: 그는 무엇을 입고 있니?

A: 그는 흰색 셔츠와 청바지를 입고 있어.

B: 아, 알겠다. 그를 찾았어.

G: 우주를 방문할 수 있으면 좋을 텐데.

M: 왜?

G: 이 놀라운 행성의 사진들을 봐요. 책으로 보는 것 말고 내 눈으로 이것들을 직접 보고 싶어요.

M: 네가 우주에 관심 있어서 기뻐. 이 책을 계속 읽어 보자.

M: 약 10년 전, 나는 밤에 자전거를 타다가 차에 치였습니다. 나는 왼쪽 다리를 잃고 6개월 동안 병원에 있었습니다. 나는 우울했고 살아야 할 이유를 찾을 수 없었어요. 하지만 부모님은 나를 지지해 주시고 사랑으로 돌봐 주셨습니다. 그분들 덕분에 나는 그 상황을 극복할 수 있었습니다. 그렇게 함으로써, 나는 삶이 모든 사람에게 의미 있는 것이 될 수 있다는 것을 알게 되었습니다. 지금은 휠체어 농구 선수로 매년 도움이 필요한 사람들을 위한 캠페인을 하고 있습니다. 매번 캠페인을 하는 동안, 나는 긍정적인 사고의 중요성에 대해 연설합니다. 어떤 사람들은 부정적인 생각을 하는 습관이 있는 것 같습니다. 그들이 좀 더 긍정적으로 생각하는 데 내 연설이 도움이 되었으면 좋겠습니다.

Ryan: 좀 어떠세요? 제가 도와드릴까요, 엄마?

Mom: 그래. 약을 좀 가져다줄 수 있니?

Ryan: 물론이죠. 마실 물도 좀 가져다 드릴게요.

Mom: 고맙구나. 내가 더 빨리 나아지면 좋을 텐데.

Ryan: 저도 그러길 바라요. 그런데 죄송해요, 엄마.

Mom: 무슨 말이니?

Ryan: 제가 아팠을 때 엄마는 온 마음을 다해 저를 돌봐 주셨잖아요. 하지만 그때 저는 감사하다는 말 한마디도 하지 않았어요.

Mom: 오, 괜찮다.

Ryan: 엄마의 사랑에 정말 감사드리고 싶어요.

Conversation 시험대비 기본평가

01 다음 대화의 빈칸에 들어갈 말을 고르시오.

> B: Excuse me. I'm afraid I'm lost. Could you give me a hand?
> W: Sure.
> B: I want to buy a shirt. Can you tell me _____?
> W: Sure. Go straight and turn left. The shop is next to the fruit store.
> B: Thank you very much.

① which shirt looks best
② how much the shirt is
③ the best gloves for my hand
④ where the nearest shop is
⑤ whether fruit is good for you

[02~03] 다음 대화를 읽고 물음에 답하시오.

> W: Excuse me, I'm looking for a birthday present for my son.
> M: Oh, can I give you a hand? (A)
> W: Yes, please. My son is 15 years old. (B)
> M: What about this colorful jacket? It is very popular. (C)
> W: It looks fine, but my son doesn't like colorful clothes.
> M: What about this green colored jacket? (D)
> W: It is very pretty. Do you have it in a large size?
> M: Yes, there is a large one here! (E)
> W: Thank you. I'll take it.

02 (A)~(E) 중에서 다음 문장이 들어가기에 가장 적절한 곳은?

> Do you have any recommendations?

① (A)　　② (B)　　③ (C)　　④ (D)　　⑤ (E)

03 위 대화의 내용과 일치하지 않는 것은?

① The woman is looking for her birthday present.
② Her son is 15 years old.
③ Her son doesn't like colorful clothes.
④ The woman will buy a green colored jacket.
⑤ The man recommended a colorful jacket at first.

01 다음 대화의 빈칸에 들어가기에 적절한 것은?

> M: I wish I were younger. Then _____
> _____!
> G: Yeah. This journey is too difficult because we aren't good at English.
> M: Do you want to study English with me when we get back to Korea?
> G: Yes, Dad! I am excited about studying with you.

① you would travel more cities
② they would study English
③ he could get back to Korea
④ I could travel with you
⑤ I would be able to study English harder

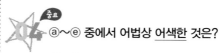

02 다음 주어진 우리말에 어울리는 영어 문장은?

> B: Excuse me. I'm afraid I'm lost. Could you give me a hand?
> W: Sure.
> B: I want to buy a shirt. 가장 가까운 상점이 어디에 있는지 알려 주시겠습니까?
> W: Sure. Go straight and turn left. The shop is next to the fruit store.
> B: Thank you very much.

① Can you show me how to go to the nearest shop?
② Can you tell me where the nearest shop is?
③ Where can you tell is the shop nearest?
④ Where the nearest shop you can tell?
⑤ The nearest ship where you can tell is?

[03~05] 다음 대화를 읽고 물음에 답하시오.

> W: Excuse me, I'm ⓐlooking for a birthday present for my son.
> M: Oh, can I ⓑgive you a hand?
> W: Yes, please. My son is 15 years old. Do you have any ⓒrecommendations?
> M: What about this colorful jacket? It is very popular.
> W: It ⓓlooks like fine, (A)_____
> M: What about this green colored jacket?
> W: It is very pretty. Do you have it in a large size?
> M: Yes, ⓔthere is a large one here!
> W: Thank you. I'll take it.

03 위 대화의 빈칸 (A)에 들어갈 말로 알맞은 것은?

① but my son doesn't like colorful clothes.
② and I want to buy this colorful jacket.
③ but is it popular these days?
④ why do you think it's popular?
⑤ do you like this colorful green jacket?

04 ⓐ~ⓔ 중에서 어법상 어색한 것은?

① ⓐ　　② ⓑ　　③ ⓒ　　④ ⓓ　　⑤ ⓔ

05 위 대화의 내용과 일치하지 않는 것은?

① The woman is a mother of 15-year-old son.
② The woman is looking for a present for her husband.
③ The woman wants help from the man to buy a present.
④ The woman's son doesn't like a colorful jacket.
⑤ The woman will buy a green jacket.

[06~07] 다음 대화를 읽고 물음에 답하시오.

> G: Dad! Look at this beautiful scenery. (가)여기에서 살 수 있으면 좋겠어요.
>
> M: It's amazing, isn't it? Standing on the top of this mountain makes me feel good.
>
> G: I'm so sad that we have to walk down soon.
>
> M: Don't be sad. You can enjoy this view again next week!

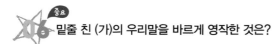

06 밑줄 친 (가)의 우리말을 바르게 영작한 것은?

① I hope to wish here.

② I want here to live.

③ I wished here I can live.

④ I wish I could live here.

⑤ You wish here you will live.

07 위 대화의 내용과 일치하지 <u>않는</u> 것은?

① They are looking at a beautiful scenery.

② They are on the top of a mountain.

③ They like the scenery at the top.

④ Standing on the top makes them feel sad.

⑤ They will be on the top again.

[08~10] 다음 대화를 읽고 물음에 답하시오.

> Ryan: How do you feel? ⓐCan I give you a hand, Mom?
>
> Mom: Yes. (가)나에게 약을 좀 가져다줄 수 있니?
>
> Ryan: Of course. ⓑI will also get you some water to drink.

> Mom: Thank you. ⓒI wish I can get better faster.
>
> Ryan: I hope you can, too. By the way, I'm sorry Mom.
>
> Mom: ⓓWhat do you mean?
>
> Ryan: When I was sick, you looked after me with all of your heart. ⓔBut back then I didn't even say a word of thanks.
>
> Mom: Oh, it's okay.
>
> Ryan: I really want to thank you for your love.

08 밑줄 친 (가)에 해당하는 영어 문장으로 가장 적절한 것은?

① Please can you give me some medicine?

② Can you please get me some medicine?

③ Will you take me to the medicine?

④ Can I bring you to some medicine?

⑤ Could you tell me some medicine?

09 ⓐ~ⓔ 중 어법상 <u>어색한</u> 것을 올바르게 고쳐 쓴 것은?

① Can I give to you a hand, Mom?

② I will also get you some water drinking.

③ I wish I could get better faster.

④ What you meant?

⑤ But back then I didn't even say no word of thanks.

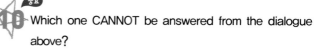

10 Which one CANNOT be answered from the dialogue above?

① Is Ryan's mom sick in bed now?

② What will Ryan take to his mom?

③ Why will Ryan give water to his mom?

④ Why does Ryan feel sorry for his mom?

⑤ What will Ryan's mom say to Ryan?

01 다음 대화의 밑줄 친 우리말을 주어진 단어를 이용하여 영작하시오.

> A: The picnic will be a lot of fun.
> B: (가)공원에 가서 소풍을 즐길 수 있으면 좋겠어요.(wish, enjoy)

➡ _____

[02~04] 다음 대화를 읽고 물음에 답하시오.

> W: Excuse me, I'm ⓐlooking for a birthday present for my son.
> M: Oh, can I give you a hand?
> W: Yes, please. My son is 15 ⓑyears old. Do you have any (A)_____?
> M: ⓒWhat about this colorful jacket? It is very popular.
> W: It looks fine, but my son doesn't like colorful clothes.
> M: What about this green ⓓcolored jacket?
> W: It is very pretty. (가)라지(L) 사이즈로 있나요?(have / do / a / you / it / large / in / size)
> M: Yes, there is a large one here!
> W: Thank you. I'll take ⓔthem.

02 내용상 빈칸 (A)에 들어가기에 적절한 한 단어를 쓰시오.(주어진 철자로 시작할 것)

➡ r_____

03 밑줄 친 ⓐ~ⓔ 중 어법상 어색한 것을 찾아 번호를 쓰고 올바르게 고치시오.

➡ _____

04 밑줄 친 (가)의 우리말을 주어진 단어를 바르게 배열하여 영작하시오.

➡ _____

05 다음 대화의 문맥이나 어법상 어색한 것을 찾아 고치시오.

> G: I wish I ⓐcould visit space.
> M: Why?
> G: Look at these ⓑamazing pictures of planets. I want ⓒto see them with my own eyes, ⓓnot from a book.
> M: I'm glad you are interested in space. Let's continue ⓔread this book.

➡ _____

[06~07] 다음 대화를 읽고 물음에 답하시오.

> B: There is no way I can carry all these things to my grandmother's house.
> G: (가)내가 도와줄게.(let, hand)
> B: Thank you very much.
> G: ⓐI will carry these books.
> B: Be careful. They are very heavy.
> G: Wow, ⓑthese are really heavy. I can't even pick them up!
> B: ⓒI wish I could drive. Then carrying heavy things wouldn't be a problem.
> G: Hey, ⓓwhy do we ask our friends for help?
> B: That's a great idea. ⓔCould you please call them for me?
> G: Sure.

06 밑줄 친 (가)의 우리말을 영어로 옮기시오. (주어진 단어 포함)

➡ _____

07 ⓐ~ⓔ 중에서 내용상 어색한 문장을 골라 바르게 고쳐 쓰시오.

➡ _____

Grammar

1 not only A but also B

Eunchong **not only** is still alive **but also** got first place in his first triathlon.
은총이는 여전히 살아 있을 뿐만 아니라 그의 첫 철인 레이스에서 1등을 했다.

- 상관접속사는 두 개의 문장이 의미와 구조가 비슷할 때 하나의 문장으로 이어주는 역할을 한다. 상관 접속사 중에서 'not only A but also B'는 'A뿐만 아니라 B도'로 해석하며, only 대신 merely, just, simply 등을 쓸 수 있다. 또한 not only A but also B에서 also는 생략 가능하다.
  - You gave us hope. You gave us courage. → You gave us **not only** hope **but also** courage.
    너는 우리에게 희망뿐 아니라 용기도 줬다.

- 'not only A but also B'는 'B as well as A'로 바꿔 쓸 수 있다.
  - **Not only** my brother **but also** my sister is a soldier. 내 오빠뿐만 아니라 내 언니도 군인이다.
    = My sister **as well as** my brother is a soldier.

- 상관접속사 'not only A but also B'에서
  (1) A와 B는 어법상 같은 것끼리 연결해 줘야 한다.
  - I enjoy **not only** playing soccer **but** (**also**) playing tennis. 나는 축구를 하는 것뿐만 아니라 테니스 치는 것 도 즐긴다.
  - **Not only** you **but also** Sally is a friend of mine. 너 뿐만 아니라 Sally도 나의 친구 중 한 명이다.
  (2) A와 B가 주어일 때, 동사는 B에 일치시킨다. ('B as well as A'에서도 B에 수의 일치)
  - **Not only** you **but also** Sally is a friend of mine. 너뿐만 아니라 Sally도 내 친구다.
    = Sally **as well as** you is a friend of mine.

- 그밖의 상관접속사에는 'both A and B(A와 B 둘 다)', 'not A but B(A가 아니라 B = B, not A)', 'either A or B(A 혹은 B 둘 중 하나)', 'neither A nor B(A도 B도 아닌)', 'not so much A as B(A라기보다는 B)', 'from A to B(A에서부터 B까지)' 등이 있다.
  - I like **both** to read books **and** to watch movies. 나는 독서와 영화 감상 둘 다 좋아한다.
  - This ring is **not** hers **but** mine. 이 반지는 그녀의 것이 아니라 내 것이다.
  - **Either** he **or** I am in charge of the task. 그도 나도 그 일에 책임이 있다.
  - **Neither** he **nor** I am able to do it. 그도 나도 그것을 할 수 없다.
  * 동사의 수의 일치
  - B에 일치: not only A but also B, B as well as A, either A or B, neither A nor B, not A but B
  - 항상 복수: both A and B

핵심 Check

1. 다음 괄호 안에서 알맞은 단어를 고르시오.
   (1) Not only you but also I (are / am) wrong.
   (2) Both Suji and Sangmin (likes / like) learning something new.
   (3) He came here not on Friday but (on Saturday / Saturday).
   (4) She is neither pretty (or / nor) intellectual.

❷ I wish 가정법 과거

> • **I wish** I **had** an umbrella. 내가 우산을 가지고 있다면 좋을 텐데.
>
> • **I wish** I **could** fly. 내가 날 수 있다면 좋을 텐데.

■ **I wish+S+과거시제 동사 ~(~라면 좋을 텐데). 종속절의 동사는 과거형**으로 써야 한다. (be동사의 경우 주어가 1, 3인칭 단수일 때 구어체에서는 were 대신에 was를 쓰기도 한다.)
  • **I wish** I **were** Superman. 내가 슈퍼맨이라면 좋을 텐데.
  • **I wish** I **could** meet her. 내가 그녀를 만난다면 좋을 텐데.

■ 현재 사실의 반대를 의미한다. 즉, 지금 무언가를 후회하거나 현재 일어날 가능성이 아주 희박한 일을 소망할 때 사용한다.
  • **I wish** I **had** a brother. 내가 남동생이 있다면 좋을 텐데.
   (= It's a pity[I am sorry] (that) I don't have a brother now.)
  • **I wish** I **were** a little taller. 내가 키가 약간 더 크다면 좋을 텐데.
   (= It's a pity[I am sorry] (that) I'm not tall.)
  • **I wish** the exam **were** easy. 시험이 쉽다면 좋을 텐데.
   (= It's a pity[I am sorry] (that) the exam is not easy.)
  * 현재 사실에 대한 반대를 나타내는 'as if+과거시제' 형태도 알아두어야 한다.
   ex) He talks **as if** he **were** rich. = In fact, he is not rich now.

■ 바라는 시점과 사건이 일어나는 시점이 동일할 때 사용
  [사건이 일어난 시점, 바라는 시점]
  • **I wish** I **took** care of him. 내가 그를 보살피면 좋았을 텐데.
   (= I am sorry I don't take care of him.)
  • **I wish** he **could call** me. 그가 나에게 전화하면 좋을 텐데.
   (= I am sorry he can't call me.)

■ **I wished+S+과거시제 동사**: ~라면 좋았을 텐데, ~하기를 바랬다(바라는 시점과 사건이 일어나는 시점이 과거로 과거 소망).
  [사건이 일어난 시점, 바라는 시점]
  • **I wished** I could visit her hometown.
   (= I was sorry I couldn't visit her hometown.)

핵심 Check

2. 괄호 안에서 알맞은 단어를 고르시오.
   (1) I wish I (know / knew) how to drive.
   (2) I wish it (is / were) not raining.
   (3) I wished the exam (am / were) easy.
   (4) I wish I (am / were) a little taller.

01 다음 우리말에 맞게 빈칸에 알맞은 단어를 쓰시오.

(1) 내가 자전거를 타면 좋을 텐데, 하지만 그럴 수 없다.
➡ I wish I _____ ride a bike, but I can't.

(2) 손을 씻는 것뿐만 아니라 발을 씻는 것도 중요하다.
➡ It's important to wash your feet _____ _____ _____ to wash your hands.

(3) 그녀는 농구뿐만 아니라 수영도 잘한다.
➡ She is good at _____ _____ playing basketball but also swimming.

02 다음 우리말을 영어로 바르게 옮긴 것은?

Ryan은 고기뿐만 아니라 채소 먹는 것도 좋아한다.

① Ryan likes to eat not meat but vegetables.
② Ryan likes to eat vegetables as well as eating meat.
③ Ryan likes eating meat and to eat vegetables.
④ Ryan likes to eat not only meat but also vegetables.
⑤ Ryan likes to eat meat as well as eating vegetables.

03 다음 문장과 의미가 같은 것을 고르시오.

I want to drink milk, but I can't because there isn't any milk now.

① I wish I buy milk.
② I wish I drink milk.
③ I wish I could drink milk.
④ I wish I wanted to drink milk.
⑤ I wish I will drink milk.

04 밑줄 친 부분을 바르게 고쳐 쓰시오.

(1) Not only Ryan but also his friends studies hard.
➡ _____

(2) I love not only to play tennis but also watching movies.
➡ _____

서답형

01 다음 〈보기〉의 표현을 활용하여 현재 이룰 가능성이 적지만 자신이 소망하는 것을 쓰시오.

┌── 보기 ──┐
(1) swim well   (2) good at singing
(3) cook well   (4) have a sister
└───────┘

➡ (1) _____
➡ (2) _____
➡ (3) _____
➡ (4) _____

중요

02 다음 빈칸에 들어갈 말로 알맞게 짝지어진 것은?

• You have to be either strong or _____.
• Either you or I _____ right.

① smart – am
② smart – are
③ to be smart – be
④ to be smart – am
⑤ to be smart – are

03 다음 각 문장의 알맞은 시점을 고르시오.

(1) I wish he would listen to my advice.
➡ [present / past]
(2) I wish people wouldn't throw trash anywhere.
➡ [present / past]
(3) I wished he would listen to my advice.
➡ [present / past]
(4) I wished people wouldn't throw trash anywhere.
➡ [present / past]

중요

04 밑줄 친 부분이 어법상 어색한 것을 모두 고르시오.

① This book is both interesting and enlightening.
② Both you and I am correct.
③ It is not a pen, but a pencil.
④ This book is not only interesting but also enlightening.
⑤ Her sisters as well as Mary is kind.

서답형

05 'I wish'를 활용하여 제시된 문장과 같은 뜻이 되도록 영작하시오.

(1) I am sorry I can't go to the park and enjoy the picnic.
➡ _____
   _____
(2) I am sorry I can't travel abroad.
➡ _____
(3) It's a pity I can't sing well.
➡ _____
(4) It's a pity I'm not tall.
➡ _____
(5) She was sorry she wasn't a nurse.
➡ _____

서답형

06 대화의 밑줄 친 우리말을 영작하시오.

M: 내가 더 젊었다면 좋을 텐데. Then I would be able to study English harder!
G: Yeah. This journey is too difficult because we aren't good at English.

➡ _____

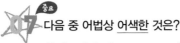 다음 중 어법상 어색한 것은?

① I wish there were better roads for disabled people.

② I wish there were more chances for them to get a job.

③ I wish I knew the answer.

④ I wish I can help them think more positively.

⑤ I wish I could vote.

서답형
08 다음 중 어법상 어색한 것은?

① She easily picked up information not only from her clients but women with whom she socialized often.

② Not merely John but also Donald knows me.

③ Teaching is not simply a mechanical job but an emotional job.

④ Not just the teacher but also the students want to read the book.

⑤ He not only teaches Spanish but English.

서답형
09 다음 우리말에 맞게 괄호 안에 주어진 단어를 활용하여 어법에 맞게 배열하시오.

(1) 너 뿐만 아니라 그녀도 해외 여행 계획이 있다.
➡ _____ a plan to travel abroad. (not only, but also, you, she, have)

➡ _____ a plan to travel abroad. (as well as, she, you, have)

(2) 아이들이 아니라 부모님들이 게임을 하고 있는 중이었다.
➡ _____ playing the game. (not, but, the kids, the parents, be)

(3) 너 또는 Kim 둘 중 한 명이 팀 리더가 될 것 같다.
➡ _____ likely to be a team leader. (either, or, you, Kim, be)

(4) 나의 엄마도 나도 결과에 만족하지 않는다.
➡ _____ satisfied with the result. (neither, nor, my mother, I, be)

(5) 작문 시험과 실용 시험 모두 자격증 취득에 필수적이다.
➡ _____ necessary to achieve the certification. (both, and, a written test, a practical exam, be)

10 다음 빈칸에 들어갈 말로 알맞은 것은?

I thank you not only for being my son but also _____ me an important life lesson.

① to teach
② teach
③ teaching
④ for teaching
⑤ for teach

11 다음 중 어법상 어색한 것을 고르면?

① Alice wishes she had long hair.

② I wish I am a bird.

③ We wish she could succeed.

④ I wished you could pass the exam.

⑤ He wished he could be happy.

12 다음 빈칸에 들어갈 말로 알맞은 것끼리 짝지어진 것을 <u>모두</u> 고르시오.

> He ___ⓐ___ that all the people from around the world ___ⓑ___ the power of positive thinking.

① wish – could know
② wish – could have
③ wishes – could know
④ wishes – could have known
⑤ wished – could know

서답형
13 다음 글을 읽고 물음에 답하시오.

> My grandmother lives in the southern part of Korea. She is a farmer. When I went ⓐ<u>to</u> her house, she showed me around the farm and ⓑ<u>told</u> me everything about farming. She not only welcomed me ⓒ<u>and</u> also treated me like the most important person in the whole world. Now, she is in the hospital. I wish I ⓓ<u>can</u> spend my time with her as we did in the past. I hope that she ⓔ<u>gets</u> healthy again.
> <The writer = the girl>

(1) ⓐ~ⓔ 중 틀린 부분을 <u>모두</u> 찾아 고치시오.

➡ _____

(2) What does the writer wish?

➡ _____
  _____
  _____

서답형
14 우리말에 맞게 문장의 빈칸에 들어갈 알맞은 어휘를 쓰시오.

(1) 이란은 세계 1위의 테러 지원국일뿐만 아니라, 이란의 지도자들은 시리아와 예멘의 비극적인 전쟁을 부채질하고 있다.

= Iran is _____ the world's number one state sponsor of terrorism, _____ Iran's leaders are fueling the tragic wars in both Syria and Yemen.

(2) 노인들이 주연으로 출연하는 광고의 수와 많은 모델의 평균 연령에서 현저한 증가가 있다.

= We see marked increase in _____ the number of ads that feature older people _____ the average age of many models.

(3) 나는 키가 더 컸으면 좋겠다.

= I wish I _____ taller.

15 다음 중 어법상 어색한 것을 고르시오.

① Neither you nor she are to blame.
② They sell books as well as newspapers.
③ She's not just my friend but my lawyer.
④ Both my mom and my dad are engineers.
⑤ Either you or he is wrong.

서답형
16 괄호 안에 주어진 어휘를 이용하여 다음 문장을 영작했을 때, 아래의 지시문에 맞는 단어를 쓰시오.

(1) 2번째와 4번째 단어를 쓰시오.
• 내가 상을 타면 좋을 텐데. (wish, I, receive, prize)

➡ _____

(2) 2번째와 5번째 단어를 쓰시오.
• 내가 당신과 함께 뛸 수 있으면 좋겠어요. (wish, I, run, you)

➡ _____

(3) 4번째에 오는 단어를 쓰시오.
• 이것은 단지 기계이기만 한 것이 아니라 예술 작품이다. (this, not, an artwork)

➡ _____

01 다음 각 문장의 의미가 같도록 주어진 조건대로 영작하시오.

(1) Not only all the furniture but also the books are for sale. (as를 이용할 것.)

➡ _____

(2) The volcano erupted not in Korea, but in Japan. (but을 쓰지 말 것.)

➡ _____

(3) Either my father or my mother is not at home. (not을 쓰지 말 것.)

➡ _____

(4) I like neither coffee nor tea. (not을 이용할 것.)

➡ _____

02 다음 문장의 빈칸을 채우시오.

(1) Not Stephen but Richard has handed in the report.
= Richard, _____ Stephen, has handed in the report.

(2) He is not only an artist but also a scientist.
= He is a scientist _____ _____ _____ an artist.

(3) Their house is neither big nor small.
= Their house is _____ either big _____ small.

03 다음 밑줄 친 부분 중 어색한 것을 찾아 바르게 고치시오.

(1) Rachel ①was impressed ②not ③only by his ④thoughtfulness but ⑤his profound knowledge.

➡ _____

(2) Neither your hat ①nor your ②shirts ③goes with this pair ④of ⑤jeans.

➡ _____

(3) She ①doesn't ②simply hate your purpose, ③merely ④she ⑤hates his purpose.

➡ _____

04 다음 문장에서 어법상 어색한 부분을 찾아 바르게 고쳐 다시 쓰시오.

(1) Throughout history, shoes have been worn not only for protection however also for decoration.

➡ _____

_____

(2) Not information but also people may move between societies.

➡ _____

_____

(3) Economic goods may take the form either of material things or services.

➡ _____

_____

05 괄호 안의 말을 사용하여 같은 뜻을 갖는 문장으로 바꿔 쓰시오.

(1) I love not only singing but also dancing.
(as well as)

➡ _____

(2) The teacher asked Tom's friends as well as Tom to come to the front.
(not only A but also B)

➡ _____

_____

06 각 문장의 괄호 안에 주어진 힌트를 참고하여 어법에 맞게 빈칸을 채우시오.

(1) The most important thing in the Olympic games is not to win but _____ (참가하다).

(2) Not only you but also he _____ (~해야 한다) to go there.

(3) You will fail not because you are incompetent but _____ (네가 게으르다).

(4) She enjoys either _____ (사무실에서 일하다) or playing outside.

(5) My brother enjoys not only walking but also _____ (그리다).

07 다음 우리말에 맞게 괄호 안의 어휘를 활용하여 빈칸을 채우시오.

이 책은 Peter에 의해서도 Jane에 의해서도 쓰여진 것이 아니다. (neither, nor)
= This book was written _____

_____.

08 다음 그림을 보고 hang out을 이용하여 문장을 완성하시오.

I _____.
= I am sorry _____.

09 대화의 흐름에 맞게 빈칸에 알맞은 말을 영작하시오.

(1) A: Why don't you drink this milk? It's fresh.
B: _____. The doctor said I shouldn't drink milk today.

(2) A: Do you want to buy those clothes?
B: Yes. But I don't have any money.

_____

10 괄호 안에 주어진 어휘를 한 번 이상 사용하여 어법에 맞게 빈칸을 채우시오.

(1) Stress affects _____

_____. (people, not, mentally, physically, but, merely, also)

(2) It isn't _____.
(simply, but, a novel, a literary classic)

(3) The solution _____

_____ in a form that the computer can understand. (must, be, but, just, detailed, very, written, not)

Reading

교과서

LOVE IS ALL YOU NEED

On October 16th, 2010, Eunchong and his dad <u>participated in</u> their
participate in = take part in: ~에 참가하다

first triathlon. It was held in Misari, Hanam. They swam 1.5 km, cycled
(좁은) 지역+그 지역이 속한 시(행정구역)

40 km, and then ran 10 km. This challenge was especially difficult for
셋 또는 셋 이상의 낱말을 열거할 때 낱말을 구분하기 위해 콤마를 사용한다.

Eunchong's dad because he had to push or pull Eunchong during the

race. Eunchong <u>couldn't talk or walk</u> because he <u>was born with</u> six
not A or B: A도, B도 아님   *be born with: ~을 가지고 태어나다*

different diseases. His skin was dark red and his brain was becoming

hard. The doctor said he would not live for long. But Eunchong <u>not</u>

<u>only</u> is still alive <u>but also</u> got first place in his first triathlon.
not only A but also B = B as well as A: A뿐만 아니라 B도

Dear Eunchong,

I thank you <u>not only</u> for being my son <u>but also</u> for teaching me an
not only A but also B = B as well as A: A뿐만 아니라 B도

important life lesson. When you were a baby, people avoided you

because of your skin color. I felt sad and wanted to <u>hide</u> you from
because(접속사)+절(주어+동사). because of+명사(구).   *숨다. ~을 숨기다*

them. Your mom hoped that you would be born with no disabilities.

participate in ~에 참가하다
triathlon 철인 레이스
be held in: ~에서 개최되다
challenge 도전; 도전하다
alive 살아 있는
hide 숨다. 숨기다

확인문제

● 다음 문장이 본문의 내용과 일치하면 T, 일치하지 <u>않으면</u> F를 쓰시오.

1 Eunchong and his dad participated in their first triathlon on October 16th, 2010. ☐

2 Eunchong and his dad swam 1.5 km, cycled 10 km, and then ran 40 km. ☐

3 Eunchong couldn't talk or walk because he was born with six different diseases. ☐

4 Eunchong is not still alive but he got first place in his first triathlon. ☐

5 When Eunchong was a baby, people avoided him because of his skin color. ☐

6 Eunchong's mom felt sad and wanted to hide Eunchong from people. ☐

She blamed herself for your sickness. But you always smiled at
주어와 목적어가 같을 때: 재귀대명사를 사용

us and held our hands. You gave us courage as well as hope. So, I
= You gave us not only hope but also courage.

promised myself that I would face the world and show you the bright
의지를 나타내는 조동사   = show the bright side of things to you

side of things. Since then we have begun our journey.
bright side of things: 밝은 면

Do you remember our first triathlon? When we began to swim,
begin: 목적어로 to부정사와 명사가 올 수 있다.

the other participants made way for us and let us go first. I was very
make way for: ~에게 길을 열어 주다   let+목적어+목적격보어(동사 원형)

touched and thankful. Some participants even cried when we passed
이어동사: 목적어가 인칭대명사인 경우 목적어는

them by. When we started cycling, many people cheered for us. But
반드시 동사와 부사 사이에 위치해야 한다.

you had to endure some strong winds and tiredness. So I cycled very
have to의 과거 형태

fast to give you a break. When we began running, your mom seemed
to부정사의 부사적 용법(목적)

to say, "I wish I could run with you." I wanted to finish the race
I wish+가정법 과거   to부정사의 명사적 용법

quickly so I could see her and let you rest. So, I ran fast. When we
let+목적어+목적격보어(동사 원형)

were almost at the finishing line, the other participants stopped and let

us go first. Eunchong, you were the winner! I hope you could tell how
let+목적어+목적격보어(동사 원형)

much everyone at those races loved you.

blame ~을 탓하다
courage 용기
since ~부터[이후]
journey 여행, 여정
participant 참가자
endure 참다, 견디다

확인문제

● 다음 문장이 본문의 내용과 일치하면 T, 일치하지 않으면 F를 쓰시오.

1 Eunchong gave his parents courage as well as hope. ☐

2 When Eunchong and his dad began to swim, they made way for other participants.
☐

3 Some participants even cried when Eunchong and his dad passed them by. ☐

4 Eunchong's dad had to endure some strong winds and tiredness. ☐

5 Eunchong's dad wanted to finish the race quickly so he could see Eunchong's mom
and let Eunchong rest. ☐

6 When Eunchong and his dad were almost at the starting line, the other participants
stopped. ☐

Thanks to you, your mom and I learned an important lesson. "Love is all
'I'와 다른 명사[대명사]를 'and'로 연결할 때 'I'는 항상 뒤에 나온다.

we need." We don't ever think, "We wish Eunchong had no disabilities"
We wish+가정법과거 구문

anymore. Instead, we are just thankful for having you. We are also happy
전치사+동명사

about many other little things. Even when we face difficulties, we are
~일 때조차도

happy. That's because we know that we can overcome any hardships when
앞 문장을 가리킨다.　　　　　　　　= get over: 극복하다

we are together and love each other. Let's continue to live happily and
continue: 목적어로 to부정사와 동명사가 올 수 있다

bravely. We will always love you and stand by you.

Love,

Dad

thanks to ~ 덕분에
hardship 어려움, 곤란

📎 **확인문제**

● 다음 문장이 본문의 내용과 일치하면 T, 일치하지 않으면 F를 쓰시오.

1 Thanks to Eunchong, his mom and dad learned an important lesson. ☐

2 Eunchong's mom and dad always think, "We wish Eunchong had no disabilities".

☐

3 Eunchong's mom and dad are just thankful for having him. ☐

4 Eunchong's mom and dad are also happy about many other great things. ☐

5 Even when Eunchong's mom and dad face difficulties, they are happy. ☐

6 Eunchong's mom and dad know that they can't overcome the hardships though they

are together and love each other. ☐

● 우리말을 참고하여 빈칸에 알맞은 말을 쓰시오.

1 LOVE IS _____

2 On October 16th, 2010, Eunchong and his dad _____ _____ their first triathlon.

3 It _____ _____ in Misari, Hanam.

4 They _____ 1.5 km, _____ 40 km, and then _____ 10 km.

5 This challenge was especially difficult for Eunchong's dad because he _____ _____ _____ _____ _____ Eunchong during the race.

6 Eunchong couldn't talk or walk because he _____ _____ _____ six different diseases.

7 His skin was dark red and his brain _____ _____ _____.

8 The doctor said he would not live _____ _____.

9 But Eunchong not only _____ _____ but also _____ _____ _____ in his first triathlon.

10 Dear Eunchong,

11 I thank you _____ _____ for being my son _____ _____ for teaching me an important life lesson.

12 When you were a baby, people avoided you _____ _____ your skin color.

13 I _____ _____ and wanted to _____ you _____ them.

14 Your mom hoped that you would be born _____ _____ _____.

1	당신에게 필요한 건 사랑이 전부다
2	2010년 10월 16일, 은총이와 그의 아빠는 그들의 첫 철인 레이스에 참가했다.
3	그것은 하남의 미사리에서 열렸다.
4	그들은 1.5 km를 수영하고, 40 km 사이클을 타고, 그런 다음 10 km를 뛰었다.
5	이 도전은 은총이 아빠에게 특히 어려웠는데 경주 동안 은총이를 밀거나 끌어야 했기 때문이다.
6	은총이는 6가지 다른 질병을 갖고 태어나서 말할 수도 걸을 수도 없었다.
7	그의 피부는 어두운 붉은색이었고 그의 두뇌는 점점 굳어가고 있었다.
8	의사는 은총이가 오래 살지 못할 거라고 했다.
9	하지만 은총이는 여전히 살아 있을 뿐만 아니라 그의 첫 철인 레이스에서 1등을 했다.
10	은총이에게.
11	나는 네가 내 아들이어서뿐만 아니라 나에게 중요한 인생의 교훈을 가르쳐 주어서 고맙구나.
12	네가 아기였을 때, 사람들이 너의 피부색 때문에 너를 피했단다.
13	나는 슬펐고 너를 그들로부터 숨기고 싶었어.
14	네 엄마는 네가 장애 없이 태어나기를 바랐지.

15 She _____ _____ _____ your sickness.

16 But you always _____ _____ us and held our hands.

17 You gave us courage _____ _____ _____ hope.

18 So, I promised _____ that I would _____ _____ _____ and show you the _____ _____ of things.

19 Since then we _____ _____ our journey.

20 Do you remember _____ _____ _____ ?

21 When we began to swim, the other participants _____ _____ _____ us and let us go first.

22 I was very _____ and _____ .

23 Some participants even cried when we _____ _____ _____ .

24 When we started cycling, many people _____ _____ us.

25 But you _____ _____ _____ some strong winds and tiredness.

26 So I cycled very fast to _____ _____ _____ _____ .

27 When we began running, your mom seemed to say, "_____ _____ _____ _____ run with you."

28 I wanted to finish the race quickly so I could see her and _____ _____ _____ .

29 So, I _____ .

30 When we were _____ at the finishing line, the other participants stopped and _____ _____ _____ .

15 네 엄마는 너의 병이 자신 때문이라고 자책도 했어.

16 하지만 너는 우리를 향해 항상 웃어주었고, 우리의 손을 잡아주었어.

17 너는 우리에게 희망뿐만 아니라 용기도 주었지.

18 그래서 나는 세상을 직면하고 너에게 세상의 밝은 면을 보여주겠다고 나 자신에게 약속했어.

19 그때부터 우리는 우리의 여정을 시작했지.

20 우리의 첫 철인 레이스를 기억하니?

21 우리가 수영을 시작했을 때, 다른 참가자들이 우리가 먼저 가도록 길을 만들어 줬어.

22 나는 정말 감동하였고 감사했단다.

23 몇몇 참가자들은 심지어 우리가 지나갈 때 울기도 했어.

24 우리가 사이클링을 시작했을 때, 많은 사람이 우리를 응원했지.

25 하지만 너는 강한 바람과 피곤함을 견뎌야만 했어.

26 그래서 나는 네가 쉴 수 있도록 아주 빨리 페달을 밟았어.

27 우리가 달리기 시작했을 때, 너의 엄마가 "당신과 함께 달릴 수 있으면 참 좋겠다." 라고 말하는 듯했어.

28 빨리 경주를 끝내서 너의 엄마를 보고 네가 쉬도록 하고 싶었어.

29 그래서 나는 빨리 달렸단다.

30 우리가 거의 결승선에 도착했을 때, 다른 참가자들이 멈췄고 우리가 먼저 가도록 해줬어.

31 Eunchong, you were the _____!

32 I hope you could _____ how much everyone _____ _____ _____ loved you.

33 _____ _____ you, your mom and I learned an important lesson.

34 "Love is _____ _____ _____."

35 We don't ever think, "We wish Eunchong _____ _____ _____" anymore.

36 _____, we are just thankful for having you.

37 We are also happy about many _____ _____ _____.

38 Even when we _____ _____, we are happy.

39 That's _____ we know that we can _____ any hardships when we _____ _____ and love each other.

40 _____ _____ to live happily and bravely.

41 We will always love you and _____ _____ _____.

42 _____,

43 Dad

31 은총아, 네가 우승자였단다!

32 아빠는 네가 그 경기에 있던 모든 사람이 너를 얼마나 사랑했는지 알았기를 바란다.

33 네 덕분에, 너의 엄마와 나는 중요한 교훈을 배웠단다.

34 "사랑이 우리가 필요한 전부다."

35 우리는 이제 더는 절대 "은총이가 장애가 없으면 좋겠다."라고 생각하지 않아.

36 대신에 우리는 너를 가진 것에 그저 감사할 뿐이야.

37 우리는 또한 많은 다른 작은 것들에 대해서도 행복해.

38 심지어 우리가 어려움에 직면할 때도, 우리는 행복하단다.

39 왜냐하면, 우리는 우리가 함께이고 서로를 사랑할 때 어떤 어려움도 극복할 수 있다는 것을 알기 때문이지.

40 우리 계속해서 행복하고 용감하게 살아가자.

41 우리는 항상 너를 사랑하고 너의 옆을 지킬게.

42 사랑하는

43 아빠가.

● 우리말을 참고하여 본문을 영작하시오.

1 당신에게 필요한 건 사랑이 전부다

➡ _____

2 2010년 10월 16일, 은총이와 그의 아빠는 그들의 첫 철인 레이스에 참가했다.

➡ _____

3 그것은 하남의 미사리에서 열렸다.

➡ _____

4 그들은 1.5 km를 수영하고, 40 km 사이클을 타고, 그런 다음 10 km를 뛰었다.

➡ _____

5 이 도전은 은총이 아빠에게 특히 어려웠는데 경주 동안 은총이를 밀거나 끌어야 했기 때문이다.

➡ _____

6 은총이는 6가지 다른 질병을 갖고 태어나서 말할 수도 걸을 수도 없었다.

➡ _____

7 그의 피부는 어두운 붉은색이었고 그의 두뇌는 점점 굳어가고 있었다.

➡ _____

8 의사는 은총이가 오래 살지 못할 거라고 했다.

➡ _____

9 하지만 은총이는 여전히 살아있을 뿐만 아니라 그의 첫 철인 레이스에서 1등을 했다.

➡ _____

10 은총이에게,

➡ _____

11 나는 네가 내 아들이어서뿐만 아니라 나에게 중요한 인생의 교훈을 가르쳐 주어서 고맙구나.

➡ _____

12 네가 아기였을 때, 사람들이 너의 피부색 때문에 너를 피했단다.

➡ _____

13 나는 슬펐고 너를 그들로부터 숨기고 싶었어.

➡ _____

14 네 엄마는 네가 장애 없이 태어나기를 바랐지.

➡ _____

15 네 엄마는 너의 병이 자신 때문이라고 자책도 했어.

➡ _____

16 하지만 너는 우리를 향해 항상 웃어주었고, 우리의 손을 잡아주었어.

➡ _____

17 너는 우리에게 희망뿐만 아니라 용기도 주었지.

➡ _____

18 그래서 나는 세상을 직면하고 너에게 세상의 밝은 면을 보여주겠다고 나 자신에게 약속했어.

➡ _____

19 그때부터 우리는 우리의 여정을 시작했지.

➡ _____

20 우리의 첫 철인 레이스를 기억하니?

➡ _____

21 우리가 수영을 시작했을 때, 다른 참가자들이 우리가 먼저 가도록 길을 만들어 줬어.

➡ _____

22 나는 정말 감동하였고 감사했단다.

➡ _____

23 몇몇 참가자들은 심지어 우리가 지나갈 때 울기도 했어.

➡ _____

24 우리가 사이클링을 시작했을 때, 많은 사람이 우리를 응원했지.

➡ _____

25 하지만 너는 강한 바람과 피곤함을 견뎌야만 했어.

➡ _____

26 그래서 나는 네가 쉴 수 있도록 아주 빨리 페달을 밟았어.

➡ _____

27 우리가 달리기 시작했을 때, 너의 엄마가 "당신과 함께 달릴 수 있으면 참 좋겠다." 라고 말하는 듯했어.

➡ _____

28 빨리 경주를 끝내서 너의 엄마를 보고 네가 쉬도록 하고 싶었어.

➡ _____

29 그래서 나는 빨리 달렸단다.

➡ _____

30 우리가 거의 결승선에 도착했을 때, 다른 참가자들이 멈췄고 우리가 먼저 가도록 해줬어.

➡ _____

31 은총아, 네가 우승자였단다!

➡ _____

32 아빠는 네가 그 경기에 있던 모든 사람이 너를 얼마나 사랑했는지 알았기를 바란다.

➡ _____

33 네 덕분에, 너의 엄마와 나는 중요한 교훈을 배웠단다.

➡ _____

34 "사랑이 우리가 필요한 전부다."

➡ _____

35 우리는 이제 더는 절대 "은총이가 장애가 없으면 좋겠다."라고 생각하지 않아.

➡ _____

36 대신에 우리는 너를 가진 것에 그저 감사할 뿐이야.

➡ _____

37 우리는 또한 많은 다른 작은 것들에 대해서도 행복해.

➡ _____

38 심지어 우리가 어려움에 직면할 때도, 우리는 행복하단다.

➡ _____

39 왜냐하면, 우리는 우리가 함께이고 서로를 사랑할 때 어떤 어려움도 극복할 수 있다는 것을 알기 때문이지.

➡ _____

_____

40 우리 계속해서 행복하고 용감하게 살아가자.

➡ _____

41 우리는 항상 너를 사랑하고 너의 옆을 지킬게.

➡ _____

42 사랑하는

➡ _____

43 아빠가.

➡ _____

[01~04] 다음 글을 읽고 물음에 답하시오.

On October 16th, 2010, Eunchong and his dad participated in their first triathlon. It ⓐ_____ in Misari, Hanam. (①) They swam ⓑ 1.5 km, cycled 40 km, and then ran 10 km. (②) This challenge was especially difficult for Eunchong's dad because he had to push or pull Eunchong during the race. (③) Eunchong couldn't talk or walk because he was born with six different diseases. (④) His skin was dark red and his brain was becoming hard. (⑤) But Eunchong not only is still alive but also got first place in his first triathlon.

서답형

01 위 글의 빈칸 ⓐ에 hold를 알맞은 형태로 쓰시오.

➡ _____

02 위 글의 흐름으로 보아, 주어진 문장이 들어가기에 가장 적절한 곳은?

The doctor said he would not live for long.

① ② ③ ④ ⑤

서답형

03 위 글의 밑줄 친 ⓑ1.5 km를 영어로 읽는 법을 쓰시오.

➡ _____

04 According to the passage, which is NOT true?

① Eunchong and his dad took part in their first triathlon on October 16th, 2010.

② Eunchong and his dad swam 1.5 km, cycled 40 km, and then ran 10 km.

③ This challenge was especially difficult for Eunchong.

④ Eunchong couldn't talk or walk because he was born with six different diseases.

⑤ During the race, Eunchong's dad to push or pull Eunchong.

[05~08] 다음 글을 읽고 물음에 답하시오.

Dear Eunchong,

I thank you not only for being my son but also for (A)teaching me an important life lesson. When you were a baby, people avoided you because of your skin color. I felt sad and wanted to hide you ⓐ_____ them. Your mom hoped that you would be born with no disabilities. She blamed herself ⓑ_____ your sickness. But you always smiled at us and held our hands. You gave us courage as well as hope. (B)So, I promised myself that I would face the world and show you the bright side of things. Since then we have begun our journey.

05 위 글의 빈칸 ⓐ와 ⓑ에 들어갈 전치사가 바르게 짝지어진 것은?

　　ⓐ　　ⓑ　　　　　　ⓐ　　ⓑ
① for – to　　　② from – for
③ from – to　　　④ for – at
⑤ at – for

06 위 글의 밑줄 친 (A)teaching과 문법적 쓰임이 다른 것을 고르시오.

① His job is teaching people how to drive a car.

② He is good at teaching children.

③ Stop teaching a fish how to swim.

④ I'm teaching history now.

⑤ Teaching students is a rewarding job.

07 위 글의 밑줄 친 (B)에서 알 수 있는 '은총이 아빠'의 성격으로 가장 알맞은 것을 고르시오.

① gloomy   ② positive

③ solemn   ④ timid

⑤ negative

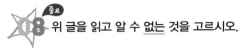

08 위 글을 읽고 알 수 없는 것을 고르시오.

① Who wrote this letter?

② For what does Eunchong's dad thank Eunchong?

③ Why did people avoid Eunchong?

④ What color was Eunchong's skin?

⑤ What did Eunchong do to his parents?

[09~11] 다음 글을 읽고 물음에 답하시오.

  Do you remember our first triathlon? When we began to swim, the other participants made way for us and let us go first. I was very touched and thankful. Some participants even cried when we passed ⓐthem by. When we started cycling, many people cheered for us. But you had to endure some strong winds and tiredness. So I cycled very fast to give you a ⓑbreak. When we began running, your mom seemed to say, "I wish I could run with you." I wanted to finish the race quickly so I could see her and let you rest. So, I ran fast. When we were almost at the finishing line, the other participants stopped and let us go first. Eunchong, you were the winner! I hope you could tell how much everyone at those races loved you.   <you: Eunchong>

서답형

09 위 글의 밑줄 친 ⓐthem이 가리키는 것을 본문에서 찾아 쓰시오.

➡ _____

10 위 글의 밑줄 친 ⓑbreak와 같은 의미로 쓰인 것을 고르시오.

① Don't break an appointment.

② Let's take a break.

③ Did you break the cup into pieces?

④ Let's break for lunch.

⑤ We could see the moon through a break in the clouds.

서답형

11 본문의 내용과 일치하도록 다음 빈칸 (A)~(C)에 알맞은 단어를 쓰시오.

> During Eunchong's team's first triathlon, in swimming, the other participants (A)_____ _____ for them and let them (B)_____ _____. In running, when they were almost at the finishing line, the other participants stopped and let them (C)_____ _____.

[12~14] 다음 글을 읽고 물음에 답하시오.

  Do you remember our first triathlon? When we began to swim, the other participants made way for us and let us go first. I was very touched and thankful. Some participants even cried when we passed them by. When we started cycling, many people cheered for us. But you had to endure some strong winds and tiredness. So I cycled very fast to give you a break. When we began running, your mom seemed to say, "I wish I could run with you." I wanted to finish the race quickly so I could see her and let you rest. So, I ran fast. When we were almost at the finishing line, the other participants stopped and let us go first. Eunchong, you were the winner! I hope you could tell how much everyone at those races loved you.   <you: Eunchong>

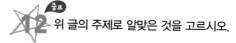

12 위 글의 주제로 알맞은 것을 고르시오.

① the difficulty of winning the triathlon
② Eunchong's love for triathlon
③ the moving story behind Eunchong's winning the triathlon
④ Eunchong's mom's hope
⑤ Eunchong's mom's love for Eunchong

서답형

13 위 글을 읽고 은총이와 그의 아버지가 철인 레이스에서 참가했던 종목을 순서대로 영어로 쓰시오.

➡ (A)＿＿＿＿ (B)＿＿＿＿ (C)＿＿＿＿

서답형

14 How could Eunchong get first place in his first triathlon? Fill in the blanks (A) and (B) with suitable words.

> Thanks to the thoughtful consideration of (A)＿＿＿＿ ＿＿＿＿ ＿＿＿＿, like giving way to them and (B)＿＿＿＿ them go first, Eunchong could get first place in his first triathlon.
>
> *thoughtful consideration: 세심한 배려

[15~17] 다음 글을 읽고 물음에 답하시오.

(A)[In / On] October 16th, 2010, Eunchong and his dad ⓐparticipated in their first triathlon. It was held in Misari, Hanam. They swam 1.5 km, cycled 40 km, and then ran 10 km. This challenge was especially difficult for Eunchong's dad because he had to push or pull Eunchong during the race. Eunchong couldn't talk or walk because he was born with six different diseases. His skin was dark red and his brain was becoming hard. The doctor said he would not live (B)[during / for] long. But Eunchong not only is still (C)[alive / live] but also got first place in his first triathlon.

서답형

15 위 글의 괄호 (A)~(C)에서 어법상 알맞은 낱말을 골라 쓰시오.

➡ (A)＿＿＿＿ (B)＿＿＿＿ (C)＿＿＿＿

16 위 글의 밑줄 친 ⓐparticipated in과 바꿔 쓸 수 없는 말을 고르시오.

① took part in
② competed in
③ entered
④ cooperated in
⑤ partook in

17 위 글의 제목으로 알맞은 것을 고르시오.

① The First Triathlon in Misari, Hanam
② Let Me Introduce Triathlon to You
③ The First Triathlon of Eunchong and His Dad
④ Eunchong with Six Different Diseases
⑤ How to Overcome a Physical Disability

[18~20] 다음 글을 읽고 물음에 답하시오.

＿＿ⓐ＿＿ you, your mom and I learned an important lesson. "Love is all we need." We don't ever think, "We wish Eunchong had no disabilities" (A)[anymore / no more]. Instead, we are just thankful for having you. We are also happy about many other little things. Even when we face difficulties, we are happy. That's because we know that we can overcome any hardships when we are together and love each other. Let's continue to live (B)[happy / happily] and (C)[brave / bravely]. We will always love you and stand by you.

Love,
Dad

18 위 글의 빈칸 ⓐ에 들어갈 알맞은 말을 <u>모두</u> 고르시오.

① Instead of   ② Thanks to

③ In spite of   ④ In addition to

⑤ Because of

서답형
19 위 글의 괄호 (A)~(C)에서 어법상 알맞은 낱말을 골라 쓰시오.

➡ (A)_____ (B)_____ (C)_____

20 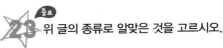 위 글의 주제로 알맞은 것을 고르시오.

① the lesson we can't learn at school

② the difficulty of facing physical disabilities

③ how to feel happy about many little things

④ overcoming hardships with the love between family members

⑤ the way to overcome physical disabilities

서답형
21 위 글의 밑줄 친 ⓐ의 우리말에 맞게 한 단어를 보충하여, 주어진 어휘를 알맞게 배열하시오.

> an important life lesson / for / you / teaching / but also / my son / being / me / I / not only / thank

➡ _____
_____.

22 위 글의 밑줄 친 ⓑhave begun과 현재완료의 용법이 <u>다른</u> 것을 <u>모두</u> 고르시오.

① She <u>has been</u> ill for a week.

② <u>Have</u> you ever <u>seen</u> a ghost?

③ How long <u>have</u> you <u>been</u> in Seoul?

④ He <u>has lived</u> in this house since last year.

⑤ I <u>have</u> just <u>finished</u> reading the book.

23 위 글의 종류로 알맞은 것을 고르시오.

① article   ② diary

③ biography   ④ essay

⑤ letter

[21~23] 다음 글을 읽고 물음에 답하시오.

Dear Eunchong,

ⓐ나는 네가 내 아들이어서뿐만 아니라 나에게 중요한 인생의 교훈을 가르쳐 주어서 고맙구나. When you were a baby, people avoided you because of your skin color. I felt sad and wanted to hide you from them. Your mom hoped that you would be born with no disabilities. She blamed herself for your sickness. But you always smiled at us and held our hands. You gave us courage as well as hope. So, I promised myself that I would face the world and show you the bright side of things. Since then we ⓑ<u>have begun</u> our journey.

[24~26] 다음 글을 읽고 물음에 답하시오.

Do you remember our first triathlon? When we began to swim, the other participants made way for us and let us go first. (①) I was very ⓐ<u>touched</u> and thankful. (②) Some participants even cried when we passed them by. (③) When we started cycling, many people cheered for us. (④) So I cycled very fast to give you a break. (⑤) When we began running, your mom seemed to say, "I wish I could run with you." I wanted to finish the race quickly so I could see her and let you rest. So, I ran fast. When we were almost at the finishing line, the other participants stopped and let us go first.

Eunchong, you were the winner! I hope you could tell how much everyone at those races loved you. <you: Eunchong>

24 위 글의 흐름으로 보아, 주어진 문장이 들어가기에 가장 적절한 곳은?

> But you had to endure some strong winds and tiredness.

① ② ③ ④ ⑤

서답형
25 위 글의 밑줄 친 @touched와 바꿔 쓸 수 있는 말을 쓰시오.

➡ _____

중요
26 Which question CANNOT be answered after reading the passage?

① What kindness did Eunchong and his dad experience while they were swimming in their first triathlon?
② Why was Eunchong's dad very touched and thankful?
③ What did Eunchong have to endure while cycling in their first triathlon?
④ How fast did Eunchong's dad run?
⑤ What happened when Eunchong and his dad were almost at the finishing line?

[27~30] 다음 글을 읽고 물음에 답하시오.

Thanks to you, your mom and I learned an important lesson. "Love is all we need." We don't ever think, "We wish Eunchong had no disabilities" anymore. __@__, we are just

thankful for having you. We are also happy about many other little things. Even when we face difficulties, we are happy. That's because we know that we can overcome any __ⓑ__ when we are together and love each other. Let's continue to live happily and bravely. ⓒWe will always love you and stand for you.

Love,
Dad

27 위 글의 빈칸 @에 들어갈 알맞은 말을 고르시오.

① In addition   ② Moreover
③ Therefore   ④ Instead
⑤ Besides

서답형
28 주어진 영영풀이를 참고하여 빈칸 ⓑ에 철자 h로 시작하는 단어를 쓰시오.

> situations in which your life is difficult or unpleasant, often because you do not have enough money

➡ _____

서답형
29 위 글의 밑줄 친 ⓒ에서 흐름상 어색한 부분을 찾아 고치시오.

➡ _____

서답형
30 다음 문장에서 위 글의 내용과 다른 부분을 찾아서 고치시오.

> When Eunchong's family face difficulties, they are unhappy.

➡ _____

[01~03] 다음 글을 읽고 물음에 답하시오.

Dear Eunchong,

I thank you not only for being my son but also for ⓐteaching me an important life lesson. When you were a baby, people avoided you because of your skin color. I felt (A)[sad / sadly] and wanted to hide you from them. Your mom hoped that you would be born with no disabilities. She blamed (B)[her / herself] for your sickness. But you always smiled at us and held our hands. You gave us courage as well as hope. So, I promised (C)[me / myself] that I would face the world and ⓑshow you the bright side of things. Since then we have begun our journey.

01 위 글의 괄호 (A)~(C)에서 어법상 알맞은 낱말을 골라 쓰시오.

➡ (A) _____ (B) _____ (C) _____

서답형
02 위 글의 밑줄 친 ⓐ와 ⓑ를 3형식 문장으로 고치시오.

➡ ⓐ _____
ⓒ _____

03 본문의 내용과 일치하도록 다음 빈칸 (A)와 (B)에 알맞은 단어를 쓰시오.

Eunchong gave two important things, (A)_____ and (B)_____, to his parents.

[04~07] 다음 글을 읽고 물음에 답하시오.

On October 16th, 2010, Eunchong and his dad participated in their first triathlon. ⓐIt was held in Misari, Hanam. They swam 1.5 km, cycled 40 km, and then ran 10 km. This challenge was especially difficult for Eunchong's dad because he had to push or pull Eunchong during the race. Eunchong couldn't talk or walk because he was born with six different diseases. His skin was dark red and his brain was becoming hard. The doctor said he would not live for long. But ⓑEunchong not only is still alive but also got first place in his first triathlon.

04 위 글의 밑줄 친 ⓐ가 가리키는 것을 본문에서 찾아 쓰시오.

➡ _____

05 위 글의 밑줄 친 ⓑ를 as well as를 사용하여 고치시오.

➡ _____
_____

06 Why was it especially difficult for Eunchong's dad to participate in the triathlon? Answer in English beginning with "Because".

➡ _____
_____

07 본문의 내용과 일치하도록 다음 빈칸 (A)~(C)에 알맞은 단어를 쓰시오.

Eunchong's dad (A)_____ or (B)_____ Eunchong while they swam 1.5 km, cycled 40 km, and then ran 10 km in their first triathlon and got (C)_____ place.

[08~10] 다음 글을 읽고 물음에 답하시오.

Do you remember our first triathlon? When we began to swim, the other participants made way for us and let us go first. I was very touched and thankful. Some participants even cried when we passed them by. When we started cycling, many people cheered for us. But you had to endure some strong winds and tiredness. So I cycled very fast to give you a (A)break. When we began running, your mom seemed to say, "ⓐ_____ _____ I could run with you." I wanted to finish the race quickly so I could see her and let you rest. So, I ran fast. When we were almost at the finishing line, the other participants stopped and let us go first. Eunchong, you were the winner! I hope you could tell how much everyone at those races loved you. <you: Eunchong>

08 위 글의 빈칸 ⓐ에 두 단어를 넣어, 은총이의 엄마의 말이 다음과 같은 뜻이 되도록 완성하시오.

> I am sorry I can't run with you.

➡ _____

09 위 글의 밑줄 친 (A)break와 바꿔 쓸 수 있는 말을 본문에서 찾아 쓰시오.

➡ _____

10 What did Eunchong and his dad do after cycling? Answer in English in a full sentence. (2 words)

➡ _____

[11~14] 다음 글을 읽고 물음에 답하시오.

Thanks to you, your mom and I learned an important lesson. "Love is all we need." We don't ever think, "We wish Eunchong had no disabilities" anymore. ⓐInstead, we are just ⓑthankful for having you. We are also happy about many other little things. Even when we face difficulties, we are happy. ⓒThat's why we know that we can overcome any hardships when we are together and love each other. Let's continue to live happily and bravely. We will always love you and stand by you.

Love,
Dad

11 위 글의 밑줄 친 ⓐInstead를 다음과 같이 바꿔 쓸 때 빈칸에 들어갈 알맞은 말을 두 단어로 쓰시오.

➡ Instead _____ _____ "We wish Eunchong had no disabilities"

12 위 글의 밑줄 친 ⓑthankful과 바꿔 쓸 수 있는 말을 쓰시오.

➡ _____

13 위 글의 밑줄 친 ⓒ에서 어법상 틀린 부분을 찾아 고치시오.

➡ _____

14 What important lesson did Eunchong's parents learn thanks to Eunchong? Answer in English in a full sentence. (7~8 words)

➡ _____

Communication Activity

We want to introduce Stevie Wonder. He is a singer from America. Although
　　　　　동사 want의 목적어로 쓰인 to부정사이다　　　　　　　　　양보의 부사절을 유도하는 접속사

he couldn't see, his hearing was excellent and he became a talented singer. His

songs are very popular and he has received many music prizes. We wish we
　　　　　　　　　　　　　　주어 wish+가정법 과거"로 "～이라면 좋을 텐데"에 해당한다.

could find our talent and become a great person like him.
　　　　　　　　　동사 become은 find와 병렬 구조이다.

해석

우리는 Stevie Wonder를 소개하려고 합니다. 그는 미국 가수입니다. 비록 그는 앞을 볼 수 없었지만, 그의 청각은 뛰어났고, 재능 있는 가수가 되었습니다. 그의 노래는 매우 인기 있었고 그는 많은 상을 받았습니다. 우리는 우리의 재능을 찾아 그와 같은 위대한 인물이 되기를 원합니다.

After You Read B

Dear Mom and Dad,

　Since 2010, you have started the journey with me. I thank you for that. When
　　　　　　　　　　　계속 용법

we participated in our first triathlon, we had to endure a lot of difficulties. But
　　= took part in　　　　　　　　　　　　　　　= lots of = many = plenty of

you never gave up on me.
　　　　give up on: ～을 단념하다

Your courage helped me see the bright side of things. I am proud of you.
　　　　　　　　　　= to see　　　　　　　　　= take pride in

Thank you for being the most wonderful parents.
　　　　　　　동명사

I love you so much!

Love,
Eunchong

엄마 아빠께
　2010년부터 당신들은 저와 함께 여정을 시작하셨죠. 그것에 대해 감사드립니다. 우리가 첫 철인 레이스에 참가했을 때, 우리는 많은 어려움을 견뎌야만 했어요. 그러나 당신들은 저를 절대 포기하지 않으셨어요. 당신들의 용기가 저로 하여금 사물의 밝은 면을 보도록 도와주었어요. 저는 두 분이 자랑스러워요. 가장 멋진 부모님들이 되어주셔서 감사드립니다. 너무 사랑해요!

　　　사랑하는
　　　은총이 올림

구문해설　• since: ～부터[이후] • journey: 여행, 여정 • participate in: ～에 참가하다 • triathlon: 철인 레이스 • endure: 참다, 견디다 • courage: 용기

Think and Write

My grandmother lives in the southern part of Korea. She is a farmer. When

I went to her house, she showed me around the farm and told me everything

about farming. She not only welcomed me but also treated me like the most
　　　　　　　not only A but also B: A뿐만 아니라 B도　　　　　　최상급

important person in the whole world. Now, she is in the hospital. I wish I
　　　　　　　　　　　　　　　　　「I wish+가정법 과거」 구문

could spend time with her as we did in the past. I hope that she gets healthy
　　　　　　　　　　　　　　　　　　　　　　　　get+형용사: ～하게 되다

again.

우리 할머니는 한국의 남부 지방에 사신다. 그녀는 농부다. 내가 그녀의 집에 갔을 때, 그녀는 나에게 농장 주위를 보여 주셨고 농사에 대한 모든 것을 말씀해 주셨다. 그녀는 나를 반겼을 뿐만 아니라 이 세상에서 가장 중요한 사람처럼 대해 주셨다. 지금 그녀는 병원에 계신다. 예전처럼 그녀와 함께 시간을 보낼 수 있으면 좋겠다. 나는 그녀가 다시 건강해지시기를 바란다.

구문해설　• southern: 남부에 위치한 • around: 주위에 • farming: 농업, 농사 • treat: 대하다, 대우하다 • whole: 전부의, 전체의 • healthy: 건강한

Words & Expressions

Conversation

01 다음 빈칸에 들어가기에 적절한 단어를 고르시오.

> A _____ consists of cycling, swimming and running.

① survival ② talent ③ courage
④ triathlon ⑤ medicine

02 다음 영영풀이에 해당하는 단어를 고르시오.

> something that makes life difficult or unpleasant

① hardship ② century
③ disease ④ victory
⑤ recommendation

03 다음 두 문장에 공통으로 알맞은 것을 고르시오.

> • She is seriously ill and in need of _____.
> • I wish my speech would _____ them think more positively.

① lend ② get ③ grow
④ give ⑤ help

04 다음 밑줄 친 단어 대신 쓸 수 있는 것은?

> The town has many <u>excellent</u> eating places.

① interesting ② big ③ various
④ old ⑤ outstanding

[05~06] 다음 우리말과 일치하도록 빈칸에 알맞은 말을 쓰시오.

05

> A: Is something wrong?
> B: Yes, I'm trying to do my homework, but it's too difficult.
> A: _____
> (let, hand)(제가 도와드리겠습니다.)
> B: Thank you so much.

06

> G: Dad! Look at this beautiful scenery. I wish I could live here.
> M: It's amazing, isn't it? _____
> _____
> (이 산의 정상에 서 있는 것이 기분 좋게 느끼도록 만들어 주는구나.)
> G: I'm so sad that we have to walk down soon.
> M: Don't be sad. You can enjoy this view again next week!

07 다음 대화의 빈칸에 들어가기에 적절하지 <u>않은</u> 것은?

> B: Excuse me, I have lost something.
> W: What have you lost?
> _____
> B: Thank you. I have lost my smartphone.
> W: Is this black smartphone yours?
> B: No, mine is red.

① Can I give you a hand?
② Let me give you a hand.
③ Do you need any help?
④ How may I help you?
⑤ Could you do me a favor?

[08~10] 다음 대화를 읽고 물음에 답하시오.

W: Excuse me, I'm looking for a birthday present for my son.

M: Oh, can I give you a hand?

W: Yes, please. (A) My son is 15 years old. Do you have any recommendations?

M: What about this colorful jacket? It is very popular. (B)

W: It looks fine, but my son (가)_____. (C)

M: What about this green colored jacket?

W: It is very pretty. (D)

M: Yes, there is a large one here!

W: Thank you. I'll take it. (E)

08 (A)~(E) 중 주어진 문장이 들어갈 곳은?

> Do you have it in a large size?

① (A)　② (B)　③ (C)　④ (D)　⑤ (E)

09 빈칸 (가)에 들어가기에 가장 적절한 것은?

① doesn't like colorful clothes
② won't wear a simple jacket
③ likes a colorful jacket
④ will wear a small sized coat
⑤ likes to buy different jackets

10 Which one CANNOT be answered from the dialogue above?

① Where is the woman at the moment?
② What does the man do?
③ What does the woman ask the man?
④ How much will the woman spend for the jacket?
⑤ What color does the woman decide to buy?

[11~13] 다음 대화를 읽고 물음에 답하시오.

Ryan: How do you feel? Can I give you a hand, Mom?

Mom: Yes. Can you please get me some medicine?

Ryan: Of course. I will also get you some water to drink.

Mom: Thank you. I wish _____.

Ryan: I hope you can, too. By the way, I'm sorry, Mom.

Mom: What do you mean?

Ryan: When I was sick, you looked after me with all of your heart. But back then I didn't even say a word of thanks.

Mom: Oh, it's okay.

Ryan: I really want to thank you for your love.

11 대화 속에 나오는 두 사람의 관계는?

① son and mother
② nephew and uncle
③ student and teacher
④ doctor and patient
⑤ customer and clerk

12 대화의 내용으로 보아 빈칸에 들어가기에 적절한 것은?

① I could give you some more help
② I could get better faster
③ you could take some more medicine
④ you could give me one hand
⑤ we could get more rest

13 위 대화를 통해서 알 수 <u>없는</u> 것은?

① Ryan is helping his mom.
② Ryan's mom is ill in bed.
③ When Ryan was sick in bed, his mom looked after him.
④ Ryan didn't say thank his mom when he was ill.
⑤ Ryan is 15 years old.

Grammar

14 다음 중 어법상 올바른 문장을 <u>모두</u> 고르시오.

① I wish all the family who live with people with disabilities would love and encourage each other.
② You gave us courage as well hope.
③ We wish Eunchong has no disabilities anymore.
④ Eunchong not only is still alive but and got first place in his first triathlon.
⑤ I wish I could run with you.

15 다음 중 어법상 어색한 문장은?

① Not only Jenny but also her friends like skating.
② The new epidemic disease has spread at an alarming rate not only in China but also Korean.
③ Neither Mr. Brady nor the other team members agree with the plan.
④ If you would like to participate in the Sixth Anniversary, you can reserve your seat either on the phone or online.
⑤ Both the mother and her baby are doing very well. *epidemic disease: 전염병

16 다음 빈칸에 들어갈 말로 가장 알맞은 것은?

> A: I wish I _____ vote.
> B: Can't you?
> A: I'm 16 years old. I have to be 19 in order to vote for President.

① to   ② can   ③ could
④ will   ⑤ as

17 다음 문장과 같은 뜻이 되도록 괄호 안의 어휘를 활용하여 영작하시오.

(1) Not only you but also I am satisfied with the result. (as well as)
➡ _____

(2) My summer vacation plan sounds like active and dynamic. (both, and)
➡ _____
_____

(3) Your decision is not good but fair. (not)
➡ _____

18 다음 빈칸에 들어갈 수 <u>없는</u> 것을 고르시오.

> Brain scans show that during calculations activity is not _____ confined to the left hemisphere, but is also present in the visual, auditory, and motor areas of the brain.
> *confine (활동·주제·지역 등을) 국한시키다.

① just   ② merely   ③ only
④ simply   ⑤ hardly

19 다음 밑줄 친 부분의 어법이 어색한 것은?

① I wish our ship was that fancy.

② I wish I had enough time.

③ Both my mom and dad are engineers.

④ Not only students but also the teacher is excited.

⑤ Students as well as the teacher is excited.

20 다음 문장과 같은 의미의 문장을 주어진 단어를 이용하여 쓰시오.

(1) I wish I could run. (pity)

➡ _____

(2) I wish I could vote. (sorry)

➡ _____

(3) I wish I were a teacher. (sorry)

➡ _____

Reading

[21~22] 다음 글을 읽고 물음에 답하시오.

On October 16th, 2010, Eunchong and his dad participated in their first triathlon. It was held in Misari, Hanam. They swam 1.5 km, cycled 40 km, and then ran 10 km. ⓐThis challenge was especially difficult for Eunchong's dad because he had to push or pull Eunchong during the race. Eunchong couldn't talk or walk because he was born with six different diseases. His skin was dark red and his brain was becoming hard. The doctor said he would not live for long. But Eunchong not only is still alive but also ⓑgot first place in his first triathlon.

21 위 글의 밑줄 친 ⓐThis challenge의 구체적인 내용을 우리말로 쓰시오.

➡ _____

_____

22 위 글의 밑줄 친 ⓑgot first place와 바꿔 쓸 수 없는 말을 고르시오.

① awarded a prize   ② came first

③ finished first   ④ won first place

⑤ took first place

[23~25] 다음 글을 읽고 물음에 답하시오.

Dear Eunchong,

I thank you not only for being my son but also for teaching me an important life lesson. When you were a baby, people avoided you because of your skin color. I felt sad and wanted to hide you from them. Your mom hoped that you would be born with no disabilities. She blamed herself for your sickness. But you always smiled at us and held our hands. You gave us courage as well as hope. So, I promised myself that I would ⓐface the world and show you the bright side of things. Since then we have begun our journey.

23 위 글의 주제로 알맞은 것을 고르시오.

① the hardship Eunchong overcame

② the reason people stared at Eunchong with cold eyes

③ the sadness that Eunchong's parents experienced

④ two important things Eunchong gave to his parents

⑤ the challenge of Eunchong and his dad

24 위 글의 밑줄 친 ⓐface와 같은 의미로 쓰인 것을 고르시오.

① Look at the north face of the mountain

② They didn't face a financial crisis.

③ Does your house face to the south?

④ He lost his face.

⑤ She looked around for a familiar face.

25 When people saw little Eunchong, how did they react? Answer in English in a full sentence.

➡ _____

[26~27] 다음 글을 읽고 물음에 답하시오.

Do you remember our first triathlon? When we began to swim, ⓐ다른 참가자들이 우리가 먼저 가도록 길을 만들어 줬어. I was very touched and thankful. Some participants even cried when we passed them by. When we started cycling, many people cheered for us. But you had to endure some strong winds and tiredness. So I cycled very fast to give you a break. When we began running, your mom seemed to say, "I wish I could run with you." I wanted to finish the race quickly so I could see her and let you rest. So, I ran fast. When we were almost at the finishing line, the other participants stopped and let us go first. Eunchong, you were the winner! I hope you could tell how much everyone at those races loved you.   <you: Eunchong>

26 위 글의 밑줄 친 ⓐ의 우리말에 맞게 주어진 어휘를 이용하여 12 단어로 영작하시오.

participants, way, for, let

➡ _____
_____

27 According to the passage, which is NOT true?

① When Eunchong and his dad began swimming, the other participants made way for them.

② When Eunchong and his dad started to cycle, many people cheered for them.

③ Eunchong's dad cycled very fast to give Eunchong a break.

④ When Eunchong and his dad were almost at the finishing line, the other participants stopped and let them go first.

⑤ Eunchong knew how much everyone at those races loved him.

[28~30] 다음 글을 읽고 물음에 답하시오.

Dear Mom and Dad,
Since 2010, you have started the journey with me. I thank you for ⓐthat. When we participated in our first triathlon, we had to endure ⓑa lot of difficulties. But you never gave up on me. Your courage helped me see the bright side of things. I am proud of you. Thank you for being the most wonderful parents. I love you so much!
                                        Love,
                                        Eunchong

28 위 글의 밑줄 친 ⓐthat이 가리키는 것을 본문에서 찾아 쓰시오.

➡ _____
_____

29 위 글의 밑줄 친 ⓑa lot of와 바꿔 쓸 수 없는 말을 고르시오.

① many   ② a number of
③ lots of   ④ plenty of
⑤ a great deal of

30 What helped Eunchong see the bright side of things? Answer in English. (3~4 words)

➡ _____

출제율 90%

01 다음 빈칸에 들어갈 말로 적절한 것은?

He has been an active _____ in the discussion.

① scenery
② farmer
③ present
④ participant
⑤ campaign

출제율 90%

02 다음 빈칸에 공통으로 들어가기에 적절한 것은?

• Can you help me look _____ my socks?
• We should make way _____ those who come after us.

① in
② for
③ on
④ with
⑤ to

출제율 100%

03 다음 제시된 단어로 자연스러운 문장을 만들 수 없는 것은?

┌─ 보기 ─┐
wheelchairs survival talent road

① When people can't walk, they ride in _____.
② Dogs have four _____.
③ My teacher told me that I had an artistic _____.
④ Animals fight for their _____.
⑤ Watch out for cars when you cross a _____.

[04~06] 다음 대화를 읽고 물음에 답하시오.

M: About 10 years ago, I was hit by a car while I ⓐwas riding a bicycle at night. I lost my left leg and stayed in the hospital ⓑfor six months. (A) I was depressed and couldn't find a reason to live. (B) However, my parents supported me and took ⓒcare of me with their love. (C) By doing so, I found out that life can be meaningful to everybody. (D) Now, I'm a wheelchair basketball player and every year I run a campaign for people in need of help. (E) During each campaign, I give a speech about the importance of ⓓpositive thinking. Some people seem to be in the habit of negative thinking. I wish my speech would help them ⓔthinking more positively.

출제율 95%

04 ⓐ~ⓔ 중에서 어법상 어색한 것은?

① ⓐ ② ⓑ ③ ⓒ ④ ⓓ ⑤ ⓔ

출제율 90%

05 (A)~(E) 중에서 다음 문장이 들어가기에 가장 적절한 곳은?

Thanks to them, I was able to overcome the situation.

① (A) ② (B) ③ (C) ④ (D) ⑤ (E)

출제율 100%

06 Which one CANNOT be answered from the dialogue above?

① When was he hit by a car?
② What was he doing when he had a car accident?
③ How did he feel after the accident?
④ Who was driving the car when the car hit him?
⑤ Who took care of him after the accident?

07 다음 우리말에 맞게 제시된 어휘를 활용하여 영작하시오.

(1) 강의를 들으면서 필기도 하는 것이 어렵게 생각 될지도 모른다. (may, find, it, both, and, the lecture, take notes)

➡ _____

_____

(2) 우리는 그의 영어뿐만 아니라 한국어도 이해할 수 있다. (could, not, also, only, but)

➡ _____

_____

(3) 그들은 기차가 아니라 비행기로 목적지에 도착 했다. (arrive, destination, but, airplane, not)

➡ _____

_____

(4) 나는 남자친구를 만나거나 집에서 쉴 예정이다. (will, boyfriend either, or, stay)

➡ _____

_____

(5) 돈도 시간도 낭비하지 마라. (waste, neither, nor)

➡ _____

08 다음 중 어법상 <u>어색한</u> 문장을 고르시오.

① Not I but my friends am good at soccer.

② Neither my boyfriend nor I am interested in playing computer games.

③ Either Mike or you are responsible for the accident.

④ My parents as well as my brother are going to come.

⑤ Both optimists and pessimists contribute to our society.

09 다음 중 어법상 <u>어색한</u> 문장을 고르시오.

① I wish she loved me.

② I wished she loved me.

③ I wish you can play the violin.

④ I wished you could play the violin.

⑤ I wish you could play the violin.

10 주어진 단어를 활용하여 다음 우리말을 영어로 옮기시오.

내 학생들뿐만 아니라 나도 그 소식을 듣고 매우 놀랐다. (not only / but also / shocked / to)

➡ _____

_____

[11~13] 다음 글을 읽고 물음에 답하시오.

Dear Eunchong,

I thank you not only for being my son but also for teaching me an important life ⓐ lesson. When you were a baby, people avoided you because of your skin color. (①) I felt sad and wanted to hide you from them. (②) She blamed herself for your sickness. (③) But you always smiled at us and held our hands. (④) You gave us courage as well as hope. (⑤) So, I promised myself that I would face the world and show you the bright side of things. Since then we have begun our journey.

11 위 글의 흐름으로 보아, 주어진 문장이 들어가기에 가장 적절한 곳은?

Your mom hoped that you would be born with no disabilities.

①　　　②　　　③　　　④　　　⑤

✏️ 출제율 90%

12 위 글의 밑줄 친 ⓐlesson과 같은 의미로 쓰인 것을 고르시오.

① She gives a lesson in music.
② I have no lesson today.
③ We have just finished Lesson Two.
④ The accident taught me a lesson I'll never forget.
⑤ Our first lesson on Tuesdays is French.

✏️ 출제율 100%

13 According to the passage, which is NOT true?

① Eunchong's dad thanks Eunchong not only for being his son but also for teaching him an important life lesson.
② When Eunchong was a baby, people avoided him because of his skin color.
③ Eunchong's dad felt sad and wanted to hide Eunchong from people.
④ Eunchong's mom blamed herself for Eunchong's sickness.
⑤ Eunchong promised himself that he would face the world.

[14~15] 다음 글을 읽고 물음에 답하시오.

Do you remember our first triathlon? When we began to swim, the other participants made way for us and let us go first. I was very touched and thankful. Some participants even cried when we passed them by. When we started cycling, many people cheered for us. But you had to endure some strong winds and tiredness. So I cycled very fast ⓐto give you a break. When we began running, your mom seemed to say, "I wish I could run with you." I wanted to finish the race quickly so I could see her and let you rest. So, I ran fast. When we were almost at the finishing line, the other participants stopped and let us go first. Eunchong, you were the winner! I hope you could tell how much everyone at those races loved you.   <you: Eunchong>

✏️ 출제율 100%

14 위 글의 제목으로 알맞은 것을 고르시오.

① Eunchong Participated in Triathlon? It Can't Be!
② Swimming Is the Hardest in Triathlon
③ Thanks to All! Your Love Led Us to Victory!
④ Too Weak to Endure Strong Winds and Tiredness
⑤ I Wish I Could Run with You!

✏️ 출제율 95%

15 아래 〈보기〉에서 위 글의 밑줄 친 ⓐto give와 to부정사의 용법이 다른 것의 개수를 고르시오.

┌─ 보기 ─┐
① I was happy to give her a chance.
② He refused to give her a chance.
③ You must be mad to give her a chance.
④ He is the last man to give her a chance.
⑤ They were kind enough to give her a chance.
└────┘

① 1개   ② 2개   ③ 3개   ④ 4개   ⑤ 5개

[16~18] 다음 글을 읽고 물음에 답하시오.

ⓐ네 덕분에, 너의 엄마와 나는 중요한 교훈을 배웠단다. "Love is all we need." We don't ever think, "We wish Eunchong had no disabilities" anymore. Instead, we are just thankful for having you. We are also happy about many other little things. Even when we face difficulties, we are happy. That's because we know that we can ⓑ<u>overcome</u> any hardships when we are together and love each other. Let's continue to live happily and bravely. We will always love you and stand by you.

Love,
Dad

✏️ 출제율 90%

16 위 글의 밑줄 친 ⓐ의 우리말에 맞게 주어진 어휘를 이용하여 11 단어로 영작하시오.

> Thanks, lesson

➡ _____

_____

✏️ 출제율 95%

17 위 글의 밑줄 친 ⓑ<u>overcome</u>과 바꿔 쓸 수 있는 말을 두 단어로 쓰시오.

➡ _____

✏️ 출제율 90%

18 What are Eunchong's parents thankful for? Answer in English in a full sentence. (6~7 words)

➡ _____

[19~21] 다음 글을 읽고 물음에 답하시오.

(A)<u>There are some things that all babies need.</u> Frederick II, the German King in the 13th century, did not let people touch or talk to some babies. Then, all of these babies soon died. For some reason, humans need love and care. Dr. Dean Ornish, the writer of the book *Love and Survival*, says love is the most important factor for a healthy life. In 2010, Lily and Summer Cobbing were born as twins. Doctors thought (B)<u>Lily, the younger sister, was too small to live.</u> The doctors weren't sure whether she could live. ⓐ , when Summer hugged Lily, Lily started to become healthy. These two stories show that not only love but also touch is very important to babies. Some scientists want to find the reason, but it's not easy to do.

✏️ 출제율 95%

19 위 글의 빈칸 ⓐ에 들어갈 알맞은 말을 고르시오.

① Therefore   ② However
③ For example   ④ Besides
⑤ That is

✏️ 출제율 90%

20 위 글의 밑줄 친 (A)가 가리키는 것 두 가지를 본문에서 찾아 쓰시오.

➡ _____

✏️ 출제율 90%

21 위 글의 밑줄 친 (B)를 복문으로 고치시오.

➡ _____

_____

[01~03] 다음 대화를 읽고 물음에 답하시오.

> B: There is no way I can carry all these things to my grandmother's house.
> G: Let me (A)_____ you a hand.
> B: Thank you very much.
> G: I will carry these books.
> B: Be careful. They are very heavy.
> G: Wow, these are really heavy. I can't even (B)_____ them up!
> B: (가)내가 운전할 수 있으면 좋을 텐데. Then carrying heavy things wouldn't be a problem.
> G: Hey, (C)_____ don't we ask our friends for help?
> B: That's a great idea. Could you please call them for me?
> G: Sure.

01 위 대화의 빈칸 (A), (B), (C)에 들어가기에 적절한 단어를 보기에서 찾아 쓰시오. (중복 사용 가능)

┌─ 보기 ├─────────────────────┐
│   how give receive get pick why   │
└──────────────────────────────┘

➡ (A)_____ (B)_____ (C)_____

02 (가)에 해당하는 우리말을 영어로 옮기시오. (5 words)

➡ _____

03 After the dialogue, what will the girl do to carry those books?

➡ She will _____ her friends.

04 괄호 안에 주어진 단어를 활용하여 같은 뜻의 문장으로 바꿔 쓰시오.

(1) It's a pity that I am not tall and strong. (wish)

➡ _____

(2) I wish I had a car. (sorry)

➡ _____

(3) I am sorry that I can't live with my son. (wish)

➡ _____

05 다음 우리말을 주어진 단어를 이용하여 영작하시오.

(1) Chris와 Pat 모두 늦었다. (both, late)

➡ _____

(2) 집에 도착했을 때 나는 피곤하기도 하고 배가 고프기도 했다. (arriving, home, both)

➡ _____

(3) Jenny와 Cathy 둘 다 파티에 오지 않았다. (neither, party)

➡ _____

(4) 그는 편지를 쓰지도 전화를 하지도 않았다. (neither, phone)

➡ _____

(5) 그녀는 스페인 사람 아니면 이탈리아 사람이다. (Spanish, Italian, either)

➡ _____

Dear Eunchong,

I thank you not only for being my son but also for teaching me an important life lesson. When you were a baby, people avoided you because of your skin color. I felt sad and wanted to hide you from them. ⓐ네 엄마는 네가 장애 없이 태어나기를 바랐지. She blamed herself for your sickness. But you always smiled at us and held our hands. ⓑYou gave us courage as well as hope. So, I promised myself that I would face the world and show you the bright side of things. Since then we have begun our journey.

06 위 글의 밑줄 친 ⓐ의 우리말에 맞게 주어진 어휘를 이용하여 11 단어로 영작하시오.

> hoped, would, with, disabilities

➡ _____

_____

07 위 글의 밑줄 친 ⓑ를 다음과 같이 바꿔 쓸 때 빈칸에 들어갈 알맞은 말을 두 단어로 쓰시오.

➡ You gave us not only _____ but also _____.

08 본문의 내용과 일치하도록 다음 빈칸 (A)~(C)에 알맞은 단어를 쓰시오.

This is a letter from (A)_____ _____ to Eunchong. In it, Eunchong's dad thanks Eunchong for teaching him an important life lesson (B)_____ _____ _____ for being his son, adding that he promised himself that he would face the world and show Eunchong the (C)_____ _____ of things.

Do you remember our first triathlon? When we began to swim, the other participants ⓐ_____ _____ _____ us and let us go first. I was very (A)[touching / touched] and thankful. Some participants even cried when we passed them by. When we started cycling, many people cheered for us. But you had to endure some strong winds and tiredness. So I cycled very fast to give you a break. When we began running, your mom seemed to say, "I (B)[hope / wish] I could run with you." I wanted to finish the race quickly so I could see her and let you rest. So, I ran fast. When we were (C)[almost / most] at the finishing line, the other participants stopped and let us go first. Eunchong, you were the winner! I hope you could tell how much everyone at those races loved you.
<you: Eunchong>

09 주어진 영영풀이를 참고하여 빈칸 ⓐ에 철자 m으로 시작하는 표현을 쓰시오. (시제를 문맥에 맞추시오.)

make enough space for somebody/something; allow somebody/something to pass

➡ _____

10 위 글의 괄호 (A)~(C)에서 문맥이나 어법상 알맞은 낱말을 골라 쓰시오.

➡ (A)_____ (B)_____ (C)_____

11 Why did Eunchong's dad cycle very fast? Answer in English using "In order to".

➡ _____

01 괄호 안에서 알맞은 낱말을 고르시오.

(1) You look sad. (Cry / Cheer) up!

(2) I am tired. I need to (rest / race).

(3) I need a light. This room is very (bright / dark).

(4) I want to travel around the world. I (special / especially) want to go to China.

(5) I didn't go camping. (Instead / Even though), I went fishing.

(6) There is going to be a soccer match. Korea will (face / avoid) Germany.

(7) I wrote a letter to my grandmother. She was (brave / touched) and cried.

(8) Wear a (bright / black) jacket on a rainy day so that drivers can see you more clearly.

02 다음은 장애인을 위해 발명한 제품을 발표한 글이다. main idea와 supporting details를 보고 빈칸을 채우시오.

Main Idea
Make a better world for everyone
Supporting Detail 1
let the disabled get on the bus more easily
Supporting Detail 2
make hidden legs next to both wheels and bright lights

I think disabled people in wheelchairs have a hard time getting on the bus. I (A)_____ they (B)_____ on the bus more easily, so I will make a wheelchair that helps them get on the bus more easily. It has (C)_____ hidden legs next to both (D)_____ (E)_____ also bright lights. The legs will appear when they are needed. The lights will light up the way when people with disabilities get on the bus. What do you think about my idea? Let's (F)_____.

03 다음 내용을 바탕으로 가족 구성원에 관한 간단한 글을 쓰시오.

Q1: Who in your family do you want to introduce?
A1: I want to introduce my mother.
Q2: Where does she live?
A2: She lives in Seoul with me.
Q3: What is your memory of her?
A3: We went to her hometown and tried farming. It was so much fun.
Q4: What do you wish you could do with her?
A4: I wish I could spend more time in her hometown.

My mom lives (A)_____ with me. Once, we went to (B)_____ and tried (C)_____. It was so much (D)_____. I wish I could spend (E)_____ in her hometown. When I grow up, I will live with her in her hometown.

단원별 모의고사

01 다음 짝지어진 단어의 관계가 같도록 빈칸에 알맞은 말을 쓰시오.

depress : depression = participate : _____

02 다음 빈칸에 들어가기에 가장 적절한 것은?

We are trying to run a political _____ here.

① experiment　　② race
③ hand　　④ care
⑤ campaign

03 다음 영영풀이에 해당하는 단어를 고르시오.

a physical or mental condition that makes it difficult for someone to use a part of their body properly

① disease　　② disability
③ present　　④ journey
⑤ view

04 다음 문장의 빈칸에 알맞은 것을 〈보기〉에서 찾아 쓰시오.

┌─ 보기 ─┐
courage challenge colorful excellent
└────────┘

(1) Climbing Mt. Everest is a big _____.

(2) Rainbows are _____.

(3) I don't have the _____ to travel alone.

(4) Your English speaking ability is _____.

[05~06] 다음 대화를 읽고 물음에 답하시오.

G: Dad! Look at this beautiful scenery. I wish I could live here.
M: It's amazing, isn't it? Standing on the top of this mountain makes me feel good.
G: I'm so sad that _____.
M: Don't be sad. You can enjoy this view again next week!

05 위 대화의 내용으로 보아 빈칸에 들어가기에 가장 적절한 것은?

① they are making a lot of noise
② we have to walk down soon
③ we were late for the train
④ it's too cold to stay on the top
⑤ we don't feel good

06 Which one of the following is NOT true according to the dialogue above?

① They are father and daughter.
② They are planning to live on the mountain.
③ They feel good on the top of the mountain.
④ The scenery is beautiful.
⑤ They will come to the mountain next week.

[07~09] 다음 글을 읽고 물음에 답하시오.

M: About 10 years ago, I was hit by a car while I was riding a bicycle at night. I lost my left leg and ⓐstayed in the hospital for six months. I was depressed and couldn't find a reason ⓑto live. However, my parents supported me and ⓒtook care of me with their love. Thanks to them, I was able to overcome the situation. By doing so, I found out that life can be ⓓmeaningless to everybody. Now, I'm a wheelchair basketball player and every year I run ⓔcampaign for people in need of help. During each campaign, I give a speech about the importance of positive thinking. Some people seem to be in the habit of negative thinking. I wish my speech would help them (가)_____.

07 ⓐ~ⓔ 중에서 문맥상 적절하지 <u>않은</u> 것은?

① ⓐ ② ⓑ ③ ⓒ ④ ⓓ ⑤ ⓔ

08 빈칸 (가)에 들어가기에 가장 적절한 것은?

① think more positively
② drive more safely
③ support their family
④ play wheelchair basketball
⑤ be in the habit of negative thinking

09 다음 중 위 글의 내용과 일치하지 <u>않는</u> 것은?

① He was 10 years old when he was hit by a car.
② He was riding a bicycle at night.
③ He stayed in the hospital for 6 months.
④ He was very depressed after the accident.
⑤ He gives a speech about the importance of positive thinking.

[10~12] 다음 대화를 읽고 물음에 답하시오.

W: Excuse me, I'm looking for a birthday present for my son. (A)
M: Oh, can I (가)give you a hand?
W: Yes, please. My son is 15 years old. (B) Do you have any recommendations?
M: What about this colorful jacket? (C)
W: It looks fine, but my son doesn't like colorful clothes. (D)
M: What about this green colored jacket?
W: It is very pretty. Do you have it in a large size? (E)
M: Yes, there is a large one here!
W: Thank you. I'll take it.

10 밑줄 친 (가) 대신 쓰기에 적절한 것은?

① ask a favor of you
② help you
③ ask you something
④ buy a green jacket
⑤ show you a new jacket

11 (A)~(E) 중에서 다음 문장이 들어가기에 가장 적절한 곳은?

It is very popular.

① (A) ② (B) ③ (C) ④ (D) ⑤ (E)

12 다음 중 위 대화의 내용과 일치하지 <u>않는</u> 것은?

① The birthday of the woman's son is coming up.
② The woman's son is ten years old.
③ The woman's son doesn't like colorful clothes.
④ The woman's son wears a large size jacket.
⑤ The woman will buy a green jacket.

13 다음 중 어법상 어색한 것은?

① I wish I were richer.
② I wish I had a bigger house.
③ I wish you would be quiet in class.
④ I wish you have more money.
⑤ I wish you would be more kind to me.

14 다음 문장과 같은 의미의 문장을 쓰시오.

(1) I wished I had more money.
➡ I was sorry _____.
(2) I wish I had more money.
➡ I am sorry _____.
(3) He wishes he used the best policy.
➡ He is sorry _____.
(4) He wished he used the best policy.
➡ He was sorry _____
_____.

15 다음 대화의 밑줄 친 우리말을 영어로 쓰시오.

A: What's wrong with you?
B: You know, tomorrow is the day, my speaking test!
A: I think you did well at the last speaking test, so don't worry.
B: Thanks, but I think I'm not good at speaking in English. 내가 영어를 유창하게 말하면 좋을 텐데. (6 words)
*fluently: 유창하게

➡ _____

16 다음 중 어색한 문장을 골라 바르게 고치시오.

① They shot firecrackers not only in New York but also in Moscow.
② Although he is Korean, he uses both spoken English and written English well.
③ He enjoyed neither talking with his wife nor listened to his wife.
④ Tsunami causes property damages as well as kills numerous people.
⑤ Although he is a famous actor, he is not arrogant but kind to others.

➡ _____
_____

17 다음 우리말을 주어진 말을 써서 두 가지로 영작하시오.

봉준호 감독은 오스카 상에서 영화 '기생충'으로 각본상뿐만 아니라 감독상도 탔다. (only, also, well)
*parasite: 기생충 original screenplay award: 각본상, the directing award: 감독상

➡ _____
_____
_____
_____
_____

18 다음 글을 보고 Jane이 바라는 것을 쓰시오.

Jane talks as if she were a famous actress. In fact, she is not a famous actor.

➡ _____

19 우리말과 일치하도록 괄호 안의 어휘를 이용하여 영작하시오.

(1) 내일이 주말이라면 얼마나 좋을까?
(wish, weekend, tomorrow)

➡ _____

(2) 지금 해변에 누워 있는 중이라면 얼마나 좋을까? (wish, lying, now)

➡ _____

(3) 네가 내일 떠나지 않으면 좋을 텐데.
(wish, leaving)

➡ _____

[20~21] 다음 글을 읽고 물음에 답하시오.

On October 16th, 2010, Eunchong and his dad participated in their first ⓐtriathlon. It was held in Misari, Hanam. They swam 1.5 km, cycled 40 km, and then ran 10 km. This challenge was especially difficult for Eunchong's dad because he had to push or pull Eunchong during the race. Eunchong couldn't talk or walk because he was born with six different diseases. His skin was dark red and his brain was becoming hard. The doctor said he would not live for long. But Eunchong not only is still alive but also got first place in his first triathlon.

20 다음 문장에서 위 글의 내용과 다른 부분을 찾아서 고치시오.

Eunchong is not still alive but got first place in his first triathlon.

➡ _____

21 다음 빈칸 (A)와 (B)에 알맞은 단어를 넣어 ⓐtriathlon에 대한 소개를 완성하시오.

A triathlon is an athletics competition in which each competitor takes part in three events, (A)_____, cycling, and (B)_____. *athletics: 운동 경기

[22~23] 다음 글을 읽고 물음에 답하시오.

Dear Eunchong,

I thank you ⓐ _____ for being my son but also for teaching me an important life lesson. When you were a baby, people avoided you because of your skin color. I felt sad and wanted to hide you from ⓑthem. Your mom hoped that you would be born with no disabilities. She blamed herself for your sickness. But you always smiled at us and held our hands. You gave us courage as well as hope. So, I promised myself that I would face the world and show you the bright side of things. Since then we have begun our journey.

22 위 글의 빈칸 ⓐ에 들어가기에 알맞은 말을 모두 고르시오.

① not only ② not just
③ nothing but ④ not simply
⑤ not merely

23 위 글의 밑줄 친 ⓑthem이 가리키는 것을 본문에서 찾아 쓰시오.

➡ _____

[24~25] 다음 글을 읽고 물음에 답하시오.

Do you remember our first triathlon? When we began ①to swim, the other participants made way for us and let us ②go first. I was very ⓐtouched and thankful. Some participants even cried when we passed them by. When we started ③cycling, many people cheered for us. But you had to endure some strong winds and tiredness. So I cycled very fast ④to give you a break. When we began ⑤running, your mom seemed to say, "I wish I could run with you." I wanted to finish the race quickly so I could see her and let you rest. So, I ran fast When we were almost at the finishing line, the other participants stopped and let us go first. Eunchong, you were the winner! I hope you could tell how much everyone at those races loved you.   <you: Eunchong>

24 다음 중 위 글의 밑줄 친 ①~⑤에 대한 설명이 옳지 <u>않은</u> 것을 <u>모두</u> 고르시오.

① swimming으로 바꿔 쓸 수 있다.
② to go로 바꿔 쓸 수 있다.
③ to cycle로 바꿔 쓸 수 있다.
④ giving으로 바꿔 쓸 수 있다.
⑤ to run으로 바꿔 쓸 수 있다.

25 위 글의 밑줄 친 ⓐtouched와 같은 의미로 쓰인 것을 고르시오.

① I <u>touched</u> him lightly on the arm.
② Everything she <u>touched</u> turned to disaster.
③ Her story <u>touched</u> us all deeply.
④ You've hardly <u>touched</u> your food.
⑤ A smile <u>touched</u> the corners of his mouth.

[26~27] 다음 글을 읽고 물음에 답하시오.

Thanks to you, your mom and I learned an important lesson. (①) "Love is all we need." (②) We don't ever think, "We wish Eunchong had no disabilities" anymore. (③) We are also happy about many other little things. (④) Even when we face difficulties, we are happy. (⑤) That's because we know that we can overcome any hardships when we are together and love each other. Let's continue to live happily and bravely. We will always love you and stand by you.

Love,
Dad

26 위 글의 흐름으로 보아, 주어진 문장이 들어가기에 가장 적절한 곳은?

Instead, we are just thankful for having you.

①   ②   ③   ④   ⑤

27 According to the passage, which is NOT true?

① Thanks to Eunchong, his parents learned an important lesson.
② Eunchong's parents think, "We wish Eunchong had no disabilities."
③ Even when Eunchong's parents face difficulties, they are happy.
④ Eunchong's parents know that they can overcome any hardships when they are together and love each other.
⑤ Eunchong's parents will always love Eunchong and stand by him.

MEMO

INSIGHT
on the textbook

교과서 파헤치기

※ 다음 영어를 우리말로 쓰시오.

01 expert _____

02 grade _____

03 carefully _____

04 disagree _____

05 convince _____

06 edit _____

07 anyway _____

08 concentrate _____

09 surface _____

10 talkative _____

11 charge _____

12 seem _____

13 strict _____

14 satisfied _____

15 cheer _____

16 scary _____

17 alone _____

18 shy _____

19 interest _____

20 career _____

21 judge _____

22 boring _____

23 place _____

24 reason _____

25 soccer field _____

26 advise _____

27 wonder _____

28 culture _____

29 exciting _____

30 introduce _____

31 look _____

32 same _____

33 mean _____

34 continue _____

35 be over _____

36 make an announcement _____

37 go over _____

38 cannot help -ing _____

39 worth -ing _____

40 come across _____

41 be in charge of ~ _____

42 turn into _____

43 have ~ in common _____

※ 다음 우리말을 영어로 쓰시오.

01	충고하다	
02	조심스럽게	
03	엄격한	
04	어쨌든	
05	말이 많은	
06	(책이나 잡지의) 표지; 다루다	
07	표면	
08	반대하다	
09	편집하다	
10	이유	
11	납득시키다, 확신시키다	
12	같은	
13	응원하다	
14	만족한	
15	궁금해 하다	
16	무서운	
17	문화	
18	관심	
19	혼자 있는	
20	~인 것 같다	
21	집중하다	

22	판단하다	
23	겉모습	
24	전문가	
25	성적	
26	요금, 책임	
27	계속하다	
28	의미하다	
29	두다, 놓다	
30	지루한	
31	직업, 이력	
32	내성적인	
33	축구장	
34	점심시간	
35	우연히 마주치다	
36	~하곤 했다	
37	확인하다	
38	~으로 되다	
39	~할 가치가 있는	
40	~을 공통으로 가지다	
41	잠시 뒤에	
42	~하지 않을 수 없다	
43	~을 책임지다	

※ 다음 영영풀이에 알맞은 단어를 <보기>에서 골라 쓴 후, 우리말 뜻을 쓰시오.

1 _____ : not interesting in any way: _____

2 _____ : without any friends or people you know: _____

3 _____ : tell them each other's names for the first time: _____

4 _____ : to make someone feel certain that something is true: _____

5 _____ : to have or express a different opinion from someone else: _____

6 _____ : to prepare something written to be published or used: _____

7 _____ : to think very carefully about something that you are doing: _____

8 _____ : tending to talk a lot or to enjoy having conversations with people: _____

9 _____ : a person with special knowledge, skill, or training in something: _____

10 _____ : demanding that people obey rules or behave in a certain way: _____

11 _____ : to form an opinion about something or someone after careful thought: _____

12 _____ : to have or express the same opinion about something as someone else: _____

13 _____ : a feeling of wanting to learn more about something or to be involved in something: _____

14 _____ : to shout as a way of showing happiness, praise, approval, or support of someone or something: _____

15 _____ : a job or profession that you have been trained for, and which you do for a long period of your life: _____

16 _____ : to tell someone what you think they should do, especially when you know more than they do about something: _____

보기

concentrate	judge	talkative	disagree
career	interest	alone	advise
expert	introduce	edit	cheer
strict	agree	convince	boring

※ 다음 우리말과 일치하도록 빈칸에 알맞은 말을 쓰시오.

해석

Everyday English 1 A-1

G: I think _____ is an _____ subject. _____ you _____?

B: I'm _____ I don't _____ _____ you. It's _____ _____ for me.

G: _____ history _____ _____ may _____ it _____.

B: I think it _____ _____ be _____ for me.

Everyday English 1 A-2

G: I _____ soccer is _____ _____ _____ _____ in our class. _____ you _____?

B: I agree. Many students _____ _____ _____ the _____ _____.

G: And many students _____ the soccer _____ at home, _____.

B: You're _____.

Everyday English 1 B

G: What _____ you _____ _____?

B: I'm looking _____ the school _____ game _____.

G: Hmm... Who _____ _____ _____ is the _____ basketball _____ in our school?

B: I _____ Jihun is _____ _____. _____ you _____?

G: No, I don't _____. I _____ Minjae is the _____ player.

B: _____ do you _____ _____?

G: His _____ _____ the basketball game _____ _____. _____ you _____?

B: But that was _____ Minjae's _____ had a _____ of _____ basketball _____.

G: _____, we are _____ to have _____ _____ _____ in our class _____ _____.

B: Yes, we are. I think our _____ is _____ _____ _____ the basketball game _____ _____.

Everyday English 2 A-2

B: Are you _____ _____ your new partner?

G: Yes, I am.

B: _____ do you _____ _____ him?

G: He is _____ and _____.

Everyday English 2 B

(Phone rings.)

G: Hello?

B: Hi, Bora! _____ me, Minsu!

G: Minsu! _____ you _____ _____ France?

B: Yes, I am.

G: _____ do you _____ your _____ in France?

B: France is _____ _____ _____ country, but I _____ Korea.

G: Are you _____ _____ your new school?

B: _____ _____ much. Everything is _____ _____ _____ Korea, _____ it's not _____ for me.

G: Do your _____ _____ you?

B: Some of them do _____ me. They are _____ _____.

G: Good for you. I _____ you the _____ _____ _____.

B: Thanks.

In Real Life

Ryan: Hey Jisu, _____ are your _____ _____ for the _____ _____ _____?

Jisu: Hi, Ryan. My group _____ are Lina, Inho, and Min.

Ryan: Are you _____ _____ your group?

Jisu: _____, I'm not. They _____ so _____ _____ me. _____ you _____?

Ryan: Well, _____ the _____ they may _____ _____ from you. But don't _____ a book _____ its _____.

Jisu: What do you _____ _____ that?

Ryan: I _____ that you _____ _____ people by their _____. You may _____ your group members when you _____ _____ them.

Jisu: Do you _____ _____ I can be _____ _____ them?

Ryan: Why _____? There could be _____ _____ about them. _____ _____ _____ your group members first.

B: 너는 새로운 짝에 만족하니?

G: 응, 그래.

B: 그에 대해서 뭐가 좋아?

G: 그는 재미있고 말하기를 좋아해.

(전화벨이 울린다.)

G: 여보세요?

B: 안녕, 보라야! 나야, 민수!

G: 민수! 프랑스에서 전화하는 거니?

B: 응, 그래.

G: 프랑스에서의 생활은 어떠니?

B: 프랑스는 아주 아름다운 나라야, 그렇지만 한국이 그리워.

G: 새로운 학교는 마음에 드니?

B: 별로야. 모든 것이 한국과 너무 달라, 그래서 나에게는 쉽지 않아.

G: 네 학급 친구들은 너를 도와주니?

B: 그들 중 몇몇은 나를 도와줘. 그들은 정말 친절해.

G: 잘됐네. 너에게 행운을 빌어.

B: 고마워.

Ryan: 안녕, 지수야. 너의 사회 과제의 모둠 멤버가 누구니?

Jisu: 안녕, Ryan. 나의 모둠 구성원은 Lina, 인호, Min이야.

Ryan: 너는 너의 모둠에 만족하니?

Jisu: 사실은 아니야. 그들은 나와 너무 달라 보여. 동의하지 않니?

Ryan: 글쎄. 표면적으로는 그들은 너와 달라 보일지도 몰라. 하지만 표지만 보고 책을 판단하지 마.

Jisu: 그게 무슨 뜻이야?

Ryan: 내 말은 네가 사람을 겉모습으로 판단해서는 안 된다는 거야. 너는 너의 모둠 구성원들을 알게 되면 그들을 좋아할지도 모르잖아.

Jisu: 너는 정말로 내가 그들과 친구가 될 수 있다고 생각하니?

Ryan: 왜 안 되겠니? 그들에게는 특별한 것이 있을 수 있어. 먼저 너의 모둠 구성원들을 이해하려고 노력해 봐.

※ 다음 우리말에 맞도록 대화를 영어로 쓰시오.

Everyday English 1 A-1

G: _____

B: _____

G: _____

B: _____

G: 나는 역사가 재미있는 과목이라고 생각해. 동의하지 않니?

B: 유감스럽게도 나는 동의하지 않아. 그것은 나에게 너무 어려워.

G: 역사 만화책을 읽는 것이 역사를 더 쉽게 만들어 줄 수 있어.

B: 나는 그것이 나한테 지루하기만 할 것 같아.

Everyday English 1 A-2

G: _____

B: _____

G: _____

B: _____

G: 나는 축구가 우리 반에서 가장 인기 있는 스포츠라고 생각해. 동의하지 않니?

B: 나도 동의해. 많은 학생들이 점심시간 동안 축구를 해.

G: 그리고 많은 학생들이 집에서 축구 경기를 시청하기도 해.

B: 네 말이 맞아.

Everyday English 1 B

G: _____

B: _____

G: _____

B: _____

G: _____

B: _____

G: _____

B: _____

G: _____

B: _____

G: 무엇을 보고 있니?

B: 학교 농구 경기 포스터를 보고 있어.

G: 음… 너는 우리 학교에서 누가 최고의 농구 선수라고 생각하니?

B: 나는 지훈이가 최고라고 생각해. 동의하지 않니?

G: 아니, 동의하지 않아. 나는 민재가 최고의 농구 선수라고 생각해.

B: 왜 그렇게 생각해?

G: 그의 학급은 작년 농구 경기에서 우승했어. 기억 안 나니?

B: 그렇지만 그것은 민재네 반에 좋은 농구 선수들이 많았기 때문이었어.

G: 어쨌든, 우리는 올해 둘 다 우리 반에 있어서 다행이야.

B: 맞아. 나는 우리 반이 올해는 농구 경기에서 우승할 거라고 생각해.

Everyday English 2 A-2

B: _____

G: _____

B: _____

G: _____

B: 너는 새로운 짝에 만족하니?
G: 응, 그래.
B: 그에 대해서 뭐가 좋아?
G: 그는 재미있고 말하기를 좋아해.

Everyday English 2 B

(Phone rings.)

G: _____

B: _____

G: _____

B: _____

G: _____

B: _____

G: _____

B: _____

G: _____

B: _____

G: _____

B: _____

(전화벨이 울린다.)
G: 여보세요?
B: 안녕, 보라야! 나야, 민수!
G: 민수! 프랑스에서 전화하는 거니?
B: 응, 그래.
G: 프랑스에서의 생활은 어떠니?
B: 프랑스는 아주 아름다운 나라야, 그렇지만 한국이 그리워.
G: 새로운 학교는 마음에 드니?
B: 별로야. 모든 것이 한국과 너무 달라, 그래서 나에게는 쉽지 않아.
G: 네 학급 친구들은 너를 도와주니?
B: 그들 중 몇몇은 나를 도와줘. 그들은 정말 친절해.
G: 잘됐네. 너에게 행운을 빌어.
B: 고마워.

In Real Life

Ryan: _____

Jisu: _____

Ryan: _____

Jisu: _____

Ryan: _____

_____

Jisu: _____

Ryan: _____

_____

Jisu: _____

Ryan: _____

Ryan: 안녕, 지수야, 너의 사회 과제의 모둠 멤버가 누구니?
Jisu: 안녕, Ryan. 나의 모둠 구성원은 Lina, 인호, Min이야.
Ryan: 너는 너의 모둠에 만족하니?
Jisu: 사실은 아니야. 그들은 나와 너무 달라 보여. 동의하지 않니?
Ryan: 글쎄. 표면적으로는 그들은 너와 달라 보일지도 몰라. 하지만 표지만 보고 책을 판단하지 마.
Jisu: 그게 무슨 뜻이야?
Ryan: 내 말은 네가 사람을 겉모습으로 판단해서는 안 된다는 거야. 너는 너의 모둠 구성원들을 알게 되면 그들을 좋아할지도 모르잖아.
Jisu: 너는 정말로 내가 그들과 친구가 될 수 있다고 생각하니?
Ryan: 왜 안 되겠니? 그들에게는 특별한 것이 있을 수 있어. 먼저 너의 모둠 구성원들을 이해하려고 노력해 봐.

※ 다음 우리말과 일치하도록 빈칸에 알맞은 것을 골라 쓰시오.

1 _____ I _____ My _____ Friends

   A. Met   B. How   C. Best

2 Mrs. Choi, my _____ _____ teacher, _____ an important

   _____.

   A. studies   B. announcement   C. social   D. made

3 "You will _____ a newspaper _____ _____.

   A. in   B. create   C. groups

4 _____ _____ your new _____ _____."

   A. out   B. check   C. members   D. group

5 Mrs. Choi started _____ _____ the _____ of the students

   in _____ group.

   A. out   B. each   C. calling   D. names

6 _____ a _____, my name _____ _____.

   A. while   B. was   C. after   D. called

7 "_____ _____, Jisu…"

   A. 4   B. group

8 "Who _____ _____ in my group?" I _____.

   A. wondered   B. be   C. will

9 Mrs. Choi _____, "Lina, Inho, _____ Min."

   A. and   B. continued

10 I _____ _____ my _____.

   A. believe   B. ears   C. couldn't

11 I _____ _____ _____ in that group.

   A. anyone   B. didn't   C. know

12 I _____ _____ _____ when I _____ with my group

   members.

   A. like   B. sat   C. crying   D. felt

13 We didn't _____ anything _____ _____.

   A. in   B. have   C. common

14 Lina _____ always _____ something _____ _____.

   A. by   B. drawing   C. herself   D. was

15 Inho never said _____, and his _____ _____ _____ to

   be soccer.

   A. interest   B. anything   C. seemed   D. only

1 가장 좋은 친구들을 어떻게 만나게 되었나

2 사회 선생님인 최 선생님께서 중요한 발표를 했다.

3 "모둠별로 신문을 만들 겁니다.

4 새 모둠의 구성원을 확인하세요."

5 최 선생님은 각 모둠의 학생들 이름을 부르기 시작했다.

6 잠시 후, 내 이름이 불렸다.

7 "모둠 4, 지수…"

8 "내 모둠의 구성원들은 누굴까?" 나는 궁금했다.

9 최 선생님은 계속 말씀하셨다. "Lina, 인호, 그리고 Min."

10 나는 내 귀를 믿을 수 없었다.

11 나는 그 모둠에 아는 사람이 하나도 없었다.

12 모둠 구성원들과 함께 앉을 때 나는 울고 싶었다.

13 우리는 공통점이 하나도 없었다.

14 Lina는 항상 혼자서 무언가를 그리고 있었다.

15 인호는 아무 말도 하지 않았으며 그의 유일한 관심은 축구 같았다.

16 Min was _____, but he always _____ his _____ in a _____.

    A. nose   B. smart   C. book   D. had

17 I _____ _____ _____ how unlucky I was.

    A. help   B. couldn't   C. thinking

18 I decided to _____ Mrs. Choi that I _____ _____ _____ my friends.

    A. be   B. convince   C. with   D. should

19 "_____ she would _____ _____ _____ the group," I thought.

    A. me   B. maybe   C. change   D. let

20 But before I could say _____, she _____ _____ her hand _____ my shoulder.

    A. placed   B. anything   C. on   D. gently

21 "I know _____ you want, Jisu," she said, "but I'm sure you will _____ _____ _____ your group members.

    A. get   B. what   C. like   D. to

22 Don't you think _____ _____ _____?"

    A. trying   B. it's   C. worth

23 I didn't really _____ her, _____ I said, "Okay," and _____ _____.

    A. away   B. believe   C. walked   D. but

24 The project wasn't _____ _____ the _____.

    A. from   B. easy   C. start

25 We couldn't _____ _____ the _____ for our newspaper.

    A. on   B. topic   C. decide

26 I _____ _____ _____ up on the project, so I asked my friend Ryan for some _____.

    A. like   B. advice   C. felt   D. giving

27 "_____ _____ _____ your group _____ first," he said.

    A. to   B. try   C. understand   D. memebers

28 _____ I _____ my group members.

    A. watched   B. carefully   C. so

29 And I _____ _____ some _____ _____ about them.

    A. across   B. facts   C. came   D. amazing

30 Lina read a _____ of Japanese comic books, so she was an _____ _____ Japanese _____.

    A. expert   B. lot   C. culture   D. on

---

16 Min은 영리했지만, 그는 항상 책만 보고 있었다.

17 나는 내가 참으로 불행하다는 생각을 하지 않을 수 없었다.

18 나는 내 친구들과 함께하겠다고 최 선생님을 설득하기로 했다.

19 "어쩌면 내가 모둠을 바꿀 수 있게 허락해 주실지 몰라." 나는 생각했다.

20 하지만 내가 말을 꺼내기도 전에, 선생님은 부드럽게 내 어깨에 손을 얹으셨다.

21 "네가 원하는 것이 뭔지 알아, 지수야." 선생님은 말했다. "하지만 네가 너의 모둠원들을 좋아하게 될 것이라고 확신해.

22 시도할 만한 가치가 있다고 생각하지 않니?"

23 나는 선생님의 말씀을 진짜로 믿진 않았지만, "네."라고 말하고 돌아섰다.

24 프로젝트는 처음부터 쉽지 않았다.

25 우리는 신문의 주제를 결정할 수 없었다.

26 나는 프로젝트를 포기하고 싶었고, 그래서 친구 Ryan에게 조언을 구했다.

27 "먼저 모둠 구성원들을 이해하려고 노력해 봐." 그는 말했다.

28 그래서 나는 모둠의 구성원들을 신중하게 살펴보았다.

29 그리고 그들에 관한 놀라운 사실들을 발견했다.

30 Lina는 일본의 만화책을 많이 읽었고, 그래서 일본 문화에 관해서는 전문가였다.

31 Inho's Korean _____ a _____ different, but that was _____ he lived in Argentina _____ he was young.

    A. because   B. bit   C. sounded   D. when

32 He knew _____ _____ about Argentina and _____ _____.

    A. its   B. lot   C. a   D. soccer

33 Min's mom was _____, and Min _____ _____ some time in Vietnam.

    A. used   B. Vietnamese   C. spend   D. to

34 He read a _____ of history books and loved _____ _____ Vietnam and its history.

    A. talk   B. lot   C. about   D. to

35 I _____ the _____ _____ for our group.

    A. of   B. perfect   C. thought   D. topic

36 We _____ _____ _____ about world culture.

    A. to   B. decided   C. write

37 I _____ Lina _____ Japanese _____.

    A. culture   B. had   C. introduce

38 Inho _____ _____ Argentina and its soccer, and Min _____ Vietnamese culture and its _____.

    A. covered   B. about   C. history   D. wrote

39 I was in _____ _____ _____ the _____ newspaper.

    A. editing   B. charge   C. whole   D. of

40 Our _____ project was _____ _____ _____.

    A. success   B. newspaper   C. great   D. a

41 We _____ an A⁺, and my group _____ _____ my best _____.

    A. became   B. received   C. friends   D. members

42 I will _____ my story _____ this _____.

    A. with   B. end   C. saying

43 Don't _____ a book _____ its _____.

    A. by   B. judge   C. cover

44 _____ _____.

    A. it   B. read

45 It _____ _____ _____ your favorite book.

    A. into   B. might   C. turn

---

31 인호의 한국어 발음은 조금 다르게 들렸는데, 그 이유는 어렸을 때 아르헨티나에서 살았기 때문이었다.

32 그는 아르헨티나와 그 나라의 축구에 관해 많은 것을 알고 있었다.

33 Min의 엄마는 베트남 사람이었고, Min은 베트남에서 약간의 시간을 보냈다.

34 그는 많은 역사책을 읽었으며, 베트남과 그 역사에 관해 이야기하는 것을 좋아했다.

35 나는 우리 모둠을 위한 완벽한 주제를 생각해 냈다.

36 우리는 세계 문화에 관해 글을 쓰기로 했다.

37 나는 Lina가 일본 문화를 소개하도록 했다.

38 인호는 아르헨티나와 축구에 관해 썼고, Min은 베트남 문화와 역사를 다뤘다.

39 나는 신문 전체를 편집하는 역할을 맡았다.

40 우리의 신문 프로젝트는 대성공이었다.

41 우리는 A⁺를 받았고, 모둠 구성원들은 나의 가장 친한 친구가 되었다.

42 나는 이 말로 내 이야기를 끝내려고 한다.

43 책을 표지로 판단하지 마라.

44 그것을 읽어라.

45 그것은 네가 가장 좋아하는 책이 될 수도 있다.

※ 다음 우리말과 일치하도록 빈칸에 알맞은 것을 골라 쓰시오.

1 _____ I _____ My _____ Friends

2 Mrs. Choi, my _____ _____ teacher, _____ an important _____.

3 "You _____ _____ a newspaper _____ _____.

4 _____ _____ your new group _____."

5 Mrs. Choi started _____ _____ the names of the students _____ _____ _____.

6 _____ _____ _____, my name _____ _____.

7 "_____ 4, Jisu…"

8 "_____ _____ _____ in my group?" I _____.

9 Mrs. Choi _____, "Lina, Inho, and Min."

10 I _____ _____ my ears.

11 I _____ _____ _____ in that group.

12 I _____ _____ _____ when I _____ _____ my group members.

13 We didn't _____ anything _____ _____.

14 Lina _____ _____ _____ something _____ _____.

15 Inho never said anything, and _____ _____ _____ _____ _____ be soccer.

1 가장 좋은 친구들을 어떻게 만나게 되었나

2 사회 선생님인 최 선생님께서 중요한 발표를 했다.

3 "모둠별로 신문을 만들 겁니다.

4 새 모둠의 구성원을 확인하세요."

5 최 선생님은 각 모둠의 학생들 이름을 부르기 시작했다.

6 잠시 후, 내 이름이 불렸다.

7 "모둠 4, 지수…"

8 "내 모둠의 구성원들은 누굴까?" 나는 궁금했다.

9 최 선생님은 계속 말씀하셨다. "Lina, 인호, 그리고 Min."

10 나는 내 귀를 믿을 수 없었다.

11 나는 그 모둠에 아는 사람이 하나도 없었다.

12 모둠 구성원들과 함께 앉을 때 나는 울고 싶었다.

13 우리는 공통점이 하나도 없었다.

14 Lina는 항상 혼자서 무언가를 그리고 있었다.

15 인호는 아무 말도 하지 않았으며 그의 유일한 관심은 축구 같았다.

16 Min was smart, but he always _____ _____ _____ _____ _____.

17 I _____ _____ _____ _____ _____ I was.

18 I decided _____ _____ Mrs. Choi that I _____ _____ _____ my friends.

19 "Maybe she would _____ _____ _____ the group," I _____.

20 But before I could say anything, she gently _____ her hand _____ my _____.

21 "I know _____ _____ _____, Jisu," she said, "but I'm sure you will _____ _____ _____ your group members.

22 _____ you think _____ _____ _____?"

23 I didn't really _____ her, but I said, "Okay," and _____ _____.

24 The project wasn't easy _____ _____ _____.

25 We _____ _____ _____ the topic for our newspaper.

26 I _____ _____ _____ up on the project, so I asked my friend Ryan for some _____.

27 "_____ _____ _____ your group members first," he said.

28 So I _____ _____ my group members.

29 And I _____ _____ some _____ _____ about them.

30 Lina read a lot of Japanese comic books, _____ she was an _____ _____ Japanese _____.

16	Min은 영리했지만, 그는 항상 책만 보고 있었다.
17	나는 내가 참으로 불행하다는 생각을 하지 않을 수 없었다.
18	나는 내 친구들과 함께하겠다고 최 선생님을 설득하기로 했다.
19	"어쩌면 내가 모둠을 바꿀 수 있게 허락해 주실지 몰라." 나는 생각했다.
20	하지만 내가 말을 꺼내기도 전에. 선생님은 부드럽게 내 어깨에 손을 얹으셨다.
21	"네가 원하는 것이 뭔지 알아, 지수야." 선생님은 말했다. "하지만 네가 너의 모둠원들을 좋아하게 될 것이라고 확신해.
22	시도할 만한 가치가 있다고 생각하지 않니?"
23	나는 선생님의 말씀을 진짜로 믿진 않았지만, "네."라고 말하고 돌아섰다.
24	프로젝트는 처음부터 쉽지 않았다.
25	우리는 신문의 주제를 결정할 수 없었다.
26	나는 프로젝트를 포기하고 싶었고. 그래서 친구 Ryan에게 조언을 구했다.
27	"먼저 모둠 구성원들을 이해하려고 노력해 봐." 그는 말했다.
28	그래서 나는 모둠의 구성원들을 신중하게 살펴보았다.
29	그리고 그들에 관한 놀라운 사실들을 발견했다.
30	Lina는 일본의 만화책을 많이 읽었고, 그래서 일본 문화에 관해서는 전문가였다.

31 Inho's Korean _____ _____ _____ different, but that was _____ he lived in Argentina when he was young.

32 He knew _____ _____ about Argentina and its soccer.

33 Min's mom was _____, and Min _____ _____ _____ some time in Vietnam.

34 He read a lot of history books and loved _____ _____ _____ Vietnam and _____ _____.

35 I _____ _____ the perfect topic for our group.

36 We _____ _____ _____ about world culture.

37 I _____ _____ _____ Japanese culture.

38 Inho _____ _____ Argentina and its soccer, and Min _____ _____ _____ and its history.

39 I _____ _____ _____ _____ the whole newspaper.

40 Our newspaper project was _____ _____ _____.

41 We _____ _____ _____, and my group members _____ my best friends.

42 I will end my story _____ _____ _____.

43 _____ _____ a book _____ _____ _____.

44 _____ it.

45 It might _____ _____ your favorite book.

31 인호의 한국어 발음은 조금 다르게 들렸는데, 그 이유는 어렸을 때 아르헨티나에서 살았기 때문이었다.

32 그는 아르헨티나와 그 나라의 축구에 관해 많은 것을 알고 있었다.

33 Min의 엄마는 베트남 사람이었고, Min은 베트남에서 약간의 시간을 보냈다.

34 그는 많은 역사책을 읽었으며, 베트남과 그 역사에 관해 이야기하는 것을 좋아했다.

35 나는 우리 모둠을 위한 완벽한 주제를 생각해 냈다.

36 우리는 세계 문화에 관해 글을 쓰기로 했다.

37 나는 Lina가 일본 문화를 소개하도록 했다.

38 인호는 아르헨티나와 축구에 관해 썼고, Min은 베트남 문화와 역사를 다뤘다.

39 나는 신문 전체를 편집하는 역할을 맡았다.

40 우리의 신문 프로젝트는 대성공이었다.

41 우리는 A⁺를 받았고, 모둠 구성원들은 나의 가장 친한 친구가 되었다.

42 나는 이 말로 내 이야기를 끝내려고 한다.

43 책을 표지로 판단하지 마라.

44 그것을 읽어라.

45 그것은 네가 가장 좋아하는 책이 될 수도 있다.

※ 다음 문장을 우리말로 쓰시오.

1 How I Met My Best Friends

➡ _____

2 Mrs. Choi, my social studies teacher, made an important announcement.

➡ _____

3 "You will create a newspaper in groups.

➡ _____

4 Check out your new group members."

➡ _____

5 Mrs. Choi started calling out the names of the students in each group.

➡ _____

6 After a while, my name was called.

➡ _____

7 "Group 4, Jisu…"

➡ _____

8 "Who will be in my group?" I wondered.

➡ _____

9 Mrs. Choi continued, "Lina, Inho, and Min."

➡ _____

10 I couldn't believe my ears.

➡ _____

11 I didn't know anyone in that group.

➡ _____

12 I felt like crying when I sat with my group members.

➡ _____

13 We didn't have anything in common.

➡ _____

14 Lina was always drawing something by herself.

➡ _____

15 Inho never said anything, and his only interest seemed to be soccer.

➡ _____

16 Min was smart, but he always had his nose in a book.

➡ _____

17 I couldn't help thinking how unlucky I was.

➡ _____

18 I decided to convince Mrs. Choi that I should be with my friends.

➡ _____

19 "Maybe she would let me change the group," I thought.

➡ _____

20 But before I could say anything, she gently placed her hand on my shoulder.

➡ _____

21 "I know what you want, Jisu," she said, "but I'm sure you will get to like your group members.

➡ _____

22 Don't you think it's worth trying?"

➡ _____

23 I didn't really believe her, but I said, "Okay," and walked away.

➡ _____

24 The project wasn't easy from the start.

➡ _____

25 We couldn't decide on the topic for our newspaper.

➡ _____

26 I felt like giving up on the project, so I asked my friend Ryan for some advice.

➡ _____

27 "Try to understand your group members first," he said.

➡ _____

28 So I carefully watched my group members.

➡ _____

29 And I came across some amazing facts about them.

➡ _____

30 Lina read a lot of Japanese comic books, so she was an expert on Japanese culture.

➡ _____

31 Inho's Korean sounded a bit different, but that was because he lived in Argentina when he was young.

➡ _____

32 He knew a lot about Argentina and its soccer.

➡ _____

33 Min's mom was Vietnamese, and Min used to spend some time in Vietnam.

➡ _____

34 He read a lot of history books and loved to talk about Vietnam and its history.

➡ _____

35 I thought of the perfect topic for our group.

➡ _____

36 We decided to write about world culture.

➡ _____

37 I had Lina introduce Japanese culture.

➡ _____

38 Inho wrote about Argentina and its soccer, and Min covered Vietnamese culture and its history.

➡ _____

39 I was in charge of editing the whole newspaper.

➡ _____

40 Our newspaper project was a great success.

➡ _____

41 We received an A⁺, and my group members became my best friends.

➡ _____

42 I will end my story with this saying.

➡ _____

43 Don't judge a book by its cover.

➡ _____

44 Read it.

➡ _____

45 It might turn into your favorite book.

➡ _____

※ 다음 괄호 안의 단어들을 우리말에 맞도록 바르게 배열하시오.

1 (I / How / My / Met / Friends / Best)
➡ _____

2 (Choi, / Mrs. / social / my / teacher, / studies / an / made / announcement. / important)
➡ _____

3 (will / "you / a / create / newspaper / groups. / in)
➡ _____

4 (out / check / new / your / members." / group)
➡ _____

5 (Choi / Mrs. / calling / started / the / out / names / the / of / in / students / group. / each)
➡ _____

6 (a / after / while, / name / my / called. / was)
➡ _____

7 (4, / "group / Jisu...")
➡ _____

8 (will / "who / in / be / group? / my // wondered. / I)
➡ _____

9 (Choi / Mrs. / continued, / "Lina, and / Min." / Inho,)
➡ _____

10 (couldn't / I / my / believe / ears.)
➡ _____

11 (didn't / I / anyone / know / that / in / group.)
➡ _____

12 (felt / I / crying / like / I / when / sat / my / with / members. / group)
➡ _____

13 (didn't / we / anything / have / common. / in)
➡ _____

14 (was / Lina / drawing / always / by / something / herself.)
➡ _____

15 (never / Inho / anything, / said / and / only / his / seemed / interest / be / to / soccer.)
➡ _____

1 가장 좋은 친구들을 어떻게 만나게 되었나

2 사회 선생님인 최 선생님께서 중요한 발표를 했다.

3 "모둠별로 신문을 만들 겁니다.

4 새 모둠의 구성원을 확인하세요."

5 최 선생님은 각 모둠의 학생들 이름을 부르기 시작했다.

6 잠시 후, 내 이름이 불렸다.

7 "모둠 4. 지수…"

8 "내 모둠의 구성원들은 누굴까?" 나는 궁금했다.

9 최 선생님은 계속 말씀하셨다. "Lina, 인호, 그리고 Min."

10 나는 내 귀를 믿을 수 없었다.

11 나는 그 모둠에 아는 사람이 하나도 없었다.

12 모둠 구성원들과 함께 앉을 때 나는 울고 싶었다.

13 우리는 공통점이 하나도 없었다.

14 Lina는 항상 혼자서 무언가를 그리고 있었다.

15 인호는 아무 말도 하지 않았으며 그의 유일한 관심은 축구 같았다.

16 (was / Min / smart, / he / but / always / his / had / nose / in / book. / a)
➡ _____

17 (couldn't / I / thinking / help / unlucky / how / was. / I)
➡ _____

18 (decided / I / convince / to / Choi / Mrs. / I / that / should / with / be / friends. / my)
➡ _____

19 (she / "maybe / let / would / change / me / group," / the / thought. / I)
➡ _____

20 (before / but / could / I / anything, / say / gently / she / her / placed / hand / on / shoulder. / my)
➡ _____
_____

21 (know / "I / you / what / want, / she / Jisu," / said, / "but / sure / I'm / will / you / to / get / like / group / your / members.)
➡ _____
_____

22 (you / don't / it's / think / trying?" / worth)
➡ _____

23 (didn't / I / believe / really / her, / I / but / said, / and / "Okay," / away. / walked)
➡ _____
_____

24 (project / the / easy / wasn't / the / from / start.)
➡ _____

25 (couldn't / we / on / decide / topic / the / our / for / newspaper.)
➡ _____

26 (felt / I / giving / like / on / up / project, / the / I / so / my / asked / Ryan / friend / some / for / advice.)
➡ _____
_____

27 (to / "try / understand / group / your / first," / members / said. / he)
➡ _____

28 (I / so / watched / carefully / group / my / members.)
➡ _____

29 (I / and / across / came / amazing / some / about / facts / them.)
➡ _____

30 (read / Lina / lot / a / Japanese / of / books, / comic / she / so / an / was / on / expert / culture. / Japanese)
➡ _____
_____

16 Min은 영리했지만, 그는 항상 책만 보고 있었다.

17 나는 내가 참으로 불행하다는 생각을 하지 않을 수 없었다.

18 나는 내 친구들과 함께하겠다고 최 선생님을 설득하기로 했다.

19 "어쩌면 내가 모둠을 바꿀 수 있게 허락해 주실지 몰라." 나는 생각했다.

20 하지만 내가 말을 꺼내기도 전에. 선생님은 부드럽게 내 어깨에 손을 얹으셨다.

21 "네가 원하는 것이 뭔지 알아. 지수야." 선생님은 말했다. "하지만 네가 너의 모둠원들을 좋아하게 될 것이라고 확신해.

22 시도할 만한 가치가 있다고 생각하지 않니?"

23 나는 선생님의 말씀을 진짜로 믿진 않았지만, "네."라고 말하고 돌아섰다.

24 프로젝트는 처음부터 쉽지 않았다.

25 우리는 신문의 주제를 결정할 수 없었다.

26 나는 프로젝트를 포기하고 싶었고. 그래서 친구 Ryan에게 조언을 구했다.

27 "먼저 모둠 구성원들을 이해하려고 노력해 봐." 그는 말했다.

28 그래서 나는 모둠의 구성원들을 신중하게 살펴보았다.

29 그리고 그들에 관한 놀라운 사실들을 발견했다.

30 Lina는 일본의 만화책을 많이 읽었고, 그래서 일본 문화에 관해서는 전문가였다.

31 (Korean / Inho's / a / sounded / different, / bit / that / but / because / was / lived / he / Argentina / in / he / when / young. / was)
➡ _____
_____

32 (knew / he / lot / a / about / and / Argentina / soccer. / its)
➡ _____

33 (mom / Min's / Vietnamese, / was / Min / and / to / used / some / spend / time / Vietnam. / in)
➡ _____

34 (read / he / lot / a / history / of / books / loved / and / talk / to / Vietnam / about / and / history. / its)
➡ _____
_____

35 (thought / I / the / of / topic / perfect / our / for / group.)
➡ _____

36 (decided / we / write / to / world / about / culture.)
➡ _____

37 (had / I / introduce / Lina / culture. / Japanese)
➡ _____

38 (wrote / Inho / Argentina / about / its / and / soccer, / Min / and / covered / culture / Vietnamese / and / history. / its)
➡ _____
_____

39 (was / I / charge / in / editing / of / whole / the / newspaper.)
➡ _____

40 (newspaper / our / was / project / a / success. / great)
➡ _____

41 (received / we / A⁺, / an / my / and / members / group / became / my / friends. / best)
➡ _____

42 (will / I / my / end / with / story / saying. / this)
➡ _____

43 (judge / don't / book / a / its / by / cover.)
➡ _____

44 (it. / read)
➡ _____

45 (might / it / into / turn / favorite / your / book.)
➡ _____

31 인호의 한국어 발음은 조금 다르게 들렸는데, 그 이유는 어렸을 때 아르헨티나에서 살았기 때문이었다.

32 그는 아르헨티나와 그 나라의 축구에 관해 많은 것을 알고 있었다.

33 Min의 엄마는 베트남 사람이었고, Min은 베트남에서 약간의 시간을 보냈다.

34 그는 많은 역사책을 읽었으며, 베트남과 그 역사에 관해 이야기하는 것을 좋아했다.

35 나는 우리 모둠을 위한 완벽한 주제를 생각해 냈다.

36 우리는 세계 문화에 관해 글을 쓰기로 했다.

37 나는 Lina가 일본 문화를 소개하도록 했다.

38 인호는 아르헨티나와 축구에 관해 썼고, Min은 베트남 문화와 역사를 다뤘다.

39 나는 신문 전체를 편집하는 역할을 맡았다.

40 우리의 신문 프로젝트는 대성공이었다.

41 우리는 A⁺를 받았고, 모둠 구성원들은 나의 가장 친한 친구가 되었다.

42 나는 이 말로 내 이야기를 끝내려고 한다.

43 책을 표지로 판단하지 마라.

44 그것을 읽어라.

45 그것은 네가 가장 좋아하는 책이 될 수도 있다.

※ 다음 우리말을 영어로 쓰시오.

1 가장 좋은 친구들을 어떻게 만나게 되었나

➡ _____

2 사회 선생님인 최 선생님께서 중요한 발표를 했다.

➡ _____

3 "모둠별로 신문을 만들 겁니다.

➡ _____

4 새 모둠의 구성원을 확인하세요."

➡ _____

5 최 선생님은 각 모둠의 학생들 이름을 부르기 시작했다.

➡ _____

6 잠시 후, 내 이름이 불렸다.

➡ _____

7 "모둠 4, 지수…"

➡ _____

8 "내 모둠의 구성원들은 누굴까?" 나는 궁금했다.

➡ _____

9 최 선생님은 계속 말씀하셨다. "Lina, 인호, 그리고 Min."

➡ _____

10 나는 내 귀를 믿을 수 없었다.

➡ _____

11 나는 그 모둠에 아는 사람이 하나도 없었다.

➡ _____

12 모둠 구성원들과 함께 앉을 때 나는 울고 싶었다.

➡ _____

13 우리는 공통점이 하나도 없었다.

➡ _____

14 Lina는 항상 혼자서 무언가를 그리고 있었다.

➡ _____

15 인호는 아무 말도 하지 않았으며 그의 유일한 관심은 축구 같았다.

➡ _____

16▷ Min은 영리했지만, 그는 항상 책만 보고 있었다.

➡ _____

17▷ 나는 내가 참으로 불행하다는 생각을 하지 않을 수 없었다.

➡ _____

18▷ 나는 내 친구들과 함께하겠다고 최 선생님을 설득하기로 했다.

➡ _____

19▷ "어쩌면 내가 모둠을 바꿀 수 있게 허락해 주실지 몰라." 나는 생각했다.

➡ _____

20▷ 하지만 내가 말을 꺼내기도 전에, 선생님은 부드럽게 내 어깨에 손을 얹으셨다.

➡ _____

21▷ "네가 원하는 것이 뭔지 알아, 지수야." 선생님은 말했다. "하지만 네가 너의 모둠원들을 좋아하게
될 것이라고 확신해.

➡ _____

22▷ 시도할 만한 가치가 있다고 생각하지 않니?"

➡ _____

23▷ 나는 선생님의 말씀을 진짜로 믿진 않았지만, "네."라고 말하고 돌아섰다.

➡ _____

24▷ 프로젝트는 처음부터 쉽지 않았다.

➡ _____

25▷ 우리는 신문의 주제를 결정할 수 없었다.

➡ _____

26▷ 나는 프로젝트를 포기하고 싶었고, 그래서 친구 Ryan에게 조언을 구했다.

➡ _____

27▷ "먼저 모둠 구성원들을 이해하려고 노력해 봐." 그는 말했다.

➡ _____

28▷ 그래서 나는 모둠의 구성원들을 신중하게 살펴보았다.

➡ _____

29▷ 그리고 그들에 관한 놀라운 사실들을 발견했다.

➡ _____

30▷ Lina는 일본의 만화책을 많이 읽었고, 그래서 일본 문화에 관해서는 전문가였다.

➡ _____

31 인호의 한국어 발음은 조금 다르게 들렸는데, 그 이유는 어렸을 때 아르헨티나에서 살았기 때문이었다.

➡ _____

_____

32 그는 아르헨티나와 그 나라의 축구에 관해 많은 것을 알고 있었다.

➡ _____

33 Min의 엄마는 베트남 사람이었고, Min은 베트남에서 약간의 시간을 보냈다.

➡ _____

34 그는 많은 역사책을 읽었으며, 베트남과 그 역사에 관해 이야기하는 것을 좋아했다.

➡ _____

35 나는 우리 모둠을 위한 완벽한 주제를 생각해냈다.

➡ _____

36 우리는 세계 문화에 관해 글을 쓰기로 했다.

➡ _____

37 나는 Lina가 일본 문화를 소개하도록 했다.

➡ _____

38 인호는 아르헨티나와 축구에 관해 썼고, Min은 베트남 문화와 역사를 다뤘다.

➡ _____

39 나는 신문 전체를 편집하는 역할을 맡았다.

➡ _____

40 우리의 신문 프로젝트는 대성공이었다.

➡ _____

41 우리는 A⁺를 받았고, 모둠 구성원들은 나의 가장 친한 친구가 되었다.

➡ _____

42 나는 이 말로 내 이야기를 끝내려고 한다.

➡ _____

43 책을 표지로 판단하지 마라.

➡ _____

44 그것을 읽어라.

➡ _____

45 그것은 네가 가장 좋아하는 책이 될 수도 있다.

➡ _____

※ 다음 우리말과 일치하도록 빈칸에 알맞은 말을 쓰시오.

Reading and Do

1. Inho's Korean sounded _____ _____ _____, but that was _____ he _____ _____ Argentina when he was young.
2. He knew _____ _____ about Argentina and _____ _____.
3. Min's mom was _____, and Min _____ _____ _____ _____ _____ in Vietnam.
4. He read _____ _____ _____ history books and _____ _____ _____ _____ Vietnam and its history.

After You Read B

1. Lina: I am _____ _____ on Japanese culture _____ I read _____ _____ _____ _____ comic books.
2. I _____ _____ _____ _____ _____ _____ about Japan.
3. Inho: My Korean may _____ _____ _____ _____ because I lived in Argentina _____ _____ _____ _____ _____.
4. I'm so glad our group _____ _____ _____ _____ _____ _____.
5. Min: I always _____ _____ _____ _____ _____ _____.
6. _____, I _____ _____ _____ Vietnam _____ I _____ some _____ _____ _____.
7. So, I _____ _____ _____ _____ and its history.
8. Jisu: _____ _____, I _____ our group members _____ nothing _____ _____.
9. But now I'm glad I didn't _____ Mrs. Choi _____ _____ my group.
10. I _____ the _____ _____.

Check Your Progress 2

1. _____ you _____ _____ your school?
2. Well, _____ _____ _____ _____ _____ _____, I wasn't.
3. I _____ know _____ in my class, and I was _____ _____ _____ _____ _____ _____ _____.
4. So I _____ _____ _____ _____.
5. But _____ _____ _____ sports day.
6. _____ sports day, _____ _____ _____ my class _____ _____ _____ _____ the games.
7. I'm _____ _____ _____ sports, but I _____ _____ _____.
8. I _____ _____ my classmates _____ the games.
9. _____ the day _____ _____, I was friends _____ my classmates.
10 Now, I _____ _____ _____ _____ my school life.

---

1. 인호의 한국어 발음은 조금 다르게 들렸는데, 그 이유는 어렸을 때 아르헨티나에서 살았기 때문이었다.
2. 그는 아르헨티나와 그 나라의 축구에 관해 많은 것을 알고 있었다.
3. Min의 엄마는 베트남 사람이었고, Min은 베트남에서 약간의 시간을 보냈다.
4. 그는 많은 역사책을 읽었으며, 베트남과 그 역사에 관해 이야기하는 것을 좋아했다.

1. Lina: 나는 일본의 만화책을 많이 읽었기 때문에 일본 문화에 관해서는 전문가이다.
2. 나는 일본에 관해 글을 쓰는 역할을 맡았다.
3. 인호: 나는 어렸을 때 아르헨티나에서 살았기 때문에 한국어 발음은 조금 다르게 들릴 수 있다.
4. 나는 우리 모둠이 프로젝트에 대해 A⁺를 받아서 너무 기쁘다.
5. Min: 나는 항상 역사책만 본다.
6. 또한 나는 베트남에서 약간의 시간을 보냈기 때문에 베트남에 대해서 잘 알고 있다.
7. 그래서 나는 베트남 문화와 역사를 다뤘다.
8. 지수: 처음에 나는 우리 모둠 구성원들이 공통점이 하나도 없다고 생각했다.
9. 그러나 이제 나는 내 모둠을 바꿔 달라고 최 선생님을 설득하지 않은 것이 기쁘다.
10. 나는 신문 전체를 편집했다.

1. 너는 학교에 만족하니?
2. 음, 올해 초에 나는 만족하지 않았어.
3. 나는 반에 아는 사람이 없었고, 나는 너무 내성적이어서 아무에게도 말을 걸지 못했어.
4. 그래서 늘 혼자였어.
5. 그러나 체육대회 이후에 모든 것이 바뀌었어.
6. 체육대회 하는 날 우리 반 학생들은 모두 이기기 위하여 최선을 다했어.
7. 나는 운동을 잘 못했지만 나는 최선을 다했어.
8. 나는 우리 반 학생들이 경기할 때 응원을 했어.
9. 그 날이 끝났을 때 나는 학급 친구들과 친구가 되었어.
10. 이제는 나는 학교 생활에 매우 만족해.

※ 다음 우리말을 영어로 쓰시오.

Reading and Do

1. 인호의 한국어 발음은 조금 다르게 들렸는데, 그 이유는 어렸을 때 아르헨티나에서 살았기 때문이었다.
➡

2. 그는 아르헨티나와 그 나라의 축구에 관해 많은 것을 알고 있었다.
➡

3. Min의 엄마는 베트남 사람이었고, Min은 베트남에서 약간의 시간을 보냈다.
➡

4. 그는 많은 역사책을 읽었으며, 베트남과 그 역사에 관해 이야기하는 것을 좋아했다.
➡

After You Read B

1. Lina: 나는 일본의 만화책을 많이 읽었기 때문에 일본 문화에 관해서는 전문가이다.
➡

2. 나는 일본에 관해 글을 쓰는 역할을 맡았다.
➡

3. 인호: 나는 어렸을 때 아르헨티나에서 살았기 때문에 한국어 발음은 조금 다르게 들릴 수 있다.
➡

4. 나는 우리 모둠이 프로젝트에 대해 A⁺를 받아서 너무 기쁘다.
➡

5. Min: 나는 항상 역사책만 본다.
➡

6. 또한 나는 베트남에서 약간의 시간을 보냈기 때문에 베트남에 대해서 잘 알고 있다.
➡

7. 그래서 나는 베트남 문화와 역사를 다뤘다.
➡

8. 지수: 처음에 나는 우리 모둠 구성원들이 공통점이 하나도 없다고 생각했다.
➡

9. 그러나 이제 나는 내 모둠을 바꿔 달라고 최 선생님을 설득하지 않은 것이 기쁘다.
➡

10. 나는 신문 전체를 편집했다.
➡

Check Your Progress 2

1. 너는 학교에 만족하니?
➡

2. 음, 올해 초에 나는 만족하지 않았어.
➡

3. 나는 반에 아는 사람이 없었고 나는 너무 내성적이어서 아무에게도 말을 걸지 못했어.
➡

4. 그래서 늘 혼자였어.
➡

5. 그러나 체육대회 이후에 모든 것이 바뀌었어.
➡

6. 체육대회 하는 날 우리 반 학생들은 모두 이기기 위하여 최선을 다했어.
➡

7. 나는 운동을 잘 못하지만 나는 최선을 다했어.
➡

8. 나는 우리 반 학생들이 경기할 때 응원을 했어.
➡

9. 그 날이 끝났을 때 나는 학급 친구들과 친구가 되었어.
➡

10. 이제는 나는 학교 생활에 매우 만족해.
➡

※ 다음 영어를 우리말로 쓰시오.

01 prevent _____

02 charge _____

03 space _____

04 already _____

05 regularly _____

06 resource _____

07 concentrate _____

08 environmental _____

09 additional _____

10 escape _____

11 cool _____

12 alone _____

13 essential _____

14 fix _____

15 information _____

16 pay _____

17 amount _____

18 character _____

19 forest _____

20 experiment _____

21 grocery _____

22 nervous _____

23 save _____

24 conference _____

25 normally _____

26 pot _____

27 price _____

28 reduce _____

29 unique _____

30 truth _____

31 waste _____

32 rooftop _____

33 consider _____

34 thickness _____

35 by oneself _____

36 had better ~ _____

37 brush off _____

38 be in danger _____

39 come up with _____

40 have no choice _____

41 stick to ~ _____

42 the same as ~ _____

43 be worth -ing _____

※ 다음 우리말을 영어로 쓰시오.

01	가격	22	자원
02	줄이다	23	필수적인
03	지불하다	24	불안한
04	글자, 성격	25	옹달샘
05	이미, 벌써	26	두께
06	숲	27	실험
07	충전하다	28	보통
08	양	29	추가적인
09	회의, 발표회	30	벗어나다, 탈출하다
10	독특한	31	가로막다
11	낭비	32	규칙적으로
12	옥상	33	사실, 진실
13	절약하다, 아끼다	34	환경의
14	공간, 우주	35	집어 들다
15	혼자 있는	36	생각해 내다
16	전체의	37	잠을 자지 않고 깨어 있다
17	식히다	38	혼자서
18	식료품	39	결코 ~ 아닌
19	데우다; 열	40	A가 ~하지 못하게 하다
20	집중하다	41	선택의 여지가 없다
21	고려하다	42	~에 달라붙다
		43	위험에 처하다

※ 다음 영영풀이에 알맞은 단어를 <보기>에서 골라 쓴 후, 우리말 뜻을 쓰시오.

1 _____ : the upper surface of a roof: _____

2 _____ : extremely important and necessary: _____

3 _____ : to go away from a place or a person: _____

4 _____ : to put something with something else: _____

5 _____ : worried or frightened about something: _____

6 _____ : without any friends or people you know: _____

7 _____ : the foods eaten or prepared for eating at one time: _____

8 _____ : to give someone money for something you buy: _____

9 _____ : a thick growth of trees and bushes that covers a large area: _____

10 _____ : not to be used in a way that is effective, useful, or sensible: _____

11 _____ : to repair something that is broken or not working properly: _____

12 _____ : something such as useful land, or minerals such as oil or coal: _____

13 _____ : to think very carefully about something that you are doing: _____

14 _____ : facts or details that tell you something about a situation, person, event, etc.: _____

15 _____ : to think about something carefully, especially before making a choice or decision: _____

16 _____ : to do something in order to find out whether something really is correct, true, or in good condition: _____

보기			
fix	waste	leave	pay
check	resource	meal	add
forest	consider	rooftop	information
concentrate	alone	essential	nervous

※ 다음 우리말과 일치하도록 빈칸에 알맞은 말을 쓰시오.

Everyday English 1 A-2(1)

B: You _____ _____. What's the _____?

G: I _____ my brother's _____. He _____ the watch so _____.

B: If I _____ you, I'd _____ _____ the _____.

G: I _____ I have _____ _____.

B: 걱정 있어 보여. 무슨 일 있니?
G: 내 동생 시계를 잃어버렸어. 그는 그 시계를 무척 좋아하는데.
B: 내가 너라면 그에게 사실대로 말하겠어.
G: 선택의 여지가 없는 것 같아.

Everyday English 1 A-2(2)

G: Oh, it's too _____ for me to _____ _____ _____.

B: Did you _____ _____ _____ last night?

G: Yeah, I just couldn't _____ well _____ _____.

B: _____ I _____ you, I'd _____ some _____ air before the next class _____.

G: 아, 나는 수업 시간에 집중하기가 너무 어려워.
B: 어젯밤에 늦게까지 안 잤니?
G: 응, 어젯밤에 잠을 잘 못 잤어.
B: 내가 너라면 다음 수업이 시작하기 전에 맑은 공기를 좀 마실 거야.

Everyday English 1 B

W: Jihu, _____ are you _____? It _____ _____ a bag _____ of fruit!

B: Yes, I _____ to a _____ store.

W: _____ me _____. Why did you _____ the apples?

B: I just _____ them _____ they were really _____.

W: We _____ have a bag of _____ at home! It's _____ a _____ of _____!

B: Oh, I didn't know that.

W: _____ I _____ you, I'd _____ what I have _____ before I _____ _____.

B: Yes, you're _____.

W: And then I'd _____ a shopping list _____ on that _____.

B: Okay, I'll _____ that next time, Mom.

W: 지후야, 무엇을 들고 있니? 마치 과일로 가득 찬 가방 같은데!
B: 네, 식료품점에 갔었어요.
W: 어디 보자. 사과를 왜 샀니?
B: 사과가 정말 싸서 그냥 샀어요.
W: 집에 이미 사과 한 봉지가 있어! 이건 정말 돈 낭비야!
B: 오, 그건 몰랐어요.
W: 내가 너라면 쇼핑을 가기 전에 무엇이 있는지 먼저 확인할 거야.
B: 네, 엄마 말씀이 맞아요.
W: 그러고 나서 그 정보를 바탕으로 쇼핑 리스트를 만들 거야.
B: 알겠어요, 다음에는 그렇게 할게요, 엄마.

Everyday English 2 A-2(1)

B: I keep _____ this _____ _____ _____ again and again.

G: I _____ the same problem _____ my computer.

B: Oh, then, do you know _____ _____ _____ this?

G: You _____ _____ _____ a program.

B: 나는 계속해서 이런 종류의 메시지를 받고 있어.
G: 내 컴퓨터에도 같은 문제가 있었어.
B: 오, 그럼, 이것을 고치는 법을 아니?
G: 어떤 프로그램을 내려받아야 해.

Everyday English 2 B

M: Do you know _____ to _____ a good _____? First, you should _____ the price of a new refrigerator. How much can you _____ on your refrigerator? The question _____ a few options for you. Next, you should _____ _____ its size. You might think that _____ ones are better. But if it's _____ big, you will _____ space and _____. _____ _____ choose the _____ size for you. The last thing you have to _____ is _____ _____ energy it uses. When you _____ at the refrigerator, there is a sticker. Choose a refrigerator with a greener _____ as it _____ _____ energy.

In Real Life

Inho: Lina, you are not _____ your phone. _____ I _____ you, I'd _____ the plug _____.

Lina: Why? I'll use the _____ later. _____ it that _____.

Inho: But you are _____ _____.

Lina: It's only _____ _____ _____.

Inho: _____, if we _____ _____ a year's _____ power, it is the same as the _____ of electricity we _____ _____ for a month.

Lina: Oh, I didn't know that.

Inho: Yeah, _____ _____ a lot of _____ like that _____ we waste _____ in our _____ _____.

Lina: Do you know _____ to _____ energy in other _____?

Inho: I hear that there's going to be an energy-saving _____ at school next week.

Lina: _____ we should _____ _____!

Check Your Progress 1

G: Do you know how to be _____ _____ _____ _____?

B: Oh, did you _____ _____ _____ them?

G: Yeah, I _____ that _____ them is really _____. But it is _____ hard to _____ all the _____.

B: If I were you, I'd try to _____ how each _____ is made first.

G: _____ do you _____?

B: _____ _____, look at this _____. A human is _____ next to a tree.

G: Oh, I see. Now I can easily _____ what the character _____ like.

M: 여러분은 좋은 냉장고를 선택하는 방법을 알고 계시나요? 우선, 새 냉장고의 가격을 고려해야 합니다. 냉장고에 얼마나 쓸 수 있나요? 그 질문은 여러분에게 몇 가지 선택지를 남겨 줍니다. 다음으로, 냉장고의 크기를 생각해야 합니다. 더 큰 것이 더 좋다고 생각할지도 모릅니다. 하지만 너무 크면 공간과 에너지를 낭비하게 될 것입니다. 여러분에게 맞는 사이즈를 고르도록 하세요. 마지막으로 고려해야 할 것은 그것이 얼마나 많은 에너지를 사용하는지 고려해야 합니다. 냉장고를 보면 스티커가 붙어 있습니다. 에너지를 적게 쓰기 때문에 녹색 스티커가 붙은 냉장고를 선택하세요.

인호: Lina야, 내 전화기를 충전하고 있지 않잖아. 내가 너라면 플러그를 뽑을 거야.

Lina: 왜? 나중에 충전기를 쓸 거야. 그렇게 놔둬.

인호: 하지만 너는 전기를 낭비하고 있는 거야.

Lina: 조금밖에 안 되잖아.

인호: 실제로 만약 우리가 1년의 대기 전력을 합하면 보통 한 달 동안 쓰는 전기량과 같아.

Lina: 오, 그건 몰랐어.

인호: 그래, 그렇게 우리가 일상생활에서 모르는 사이에 낭비하는 것들이 많이 있어.

Lina: 에너지를 절약하는 다른 방법들을 아니?

인호: 다음 주에 학교에서 에너지 절약 회의가 있을 거라고 들었어.

Lina: 그럼 같이 가야겠구나!

G: 너는 어떻게 하면 한자를 잘하는지 아니?

B: 오, 너는 그것들을 배우기 시작했니?

G: 응, 그것들을 배우는 게 정말 도움이 된다고 들었어. 하지만 모든 글자를 기억하는 게 너무 힘들어.

B: 내가 너라면 먼저 각 글자가 어떻게 만들어졌는지 이해하려고 할 거야.

G: 무슨 말이니?

B: 예를 들면, 이 글자를 봐. 사람이 나무 옆에 서 있잖아.

G: 아, 알겠다. 이제 그 글자가 어떻게 생겼는지 쉽게 기억할 수 있어.

※ 다음 우리말에 맞도록 대화를 영어로 쓰시오.

Everyday English 1 A-2(1)

B: _____

G: _____

B: _____

G: _____

B: 걱정 있어 보여. 무슨 일 있니?
G: 내 동생 시계를 잃어버렸어. 그는 그 시계를 무척 좋아하는데.
B: 내가 너라면 그에게 사실대로 말하겠어.
G: 선택의 여지가 없는 것 같아.

Everyday English 1 A-2(2)

G: _____

B: _____

G: _____

B: _____

G: 아, 나는 수업 시간에 집중하기가 너무 어려워.
B: 어젯밤에 늦게까지 안 잤니?
G: 응, 어젯밤에 잠을 잘 못 잤어.
B: 내가 너라면 다음 수업이 시작하기 전에 맑은 공기를 좀 마실 거야.

Everyday English 1 B

W: _____

B: _____

W: _____

B: _____

W: _____

B: _____

W: _____

B: _____

W: _____

B: _____

W: 지후야, 무엇을 들고 있니? 마치 과일로 가득 찬 가방 같은데!
B: 네, 식료품점에 갔었어요.
W: 어디 보자. 사과를 왜 샀니?
B: 사과가 정말 싸서 그냥 샀어요.
W: 집에 이미 사과 한 봉지가 있어! 이건 정말 돈 낭비야!
B: 오, 그건 몰랐어요.
W: 내가 너라면 쇼핑을 가기 전에 무엇이 있는지 먼저 확인할 거야.
B: 네, 엄마 말씀이 맞아요.
W: 그러고 나서 그 정보를 바탕으로 쇼핑 리스트를 만들 거야.
B: 알겠어요, 다음에는 그렇게 할게요, 엄마.

Everyday English 2 A-2(1)

B: _____

G: _____

B: _____

G: _____

B: 나는 계속해서 이런 종류의 메시지를 받고 있어.
G: 내 컴퓨터에도 같은 문제가 있었어.
B: 오, 그럼, 이것을 고치는 법을 아니?
G: 어떤 프로그램을 내려받아야 해.

Everyday English 2 B

M: _____

_____

_____

_____

_____

_____

_____

M: 여러분은 좋은 냉장고를 선택하는 방법을 알고 계시나요? 우선, 새 냉장고의 가격을 고려해야 합니다. 냉장고에 얼마나 쓸 수 있나요? 그 질문은 여러분에게 몇 가지 선택지를 남겨 줍니다. 다음으로, 냉장고의 크기를 생각해야 합니다. 더 큰 것이 더 좋다고 생각할지도 모릅니다. 하지만 너무 크면 공간과 에너지를 낭비하게 될 것입니다. 여러분에게 맞는 사이즈를 고르도록 하세요. 마지막으로 고려해야 할 것은 그것이 얼마나 많은 에너지를 사용하는지 고려해야 합니다. 냉장고를 보면 스티커가 붙어 있습니다. 에너지를 적게 쓰기 때문에 녹색 스티커가 붙은 냉장고를 선택하세요.

In Real Life

Inho: _____

Lina: _____

Inho: _____

Lina: _____

Inho: _____

_____

Lina: _____

Inho: _____

_____

Lina: _____

Inho: _____

_____

Lina: _____

인호: Lina야, 내 전화기를 충전하고 있지 않잖아. 내가 너라면 플러그를 뽑을 거야.

Lina: 왜? 나중에 충전기를 쓸 거야. 그렇게 놔둬.

인호: 하지만 너는 전기를 낭비하고 있는 거야.

Lina: 조금밖에 안 되잖아.

인호: 실제로 만약 우리가 1년의 대기 전력을 합하면 보통 한 달 동안 쓰는 전기량과 같아.

Lina: 오, 그건 몰랐어.

인호: 그래, 그렇게 우리가 일상생활에서 모르는 사이에 낭비하는 것들이 많이 있어.

Lina: 에너지를 절약하는 다른 방법들을 아니?

인호: 다음 주에 학교에서 에너지 절약 회의가 있을 거라고 들었어.

Lina: 그럼 같이 가야겠구나!

Check Your Progress 1

G: _____

B: _____

G: _____

_____

B: _____

G: _____

B: _____

G: _____

G: 너는 어떻게 하면 한자를 잘하는지 아니?

B: 오, 너는 그것들을 배우기 시작했니?

G: 응, 그것들을 배우는 게 정말 도움이 된다고 들었어. 하지만 모든 글자를 기억하는 게 너무 힘들어.

B: 내가 너라면 먼저 각 글자가 어떻게 만들어졌는지 이해하려고 할 거야.

G: 무슨 말이니?

B: 예를 들면, 이 글자를 봐. 사람이 나무 옆에 서 있잖아.

G: 아, 알겠다. 이제 그 글자가 어떻게 생겼는지 쉽게 기억할 수 있어.

Step1

※ 다음 우리말과 일치하도록 빈칸에 알맞은 것을 골라 쓰시오.

1 _____ _____
A. Conference   B. Energy-Saving

2 _____ to the _____ _____.
A. Energy-Saving   B. welcome   C. Conference

3 The Earth _____ _____ _____.
A. in   B. is   C. danger

4 The _____ is _____ _____ every day.
A. dirtier   B. air   C. getting

5 _____ and more animals _____ _____.
A. dying   B. more   C. are

6 This is _____ we are _____ a _____ of _____.
A. wasting   B. because   C. energy   D. lot

7 So _____ can we _____ _____?
A. save   B. how   C. energy

8 Three _____ _____ clubs are here to _____ their
_____.
A. share   B. different   C. activities   D. environment

9 The _____ ideas we _____, the more _____ we can
_____!
A. share   B. save   C. energy   D. more

10 Jimin: _____, _____.
A. friends   B. hello

11 A _____ months ago, I was surprised to see some _____
classrooms _____ the lights _____.
A. empty   B. on   C. few   D. with

12 That's _____ right _____ _____.
A. at   B. not   C. all

13 _____ is essential _____ all students _____ _____
fewer resources at school.
A. for   B. use   C. it   D. to

14 So we have designed some _____ _____ _____ and put
them on the _____.
A. saving   B. switches   C. resource   D. stickers

---

1 에너지 절약 회의

2 에너지 절약 회의에 오신 것을 환영합니다.

3 지구는 지금 위험에 처해 있습니다.

4 공기는 매일 더러워지고 있습니다.

5 점점 더 많은 동물이 죽어가고 있습니다.

6 이것은 우리가 많은 에너지를 낭비하고 있기 때문입니다.

7 그렇다면 우리는 어떻게 에너지를 절약할 수 있을까요?

8 세 개의 다른 환경 동아리들이 그들의 활동을 공유하기 위해 여기에 있습니다.

9 우리가 더 많은 아이디어를 공유할수록, 우리는 더 많은 에너지를 절약할 수 있습니다!

10 지민: 친구들, 안녕하세요.

11 몇 달 전에, 저는 전등이 켜진 몇 개의 빈 교실을 보고 놀랐습니다.

12 그것은 전혀 옳지 않습니다.

13 모든 학생이 학교에서 더 적은 자원을 사용하는 것이 필수적입니다.

14 그래서 우리는 몇 장의 자원 절약 스티커를 디자인해서 스위치에 붙였습니다.

15 They tell us which light should be _____ on, _____ that we can _____ _____ electricity.

A. so   B. less   C. turned   D. waste

16 They also tell the _____ student who _____ the classroom to _____ _____ the lights.

A. off   B. last   C. turn   D. leaves

17 We also _____ some tickets _____ the _____ in the _____.

A. on   B. put   C. restrooms   D. mirrors

18 They help students _____ _____ _____ water.

A. to   B. not   C. waste

19 The more _____ we _____ up, the more _____ we can _____ at school.

A. resources   B. stickers   C. save   D. put

20 **Dongsu:** _____, _____.

A. everyone   B. hi

21 A lot of energy _____ _____ to _____ and _____ our school.

A. heat   B. is   C. cool   D. used

22 It is _____ for students to _____ the _____ of energy we _____.

A. amount   B. important   C. reduce   D. use

23 We did an _____ last winter and found that bubble _____ can _____ to _____ energy.

A. wrap   B. experiment   C. save   D. help

24 _____ _____ this _____.

A. at   B. look   C. chart

25 In Classroom A we _____ bubble _____ _____ the windows and in Classroom B we _____.

A. on   B. put   C. wrap   D. didn't

26 When we _____ _____ the heater, the _____ was 16 ℃ in _____ classrooms.

A. both   B. off   C. turned   D. temperature

27 Sixty minutes _____, the temperature in Classroom B _____ _____ _____ 7 ℃.

A. went   B. to   C. later   D. down

28 But _____ was 9 ℃ _____ Classroom A!

A. in   B. it

29 We learned that bubble wrap only _____ a _____ heat _____ _____ the building.

A. escape   B. lets   C. from   D. little

15 그것들은 어떤 전등이 켜질 것인지 알려 줘서, 우리는 전기를 덜 낭비할 수 있습니다.

16 그것들은 또한 교실을 떠나는 마지막 학생이 전등을 꺼야 한다고 알려 줍니다.

17 우리는 또한 화장실에 있는 거울에도 몇 장의 스티커를 붙였습니다.

18 그것들은 학생들이 물을 낭비하지 않도록 도와줍니다.

19 우리가 더 많은 스티커들을 붙일수록, 학교에서 더 많은 자원을 절약할 수 있습니다.

20 동수: 모두 안녕하세요.

21 많은 에너지가 우리 학교의 난방과 냉방을 위해 사용됩니다.

22 우리가 사용하는 에너지양을 학생들이 줄이는 것이 중요합니다.

23 우리는 지난겨울 실험을 해서 뽁뽁이가 에너지를 절약하는 데에 도움이 된다는 것을 발견했습니다.

24 이 도표를 보세요.

25 우리는 교실 A에는 창문에 뽁뽁이를 붙였고 교실 B에는 붙이지 않았습니다.

26 우리가 히터를 껐을 때, 두 교실 온도는 모두 16℃였습니다.

27 60분 뒤, 교실 B의 온도는 7℃로 내려갔습니다.

28 하지만 교실 A는 9℃였어요!

29 우리는 뽁뽁이가 오직 적은 양의 열만 건물에서 빠져나가게 한다는 것을 알았습니다.

30 _____ we started _____ _____ wrap _____ the school windows.

    A. on   B. so   C. putting   D. bubble

31 This will also _____ heat _____ _____ _____ the classroom in the summer.

    A. into   B. prevent   C. getting   D. from

32 The _____ bubble wrap we _____ on the windows, the _____ our summer will _____!

    A. cooler   B. more   C. put   D. become

33 Minwoo: _____, _____.

    A. friends   B. hello

34 We decided to _____ a garden _____ the _____ of the school to _____ energy.

    A. rooftop   B. save   C. on   D. make

35 _____ a _____ people know _____ it _____.

    A. few   B. works   C. only   D. how

36 It's _____ _____ bubble _____.

    A. like   B. wrap   C. just

37 It _____ heat _____ getting _____ and _____ of the buildings.

    A. from   B. out   C. prevents   D. in

38 So when we have _____ gardens on our buildings, we can _____ some of the energy we _____ to _____ the buildings in the summer.

    A. use   B. save   C. cool   D. rooftop

39 Also, the _____ air from the _____ garden helps to _____ the _____ city.

    A. whole   B. fresh   C. cool   D. rooftop

40 So _____ is necessary _____ us students _____ more rooftop gardens at our school!

    A. make   B. for   C. it   D. to

41 The more _____ our rooftops _____, the _____ our school will use!

    A. energy   B. beautiful   C. less   D. become

42 MC: It's very clever _____ you to _____ _____ _____ such great ideas!

    A. come   B. of   C. with   D. up

43 These are _____ _____ _____ _____ at school or _____ home.

    A. at   B. worth   C. all   D. trying

44 Thank you _____ your _____ ideas and _____!

    A. for   B. activities   C. unique

30 그래서 우리는 학교 창문에 뽁뽁이를 붙이기 시작했습니다.

31 이것이 여름에 열이 교실로 들어오는 것 또한 막아 줄 것입니다.

32 우리가 창문에 더 많은 뽁뽁이를 붙일수록, 우리의 여름도 더 시원해질 거예요!

33 민우: 안녕하세요, 친구들.

34 우리는 에너지를 절약하기 위해 학교 옥상에 정원을 만들기로 했습니다.

35 오직 몇몇 사람들만이 그것이 어떻게 작용하는지 알고 있습니다.

36 그것은 마치 뽁뽁이와 같습니다.

37 그것은 열기가 건물 안팎으로 드나드는 것을 막습니다.

38 그래서 건물에 옥상정원을 가지고 있으면, 우리는 여름에 건물을 식히기 위해 사용하는 에너지 일부를 절약할 수 있습니다.

39 또한, 옥상정원에서 나오는 신선한 공기는 도시 전체를 식히는 것을 도와줍니다.

40 그래서 우리 학생들이 우리 학교에 더 많은 옥상정원을 만드는 것이 필요합니다!

41 우리의 옥상이 더 아름다워질수록, 우리 학교는 에너지를 덜 사용하게 될 겁니다!

42 진행자: 이런 멋진 아이디어를 떠올리다니 여러분은 아주 똑똑하군요!

43 학교나 집에서 모두 해볼 만한 것들 입니다.

44 여러분의 고유한 아이디어와 활동에 감사합니다!

※ 다음 우리말과 일치하도록 빈칸에 알맞은 것을 골라 쓰시오.

1 _____ Conference

2 _____ _____ the _____ Conference.

3 The Earth _____ _____ _____.

4 The air is _____ _____ _____ _____.

5 _____ _____ _____ animals are dying.

6 This is _____ we _____ _____ a lot of energy.

7 So _____ can we _____ _____?

8 Three different environmental clubs are here _____ _____ _____ _____.

9 _____ _____ _____ we share, _____ _____ _____ we can _____!

10 Jimin: Hello, _____.

11 _____ _____ months ago, I was surprised to see some empty classrooms _____ _____ _____ _____.

12 That's _____ right _____ _____.

13 It is essential _____ all students _____ _____ _____ _____ at school.

14 So we have designed some _____ _____ _____ and _____ them _____ the switches.

15 They tell us which light should _____ _____ _____, _____ _____ we can waste _____ _____.

16 They also tell the _____ student who leaves the classroom _____ _____ _____ the lights.

17 We also _____ _____ _____ _____ the mirrors in the restrooms.

18 They _____ students _____ _____ _____ water.

19 _____ _____ _____ we _____ _____, _____ _____ _____ we can save at school.

20 Dongsu: Hi, _____.

21 A lot of energy _____ _____ to heat and cool our school.

22 _____ is important _____ students _____ _____ the _____ _____ _____ we use.

23 We _____ _____ _____ last winter and found that _____ _____ can _____ _____ _____ energy.

24 _____ _____ this chart.

25 In Classroom A we _____ bubble wrap _____ the windows and in Classroom B we didn't.

26 When we _____ _____ the heater, the _____ was 16 ℃ in _____ classrooms.

27 Sixty minutes _____, the temperature in Classroom B _____ _____ _____ 7 ℃.

28 But _____ was 9 ℃ in Classroom A!

29 We learned that bubble wrap only _____ a little heat _____ _____ the building.

15 그것들은 어떤 전등이 켜질 것인지 알려 줘서, 우리는 전기를 덜 낭비할 수 있습니다.

16 그것들은 또한 교실을 떠나는 마지막 학생이 전등을 꺼야 한다고 알려 줍니다.

17 우리는 또한 화장실에 있는 거울에도 몇 장의 스티커를 붙였습니다.

18 그것들은 학생들이 물을 낭비하지 않도록 도와줍니다.

19 우리가 더 많은 스티커들을 붙일수록, 학교에서 더 많은 자원을 절약할 수 있습니다.

20 동수: 모두 안녕하세요.

21 많은 에너지가 우리 학교의 난방과 냉방을 위해 사용됩니다.

22 우리가 사용하는 에너지양을 학생들이 줄이는 것이 중요합니다.

23 우리는 지난겨울 실험을 해서 뽁뽁이가 에너지를 절약하는 데에 도움이 된다는 것을 발견했습니다.

24 이 도표를 보세요.

25 우리는 교실 A에는 창문에 뽁뽁이를 붙였고 교실 B에는 붙이지 않았습니다.

26 우리가 히터를 껐을 때, 두 교실 온도는 모두 16℃였습니다.

27 60분 뒤, 교실 B의 온도는 7℃로 내려갔습니다.

28 하지만 교실 A는 9℃였어요!

29 우리는 뽁뽁이가 오직 적은 양의 열만 건물에서 빠져나가게 한다는 것을 알았습니다.

30 So we started _____ bubble wrap _____ the school windows.

31 This will also _____ heat _____ _____ _____ the classroom in the summer.

32 _____ _____ _____ _____ we _____ _____ the windows, _____ _____ our summer will become!

33 Minwoo: Hello, _____.

34 We decided _____ _____ a garden _____ _____ _____ of the school _____ _____ _____.

35 _____ _____ _____ people know _____ _____ _____.

36 _____ _____ _____ bubble wrap.

37 It _____ heat _____ getting _____ _____ _____ the buildings.

38 So when we have _____ _____ on our buildings, we can save some of the energy _____ _____ _____ _____ the buildings in the summer.

39 Also, the fresh air from the rooftop garden _____ _____ _____ the _____ _____.

40 So it _____ necessary _____ us students _____ _____ more rooftop gardens at our school!

41 _____ _____ _____ our rooftops become, _____ _____ our school will use!

42 MC: It's very _____ _____ you _____ _____ _____ such great ideas!

43 These are all _____ _____ at school or at home.

44 Thank you for your _____ ideas and _____!

30 그래서 우리는 학교 창문에 뽁뽁이를 붙이기 시작했습니다.

31 이것이 여름에 열이 교실로 들어오는 것 또한 막아 줄 것입니다.

32 우리가 창문에 더 많은 뽁뽁이를 붙일수록, 우리의 여름도 더 시원해질 거예요!

33 민우: 안녕하세요, 친구들.

34 우리는 에너지를 절약하기 위해 학교 옥상에 정원을 만들기로 했습니다.

35 오직 몇몇 사람들만이 그것이 어떻게 작용하는지 알고 있습니다.

36 그것은 마치 뽁뽁이와 같습니다.

37 그것은 열기가 건물 안팎으로 드나드는 것을 막습니다.

38 그래서 건물에 옥상정원을 가지고 있으면, 우리는 여름에 건물을 식히기 위해 사용하는 에너지 일부를 절약할 수 있습니다.

39 또한, 옥상정원에서 나오는 신선한 공기는 도시 전체를 식히는 것을 도와줍니다.

40 그래서 우리 학생들이 우리 학교에 더 많은 옥상정원을 만드는 것이 필요합니다!

41 우리의 옥상이 더 아름다워질수록, 우리 학교는 에너지를 덜 사용하게 될 겁니다!

42 진행자: 이런 멋진 아이디어를 떠올리다니 여러분은 아주 똑똑하군요!

43 학교나 집에서 모두 해볼 만한 것들 입니다.

44 여러분의 고유한 아이디어와 활동에 감사합니다!

※ 다음 문장을 우리말로 쓰시오.

1   Energy-Saving Conference

➡ _____

2   Welcome to the Energy-Saving Conference.

➡ _____

3   The Earth is in danger.

➡ _____

4   The air is getting dirtier every day.

➡ _____

5   More and more animals are dying.

➡ _____

6   This is because we are wasting a lot of energy.

➡ _____

7   So how can we save energy?

➡ _____

8   Three different environmental clubs are here to share their activities.

➡ _____

9   The more ideas we share, the more energy we can save!

➡ _____

10   Jimin: Hello, friends.

➡ _____

11   A few months ago, I was surprised to see some empty classrooms with the lights on.

➡ _____

12   That's not right at all.

➡ _____

13   It is essential for all students to use fewer resources at school.

➡ _____

14   So we have designed some resource saving stickers and put them on the switches.

➡ _____

15 They tell us which light should be turned on, so that we can waste less electricity.

➡ _____

16 They also tell the last student who leaves the classroom to turn off the lights.

➡ _____

17 We also put some stickers on the mirrors in the restrooms.

➡ _____

18 They help students not to waste water.

➡ _____

19 The more stickers we put up, the more resources we can save at school.

➡ _____

20 Dongsu: Hi, everyone.

➡ _____

21 A lot of energy is used to heat and cool our school.

➡ _____

22 It is important for students to reduce the amount of energy we use.

➡ _____

23 We did an experiment last winter and found that bubble wrap can help to save energy.

➡ _____

24 Look at this chart.

➡ _____

25 In Classroom A we put bubble wrap on the windows and in Classroom B we didn't.

➡ _____

26 When we turned off the heater, the temperature was 16 °C in both classrooms.

➡ _____

27 Sixty minutes later, the temperature in Classroom B went down to 7 °C.

➡ _____

28 But it was 9 °C in Classroom A!

➡ _____

29 We learned that bubble wrap only lets a little heat escape from the building.

➡ _____

30 So we started putting bubble wrap on the school windows.

➡ _____

31 This will also prevent heat from getting into the classroom in the summer.

➡ _____

32 The more bubble wrap we put on the windows, the cooler our summer will become!

➡ _____

33 Minwoo: Hello, friends.

➡ _____

34 We decided to make a garden on the rooftop of the school to save energy.

➡ _____

35 Only a few people know how it works.

➡ _____

36 It's just like bubble wrap.

➡ _____

37 It prevents heat from getting in and out of the buildings.

➡ _____

38 So when we have rooftop gardens on our buildings, we can save some of the energy we use to cool the buildings in the summer.

➡ _____

39 Also, the fresh air from the rooftop garden helps to cool the whole city.

➡ _____

40 So it is necessary for us students to make more rooftop gardens at our school!

➡ _____

41 The more beautiful our rooftops become, the less energy our school will use!

➡ _____

42 MC: It's very clever of you to come up with such great ideas!

➡ _____

43 These are all worth trying at school or at home.

➡ _____

44 Thank you for your unique ideas and activities!

➡ _____

※ 다음 괄호 안의 단어들을 우리말에 맞도록 바르게 배열하시오.

1 (Conference / Energy-Saving)
➡ _____

2 (to / welcome / the / Conference. / Energy-Saving)
➡ _____

3 (Earth / the / in / is / danger.)
➡ _____

4 (air / the / getting / is / every / dirtier / day.)
➡ _____

5 (and / more / animals / more / dying. / are)
➡ _____

6 (is / this / because / are / we / a / wasting / lot / energy. / of)
➡ _____

7 (how / so / we / can / energy? / save)
➡ _____

8 (different / three / clubs / environmental / here / are / share / to / activities. / their)
➡ _____

9 (more / the / we / ideas / share / more / the / we / energy / save! / can)
➡ _____

10 (Jimin: / friends. / hello,)
➡ _____

11 (few / a / ago, / months / was / I / to / surprised / some / see / classrooms / empty / the / with / on. / lights)
➡ _____
_____

12 (not / that's / at / all. / right)
➡ _____

13 (is / it / for / essential / students / all / use / to / resources / fewer / school. / at)
➡ _____

14 (we / so / designed / have / resource / some / stickers / saving / and / them / put / the / on / switches.)
➡ _____
_____

1 에너지 절약 회의

2 에너지 절약 회의에 오신 것을 환영합니다.

3 지구는 지금 위험에 처해 있습니다.

4 공기는 매일 더러워지고 있습니다.

5 점점 더 많은 동물이 죽어가고 있습니다.

6 이것은 우리가 많은 에너지를 낭비하고 있기 때문입니다.

7 그렇다면 우리는 어떻게 에너지를 절약할 수 있을까요?

8 세 개의 다른 환경 동아리들이 그들의 활동을 공유하기 위해 여기에 있습니다.

9 우리가 더 많은 아이디어를 공유할수록, 우리는 더 많은 에너지를 절약할 수 있습니다!

10 지민: 친구들, 안녕하세요.

11 몇 달 전에, 저는 전등이 켜진 몇 개의 빈 교실을 보고 놀랐습니다.

12 그것은 전혀 옳지 않습니다.

13 모든 학생이 학교에서 더 적은 자원을 사용하는 것이 필수적입니다.

14 그래서 우리는 몇 장의 자원 절약 스티커를 디자인해서 스위치에 붙였습니다.

15 (tell / they / which / us / should / light / turned / be / on, / that / so / can / we / waste / electricity. / less)
➡ _____
_____

16 (also / they / the / tell / student / last / leaves / who / classroom / the / to / off / turn / lights. / the)
➡ _____

17 (also / we / some / put / stickers / the / on / mirrors / the / in / restrooms.)
➡ _____

18 (help / they / not / students / waste / to / water.)
➡ _____

19 (more / the / we / stickers / up, / put / more / the / resources / can / we / at / save / school.)
➡ _____

20 (Dongsu: / everyone. / hi,)
➡ _____

21 (lot / a / of / is / energy / to / used / and / heat / our / cool / school.)
➡ _____

22 (is / it / for / important / to / students / the / reduce / of / amount / we / energy / use.)
➡ _____

23 (did / we / an / last / experiment / winter / and / that / found / wrap / bubble / help / can / save / to / energy.)
➡ _____
_____

24 (at / look / chart. / this)
➡ _____

25 (Classroom / in / we / A / bubble / put / on / wrap / the / and / windows / in / B / Classroom / didn't. / we)
➡ _____

26 (we / when / off / turned / heater, / the / temperature / the / 16 ℃ / was / both / in / classrooms.)
➡ _____
_____

27 (minutes / sixty / later, / temperature / the / Classroom / in / down / went / B / 7 ℃ / to)
➡ _____

28 (it! / but / 9℃ / was / Classroom / in / A!)
➡ _____

29 (learned / we / bubble / that / only / wrap / lets / heat / a / little / from / escape / building. / the)
➡ _____
_____

15 그것들은 어떤 전등이 켜질 것인지 알려 줘서, 우리는 전기를 덜 낭비할 수 있습니다.

16 그것들은 또한 교실을 떠나는 마지막 학생이 전등을 꺼야 한다고 알려 줍니다.

17 우리는 또한 화장실에 있는 거울에도 몇 장의 스티커를 붙였습니다.

18 그것들은 학생들이 물을 낭비하지 않도록 도와줍니다.

19 우리가 더 많은 스티커들을 붙일수록, 학교에서 더 많은 자원을 절약할 수 있습니다.

20 동수: 모두 안녕하세요.

21 많은 에너지가 우리 학교의 난방과 냉방을 위해 사용됩니다.

22 우리가 사용하는 에너지양을 학생들이 줄이는 것이 중요합니다.

23 우리는 지난겨울 실험을 해서 뽁뽁이가 에너지를 절약하는 데에 도움이 된다는 것을 발견했습니다.

24 이 도표를 보세요.

25 우리는 교실 A에는 창문에 뽁뽁이를 붙였고 교실 B에는 붙이지 않았습니다.

26 우리가 히터를 껐을 때, 두 교실 온도는 모두 16℃였습니다.

27 60분 뒤, 교실 B의 온도는 7℃로 내려갔습니다.

28 하지만 교실 A는 9℃였어요!

29 우리는 뽁뽁이가 오직 적은 양의 열만 건물에서 빠져나가게 한다는 것을 알았습니다.

30 (we / so / putting / started / wrap / bubble / the / on / windows. / school)

➡ _____

31 (will / this / prevent / also / from / heat / into / getting / the / in / classroom / summer. / the)

➡ _____

32 (more / the / wrap / bubble / put / we / the / on / windows, / cooler / the / summer / our / become! / will)

➡ _____
_____

33 (Minwoo: / friends. / hello,)

➡ _____

34 (decided / we / make / to / garden / a / the / on / of / rooftop / school / the / save / to / energy.)

➡ _____
_____

35 (a / only / people / few / how / know / works. / it)

➡ _____

36 (just / it's / bubble / like / wrap.)

➡ _____

37 (prevents / it / from / heat / in / getting / and / of / out / buildings. / the)

➡ _____

38 (when / so / have / we / gardens / rooftop / our / on / buildings, / can / we / save / of / some / the / we / energy / to / use / cool / buildings / the / in / summer. / the)

➡ _____

39 (the / also, / air / fresh / the / from / garden / rooftop / to / helps / cool / the / city. / whole)

➡ _____

40 (it / so / necessary / is / us / for / to / students / more / make / gardens / rooftop / at / school! / our)

➡ _____
_____

41 (more / the / our / beautiful / become, / rooftops / less / the / our / energy / school / use! / will)

➡ _____
_____

42 (MC: / very / it's / of / clever / you / come / to / with / up / great / such / ideas!)

➡ _____

43 (are / these / worth / all / at / trying / school / or / home. / at)

➡ _____

44 (you / thank / your / for / ideas / unique / activities! / and)

➡ _____

30 그래서 우리는 학교 창문에 뽁뽁이를 붙이기 시작했습니다.

31 이것이 여름에 열이 교실로 들어오는 것 또한 막아 줄 것입니다.

32 우리가 창문에 더 많은 뽁뽁이를 붙일수록, 우리의 여름도 더 시원해질 거예요!

33 민우: 안녕하세요, 친구들.

34 우리는 에너지를 절약하기 위해 학교 옥상에 정원을 만들기로 했습니다.

35 오직 몇몇 사람들만이 그것이 어떻게 작용하는지 알고 있습니다.

36 그것은 마치 뽁뽁이와 같습니다.

37 그것은 열기가 건물 안팎으로 드나드는 것을 막습니다.

38 그래서 건물에 옥상정원을 가지고 있으면, 우리는 여름에 건물을 식히기 위해 사용하는 에너지 일부를 절약할 수 있습니다.

39 또한, 옥상정원에서 나오는 신선한 공기는 도시 전체를 식히는 것을 도와줍니다.

40 그래서 우리 학생들이 우리 학교에 더 많은 옥상정원을 만드는 것이 필요합니다!

41 우리의 옥상이 더 아름다워질수록, 우리 학교는 에너지를 덜 사용하게 될 겁니다!

42 진행자: 이런 멋진 아이디어를 떠올리다니 여러분은 아주 똑똑하군요!

43 학교나 집에서 모두 해볼 만한 것들 입니다.

44 여러분의 고유한 아이디어와 활동에 감사합니다!

※ 다음 우리말을 영어로 쓰시오.

1 에너지 절약 회의

➡ _____

2 에너지 절약 회의에 오신 것을 환영합니다.

➡ _____

3 지구는 지금 위험에 처해 있습니다.

➡ _____

4 공기는 매일 더러워지고 있습니다.

➡ _____

5 점점 더 많은 동물이 죽어가고 있습니다.

➡ _____

6 이것은 우리가 많은 에너지를 낭비하고 있기 때문입니다.

➡ _____

7 그렇다면 우리는 어떻게 에너지를 절약할 수 있을까요?

➡ _____

8 세 개의 다른 환경 동아리들이 그들의 활동을 공유하기 위해 여기에 있습니다.

➡ _____

9 우리가 더 많은 아이디어를 공유할수록, 우리는 더 많은 에너지를 절약할 수 있습니다!

➡ _____

10 지민: 친구들, 안녕하세요.

➡ _____

11 몇 달 전에, 저는 전등이 켜진 몇 개의 빈 교실을 보고 놀랐습니다.

➡ _____

12 그것은 전혀 옳지 않습니다.

➡ _____

13 모든 학생이 학교에서 더 적은 자원을 사용하는 것이 필수적입니다.

➡ _____

14 그래서 우리는 몇 장의 자원 절약 스티커를 디자인해서 스위치에 붙였습니다.

➡ _____

15 그것들은 어떤 전등이 켜질 것인지 알려 줘서, 우리는 전기를 덜 낭비할 수 있습니다.

➡ _____

16 그것들은 또한 교실을 떠나는 마지막 학생이 전등을 꺼야 한다고 알려 줍니다.

➡ _____

17 우리는 또한 화장실에 있는 거울에도 몇 장의 스티커를 붙였습니다.

➡ _____

18 그것들은 학생들이 물을 낭비하지 않도록 도와줍니다.

➡ _____

19 우리가 더 많은 스티커들을 붙일수록, 학교에서 더 많은 자원을 절약할 수 있습니다.

➡ _____

20 동수: 모두 안녕하세요.

➡ _____

21 많은 에너지가 우리 학교의 난방과 냉방을 위해 사용됩니다.

➡ _____

22 우리가 사용하는 에너지양을 학생들이 줄이는 것이 중요합니다.

➡ _____

23 우리는 지난겨울 실험을 해서 뽁뽁이가 에너지를 절약하는 데에 도움이 된다는 것을 발견했습니다.

➡ _____

24 이 도표를 보세요.

➡ _____

25 우리는 교실 A에는 창문에 뽁뽁이를 붙였고 교실 B에는 붙이지 않았습니다.

➡ _____

26 우리가 히터를 껐을 때, 두 교실 온도는 모두 16℃였습니다.

➡ _____

27 60분 뒤, 교실 B의 온도는 7℃로 내려갔습니다.

➡ _____

28 하지만 교실 A는 9℃였어요!

➡ _____

29 우리는 뽁뽁이가 오직 적은 양의 열만 건물에서 빠져나가게 한다는 것을 알았습니다.

➡ _____

30 그래서 우리는 학교 창문에 뽁뽁이를 붙이기 시작했습니다.

➡ _____

31 이것이 여름에 열이 교실로 들어오는 것 또한 막아 줄 것입니다.

➡ _____

32 우리가 창문에 더 많은 뽁뽁이를 붙일수록, 우리의 여름도 더 시원해질 거예요!

➡ _____

33 민우: 안녕하세요, 친구들.

➡ _____

34 우리는 에너지를 절약하기 위해 학교 옥상에 정원을 만들기로 했습니다.

➡ _____

35 오직 몇몇 사람들만이 그것이 어떻게 작용하는지 알고 있습니다.

➡ _____

36 그것은 마치 뽁뽁이와 같습니다.

➡ _____

37 그것은 열기가 건물 안팎으로 드나드는 것을 막습니다.

➡ _____

38 그래서 건물에 옥상정원을 가지고 있으면, 우리는 여름에 건물을 식히기 위해 사용하는 에너지 일부를 절약할 수 있습니다.

➡ _____

_____

39 또한, 옥상정원에서 나오는 신선한 공기는 도시 전체를 식히는 것을 도와줍니다.

➡ _____

40 그래서 우리 학생들이 우리 학교에 더 많은 옥상정원을 만드는 것이 필요합니다!

➡ _____

41 우리의 옥상이 더 아름다워질수록, 우리 학교는 에너지를 덜 사용하게 될 겁니다!

➡ _____

42 진행자: 이런 멋진 아이디어를 떠올리다니 여러분은 아주 똑똑하군요!

➡ _____

43 학교나 집에서 모두 해볼 만한 것들입니다.

➡ _____

44 여러분의 고유한 아이디어와 활동에 감사합니다!

➡ _____

※ 다음 우리말과 일치하도록 빈칸에 알맞은 말을 쓰시오.

Communication Activity

1. A: Do you know _____ _____ _____ _____?
2. B: _____ _____ I do. _____ we use a cup _____ _____ _____ _____ _____, we can _____ _____.
3. A: That's a great idea. _____ _____ oil? Do you know _____ _____ _____ _____?
4. C: We _____ _____ oil by ….

1. A: 어떻게 물을 아끼는지 아니?
2. B: 물론이지. 양치질할 때 컵을 사용하면 물을 아낄 수 있어.
3. A: 좋은 생각이야. 기름은 어때? 기름은 어떻게 아끼는지 아니?
4. C: 우리는 기름을 ..... 아낄 수 있어.

Before You Read A

1. I _____ _____ _____ glass or plastic bottles.
2. I _____ _____ _____ when I go to _____ _____ _____.
3. I _____ the plug _____ _____ I _____ _____ _____ my computer.
4. I _____ _____ _____. (Or I _____ _____ _____.)
5. I _____ _____ the light _____ it is _____.
6. I _____ _____ _____ when I study.
7. I open the door of the refrigerator _____ _____ _____ _____ _____.
8. I _____ _____ _____ the time for _____ _____ _____.

1. 나는 유리나 플라스틱 병들을 재활용하려고 노력한다.
2. 나는 2층에 갈 때 계단을 사용한다.
3. 나는 컴퓨터를 사용하지 않을 때 플러그를 뽑는다.
4. 나는 학교에 걸어간다. (혹은 나는 학교에 자전거를 타고 간다.)
5. 나는 환할 때 불을 끈다.
6. 나는 공부할 때 헌 종이를 사용한다.
7. 나는 필요할 때만 냉장고 문을 연다.
8. 나는 샤워하는 시간을 줄이려고 노력한다.

After You Read

1. This chart _____ _____ _____ _____ _____ _____ in Classroom A and in Classroom B.
2. In Classroom A the students _____ _____ _____ _____ _____ and in Classroom B they didn't.
3. _____ the heater was _____ _____, the temperatures were _____ _____ _____ _____ _____ _____.
4. _____ _____ _____, the temperature in Classroom B _____ _____ _____ 7 ℃.
5. But the temperature in Classroom A _____ _____ _____ _____ in Classroom B. It was 9 ℃.
6. This is _____ bubble wrap only _____ _____ _____ _____ _____ from the building.

1. 이 도표는 교실 A와 B에서 온도가 어떻게 변했는지를 보여준다.
2. 교실 A에서는 학생들이 창문에 뽁뽁이를 붙였고, 교실 B에서는 붙이지 않았다.
3. 난방기가 꺼졌을 때, 온도가 양쪽 방에서 같았다.
4. 60분 뒤에 교실 B의 온도는 7도로 내려갔다.
5. 그러나 교실 A의 온도는 교실 B의 온도보다 높았다. 온도는 9도였다.
6. 이것은 뽁뽁이가 아주 작은 열만 건물에서 빠져나갈 수 있도록 했기 때문이다.

※ 다음 우리말을 영어로 쓰시오.

Communication Activity

1. A: 어떻게 물을 아끼는지 아니?
   ➡ _____

2. B: 물론이지. 양치질할 때 컵을 사용하면 물을 아낄 수 있어.
   ➡ _____

3. A: 좋은 생각이야. 기름은 어때? 기름은 어떻게 아끼는지 아니?
   ➡ _____

4. C: 우리는 기름을 ..... 아낄 수 있어.
   ➡ _____

Before You Read A

1. 나는 유리나 플라스틱 병들을 재활용하려고 노력한다.
   ➡ _____

2. 나는 2층에 갈 때 계단을 사용한다.
   ➡ _____

3. 나는 컴퓨터를 사용하지 않을 때 플러그를 뽑는다.
   ➡ _____

4. 나는 학교에 걸어간다. (혹은 나는 학교에 자전거를 타고 간다.)
   ➡ _____

5. 나는 환할 때 불을 끈다.
   ➡ _____

6. 나는 공부할 때 헌 종이를 사용한다.
   ➡ _____

7. 나는 필요할 때만 냉장고 문을 연다.
   ➡ _____

8. 나는 샤워하는 시간을 줄이려고 노력한다.
   ➡ _____

After You Read

1. 이 도표는 교실 A와 B에서 온도가 어떻게 변했는지를 보여준다.
   ➡ _____

2. 교실 A에서는 학생들이 창문에 뽁뽁이를 붙였고, 교실 B에서는 붙이지 않았다.
   ➡ _____

3. 난방기가 꺼졌을 때, 온도가 양쪽 방에서 같았다.
   ➡ _____

4. 60분 뒤에 교실 B의 온도는 7도로 내려갔다.
   ➡ _____

5. 그러나 교실 A의 온도는 교실 B의 온도보다 높았다. 온도는 9도였다.
   ➡ _____

6. 이것은 뽁뽁이가 아주 작은 열만 건물에서 빠져나갈 수 있도록 했기 때문이다.
   ➡ _____

※ 다음 영어를 우리말로 쓰시오.

01 challenge _____

02 recommendation _____

03 scenery _____

04 blame _____

05 research _____

06 century _____

07 view _____

08 result _____

09 relationship _____

10 triathlon _____

11 colorful _____

12 depression _____

13 skin _____

14 cheer _____

15 survival _____

16 disease _____

17 endure _____

18 courage _____

19 face _____

20 disability _____

21 hardship _____

22 bravely _____

23 comfortably _____

24 bright _____

25 achievement _____

26 support _____

27 depressed _____

28 cycle _____

29 tiredness _____

30 journey _____

31 touched _____

32 overcome _____

33 participant _____

34 present _____

35 be proud of _____

36 thanks to _____

37 A as well as B _____

38 give a hand _____

39 take care of _____

40 with all of one's heart _____

41 get through _____

42 participate in _____

43 not only A but also B _____

※ 다음 우리말을 영어로 쓰시오.

01	선물
02	해외에
03	감사하는
04	추천
05	다채로운
06	(기분이) 우울한
07	100년, 세기
08	성취, 달성
09	응원하다
10	피곤함
11	조사
12	지지하다
13	자전거를 타다
14	(신체적, 정신적) 장애
15	관계
16	의미 있는
17	질병
18	생존
19	요인
20	용감하게
21	참다, 견디다

22	결과
23	경치
24	밝은, 발랄한
25	피부
26	탁월한
27	여행, 여정
28	어려움, 곤란
29	극복하다
30	참가자
31	용기
32	철인 레이스
33	~부터[이후]
34	직면하다
35	포기하다
36	~을 돌보다
37	그런데
38	~을 자랑스러워하다
39	~ 덕분에
40	통과하다, 연락이 닿다
41	~에 참가하다
42	곁을 지키다, 대기하다
43	B 뿐만 아니라 A도

※ 다음 영영풀이에 알맞은 단어를 <보기>에서 골라 쓴 후, 우리말 뜻을 쓰시오.

1 _____ : to ride a bicycle: _____

2 _____ : in or to a foreign country: _____

3 _____ : still living and not dead: _____

4 _____ : a period of 100 years: _____

5 _____ : someone who is taking part in an activity or event: _____

6 _____ : something that makes life difficult or unpleasanr: _____

7 _____ : an illness affecting humans, animals, or plants, often caused by infection:

_____

8 _____ : full of bright colors or having a lot of different colors: _____

9 _____ : a very large round object in space that moves around the Sun or another

star: _____

10 _____ : to successfully control a feeling or problem that prevents you from

achieving something: _____

11 _____ : a sports competition in which competitors run, swim, and cycle long

distances: _____

12 _____ : a view of natural features such as mountains, hills, valleys, etc. that is

pleasing to look at: _____

13 _____ : something that you give to someone especially as a way of showing

affection or thanks: _____

14 _____ : a careful study of a subject, especially in order to discover new facts or

information about it: _____

15 _____ : to experience and deal with something that is painful or unpleasant,

especially without complaining: _____

16 _____ : a physical or mental condition that makes it difficult for someone to use

a part of their body properly: _____

보기	research	disability	colorful	disease
	planet	present	alive	cycle
	endure	triathlon	hardship	participant
	scenery	abroad	overcome	century

※ 다음 우리말과 일치하도록 빈칸에 알맞은 말을 쓰시오.

해석

Everyday English 1 A-1

B: _____ me. I'm _____ I'm lost. _____ you _____ me a _____?

W: Sure.

B: I _____ to buy a _____. Can you _____ me _____ _____ _____ _____ _____?

W: Sure. _____ _____ and _____ _____. The shop is _____ _____ the fruit _____.

B: Thank you very _____.

B: 실례합니다. 제가 길을 잃은 것 같아요. 도와주실 수 있을까요?
W: 물론이지.
B: 셔츠를 사고 싶은데요. 가장 가까운 상점이 어디에 있는지 알려 주실래요?
W: 물론이지. 곧장 가다가 왼쪽으로 돌아. 과일 가게 옆에 그 상점이 있어.
B: 정말 고맙습니다.

Everyday English 1 A-2

B: _____ me, I have _____ something.

W: What _____ you _____? Let me _____ you a _____.

B: Thank you. I _____ _____ my _____.

W: _____ this black _____ _____?

B: No, _____ is red.

B: 실례합니다. 제가 뭘 잃어버렸어요.
W: 무엇을 잃어버렸니? 내가 도와줄게.
B: 고맙습니다. 제 스마트폰을 잃어버렸어요.
W: 이 검정색 스마트폰이 네 거니?
B: 아니요, 제 것은 빨간색이에요.

Everyday English 1 B

W: Excuse me, I'm _____ _____ a birthday _____ for my son.

M: Oh, _____ I _____ a _____?

W: Yes, please. My _____ is 15 _____ old. Do you _____ any _____?

M: What _____ this _____ _____? It is very _____.

W: It looks _____, but my son doesn't like _____ _____.

M: _____ about this _____ colored _____?

W: It is very _____. Do you have it in a _____ size?

M: Yes, there is a large _____ here!

W: Thank you. I'll _____ _____.

W: 실례합니다만, 아들 생일 선물을 찾고 있는데요.
M: 아, 제가 도와드릴까요?
W: 네, 제 아들은 15살이에요. 추천해 주실 만한 것이 있나요?
M: 이 컬러풀한 재킷은 어떠세요? 아주 인기가 많아요.
W: 괜찮아 보이지만 제 아들은 컬러풀한 옷을 좋아하지 않아요.
M: 이 녹색 재킷은 어떠세요?
W: 아주 예쁘군요. 라지(L) 사이즈로 있나요?
M: 네, 여기 라지(L) 사이즈가 있어요!
W: 고맙습니다. 그걸로 살게요.

Everyday English 1 C

A: I have _____ my brother. I don't _____ _____ _____ _____.

B: _____ I give you a _____?

A: Yes, please.

B: What _____ your brother _____ _____?

A: He _____ short and _____ _____ _____.

A: 내 남동생을 잃어버렸어. 어떻게 하면 좋을지 모르겠어.
B: 내가 도와줄까?
A: 그래.
B: 네 남동생은 어떻게 생겼니?
A: 그는 키가 작고 갈색 머리를 하고 있어.

B: What _____ he _____?

A: He is wearing a _____ _____ and _____ _____.

B: Oh, I _____. I have _____ him.

Everyday English 2 A-1

G: I _____ I _____ visit _____.

M: _____?

G: Look at _____ _____ pictures of _____. I want to see them _____ my _____ _____, not _____ a book.

M: I'm _____ you are _____ _____ space. Let's _____ _____ this _____.

Everyday English 2 B

M: About 10 _____ ago, I was _____ by a car _____ I was _____ a bicycle at night. I _____ my left leg and _____ in the hospital _____ six months. I was _____ and couldn't _____ a reason to _____. However, my parents _____ me and _____ care of me _____ their love. Thanks to them, I was _____ to _____ the situation. _____ doing so, I found _____ that life can be _____ to everybody. Now, I'm a _____ basketball _____ and every year I _____ a campaign for people _____ need of _____. During each _____, I give a _____ about the _____ of _____ thinking. Some people _____ to be in the _____ of _____ thinking. I _____ my speech would _____ them _____ _____ _____.

In Real Life

Ryan: _____ do you _____? Can I _____ you a _____, Mom?

Mom: Yes. Can you _____ get me some _____?

Ryan: Of _____. I will also _____ you some _____ to drink.

Mom: Thank you. I _____ I _____ _____ _____ faster.

Ryan: I _____ you can, _____. By the _____, I'm _____ Mom.

Mom: What do you _____?

Ryan: When I was _____, you _____ me with all of your _____. But _____ then I didn't _____ a word of _____.

Mom: Oh, it's _____.

Ryan: I really _____ to _____ you _____ your love.

B: 그는 무엇을 입고 있니?

A: 그는 흰색 셔츠와 청바지를 입고 있어.

B: 아, 알겠다. 그를 찾았어.

G: 우주를 방문할 수 있으면 좋을 텐데.

M: 왜?

G: 이 놀라운 행성의 사진들을 봐요. 책으로 보는 것 말고 내 눈으로 이것들을 직접 보고 싶어요.

M: 네가 우주에 관심 있어서 기뻐. 이 책을 계속 읽어 보자.

M: 약 10년 전, 나는 밤에 자전거를 타다가 차에 치였습니다. 나는 왼쪽 다리를 잃고 6개월 동안 병원에 있었습니다. 나는 우울했고 살아야 할 이유를 찾을 수 없었어요. 하지만 부모님은 나를 지지해 주시고 사랑으로 돌봐 주셨습니다. 그분들 덕분에 나는 그 상황을 극복할 수 있었습니다. 그렇게 함으로써, 나는 삶이 모든 사람에게 의미 있는 것이 될 수 있다는 것을 알게 되었습니다. 지금은 휠체어 농구 선수로 매년 도움이 필요한 사람들을 위한 캠페인을 하고 있습니다. 매번 캠페인을 하는 동안, 나는 긍정적인 사고의 중요성에 대해 연설합니다. 어떤 사람들은 부정적인 생각을 하는 습관이 있는 것 같습니다. 그들이 좀 더 긍정적으로 생각하는 데 내 연설이 도움이 되었으면 좋겠습니다.

Ryan: 좀 어떠세요? 제가 도와드릴까요, 엄마?

Mom: 그래. 약을 좀 가져다줄 수 있니?

Ryan: 물론이죠. 마실 물도 좀 가져다드릴게요.

Mom: 고맙구나. 내가 더 빨리 나아지면 좋을 텐데.

Ryan: 저도 그러길 바라요. 그런데 죄송해요, 엄마.

Mom: 무슨 말이니?

Ryan: 제가 아팠을 때 엄마는 온 마음을 다해 저를 돌봐 주셨잖아요. 하지만 그때 저는 감사하다는 말 한마디도 하지 않았어요.

Mom: 오, 괜찮다.

Ryan: 엄마의 사랑에 정말 감사드리고 싶어요.

※ 다음 우리말에 맞도록 대화를 영어로 쓰시오.

Everyday English 1 A-1

B: _____

W: _____

B: _____

W: _____

B: _____

Everyday English 1 A-2

B: _____

W: _____

B: _____

W: _____

B: _____

Everyday English 1 B

W: _____

M: _____

W: _____

M: _____

W: _____

M: _____

W: _____

M: _____

W: _____

Everyday English 1 C

A: _____

B: _____

A: _____

B: _____

A: _____

해석

B: 실례합니다. 제가 길을 잃은 것 같아요. 도와주실 수 있을까요?
W: 물론이지.
B: 셔츠를 사고 싶은데요. 가장 가까운 상점이 어디에 있는지 알려 주실래요?
W: 물론이지. 곧장 가다가 왼쪽으로 돌아. 과일 가게 옆에 그 상점이 있어.
B: 정말 고맙습니다.

B: 실례합니다. 제가 뭘 잃어버렸어요.
W: 무엇을 잃어버렸니? 내가 도와줄게.
B: 고맙습니다. 제 스마트폰을 잃어버렸어요.
W: 이 검정색 스마트폰이 네 거니?
B: 아니요, 제 것은 빨간색이에요.

W: 실례합니다만, 아들 생일 선물을 찾고 있는데요.
M: 아, 제가 도와드릴까요?
W: 네, 제 아들은 15살이에요. 추천해 주실 만한 것이 있나요?
M: 이 컬러풀한 재킷은 어떠세요? 아주 인기가 많아요.
W: 괜찮아 보이지만 제 아들은 컬러풀한 옷을 좋아하지 않아요.
M: 이 녹색 재킷은 어떠세요?
W: 아주 예쁘군요. 라지(L) 사이즈로 있나요?
M: 네, 여기 라지(L) 사이즈가 있어요!
W: 고맙습니다. 그걸로 살게요.

A: 내 남동생을 잃어버렸어. 어떻게 하면 좋을지 모르겠어.
B: 내가 도와줄까?
A: 그래.
B: 네 남동생은 어떻게 생겼니?
A: 그는 키가 작고 갈색 머리를 하고 있어.

B: _____

A: _____

B: _____

B: 그는 무엇을 입고 있니?
A: 그는 흰색 셔츠와 청바지를 입고 있어.
B: 아, 알겠다. 그를 찾았어.

Everyday English 2 A-1

G: _____

M: _____

G: _____

_____

M: _____

G: 우주를 방문할 수 있으면 좋을 텐데.
M: 왜?
G: 이 놀라운 행성의 사진들을 봐요. 책으로 보는 것 말고 내 눈으로 이것들을 직접 보고 싶어요.
M: 네가 우주에 관심 있어서 기뻐. 이 책을 계속 읽어 보자.

Everyday English 2 B

M: _____

_____

_____

_____

_____

_____

_____

_____

M: 약 10년 전, 나는 밤에 자전거를 타다가 차에 치였습니다. 나는 왼쪽 다리를 잃고 6개월 동안 병원에 있었습니다. 나는 우울했고 살아야 할 이유를 찾을 수 없었어요. 하지만 부모님은 나를 지지해 주시고 사랑으로 돌봐 주셨습니다. 그분들 덕분에 나는 그 상황을 극복할 수 있었습니다. 그렇게 함으로써, 나는 삶이 모든 사람에게 의미 있는 것이 될 수 있다는 것을 알게 되었습니다. 지금은 휠체어 농구 선수로 매년 도움이 필요한 사람들을 위한 캠페인을 하고 있습니다. 매번 캠페인을 하는 동안, 나는 긍정적인 사고의 중요성에 대해 연설합니다. 어떤 사람들은 부정적인 생각을 하는 습관이 있는 것 같습니다. 그들이 좀 더 긍정적으로 생각하는 데 내 연설이 도움이 되었으면 좋겠습니다.

In Real Life

Ryan: _____

Mom: _____

Ryan: _____

Mom: _____

Ryan: _____

Mom: _____

Ryan: _____

Mom: _____

Ryan: _____

Ryan: 좀 어떠세요? 제가 도와드릴까요, 엄마?
Mom: 그래. 약을 좀 가져다줄 수 있니?
Ryan: 물론이죠. 마실 물도 좀 가져다드릴게요.
Mom: 고맙구나. 내가 더 빨리 나아지면 좋을 텐데.
Ryan: 저도 그러길 바라요. 그런데 죄송해요, 엄마.
Mom: 무슨 말이니?
Ryan: 제가 아팠을 때 엄마는 온 마음을 다해 저를 돌봐 주셨잖아요. 하지만 그때 저는 감사하다는 말 한마디도 하지 않았어요.
Mom: 오, 괜찮다.
Ryan: 엄마의 사랑에 정말 감사드리고 싶어요.

※ 다음 우리말과 일치하도록 빈칸에 알맞은 것을 골라 쓰시오.

1 LOVE IS _____ _____ _____

    A. NEED   B. YOU   C. ALL

2 _____ October 16th, 2010, Eunchong and his dad _____ _____ their first _____.

    A. in   B. on   C. participated   D. triathlon

3 It _____ _____ _____ Misari, Hanam.

    A. held   B. was   C. in

4 They _____ 1.5 km, _____ 40 km, and then _____ 10 km.

    A. cycled   B. swam   C. ran

5 This _____ was especially _____ for Eunchong's dad because he _____ to _____ or pull Eunchong during the race.

    A. difficult   B. push   C. challenge   D. had

6 Eunchong couldn't talk or walk _____ he was _____ _____ six different _____.

    A. born   B. because   C. diseases   D. with

7 His _____ was dark red and his _____ was _____ _____.

    A. hard   B. skin   C. brain   D. becoming

8 The doctor _____ he _____ not live _____ _____.

    A. would   B. long   C. said   D. for

9 But Eunchong not only is _____ _____ but also _____ first _____ in his first triathlon.

    A. place   B. alive   C. got   D. still

10 _____ _____,

    A. Eunchong,   B. Dear

11 I thank you not _____ for _____ my son but _____ for teaching me an important life _____.

    A. lesson   B. being   C. also   D. only

12 When you were a baby, people _____ you _____ _____ your _____ color.

    A. avoided   B. of   C. skin   D. because

13 I _____ _____ and wanted to _____ you _____ them.

    A. sad   B. from   C. hide   D. felt

14 Your mom hoped that you would be _____ _____ _____.

    A. no   B. born   C. disabilities   D. with

---

1 당신에게 필요한 건 사랑이 전부다

2 2010년 10월 16일, 은총이와 그의 아빠는 그들의 첫 철인 레이스에 참가했다.

3 그것은 하남의 미사리에서 열렸다.

4 그들은 1.5 km를 수영하고, 40 km 사이클을 타고, 그런 다음 10 km를 뛰었다.

5 이 도전은 은총이 아빠에게 특히 어려웠는데 경주 동안 은총이를 밀거나 끌어야 했기 때문이다.

6 은총이는 6가지 다른 질병을 갖고 태어나서 말할 수도 걸을 수도 없었다.

7 그의 피부는 어두운 붉은색이었고 그의 두뇌는 점점 굳어가고 있었다.

8 의사는 은총이가 오래 살지 못할 거라고 했다.

9 하지만 은총이는 여전히 살아 있을 뿐만 아니라 그의 첫 철인 레이스에서 1등을 했다.

10 은총이에게,

11 나는 네가 내 아들이어서뿐만 아니라 나에게 중요한 인생의 교훈을 가르쳐 주어서 고맙구나.

12 네가 아기였을 때, 사람들이 너의 피부색 때문에 너를 피했단다.

13 나는 슬펐고 너를 그들로부터 숨기고 싶었어.

14 네 엄마는 네가 장애 없이 태어나기를 바랐지.

15 She _____ _____ _____ your _____ .

    A. sickness   B. blamed   C. for   D. herself

16 But you always _____ _____ us and _____ our hands.

    A. at   B. smiled   C. held

17 You gave us _____ as _____ as _____ .

    A. hope   B. courage   C. well

18 So, I promised _____ that I would _____ the world and show you the _____ _____ of things.

    A. face   B. side   C. bright   D. myself

19 _____ then we _____ _____ our _____ .

    A. begun   B. since   C. journey   D. have

20 Do you remember _____ _____ _____ ?

    A. first   B. our   C. triathlon

21 When we began to swim, the _____ participants _____ _____ for us and _____ us go first.

    A. made   B. let   C. other   D. way

22 I _____ very _____ and _____ .

    A. thankful   B. touched   C. was

23 Some participants even _____ when we _____ _____ _____ .

    A. them   B. cried   C. by   D. passed

24 _____ we started _____ , many people _____ _____ us.

    A. for   B. cycling   C. cheered   D. when

25 But you _____ _____ _____ some strong winds and _____ .

    A. to   B. endure   C. tiredness   D. had

26 So I _____ very fast to _____ you a _____ .

    A. break   B. cycled   C. give

27 When we began _____ , your mom _____ to say, "I _____ I _____ run with you."

    A. seemed   B. could   C. running   D. wish

28 I wanted to _____ the race quickly _____ I could see her and _____ you _____ .

    A. rest   B. so   C. let   D. finish

29 So, I _____ _____ .

    A. fast   B. ran

30 When we were _____ at the _____ line, the other _____ stopped and _____ us go first.

    A. let   B. almost   C. participants D. finishing

---

15 네 엄마는 너의 병이 자신 때문이라고 자책도 했어.

16 하지만 너는 우리를 향해 항상 웃어주었고, 우리의 손을 잡아주었어.

17 너는 우리에게 희망뿐만 아니라 용기도 주었지.

18 그래서 나는 세상을 직면하고 너에게 세상의 밝은 면을 보여주겠다고 나 자신에게 약속했어.

19 그때부터 우리는 우리의 여정을 시작했지.

20 우리의 첫 철인 레이스를 기억하니?

21 우리가 수영을 시작했을 때, 다른 참가자들이 우리가 먼저 가도록 길을 만들어 줬어.

22 나는 정말 감동하였고 감사했단다.

23 몇몇 참가자들은 심지어 우리가 지나갈 때 울기도 했어.

24 우리가 사이클링을 시작했을 때, 많은 사람이 우리를 응원했지.

25 하지만 너는 강한 바람과 피곤함을 견뎌야만 했어.

26 그래서 나는 네가 쉴 수 있도록 아주 빨리 페달을 밟았어.

27 우리가 달리기 시작했을 때, 너의 엄마가 "당신과 함께 달릴 수 있으면 참 좋겠다." 라고 말하는 듯했어.

28 빨리 경주를 끝내서 너의 엄마를 보고 네가 쉬도록 하고 싶었어.

29 그래서 나는 빨리 달렸단다.

30 우리가 거의 결승선에 도착했을 때, 다른 참가자들이 멈췄고 우리가 먼저 가도록 해줬어.

31 Eunchong, you _____ _____ _____ !

    A. the   B. were   C. winner

32 I hope you could _____ how much everyone _____ _____ _____ loved you.

    A. at   B. tell   C. races   D. those

33 _____ _____ you, your mom and I _____ an important _____ .

    A. lesson   B. to   C. thanks   D. learned

34 "Love is _____ _____ _____ ."

    A. we   B. all   C. need

35 We don't ever think, "We wish Eunchong _____ _____ _____ " _____ .

    A. no   B. anymore   C. disabilities   D. had

36 _____ , we are just _____ _____ _____ you.

    A. having   B. thankful   C. instead   D. for

37 We are also happy about _____ _____ _____ _____ .

    A. other   B. things   C. little   D. many

38 _____ when we _____ _____ , we are happy.

    A. difficulties   B. even   C. face

39 That's _____ we know that we can _____ any _____ when we are _____ and love each other.

    A. overcome   B. because   C. together   D. hardships

40 _____ _____ to live happily and _____ .

    A. continue   B. let's   C. bravely

41 We will always love you and _____ _____ _____ .

    A. by   B. stand   C. you

42 Love,

43 Dad

---

31 은총아, 네가 우승자였단다!

32 아빠는 네가 그 경기에 있던 모든 사람이 너를 얼마나 사랑했는지 알았기를 바란다.

33 네 덕분에, 너의 엄마와 나는 중요한 교훈을 배웠단다.

34 "사랑이 우리가 필요한 전부다."

35 우리는 이제 더는 절대 "은총이가 장애가 없으면 좋겠다."라고 생각하지 않아.

36 대신에 우리는 너를 가진 것에 그저 감사할 뿐이야.

37 우리는 또한 많은 다른 작은 것들에 대해서도 행복해.

38 심지어 우리가 어려움에 직면할 때도, 우리는 행복하단다.

39 왜냐하면, 우리는 우리가 함께이고 서로를 사랑할 때 어떤 어려움도 극복할 수 있다는 것을 알기 때문이지.

40 우리 계속해서 행복하고 용감하게 살아가자.

41 우리는 항상 너를 사랑하고 너의 옆을 지킬게.

42 사랑하는

43 아빠가.

※ 다음 우리말과 일치하도록 빈칸에 알맞은 것을 골라 쓰시오.

1 LOVE IS _____ _____ _____

2 _____ October 16th, 2010, Eunchong and his dad _____ _____ their _____ _____.

3 It _____ _____ _____ Misari, Hanam.

4 They _____ 1.5 km, _____ 40 km, and then _____ 10 km.

5 This challenge was especially difficult for Eunchong's dad because he _____ _____ _____ _____ _____ Eunchong _____ _____ _____.

6 Eunchong couldn't talk or walk because he _____ _____ _____ _____ _____ _____.

7 His skin was dark red and his brain _____ _____ _____.

8 The doctor _____ he _____ not live _____ _____.

9 But Eunchong not only _____ _____ _____ but also _____ _____ _____ in his first triathlon.

10 _____ Eunchong,

11 I thank you _____ _____ for _____ my son _____ _____ for _____ me an important life _____.

12 When you were a baby, people _____ you _____ _____ _____ _____.

13 I _____ _____ and wanted to _____ you _____ them.

14 Your mom hoped that you would _____ _____ _____ _____ _____.

1 당신에게 필요한 건 사랑이 전부다

2 2010년 10월 16일, 은총이와 그의 아빠는 그들의 첫 철인 레이스에 참가했다.

3 그것은 하남의 미사리에서 열렸다.

4 그들은 1.5 km를 수영하고, 40 km 사이클을 타고, 그런 다음 10 km를 뛰었다.

5 이 도전은 은총이 아빠에게 특히 어려웠는데 경주 동안 은총이를 밀거나 끌어야 했기 때문이다.

6 은총이는 6가지 다른 질병을 갖고 태어나서 말할 수도 걸을 수도 없었다.

7 그의 피부는 어두운 붉은색이었고 그의 두뇌는 점점 굳어가고 있었다.

8 의사는 은총이가 오래 살지 못할 거라고 했다.

9 하지만 은총이는 여전히 살아 있을 뿐만 아니라 그의 첫 철인 레이스에서 1등을 했다.

10 은총이에게,

11 나는 네가 내 아들이어서뿐만 아니라 나에게 중요한 인생의 교훈을 가르쳐 주어서 고맙구나.

12 네가 아기였을 때, 사람들이 너의 피부색 때문에 너를 피했단다.

13 나는 슬펐고 너를 그들로부터 숨기고 싶었어.

14 네 엄마는 네가 장애 없이 태어나기를 바랐지.

15 She _____ _____ _____ your _____.

16 But you always _____ _____ us and _____ our hands.

17 You gave us courage _____ _____ _____ hope.

18 So, I promised _____ that I would _____ _____ _____ and show you the _____ _____ of things.

19 _____ then we _____ _____ our journey.

20 Do you remember _____ _____ _____?

21 When we began to swim, the other participants _____ _____ _____ us and _____ us _____ first.

22 I was very _____ and _____.

23 Some participants _____ _____ when we _____ _____ _____.

24 When we started _____, many people _____ _____ us.

25 But you _____ _____ _____ some strong _____ and _____.

26 So I cycled very fast to _____ _____ _____ _____.

27 When we began running, your mom _____ _____ say, "_____ _____ _____ _____ run _____ you."

28 I wanted to finish the race quickly _____ I could see her and _____ _____ _____.

29 So, I _____ _____.

30 When we were _____ at the _____ _____, the other participants stopped and _____ _____ _____ _____ _____.

---

15 네 엄마는 너의 병이 자신 때문이라고 자책도 했어.

16 하지만 너는 우리를 향해 항상 웃어주었고, 우리의 손을 잡아주었어.

17 너는 우리에게 희망뿐만 아니라 용기도 주었지.

18 그래서 나는 세상을 직면하고 너에게 세상의 밝은 면을 보여주겠다고 나 자신에게 약속했어.

19 그때부터 우리는 우리의 여정을 시작했지.

20 우리의 첫 철인 레이스를 기억하니?

21 우리가 수영을 시작했을 때, 다른 참가자들이 우리가 먼저 가도록 길을 만들어 줬어.

22 나는 정말 감동하였고 감사했단다.

23 몇몇 참가자들은 심지어 우리가 지나갈 때 울기도 했어.

24 우리가 사이클링을 시작했을 때, 많은 사람이 우리를 응원했지.

25 하지만 너는 강한 바람과 피곤함을 견뎌야만 했어.

26 그래서 나는 네가 쉴 수 있도록 아주 빨리 페달을 밟았어.

27 우리가 달리기 시작했을 때, 너의 엄마가 "당신과 함께 달릴 수 있으면 참 좋겠다." 라고 말하는 듯했어.

28 빨리 경주를 끝내서 너의 엄마를 보고 네가 쉬도록 하고 싶었어.

29 그래서 나는 빨리 달렸단다.

30 우리가 거의 결승선에 도착했을 때, 다른 참가자들이 멈췄고 우리가 먼저 가도록 해줬어.

31 Eunchong, you were the _____!

32 I hope you could _____ _____ _____ everyone _____ _____ _____ loved you.

33 _____ _____ you, your mom and I _____ an important _____.

34 "Love is _____ _____ _____."

35 We don't ever think, "We wish Eunchong _____ _____ _____" _____.

36 _____, we are just _____ _____ _____ you.

37 We are also happy about many _____ _____ _____.

38 _____ _____ we _____ _____, we are happy.

39 That's _____ we know that we can _____ any hardships when we _____ _____ and love _____ _____.

40 _____ _____ to live _____ and _____.

41 We will always love you and _____ _____ _____.

42 _____,

43 Dad

---

31 은총아, 네가 우승자였단다!

32 아빠는 네가 그 경기에 있던 모든 사람이 너를 얼마나 사랑했는지 알았기를 바란다.

33 네 덕분에, 너의 엄마와 나는 중요한 교훈을 배웠단다.

34 "사랑이 우리가 필요한 전부다."

35 우리는 이제 더는 절대 "은총이가 장애가 없으면 좋겠다."라고 생각하지 않아.

36 대신에 우리는 너를 가진 것에 그저 감사할 뿐이야.

37 우리는 또한 많은 다른 작은 것들에 대해서도 행복해.

38 심지어 우리가 어려움에 직면할 때도, 우리는 행복하단다.

39 왜냐하면, 우리는 우리가 함께이고 서로를 사랑할 때 어떤 어려움도 극복할 수 있다는 것을 알기 때문이지.

40 우리 계속해서 행복하고 용감하게 살아가자.

41 우리는 항상 너를 사랑하고 너의 옆을 지킬게.

42 사랑하는

43 아빠가.

※ 다음 문장을 우리말로 쓰시오.

1 LOVE IS ALL YOU NEED

➡ _____

2 On October 16th, 2010, Eunchong and his dad participated in their first triathlon.

➡ _____

3 It was held in Misari, Hanam.

➡ _____

4 They swam 1.5 km, cycled 40 km, and then ran 10 km.

➡ _____

5 This challenge was especially difficult for Eunchong's dad because he had to push or pull Eunchong during the race.

➡ _____

6 Eunchong couldn't talk or walk because he was born with six different diseases.

➡ _____

7 His skin was dark red and his brain was becoming hard.

➡ _____

8 The doctor said he would not live for long.

➡ _____

9 But Eunchong not only is still alive but also got first place in his first triathlon.

➡ _____

10 Dear Eunchong,

➡ _____

11 I thank you not only for being my son but also for teaching me an important life lesson.

➡ _____

12 When you were a baby, people avoided you because of your skin color.

➡ _____

13 I felt sad and wanted to hide you from them.

➡ _____

14 Your mom hoped that you would be born with no disabilities.

➡ _____

15 She blamed herself for your sickness.

➡ _____

16 But you always smiled at us and held our hands.

➡ _____

17 You gave us courage as well as hope.

➡ _____

18 So, I promised myself that I would face the world and show you the bright side of things.

➡ _____

19 Since then we have begun our journey.

➡ _____

20 Do you remember our first triathlon?

➡ _____

21 When we began to swim, the other participants made way for us and let us go first.

➡ _____

22 I was very touched and thankful.

➡ _____

23 Some participants even cried when we passed them by.

➡ _____

24 When we started cycling, many people cheered for us.

➡ _____

25 But you had to endure some strong winds and tiredness.

➡ _____

26 So I cycled very fast to give you a break.

➡ _____

27 When we began running, your mom seemed to say, "I wish I could run with you."

➡ _____

28 I wanted to finish the race quickly so I could see her and let you rest.

➡ _____

29 So, I ran fast.

➡ _____

30 When we were almost at the finishing line, the other participants stopped and let us go first.

➡ _____

31 Eunchong, you were the winner!

➡ _____

32 I hope you could tell how much everyone at those races loved you.

➡ _____

33 Thanks to you, your mom and I learned an important lesson.

➡ _____

34 "Love is all we need."

➡ _____

35 We don't ever think, "We wish Eunchong had no disabilities" anymore.

➡ _____

36 Instead, we are just thankful for having you.

➡ _____

37 We are also happy about many other little things.

➡ _____

38 Even when we face difficulties, we are happy.

➡ _____

39 That's because we know that we can overcome any hardships when we are together and love each other.

➡ _____

40 Let's continue to live happily and bravely.

➡ _____

41 We will always love you and stand by you.

➡ _____

42 Love,

➡ _____

43 Dad

➡ _____

※ 다음 괄호 안의 단어들을 우리말에 맞도록 바르게 배열하시오.

1 (IS / LOVE / YOU / ALL / NEED)
➡ _____

2 (October / on / 2010, / 16th, / Eunchong / his / and / participated / dad / their / in / triathlon. / first)
➡ _____
_____

3 (was / it / in / held / Hanam. / Misair,)
➡ _____

4 (swam / they / 1.5 km, / 40 km, / cycled / then / and / 10 km. / ran)
➡ _____

5 (challenge / this / especially / was / for / difficult / dad / Eunchong's / because / had / he / push / to / or / Eunchong / pull / the / during / race.)
➡ _____
_____

6 (couldn't / Eunchong / or / talk / because / walk / was / he / born / six / with / diseases. / different)
➡ _____
_____

7 (skin / his / dark / was / and / red / brain / his / was / hard. / becoming)
➡ _____

8 (doctor / the / he / said / not / would / for / live / long.)
➡ _____

9 (Eunchong / but / only / not / still / is / but / alive / also / first / got / in / place / his / triathlon. / first)
➡ _____
_____

10 (Eunchong, / Dear)
➡ _____

11 (thank / I / not / you / for / only / being / son / my / also / but / teaching / for / an / me / life / important / lesson.)
➡ _____
_____

12 (you / when / a / were / baby, / avoided / people / because / you / your / of / color. / skin)
➡ _____
_____

13 (felt / I / and / wanted / sad / hide / to / from / you / them.)
➡ _____

14 (mom / your / that / hoped / would / you / be / born / no / with / disabilties.)
➡ _____
_____

1 당신에게 필요한 건 사랑이 전부다

2 2010년 10월 16일, 은총이와 그의 아빠는 그들의 첫 철인 레이스에 참가했다.

3 그것은 하남의 미사리에서 열렸다.

4 그들은 1.5 km를 수영하고, 40 km 사이클을 타고, 그런 다음 10 km를 뛰었다.

5 이 도전은 은총이 아빠에게 특히 어려웠는데 경주 동안 은총이를 밀거나 끌어야 했기 때문이다.

6 은총이는 6가지 다른 질병을 갖고 태어나서 말할 수도 걸을 수도 없었다.

7 그의 피부는 어두운 붉은색이었고 그의 두뇌는 점점 굳어가고 있었다.

8 의사는 은총이가 오래 살지 못할 거라고 했다.

9 하지만 은총이는 여전히 살아 있을 뿐만 아니라 그의 첫 철인 레이스에서 1등을 했다.

10 은총이에게,

11 나는 네가 내 아들이어서뿐만 아니라 나에게 중요한 인생의 교훈을 가르쳐 주어서 고맙구나.

12 네가 아기였을 때, 사람들이 너의 피부색 때문에 너를 피했단다.

13 나는 슬펐고 너를 그들로부터 숨기고 싶었어.

14 네 엄마는 네가 장애 없이 태어나기를 바랐지.

15 (blamed / she / for / herself / sickness. / your)

➡ _____

16 (you / but / smiled / always / us / at / and / our / held / hands.)

➡ _____

17 (gave / you / us / as / courage / as / well / hope.)

➡ _____

18 (I / so, / myself / promised / that / would / I / face / world / the / and / you / show / bright / the / of / side / things.)

➡ _____

_____

19 (then / since / have / we / our / begun / journey.)

➡ _____

20 (you / do / our / remember / triathlon? / first)

➡ _____

21 (we / when / to / began / swim, / other / the / made / participants / way / us / for / and / us / let / first. / go)

➡ _____

_____

22 (was / I / touched / very / thankful. / and)

➡ _____

23 (participants / some / cried / even / we / when / them / passed / by.)

➡ ` _____

24 (we / when / cycling, / started / people / many / for / cheered / us.)

➡ _____

25 (you / had / but / endure / to / strong / some / and / winds / tiredness.)

➡ _____

26 (I / so / very / cycled / to / fast / you / give / break. / a)

➡ _____

27 (we / when / running, / began / mom / your / to / seemed / say, / wish / "I / could / I / run / you." / with)

➡ _____

_____

28 (wanted / I / finish / to / race / the / so / quickly / could / I / see / her / let / and / rest. / you)

➡ _____

_____

29 (I / so, / fast. / ran)

➡ _____

30 (we / when / almost / were / the / at / line, / finishing / other / the / stopped / participants / and / us / let / first. / go)

➡ _____

_____

---

15 네 엄마는 너의 병이 자신 때문 이라고 자책도 했어.

16 하지만 너는 우리를 향해 항상 웃어주었고, 우리의 손을 잡아 주었어.

17 너는 우리에게 희망뿐만 아니라 용기도 주었지.

18 그래서 나는 세상을 직면하고 너에게 세상의 밝은 면을 보여 주겠다고 나 자신에게 약속했어.

19 그때부터 우리는 우리의 여정을 시작했지.

20 우리의 첫 철인 레이스를 기억 하니?

21 우리가 수영을 시작했을 때, 다 른 참가자들이 우리가 먼저 가 도록 길을 만들어 줬어.

22 나는 정말 감동하였고 감사했단다.

23 몇몇 참가자들은 심지어 우리가 지나갈 때 울기도 했어.

24 우리가 사이클링을 시작했을 때, 많은 사람이 우리를 응원했지.

25 하지만 너는 강한 바람과 피곤 함을 견뎌야만 했어.

26 그래서 나는 네가 쉴 수 있도록 아주 빨리 페달을 밟았어.

27 우리가 달리기 시작했을 때, 너 의 엄마가 "당신과 함께 달릴 수 있으면 참 좋겠다." 라고 말 하는 듯했어.

28 빨리 경주를 끝내서 너의 엄마를 보고 네가 쉬도록 하고 싶었어.

29 그래서 나는 빨리 달렸단다.

30 우리가 거의 결승선에 도착했을 때, 다른 참가자들이 멈췄고 우 리가 먼저 가도록 해줬어.

31 (you / Eunchong, / were / winner! / the)

➡ _____

32 (hope / I / could / you / how / tell / everyone / much / those / at / loved / races / you.)

➡ _____

33 (to / thanks / you, / mom / your / I / and / learned / important / an / lesson.)

➡ _____

34 (is / "love / all / need." / we)

➡ _____

35 (don't / we / think, / ever / "we / Eunchong / wish / no / had / anymore. / disabilities")

➡ _____

36 (we / instead, / are / just / for / thankful / you. / having)

➡ _____

37 (are / we / happy / also / many / about / little / other / things.)

➡ _____

38 (when / even / face / we / difficulties, / are / we / happy.)

➡ _____

39 (because / that's / know / we / that / can / we / overcome / hardships / any / we / when / together / are / love / and / other. / each)

➡ _____

➡ _____

40 (continue / let's / live / to / bravely. / and / happily)

➡ _____

41 (will / we / love / always / you / and / by / stand / you.)

➡ _____

42 (love,)

➡ _____

43 (Dad)

➡ _____

---

31 은총아, 네가 우승자였단다!

32 아빠는 네가 그 경기에 있던 모든 사람이 너를 얼마나 사랑했는지 알았기를 바란다.

33 네 덕분에, 너의 엄마와 나는 중요한 교훈을 배웠단다.

34 "사랑이 우리가 필요한 전부다."

35 우리는 이제 더는 절대 "은총이가 장애가 없으면 좋겠다."라고 생각하지 않아.

36 대신에 우리는 너를 가진 것에 그저 감사할 뿐이야.

37 우리는 또한 많은 다른 작은 것들에 대해서도 행복해.

38 심지어 우리가 어려움에 직면할 때도, 우리는 행복하단다.

39 왜냐하면, 우리는 우리가 함께이고 서로를 사랑할 때 어떤 어려움도 극복할 수 있다는 것을 알기 때문이지.

40 우리 계속해서 행복하고 용감하게 살아가자.

41 우리는 항상 너를 사랑하고 너의 옆을 지킬게.

42 사랑하는

43 아빠가.

※ 다음 우리말을 영어로 쓰시오.

1 당신에게 필요한 건 사랑이 전부다

➡ _____

2 2010년 10월 16일, 은총이와 그의 아빠는 그들의 첫 철인 레이스에 참가했다.

➡ _____

3 그것은 하남의 미사리에서 열렸다.

➡ _____

4 그들은 1.5 km를 수영하고, 40 km 사이클을 타고, 그런 다음 10 km를 뛰었다.

➡ _____

5 이 도전은 은총이 아빠에게 특히 어려웠는데 경주 동안 은총이를 밀거나 끌어야 했기 때문이다.

➡ _____

_____

6 은총이는 6가지 다른 질병을 갖고 태어나서 말할 수도 걸을 수도 없었다.

➡ _____

7 그의 피부는 어두운 붉은색이었고 그의 두뇌는 점점 굳어가고 있었다.

➡ _____

8 의사는 은총이가 오래 살지 못할 거라고 했다.

➡ _____

9 하지만 은총이는 여전히 살아있을 뿐만 아니라 그의 첫 철인 레이스에서 1등을 했다.

➡ _____

10 은총이에게,

➡ _____

11 나는 네가 내 아들이어서뿐만 아니라 나에게 중요한 인생의 교훈을 가르쳐 주어서 고맙구나.

➡ _____

12 네가 아기였을 때, 사람들이 너의 피부색 때문에 너를 피했단다.

➡ _____

13 나는 슬펐고 너를 그들로부터 숨기고 싶었어.

➡ _____

14 네 엄마는 네가 장애 없이 태어나기를 바랐지.

➡ _____

15 네 엄마는 너의 병이 자신 때문이라고 자책도 했어.

➡ _____

16 하지만 너는 우리를 향해 항상 웃어주었고, 우리의 손을 잡아주었어.

➡ _____

17 너는 우리에게 희망뿐만 아니라 용기도 주었지.

➡ _____

18 그래서 나는 세상을 직면하고 너에게 세상의 밝은 면을 보여주겠다고 나 자신에게 약속했어.

➡ _____

19 그때부터 우리는 우리의 여정을 시작했지.

➡ _____

20 우리의 첫 철인 레이스를 기억하니?

➡ _____

21 우리가 수영을 시작했을 때, 다른 참가자들이 우리가 먼저 가도록 길을 만들어 줬어.

➡ _____

22 나는 정말 감동하였고 감사했단다.

➡ _____

23 몇몇 참가자들은 심지어 우리가 지나갈 때 울기도 했어.

➡ _____

24 우리가 사이클링을 시작했을 때, 많은 사람이 우리를 응원했지.

➡ _____

25 하지만 너는 강한 바람과 피곤함을 견뎌야만 했어.

➡ _____

26 그래서 나는 네가 쉴 수 있도록 아주 빨리 페달을 밟았어.

➡ _____

27 우리가 달리기 시작했을 때, 너의 엄마가 "당신과 함께 달릴 수 있으면 참 좋겠다." 라고 말하는 듯했어.

➡ _____

28 빨리 경주를 끝내서 너의 엄마를 보고 네가 쉬도록 하고 싶었어.

➡ _____

29 그래서 나는 빨리 달렸단다.

➡ _____

30 우리가 거의 결승선에 도착했을 때, 다른 참가자들이 멈췄고 우리가 먼저 가도록 해줬어.

➡ _____

31 은총아, 네가 우승자였단다!

➡ _____

32 아빠는 네가 그 경기에 있던 모든 사람이 너를 얼마나 사랑했는지 알았기를 바란다.

➡ _____

33 네 덕분에, 너의 엄마와 나는 중요한 교훈을 배웠단다.

➡ _____

34 "사랑이 우리가 필요한 전부다."

➡ _____

35 우리는 이제 더는 절대 "은총이가 장애가 없으면 좋겠다."라고 생각하지 않아.

➡ _____

36 대신에 우리는 너를 가진 것에 그저 감사할 뿐이야.

➡ _____

37 우리는 또한 많은 다른 작은 것들에 대해서도 행복해.

➡ _____

38 심지어 우리가 어려움에 직면할 때도, 우리는 행복하단다.

➡ _____

39 왜냐하면, 우리는 우리가 함께이고 서로를 사랑할 때 어떤 어려움도 극복할 수 있다는 것을 알기 때문이지.

➡ _____

_____

40 우리 계속해서 행복하고 용감하게 살아가자.

➡ _____

41 우리는 항상 너를 사랑하고 너의 옆을 지킬게.

➡ _____

42 사랑하는

➡ _____

43 아빠가.

➡ _____

※ 다음 우리말과 일치하도록 빈칸에 알맞은 말을 쓰시오.

Communication Activity

1. We _____ _____ _____ Stevie Wonder.

2. He is _____ _____ _____ _____.

3. _____ he _____ _____, his hearing was excellent and he _____ _____ _____ _____.

4. His songs _____ _____ _____ and he _____ _____ many _____ _____.

5. We _____ we _____ _____ our talent and _____ a great person _____ _____.

1. 우리는 Stevie Wonder를 소개하려고 합니다.
2. 그는 미국 가수입니다.
3. 비록 그는 앞을 볼 수 없었지만 그의 청각은 뛰어났고 재능 있는 가수가 되었습니다.
4. 그의 노래는 매우 인기 있었고 그는 많은 상을 받았습니다.
5. 우리는 우리의 재능을 찾아 그와 같은 위대한 인물이 되기를 원합니다.

After You Read B

1. _____ Mom and Dad,

2. _____ 2010, you _____ _____ the journey _____ _____.

3. I _____ _____ for that.

4. When we _____ _____ our first triathlon, we _____ _____ _____ a lot of _____.

5. But you _____ _____ _____ _____ me.

6. Your courage _____ me _____ the _____ _____ _____.

7. I _____ _____ _____ you.

8. Thank you _____ _____ the _____ _____ _____.

9. I love you _____ _____!

Love,
Eunchong

1. 엄마 아빠께
2. 2010년부터 당신들은 저와 함께 여정을 시작하셨죠.
3. 그것에 대해 감사드립니다.
4. 우리가 첫 철인 레이스에 참가했을 때, 우리는 많은 어려움을 견뎌야만 했어요.
5. 그러나 당신들은 저를 절대 포기하지 않으셨어요.
6. 당신들의 용기가 저로 하여금 사물의 밝은 면을 보도록 도와주었어요.
7. 저는 두 분이 자랑스러워요.
8. 가장 멋진 부모님들이 되어주셔서 감사드립니다.
9. 너무 사랑해요!

사랑하는
은총이 올림

Think and Write

1. My grandmother _____ _____ _____ _____ _____ _____ Korea.

2. She _____ _____ _____.

3. When I _____ _____ her house, she _____ _____ _____ _____ and told me everything about farming.

4. She _____ _____ welcomed me _____ _____ treated me _____ _____ _____ _____ _____ _____ in the whole world.

5. Now, she _____ _____ _____ _____ _____.

6. I _____ I _____ spend time _____ her _____ _____ _____ _____ _____.

7. I hope _____ _____ _____ _____ again.

1. 우리 할머니는 한국의 남부 지방에 사신다.
2. 그녀는 농부다.
3. 내가 그녀의 집에 갔을 때, 그녀는 나에게 농장 주위를 보여 주셨고 농사에 대한 모든 것을 말씀해 주셨다.
4. 그녀는 나를 반겼을 뿐만 아니라 이 세상에서 가장 중요한 사람처럼 대해 주셨다.
5. 지금 그녀는 병원에 계신다.
6. 예전처럼 그녀와 함께 시간을 보낼 수 있으면 좋겠다.
7. 나는 그녀가 다시 건강해지시기를 바란다.

※ 다음 우리말을 영어로 쓰시오.

Communication Activity

1. 우리는 Stevie Wonder를 소개하려고 합니다.
   ➡ _____

2. 그는 미국 가수입니다.
   ➡ _____

3. 비록 그는 앞을 볼 수 없었지만 그의 청각은 뛰어났고 재능 있는 가수가 되었습니다.
   ➡ _____

4. 그의 노래는 매우 인기 있었고 그는 많은 상을 받았습니다.
   ➡ _____

5. 우리는 우리의 재능을 찾아서 그와 같은 위대한 인물이 되기를 원합니다.
   ➡ _____

After You Read B

1. 엄마 아빠께
   ➡ _____

2. 2010년부터 당신들은 저와 함께 여정을 시작하셨죠.
   ➡ _____

3. 그것에 대해 감사드립니다.
   ➡ _____

4. 우리가 첫 철인 레이스에 참가했을 때, 우리는 많은 어려움을 견뎌야만 했어요.
   ➡ _____

5. 그러나 당신들은 저를 절대 포기하지 않으셨어요.
   ➡ _____

6. 당신들의 용기가 저로 하여금 사물의 밝은 면을 보도록 도와주었어요.
   ➡ _____

7. 저는 두 분이 자랑스러워요.
   ➡ _____

8. 가장 멋진 부모님들이 되어주셔서 감사드립니다.
   ➡ _____

9. 너무 사랑해요!
   ➡ _____

Think and Write

1. 우리 할머니는 한국의 남부 지방에 사신다.
   ➡ _____

2. 그녀는 농부다.
   ➡ _____

3. 내가 그녀의 집에 갔을 때, 그녀는 나에게 농장 주위를 보여 주셨고 농사에 대한 모든 것을 말씀해 주셨다.
   ➡ _____

4. 그녀는 나를 반겼을 뿐만 아니라 이 세상에서 가장 중요한 사람처럼 대해 주셨다.
   ➡ _____

5. 지금 그녀는 병원에 계신다.
   ➡ _____

6. 예전처럼 그녀와 함께 시간을 보낼 수 있으면 좋겠다.
   ➡ _____

7. 나는 그녀가 다시 건강해지시기를 바란다.
   ➡ _____

MEMO

영어 기출 문제집

영어 기출 문제집

1학기

정답 및 해설

금성 | 최인철

중 3

영어 기출 문제집

1학기

정답 및 해설

금성 | 최인철

중 3

Don't Judge a Book by Its Cover

p.08

| 01 ④ | 02 ① | 03 ② | 04 ⑤ |
| 05 ⑤ | 06 ③ | 07 ② | |

01 주어진 단어는 동의어 관계이다. boring 지루한, dull 지루한 – cause 원인, reason 이유

02 주어진 단어는 반의어 관계이다. carefully 조심스럽게, carelessly 부주의하게 generous 관대한, strict 엄격한

03 '다른 사람보다 많이 알아서 그 사람에게 무엇을 해야 할지 말해 주다'는 '충고하다'에 해당한다. destroy 파괴하다 take 가지고 가다 agree 동의하다 convince 확신을 주다

04 'I'm afraid'는 상대방의 의견과 다를 때 자연스럽게 자신의 동의하지 않는 의견을 유도하는 말이다.

05 "표지만 보고 책을 판단하지 마라."는 말을 들어 보셨나요? / 표지만 보고 책을 판단하지 마라. = Don't[Never] judge a book by its cover.

06 'grade'는 '성적, 학년, 등급'의 의미로 여기서는 '성적'이라는 의미로 쓰였다.

07 ① create, 그 프로젝트는 조별로 신문을 만드는 것이다. ② introduce, Lina는 일본 문화를 소개할 것이다. ③ expert, Lina는 일본문화의 전문가이다. ④ charge, 지수는 전체 신문 편집을 책임졌다. ⑤ help, 나는 내가 매우 불행하다고 생각하지 않을 수 없었다.

p.09

01 (a)nnouncement
02 (a)gree
03 (c)over
04 (j)ob
05 (1) while (2) (c)heered (3) (c)onvinced
    (4) (c)arefully
06 (1) worth (2) shy (3) concentrate (4) came

01 make an announcement 발표하다

02 '다른 사람과 같은 의견을 가지거나 같은 의견을 표현하다'는 '동의하다'에 해당한다.

03 '겉모습만으로 판단하지 마라'에 해당하는 영어 속담으로 'Don't judge a book by its cover.'이다.

04 주어진 단어는 동의어 관계이다. boring 지루한 – dull 지루한 career 직업, 이력 – job 직업

05 (1) 잠시 후에 after a while (2) 응원하다 cheer (3) 확신을 심어 주다 convince (4) 주의 깊게 carefully

06 (1) 그것이 시도할 가치가 있다고 생각하지 않으세요? 가치있는 worth (2) 나는 너무 내성적이어서 누구와도 이야기할 수 없었다. 내성적인 shy (3) 뒷자리에 앉을 때는 집중하기가 더 어렵다. concentrate 집중하다 (4) 나는 그들에 관한 몇 가지 놀라운 사실을 우연히 발견했다. come across 우연히 발견하다

p.10~11

1 agree / afraid 2 (B) → (C) → (A)
3 satisfied 4 (C) → (A) → (B)

02 '동의 여부를 묻는 질문에 (B) 동의하지 않는다는 점을 밝힌 후, 자신의 생각을 말하고 (C) 또 다른 질문을 한 것에 대하여 (A) 그 대답을 하는 순서가 적절하다.

04 '(C) 수학 선생님이 좋으냐는 질문에 아니라고 대답한다. → (A) 좋아하지 않는다는 대답에 수학 선생님의 장점을 이야기한다. (B) 그 장점에 동의하지만 만족하지 못하는 단점도 말한다.

p.12

1 F 2 T 3 T 4 F

p.14~15

Everyday English 1 A-2

history, interesting, Don't, agree / afraid, agree, too hard / Reading, comic books, make / would just, boring

Everyday English 1 A-2

think, popular sport, Don't, agree / play soccer during / watch, games

Everyday English 1 B

looking / at, basketball, poster / do you think, best, player / think, Don't, agree / agree, think, best / Why, think so / class won, Don't, remember / because, class, good, players / Anyway, lucky, both of them / class, win, this year

Everyday English 2 A-2
satisfied with / What, like / fun, talkative

Everyday English 2 B
It's / Are, calling from / How, like, life / such a beautiful / happy with / Not so, so different, easy / classmates help / help, really nice / wish, best

In Real Life
who, group members, social / members / satisfied with / Actually, seem, different / on, surface, seem different, judge, by, cover / mean by / mean, shouldn't judge, looks, like, get to know / really think, friends with / not, special, Try, understand

시험대비 기본평가 p.16

01 ①   02 ④   03 satisfied   04 ①

01 'I don't agree with you.'를 보면 앞에 나온 interesting과 반대의 의미가 될 수 있는 내용이 적절하다.

02 이어지는 'I'm happy with you.'를 보면 빈칸에는 '당연하죠.'가 들어가는 것이 자연스럽다.

03 사람이 만족하는 것이므로 과거분사형의 형용사로 고친다.

04 이어지는 대답이 긍정적인 것으로 보아 앞 사람의 대화에 동의하는 내용이 들어가는 것이 적절하다.

시험대비 실력평가 p.17~18

01 ②   02 ⑤   03 ①
04 (B) → (D) → (A) → (C)   05 ②
06 But you shouldn't judge people by their looks.
07 ⑤   08 ⑤   09 ④   10 ⑤

01 이어지는 대답에 좋은 성적을 받았다고 하는 것으로 보아 성적에 만족하는지 여부를 물어본 것을 알 수 있다. scary 무서운 convinced 확신하는

02 (A) 새로운 짝에 대하여 만족 여부를 묻는 'Are you satisfied with ~?'가 적절하다. (B) 동사 like의 목적어가 되는 의문대명사 What이 적절하다.

03 뒤에 앉는 것이 불리하다는 말에 동의하지만 자신은 키가 커서 뒤에 앉는 것을 선호한다는 말을 하기 때문에 빈칸에는 앞의 말에 동의하는 의미의 ①이 적절하다.

04 '무엇을 보고 있느냐?'는 질문에 (B) 자신이 보고 있는 것이 무

엇인지 대답한다. (D) 이어지는 대화에 '동의하지 않는다.'는 대답으로 보아 동의 여부를 묻는다. (A) 동의하지 않는 이유를 물어보고 그 이유를 대답한다. (C) 우리 반이 우승할 것이라고 하는 것으로 보아 그 근거가 앞에 놓인다는 것을 알 수 있다.

05 'Are you satisfied with ~?'대신 'Are you happy with ~?'라고 할 수 있다.

06 Don't judge a book by its cover.'는 '사람을 외모로 판단하지 마라.'에 해당하므로 'You shouldn't judge people by their looks.'의 의미이다.

07 '~으로 …을 의미하다'는 'mean by ~'를 쓴다.

08 모둠 구성원에 대한 불만이 있는 지수에게 라이언이 겉모습만으로는 판단하지 말라고 조언을 하는 것으로 보아 지수는 자신의 모둠 구성원들에 대해서 다시 생각해볼 것이라고 추측할 수 있다.

09 밑줄 친 (A)는 '운동회 날이 좋았다.'는 앞의 말에 동의하는 표현이다.

10 위 대화에서 언급한 sports day는 이미 지나간 행사이기 때문에 앞으로 일어날 일인 것처럼 설명한 것은 위 대화의 내용과 일치하지 않는다.

서술형 시험대비 p.19

01 How do you like your life in France?
02 different
03 ⓓ → really nice[kind]
04 (a)fraid
05 Are you satisfied with your group?
06 the surface they may seem different from you.

01 '~가 마음에 드니?'라고 만족하는지를 묻는 말은 'How do you like ~?'라고 한다.

02 "it's not easy for me"라고 하는 것으로 보아 프랑스에서의 생활이 한국과 다르다는 이야기를 하는 것으로 생각할 수 있다.

03 한국과 다른 프랑스에서 생활이 쉽지는 않지만 주변에서 도와주는 사람들이 있다는 말로 이 사람들은 무례한 것이 아니라 친절하다고 해야 한다.

04 반대하는 의견을 말할 때 유감을 표현하는 말은 'I'm afraid.'에 이어서 말한다.

05 "~에 만족하니?"의 의미는 "Are you satisfied with ~?"이다.

06 표면적으로 = on the surface, 그들은 달라 보일 수도 있다 = they may seem different이라고 생각할 수 있다.

시험대비 기본평가   p.22

핵심 Check   p.20~21

1 (1) go   (2) do   (3) read
2 (1) going   (2) is worth buying   (3) couldn't help telling   (4) watching

시험대비 기본평가   p.22

01 (1) listen → listening   (2) stopped → stop
     (3) laugh → laughing   (4) to go → go
     (5) repair → repaired   (6) do → done
02 ①   **03** ④
04 (1) Some schools don't make students wear school uniforms.
     (2) We are used to living in a busy city.

01 (1) 'be worth -ing' 형태이므로 listening, (2) 사역동사 make의 목적격보어로 원형부정사가 오므로 stop, (3) 'can't[couldn't]+help -ing' 형태이므로 laughing, (4) 사역동사 let+목적어+목적격 보어(능동관계)로 go, (5) 사역동사 have가 있는 문장으로 지붕(목적어)이 스스로 '고치는' 것이 아니라 '고쳐지는(목적격 보어)' 것으로 수동이므로 repaired (6) get+목적어+목적보어(수동 관계)로 done이 적절하다.
02 'feel like -ing'이므로 'She felt like eating cheese cake.' 가 되어야 한다.
03 make는 사역동사이므로 목적격보어에 do가 와야 한다.
04 (1) 사역동사 make가 있는 문장이므로 목적격보어로 원형부정 사가 온다. (2) 'be used to -ing: ~하는 것에 익숙하다' 구문이 므로 어순에 주의해야 한다.

시험대비 실력평가   p.23~25

01 doing → do   **02** ⑤
03 (1) going   (2) visiting   (3) making   (4) keeping
04 ②   **05** ②
06 (1) couldn't help feeling   (2) couldn't help agreeing
07 ④   **08** ③   **09** ④   **10** ④
11 ②   **12** ①, ④   **13** ⑤   **14** ②
15 ②, ③, ⑤
16 (1) to introduce → introduce
     (2) using → use
     (3) to empty → empty   **17** ②
18 (A) crying   (B) thinking   (C) change   (D) spend

     (E) trying   **19** ②
20 (1) had, show   (2) let, to

01 'can't help but 동사원형' 어순이므로 doing이 아닌 do가 와 야 한다. can't help -ing = can't help but 동사원형: ~하지 않을 수 없다
02 'look forward to -ing'와 'couldn't help -ing' 구문이므로 공 통으로 looking이 와야 한다.
03 (1) feel like -ing 구문 / 점심 후에, 그녀는 산책하고 싶어 했 다. (2) be worth -ing 구문 / 그 호수는 방문할 만한 가치가 있 다. (3) be busy -ing 구문 / 그의 마음은 내일의 계획을 짜느 라 바빴다. (4) be used to -ing 구문 / 나는 매일 일기를 쓰는 데 익숙하다.
04 ① be worth -ing 구문 ③ cannot help -ing 구문 ④ 사역동 사+목적어+목적격보어(원형부정사) ⑤ 5형식 문장(주어+동사 +목적어+목적격보어)에서 목적격보어로 원형부정사를 사용.
05 (1) let+목적어+목적격보어(원형부정사) / 나의 부모님은 내가 파티에 가는 것을 절대 허락하지 않을 것이다. (2) have+목적어 +목적격보어(원형부정사) / 나의 영어 선생님은 우리가 많은 영 어책을 읽게 했다. (3) can't help but 동사원형 / 너는 그녀를 존경하지 않을 수 없다.
06 <보기> 나는 진실을 말하지 않을 수 없었다. can't[couldn't] help -ing = can't[couldn't] help but 동사원형: ~하지 않을 수 없다 (1) 나는 엄마에게 죄송하다고 느끼지 않을 수 없었다. (2) 나는 그의 의견에 동의할 수밖에 없었다.
07 used to 동사원형: ~하곤 했다, 사역동사+목적어+목적격보어(원 형부정사)
08 사역동사가 있는 문장의 쓰임에 대해 묻는 질문이다. '사역동사 (have, make, let)+목적어+목적격보어(원형부정사)' 어순을 확인한다.
09 be worth -ing: ~할 가치가 있다
10 ⓐ '축구를 하곤 했다'이므로 'used to play' ⓑ '말을 걸어오는 데 익숙하지 않다'이므로 'am not used to being'
11 '사역동사 let+목적어+목적격보어(원형부정사)'와 내용상 목적어 로 me가 되어야 한다.
12 ① 사역동사 let+목적어+목적격보어(원형부정사) ④ cannot help -ing: ~하지 않을 수 없다
13 첫 번째 문장은 '그는 낚시를 가곤 했다'는 의미이므로 빈칸에 'used to'가 들어가야 적절하다. 두 번째 문장은 '그는 그 기계를 사용하는 데 익숙하다'는 의미로 'be used to -ing' 구문이므로 공통으로 들어가 말은 'used to'이다.
14 준사역동사 help의 5형식 어순은 'help+목적어+목적격보 어(원형부정사/to부정사)'이다. ① packing → (to) pack ③ cleaning → (to) clean ④ moving → (to) move ⑤ finding → (to) find

15 주어진 문장과 ②, ③, ⑤번은 사역동사로 쓰인 문장이다.

16 (1) 사역동사 let+목적어+목적격보어(원형부정사) (2) 사역동사 let+목적어+목적격보어(원형부정사) (3) 사역동사 have+목적어+목적격보어(원형부정사)

17 사역동사 have를 찾는다.

18 (A) feel like -ing 구문이므로 crying. (B) couldn't help -ing 구문이므로 thinking, (C) 사역동사(5형식동사)+목적어+목적격보어(원형부정사) change, (D) 'used to 동사원형: ~하곤 했다' 구문이므로 spend, (E) be worth -ing 구문이므로 trying이 적절하다.

19 사역동사 make를 찾는다.

20 (1) 어법에 맞게 배열하면, 'Flight attendants had the passengers show their tickets.'이다. (2) 어법에 맞게 배열하면, 'Alice's parents let her go to Egypt by herself.'이다.

서술형 시험대비
p.26~27

01 (1) I felt like giving up the attempt.
   (2) These projects are worth doing.
   (3) May I have the scarf wrapped?

02 (1) couldn't help listening
   (2) helped the United States (to) win
   (3) it is worth trying

03 My dad made me do it.

04 (1) I felt like crying when I sat with my group members.
   (2) I couldn't help thinking how unlucky I was.
   (3) She would let me change the group.
   (4) It is no use learning such a thing.
   (5) Do you have any difficulties living with him?

05 am used to driving

06 (1) clean (2) have (3) help (4) sit

07 (1) Alice is used to using a computer.
   (2) Alice is busy working these days.
   (3) Alice is looking[looks] forward to taking a rest.

08 (1) helped[helps] me (to) pack my luggage
   (2) In trying to protect the child

09 (1) help thinking[help but think]
   (2) used to spend (3) is used to reading

10 you felt like giving up this project

11 She is used to solving difficult problems.

01 (1) feel like -ing: ~하고 싶다 (2) be worth -ing: ~할 가치가 있다 (3) 사역동사 have+목적어+목적격보어(수동관계)

02 관용어 표현 제대로 알기 (1) 듣지 않을 수 없었다 (2) 미국이 이기게 도왔다 (3) 시도할 가치가 있다

03 과거에 부탁한 것이기 때문에 make의 과거형 made가 적절하다. 사역동사 make+목적어+목적격보어(원형부정사)

04 (1) feel like -ing: ~하고 싶다 to cry → crying (2) couldn't help -ing(= couldn't help but 동사원형). to think → thinking 또는 but think (3) 사역동사 let+목적어+목적격보어(능동 관계) to change → change (4) It's no use -ing: ~해 봐야 소용없다 to learn → learning (5) have any difficulties -ing: ~하는 데 어려움이 있다. to live → living

05 because 뒤에 나온 문장에서 빈칸에 올 시제의 힌트를 얻을 수 있다. 'have lived'가 있으므로 빈칸의 시제는 현재형이고, '~에 익숙하다'는 'be used to -ing'이다.

06 사역동사의 어순을 확인한다. 사역동사+목적어+목적격보어(원형부정사)

07 (1) Alice는 게임프로그래머이며 컴퓨터를 항상 사용하므로 '컴퓨터 사용에 익숙하다.'는 표현으로 고쳐 쓸 수 있다. (2) Alice는 요즘 밤늦게까지 일을 하므로 '일하느라 바쁘다.'라는 표현으로 고쳐 쓸 수 있다. (3) Alice는 휴식을 원하고 있으므로 'look forward to -ing' 표현으로 고쳐 쓸 수 있다.

08 (1) 'help+목적어+목적격보어(원형부정사/to부정사)' 어순을 확인한다. (2) 동명사의 관용 표현 'in+-ing'를 확인한다.

09 (1) '~라고 생각하지 않을 수 없었다.'이므로 'help thinking 또는 help but think' (2) '시간을 보내곤 했다.'이므로 'used to spend' (3) '~에 익숙하다'는 'be used to -ing'이므로 'is used to reading'이 적절하다.

10 'feel like -ing' 구문이고 어법에 맞게 어순 배치를 해야 하므로 you felt like giving up this project가 답이다.

11 be used to -ing: ~하는 데 익숙하다

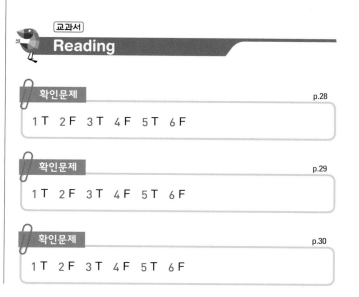

교과서
Reading

확인문제
p.28

1 T 2 F 3 T 4 F 5 T 6 F

확인문제
p.29

1 T 2 F 3 T 4 F 5 T 6 F

확인문제
p.30

1 T 2 F 3 T 4 F 5 T 6 F

01 How

02 social studies, announcement

03 in groups

04 Check out

05 calling out

06 was called

07 Group

08 Who will be

09 continued

10 couldn't believe

11 didn't know anyone

12 felt like crying

13 have, in common

14 was always drawing

15 his only interest

16 had his nose in a book

17 couldn't help thinking

18 should be with

19 let me change

20 placed, on

21 what you want, get to like

22 it's worth trying

23 walked away

24 from the start

25 decide on

26 felt like giving

27 Try to understand

28 carefully watched

29 came across

30 expert on

31 a bit, because

32 a lot

33 Vietnamese, used to spend

34 to talk about

35 thought of

36 to write

37 had Lina introduce

38 wrote about, covered

39 was in charge of editing

40 a great success

41 received an A⁺

42 with this saying

43 by its cover

44 Read

45 turn into

1 How I Met My Best Friends

2 Mrs. Choi, my social studies teacher, made an important announcement.

3 "You will create a newspaper in groups.

4 Check out your new group members."

5 Mrs. Choi started calling out the names of the students in each group.

6 After a while, my name was called.

7 "Group 4, Jisu···"

8 "Who will be in my group?" I wondered.

9 Mrs. Choi continued, "Lina, Inho, and Min."

10 I couldn't believe my ears.

11 I didn't know anyone in that group.

12 I felt like crying when I sat with my group members.

13 We didn't have anything in common.

14 Lina was always drawing something by herself.

15 Inho never said anything, and his only interest seemed to be soccer.

16 Min was smart, but he always had his nose in a book.

17 I couldn't help thinking how unlucky I was.

18 I decided to convince Mrs. Choi that I should be with my friends.

19 "Maybe she would let me change the group," I thought.

20 But before I could say anything, she gently placed her hand on my shoulder.

21 "I know what you want, Jisu," she said, "but I'm sure you will get to like your group members.

22 Don't you think it's worth trying?"

23 I didn't really believe her, but I said, "Okay," and walked away.

24 The project wasn't easy from the start.

25 We couldn't decide on the topic for our newspaper.

26 I felt like giving up on the project, so I asked my friend Ryan for some advice.

27 "Try to understand your group members first," he said.

28 So I carefully watched my group members.

29 And I came across some amazing facts about them.

30 Lina read a lot of Japanese comic books, so she was an expert on Japanese culture.

31 Inho's Korean sounded a bit different, but that was because he lived in Argentina when he was young.

32 He knew a lot about Argentina and its soccer.

33 Min's mom was Vietnamese, and Min used to spend some time in Vietnam.

34 He read a lot of history books and loved to talk about Vietnam and its history.

35 I thought of the perfect topic for our group.

36 We decided to write about world culture.

37 I had Lina introduce Japanese culture.

38 Inho wrote about Argentina and its soccer, and Min covered Vietnamese culture and its history.

39 I was in charge of editing the whole newspaper.

40 Our newspaper project was a great success.

41 We received an A⁺, and my group members became my best friends.

42 I will end my story with this saying.

43 Don't judge a book by its cover.

44 Read it.

45 It might turn into your favorite book.

시험대비 실력평가
p.37~41

01 ②　　　02 ②, ③, ⑤　　03 ⑤　　　04 ④

05 ②, ⑤　　06 share　　07 expert

08 Min's mom was Vietnamese, and Min used to spend some time in Vietnam.

09 ③　　　10 ③　　　11 alone

12 lucky → unlucky　　13 ②, ⑤

14 (1) Lina: 일본의 만화책을 많이 읽었고, 그래서 일본 문화에 관해서는 전문가였다.

(2) 인호: 한국어 발음이 조금 다르게 들린 이유는 어렸을 때 아르헨티나에서 살았기 때문이고, 아르헨티나와 그 나라의 축구에 관해 많은 것을 알고 있었다.

(3) Min: 엄마가 베트남 사람이고, Min은 베트남에서 약간의 시간을 보냈다. 그는 많은 역사책을 읽었으며, 베트남과 그 역사에 관해 이야기하는 것을 좋아했다.

15 Vietnam　16 ③　　　17 ②　　　18 ④

19 best friend　　20 crying　　21 ④

22 ②　　　23 convincing → to convince

24 ①, ④　　25 ④

26 (A) introduce　(B) editing　(C) a great success

27 ③　　　28 (A) by its cover　(B) reading it

01 ⓐ in groups: 그룹을 지어, ⓑ sit with ~와 같이 앉다

02 (A)와 ②, ③, ⑤: 동명사, ①, ④: 현재분사

03 ⑤ 지수는 자신의 모둠에 아는 사람이 하나도 없었다. ③ belong to ~: ~ 소속이다

04 주어진 문장의 But에 주목한다. ④번 앞 문장의 내용과 상반되

는 내용이 뒤에 이어지므로 ④번이 적절하다.

05 ⓑ와 ②, ⑤: 관심, ① 이자, ③ ~의 관심[흥미]을 끌다, (~에) 관심[흥미]을 보이다(동사), ④ 이익

06 have ~ in common = share: 공통점이 있다

07 expert: 전문가, 어떤 것을 하는 데 매우 노련한 또는 특정한 주제에 대해 많이 아는 사람

08 used to+동사 원형': 과거의 상태를 나타내거나, 예전에 했었던 규칙적인 습관을 나타냄. '예전에는 ~했다'

09 ③ '인호가 어렸을 때 왜 아르헨티나에서 살았는지'는 대답할 수 없다. ① By reading a lot of Japanese comic books. ② Because he lived in Argentina when he was young. ④ He knew a lot about Argentina and its soccer. ⑤ He loved to talk about Vietnam and its history.

10 선행사를 포함하는 관계대명사 what이 적절하다.

11 by oneself = alone: 혼자

12 글의 첫 부분에서 '우리는 공통점이 하나도 없었다.'라고 했고 ⓑ 다음 문장에서 '나는 내 친구들과 함께하겠다고 최 선생님을 설득하기로 했다.'라고 했기 때문에, 나는 내가 '불행하다'는 생각을 하지 않을 수 없었다고 하는 것이 적절하다.

13 ⓐ와 ①, ③, ④: 동명사, ②, ⑤: 현재분사

14 뒤에 이어지는 Lina, 인호, Min에 대한 설명을 쓰는 것이 적절하다.

16 이 글은 '지수가 모둠 구성원들을 이해하려고 노력해서 발견하게 된 그들에 관한 놀라운 사실들'에 관한 글이므로, 주제로는 ③번 '먼저 모둠 구성원들을 이해하기'가 적절하다.

17 이 글은 '책을 표지로 판단하지 마라. 읽어라. 네가 가장 좋아하는 책이 될 수도 있다.'는 내용의 글이므로, 제목으로는 ②번 그 것을 '어떻게 보이느냐가 아니라 무엇을 말하느냐'가 적절하다. ③ cooperation: 협동, policy: 정책, 방침, ④ matter: 중요하다, ⑤ 빛난다고 모두 금은 아니다.(매력적인 것이 실제로는 거의 가치가 없을 수도 있다는 것을 뜻하는 속담)

18 ⓐ와 ④: 책임, in charge of ~을 담당하는, ① (서비스에 대한) 요금, ② 충전하다(동사), ③ 비난하다, 고소[고발]하다(동사), ⑤ (요금을) 청구하다(동사)

19 '가장 친한 친구'를 가리킨다.

20 feel like ~ing: ~하고 싶다

21 이 글은 '지수가 신문을 같이 만들 새 모둠의 구성원들 중에 아는 사람이 하나도 없어서 모둠 구성원들과 함께 앉을 때 울고 싶었다.'는 내용의 글이므로, 제목으로는 ④번 '믿을 수 없어! 나는 저들 중 아무도 몰라!'가 적절하다.

22 ③ 중반부의 '"Who will be in my group?" I wondered.'를 통해 'expectant'를, 마지막 부분의 'I felt like crying when I sat with my group members.'를 통해 'disappointed'를 찾을 수 있다. ① upset: 속상한 ② expectant: 기대하는, disappointed: 실망한, ③ bored: 지루한, nervous: 초조한

23 decide는 목적어로 to부정사를 취하는 동사이다.

24 come/get/grow to부정사: ~하게 되다

25 '최 선생님이 지수가 원하는 것이 뭔지를 어떻게 아셨는지'는 대답 할 수 없다. ① Lina. ② It seemed to be soccer. ③ Min. ⑤ She was sure Jisu would get to like her group members.

26 (A) 'have+사람+원형부정사'이므로 introduce가 적절하다. (B) edit의 동명사는 editing이 적절하다. (C) 구체적인 성공 사례를 나타낼 때는 success가 셀 수 있는 명사로 쓰인 것이므로 a great success가 적절하다.

27 ⓐ와 ③: 다루다, 포함시키다, ① 씌우다[가리다], ② 덮다, ④ (언급된 거리를) 가다[이동하다], ⑤ (물건에) 덮개를 씌우다, 뚜 껑을 덮다

28 처음에 지수는 그녀의 모둠 구성원들이 공통점이 하나도 없다고 생각하고 모둠을 바꿔 달라고 최 선생님을 설득하기로 했다. 즉, 그녀는 책을 '표지로' 판단하고 '그것을 읽기를' 거의 포기할 뻔 했 다.

역사에 관해 이야기하는 것을 좋아했다.

07 형용사 뒤에 명사 형태로 쓰는 것이 적절하다.

08 start는 동명사와 to부정사를 모두 목적어로 취할 수 있는 동사이 다.

09 '모둠 4'를 가리킨다.

10 지수가 그녀 모둠의 구성원들의 이름을 들었을 때, 그녀는 그 모 둠에 '아는 사람이 하나도 없었기' 때문에 '자신의 귀'를 믿을 수 없었다. 모둠 구성원들과 함께 앉을 때 그녀는 울고 싶은 마음이 들었다.

11 bookworm: 책벌레, have one's nose in a book: 책벌레이 다

12 be worth doing = be worth while to do: ~할 가치가 있다

13 지수는 그녀의 모둠원들이 '공통점'이 하나도 없다고 생각해서 자신의 친구들과 함께 하겠다고 최 선생님을 '설득하기로' 했지 만, 선생님은 지수에게 모둠원들을 좋아하게 되도록 시도해보라 고 충고하셨다.

🦉 서술형 시험대비   p.42~43

01 to introduce

02 They decided to write about world culture.

03 (1) Lina: 일본 문화를 소개하는 역할
(2) 인호: 아르헨티나와 그 나라의 축구에 관해 글을 쓰는 역할
(3) Min: 베트남의 문화와 역사를 다루는 역할
(4) 지수: 신문 전체를 편집하는 역할

04 my group members 또는 Lina, Inho and Min

05 in Argentina

06 (A) Vietnam (B) history books

07 announcement

08 Mrs. Choi started calling out the names of the students in each group.

09 Group 4

10 (A) her ears (B) didn't know

11 bookworm

12 while

13 (A) in common (B) to convince

---

01 have+사람+원형부정사 = get+사람+to부정사

02 그들은 세계 문화에 관해 글을 쓰기로 했다.

03 글의 전반부의 내용을 쓰는 것이 적절하다.

04 '나의 모둠 구성원들' 또는 'Lina, 인호 그리고 Min'을 가리킨 다.

05 어렸을 때 '아르헨티나에서' 살았기 때문이었다.

06 Min의 엄마는 '베트남' 출신이고, Min은 베트남에서 약간의 시 간을 보냈다. 그는 많은 '역사책'을 읽었으며, 베트남과 베트남의

🦫 영역별 핵심문제   p.45~49

01 ④	02 ①	03 ⑤	04 ①
05 ⑤	06 ③	07 ④	

08 Who do you think is the best basketball player in our school?

09 ①	10 ②
11 ①	12 ③	13 ①

14 (1) It's no use buying that early.
(2) She has trouble sleeping these days.
(3) He spent ten years finding out the truth.
(4) On looking at the police, the pickpocket started to run away.
(5) In crossing the street, he met with the accident.

15 ④	16 ①, ③
17 (1) picking (2) traveling	18 ④	19 certain
20 ②	

21 Inho's Korean sounded a bit different

22 ③	23 ⑤

24 I was in charge of editing the whole newspaper.

25 ④	26 ②, ④, ⑤	27 ③

---

01 'win'은 '이기다, 우승하다, 수상하다'의 의미를 가진다. 여기서 는 '우승하다'의 의미이다.

02 '여러분이 훈련을 받고, 생애의 오랜 기간 동안 해온 일이나 직 업'은 'career'를 가리킨다.

03 cheer 응원하다 advise 충고하다 consult 상담하다 continue 계속하다 introduce 소개하다 encourage 격려하다

04 (A) 상대의 질문에 대하여 긍정적인 대답을 하고 (C) 그 대답에 대한 이유를 질문하고 (B) 그 이유에 대한 대답을 하는 순서가

자연스럽다.

05 뒤에 있는 자리에 앉으면 집중하기 힘들다는 단점에 동의한다고 한 다음 but으로 이어지는 대조적인 연결을 통해서 반대되는 입장을 설명하기 때문에 뒤에 앉기로 선택한다는 내용이 적절하다.

06 '내 뒤에 앉는 사람들'은 'those who sit behind'이다.

07 소녀의 'Don't you agree?'라는 질문에 'That's true,'라고 대답하는 것으로 보아 소년은 소녀의 의견에 동의한다는 것을 알 수 있다.

08 '누가 ~라고 생각하니?'는 'Who do you think ~?'라고 해야 한다.

09 (B)는 상대의 말에 동의하지 않는다는 말이다.

10 민재가 가장 좋은 선수라고 말한 것에 대한 이유로 그의 반이 시합에서 우승했다고 하는 것이 적절하다.

11 ① get+목적어+목적보어(수동 관계) ② get+목적어+목적보어(수동 관계) stealing → stolen ③ get+목적어+목적보어(능동 관계) study → to study ④ get+목적어+목적보어(능동 관계) do → to do ⑤ get+목적어+목적보어(수동 관계) to wash → washed

12 ①, ② 'be worth -ing'이므로 to try → trying, to watching → watching ④ 'cannot help –ing 또는 cannot help but 동사원형'이므로 to leave → leaving 또는 to leave → but leave ⑤ 'look forward to -ing'이므로 have → having

13 'be used to -ing: ~하는 데 익숙하다.'와 'feel like -ing: ~하고 싶다'이므로 'speaking - reading'이 적절하다.

15 ④번은 사역동사로 쓰인 것이 아니지만 나머지는 모두 사역동사로 쓰였다.

16 ① look forward to -ing: ~하는 것을 고대하다[기대하다] to travel → to traveling ③ couldn't help -ing: ~하지 않을 수 없었다. to feel → feeling

17 (1) 'feel like -ing'이므로 picking (2) 'be worth -ing'이므로 traveling이 적절하다.

18 진행형+always/constantly/continuously/forever: 습관, 불평, 짜증, 비난을 나타낸다. ④ immediately: 즉시

19 I'm sure = It's certain

20 이 글은 '지수는 그녀의 모둠원들이 공통점이 하나도 없다고 생각해서 자신의 친구들과 함께 하겠다고 최 선생님을 설득하기로 했지만, 선생님은 지수에게 모둠원들을 좋아하게 되도록 시도해 보라고 충고하셨다.'는 내용의 글이므로, 제목으로는 ②번 '어서 해 봐! 그것은 해 볼 가치가 있어!'가 적절하다.

21 '인호의 한국어 발음이 조금 다르게 들린 것'을 가리킨다.

22 a great deal of = much

23 모둠의 구성원들에 관한 놀라운 사실들을 발견한 사람은 '지수'였다.

24 in charge of ~을 담당하는

25 당신은 어떤 것의 가치를 그것의 겉모습만으로 예단해서는 안 된다. prejudge: 예단[속단]하다, 편견; appearance: (겉)모습, 외모, ① 성격, ② 질, ③ 도덕성, ⑤ 특징

26 ② explorer: 탐험가, ④ professor: 교수 ⑤ amateur: 아마추어, 비전문가

27 Min이 항상 역사책만 보는 이유는 알 수 없다. ① Because she read a lot of Japanese comic books. ② In Argentina. ④ He covered Vietnamese culture and its history. ⑤ Jisu did.

단원별 예상문제   p.50~53

01 ③	02 ⑤	03 ⑤	04 ①
05 ⑤	06 ⑤	07 ②	08 ⑤
09 ①	10 I wish you the best of luck.		
11 ⑤			

12 (1) They couldn't help telling me the news.
(2) I feel like sleeping all day long.
(3) I am used to taking a walk in the morning.
(4) On lying on the floor, he fell asleep.
(5) They had difficulty getting jobs.
(6) This car needs repairing.
(7) I'm looking forward to attending the meeting.

13 Your food is worth waiting for.

14 Mrs. Choi called my name   15 ⑤

16 I couldn't help thinking how unlucky I was.

17 to change 18 ⑤   19 ③, ⑤   20 ①
21 ③   22 ②

01 주어진 두 단어는 반의어 관계이다. agree 동의하다 disagree 반대하다 cause 이유 result 결과

02 ⑤ interest는 '흥미, 관심'이라는 뜻이다.

03 체육 대회에 만족한다고 했으므로 체육 대회를 긍정적으로 나타내는 표현이 필요하다.

04 '친구들이나 아는 사람이 없는'이 나타내는 것은 '외로운'이다.

05 ⑤ '그녀가 부드럽게 내 어깨에 손을 올려놓았다.'의 의미로 'put'이나 'placed'가 적절하다.

06 (C) 누가 제일 훌륭한 singer냐는 질문에 대하여 (B) 수지라고 대답하고 동의하는지 물어본다. (A) 앞의 질문에 동의하지 않는다는 대답과 함께 거기에 대한 이유를 덧붙이는 순서가 자연스러운 배열이다.

07 이어지는 내용으로 보아 프랑스에서 전화를 거는 것이냐는 질문에 대하여 긍정의 대답을 했음을 알 수 있다.

9

08 ⑤ 프랑스에서의 생활이 힘든 이유가 나오도록 부정적인 내용을 소개해야 한다.

09 ① 'Hi, Bora! It's me, Minsu!'라고 하는 것으로 보아 전화를 거는 사람이 민수라는 것을 알 수 있다.

10 '행운을 빌어요.'의 의미로 상대방에게 행운을 비는 말은 'wish+사람+the best of luck'이다.

11 ⑤ 주어+동사+목적어+목적격보어(형용사)

12 (1) couldn't help -ing: ~하지 않을 수 없었다 (2) feel like -ing: ~하고 싶다 (3) be used to -ing: ~하는 데 익숙하다 (4) on -ing: ~하자마자 (6) need -ing : ~할 필요가 있다 (7) look forward to -ing: ~을 고대하다[기대하다]

13 wait for: (~을) 기다리다

14 'Mrs. Choi'를 주어로 해서 능동태로 고치는 것이 적절하다.

15 '발표를 들었을 때 지수 모둠의 구성원들이 어떻게 느꼈는지'는 대답할 수 없다. ① She teaches social studies. ② She announced that Jisu's class would create a newspaper in groups. ③ Group 4. ④ No.

16 'help'를 보충하면 된다. cannot help -ing: ~하지 않을 수 없다

17 let+목적어+원형부정사 = allow+목적어+to부정사

18 ⓐ decide on: ~으로 정하다, ⓑ ask A for B: A에게 B를 부탁하다, 청하다

19 come across = run into = bump into = run across = happen to meet = meet by chance: 우연히 만나다, ③ take up: (시간·공간을) 차지하다, ⑤ run through: 다 써 버리다

20 ① 프로젝트는 처음부터 쉽지 않았다.

21 주어진 문장의 this saying에 주목한다. ③번 다음 문장의 속담을 가리키므로 ③번이 적절하다.

22 '지수'는 'Lina'가 일본 문화를 소개하도록 했다.

서술형 실전문제 p.54~55

01 Are you satisfied with your grades?

02 Don't you agree?

03 He is used to handling the ball.

04 is looking forward to watching Lionel Messi playing[play]

05 felt like fighting

06 (1) Lina: 항상 혼자서 무언가를 그리고 있었다.
   (2) 인호: 아무 말도 하지 않았으며 그의 유일한 관심은 축구 같았다.
   (3) Min: 영리했지만, 그는 항상 책만 보고 있었다.

07 (1) but think   (2) help but   (3) to think

08 Don't you think it's worth trying?

09 (A) advice   (B) amazing   (C) sounded

10 group members

11 Japanese culture

01 상대방에게 만족하는지 묻는 말은 'Are you satisfied with ~?' 또는 'Are you happy with ~?'이다.

02 이어지는 'Well, I don't.'이라는 대답과 보라의 생각과 달리 'working with others'가 어렵다는 말을 하는 것으로 보아 동의하는지 여부를 묻는 말이 들어가는 것이 자연스럽다.

03 be used to -ing: ~하는 데 익숙하다

04 위 대화에서 소녀는 이번 여름 방학 동안 스페인에 가서 Lionel Messi가 경기하는 것을 보려고 한다.

05 지문에서 변호사 간디는 사람들이 그들의 나라를 위해 싸워야 한다고 말했으므로 felt like fighting이 와야 한다.

06 ⓐ 다음에 나오는 내용을 쓰는 것이 적절하다.

07 can't help -ing = can't but+동사원형 = can't help but+동사원형 = have no choice but to 동사원형: ~하지 않을 수 없다

08 be worth -ing ~할 가치가 있다

09 (A) advice는 셀 수 없는 명사이므로 단수가 적절하다. (B) 감정을 나타내는 동사는 감정을 유발할 때 현재분사를 쓰는 것이 적절하므로 amazing이 적절하다. (C) 감각동사 sounded 다음에 형용사 보어 different가 있으므로 sounded가 적절하다. sound like+명사

10 먼저 그녀의 '모둠 구성원들'을 이해하기를 원했기 때문이다.

11 Lina는 일본의 만화책을 많이 읽었기 때문에 '일본 문화'에 관해서는 전문가였다.

창의사고력 서술형 문제 p.56

|모범답안|

01 (A) make   (B) like crying   (C) help thinking
   (D) felt like giving   (E) good at introducing
   (F) playing   (G) spend   (H) Don't judge a book by its cover

02 (A) First   (B) from each other   (C) new friends
   (D) to work with others   (E) doing

단원별 모의고사 p.57~60

01 ①   02 talkative

03 (1) (c)ommon   (2) (p)erfect   (3) (c)ulture   (4) (a)mazing

04 (1) announcement   (2) while   (3) crying   (4) carefully

05 ②

06 Reading history comic books may make it easier

07 ⑤   08 ②   09 ②   10 ④

11 (1) She helped the United States win the first FIFA
   Women's World Cup.

   (2) I feel like going for a walk tomorrow morning.

12 My room needs cleaning.

   My room needs to be cleaned.

13 ②, I feel like going on a trip.   14 ④

15 (1) I don't feel like having lunch now.

   (2) Lisa didn't feel like drinking something cold.

   (3) I saw him get on the bus.

   (4) He made us understand his plan through the sign
   language.

   (5) She let the breeze from an electric fan blow her
   hair dry.

16 ④   17 alone → in groups   18 ②

19 Mrs. Choi 20 ④   21 ③

22 (C) to → on   23 why → because

01 '다른 사람과 다른 의견을 가지거나 표현하다'는 '반대하다 disagree'에 해당한다. advise 충고하다 edit 편집하다 cheer 응원하다 continue 계속하다

02 be동사의 보어로 형용사가 적절하다. 동사 talk의 형용사 'talkative'가 적절하다.

03 (1) 공통점을 가지다 have in common (2) 완벽한 perfect (3) 문화 culture (4) 놀라운 amazing

04 (1) 사회 선생님인 최 선생님이 중요한 발표를 하셨다. (2) 잠시 후 내 이름이 불렸다. (3) 모둠 구성원들과 앉았을 때 울고 싶었다. (4) 그래서 나는 우리 조원들을 조심스럽게 살폈다.

05 대답에 'I don't agree.'가 있으므로 동의 여부를 묻는 질문이라는 것을 알 수 있다.

06 역사 만화책을 읽는 것 = reading history comic books

07 두 사람의 대화의 주제는 'history'이다. 소년이 history를 어려워하기 때문에 재미있게 공부하는 한 가지 방법으로 만화책 읽기를 소개하지만 중심 소재는 역사 과목이라고 하는 것이 적절하다.

08 학교에서 가장 우수한 농구선수를 물어보는 질문이기 때문에 사람을 나타내는 의문사로 동사 is의 주어가 되는 Who가 적절하다.

09 'No, I don't agree.'라는 대답이 나오는 것으로 보아 주어진 문장이 들어갈 곳은 ⓑ이다.

10 두 사람의 대화에서 작년에 우승한 학급은 민재네 반이라고 나와 있으므로 ④는 대화의 내용과 일치하지 않는다.

11 (1) help+목적어+목적격보어(원형부정사) (2) feel like -ing: ~하고 싶다

12 need+-ing: ~할 필요가 있다(= need to be 과거분사)

14 ①, ②, ③, ⑤는 사역동사이고, ④는 3형식 문장이다.

15 (1), (2) 각각 'feel like -ing: ~하고 싶다.' (3), (4), (5) '주어+동사+목적어+목적격보어(원형부정사)'인 사역[지각]동사의 어순을 확인한다.

16 ⓐ와 ①, ②, ③, ⑤: 전치사, ① (외관·내용 등이) ~을 닮아, 유사하여; ~일 것 같아, ② look like A ~: ~이 일어날 듯하여, ~할 징조를 나타내어, ③, ⑤: ~와 (똑)같이[마찬가지로], ~처럼, ④ 좋아하다(동사)

17 학생들은 '혼자' 신문을 만드는 것이 아니라, '모둠별'로 신문을 만들 것이다.

18 '우리는 공통점이 하나도 없었다.'에 어울리는 속담으로는 ②번 '취향도 가지가지다. (사람의 마음은 가지각색이다).'가 적절하다. ① 사공이 많으면 배가 산으로 올라간다. (어떤 일에 관여하는 사람이 너무 많으면 일을 망친다는 뜻) ③ 어려울 때 친구가 진정한 친구다. ④ 백지장도 맞들면 낫다. (두 사람의 지혜가 한 사람의 지혜보다 낫다). ⑤ 유유상종(같은 유형의 사람들은 서로 함께 모이는 경향이 있다).

19 '최 선생님'을 가리킨다.

20 지수는 자신이 불행하다는 생각을 '하지 않을 수 없었다.'

21 ③번 다음 문장의 So에 주목한다. 주어진 문장의 충고의 결과가 나오고 있으므로 ③번이 적절하다.

22 give up on: ~을 단념하다

23 why 다음에 앞 내용에 대한 이유가 이어지고 있기 때문에, why를 because로 고치는 것이 적절하다.

Waste Not, Want Not

시험대비 실력평가 p.64

01 ② 02 ① 03 ④
04 (1) save (2) waste (3) experiment (4) decide
05 ⑤ 06 ④ 07 ②

01 주어진 단어는 유의어 관계이다. add 더하다, sum 합을 내다, alone 혼자 있는, isolated 고립된

02 주어진 단어는 반의어 관계이다. charge 충전하다 discharge 방출하다 cool 식히다 heat 데우다

03 "대단히 중요하고 필요한"은 "essential 필수적인"에 해당한다.

04 (1) 어떻게 에너지를 절약할 수 있을까요? (2) 그것들은 학생들이 물을 낭비하지 않도록 도와준다. (3) 우리는 지난 겨울에 실험을 했다. (4) 우리는 학교 지붕에 정원을 만들기로 결정할 것이다.

05 동생의 시계를 잃어버리고 고민하는 소녀에게 사실대로 이야기하라는 조언을 하고 있다.

06 price 가격 exercise 운동, 연습 amount 합계, 금액 character 특징, 글자 cost 비용, 가격 pot 화분

07 ② "empty"는 "비어 있는"이라는 뜻이다.

서술형 시험대비 p.65

01 up
02 at
03 (1) order (2) choose (3) electricity (4) energy
04 (n)ervous
05 additional
06 (1) danger (2) (l)eaves (3) temperature (4) cool

01 • 너는 어젯밤에 밤늦게까지 깨어 있었니? stay up 깨어 있다 / • 네가 그런 대단한 생각을 해낸 것은 매우 현명하다! come up with 생각해 내다

02 • 나는 그가 네 아이디어를 전혀 이해하지 못한다고 생각한다. not ~ at all = 전혀 ~가 아닌 / 내가 테니스를 조금도 잘할 거라고는 생각하지 않지만 한번 시도는 해 보겠어요. be good at ~ = ~을 잘하다

03 (1) 네가 원하는 음식을 모두 확인하고 주문 버튼을 눌러라. (2) 너는 어떻게 좋은 냉장고를 선택하는지 아니? (3) 그것들은 어느

등불이 켜져야 하는지 알려주어서 우리가 에너지를 더 적게 낭비하도록 해준다. (4) 학교를 난방하고, 또 냉방하기 위하여 많은 에너지가 사용된다.

04 주어진 단어는 반의어 관계이다. spend 쓰다, 보내다, save 아끼다, 절약하다, nervous 불안한, calm 차분한

05 동사 add의 형용사 additional이 적절하다.

06 (1) 위험에 빠진 = in danger (2) 떠나다 = leave (3) 온도 = temperature (4) 냉방하다 = cool

Conversation

핵심 Check p.66~67

1 ② 2 ④
3 Do you know how to use this washing machine

01 소녀가 처한 곤란함에 대하여 충고하는 의미로 "If I were you"가 적절하고, "You'd better + 동사원형", "Why don't you + 동사원형?"도 충고하는 표현으로 쓸 수 있다.

02 이어지는 소녀의 응답이 식당을 이용하는 방법이므로 질문도 식당을 이용하는 방법이 적절하다.

교과서 대화문 익히기

Check(√) True or False p.68

1 F 2 T 3 T 4 F

교과서 확인학습 p.70~71

Everday English 1 A-2(1)
look, problem / lost, watch, loves, much / were, truth / guess, choice

Everday English 1 A-2(2)
hard, concentrate / stay / sleep / If, were, get, fresh, starts

Everday English 1 - B
what, holding, like, full / went, grocery / Let, buy / bought, because, cheap / already, apples, such, money / If, were, check, first, shopping / make, based, information / do

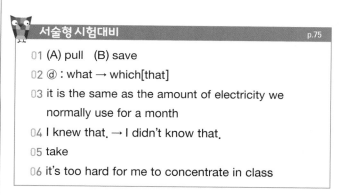

시험대비 기본평가   p.72

| 01 ④ | 02 ③ | 03 ④ | 04 ① |

01 밤늦게까지 자지 않아서 수업에 집중하기 어렵다는 내용으로 '집중하다 = concentrate'가 적절하다. get some fresh air = 신선한 공기를 마시다, 기분전환을 하다

02 컴퓨터의 문제를 해결하는 '방법'을 대답하고 있으므로 질문도 방법을 나타내는 'how to'가 적절하다.

03 주어진 문장은 단계별 과정에서 앞에 나온 과정 다음 단계를 묻는 질문으로 (D)가 적절한 위치이다.

04 이 대화에서는 기계 사용법을 소년이 설명하는 것이 아니라 소녀가 설명하고 있다.

시험대비 실력평가   p.73~74

01 ③	02 ③	03 ⑤	04 ①
05 ⑤	06 ②	07 ⑤	08 ③
09 (A) price (B) size		10 ④	11 ③

01 (B) 전기 절약 방법을 질문하고 (C) 거기에 대한 대답으로 전자 제품의 전원을 끄는 것과 (A) 추가로 플러그를 뽑는 것을 알려 준다.

02 화분을 바꾸면 식물이 더 크게 자랄 것이라고 설명하는 것으로 보아 ③이 적절하다.

03 소녀가 가르쳐 주겠다는 내용이 소년이 질문한 것이므로 'how to move'가 적절하다.

04 그 식물은 소녀가 아니라 그의 여동생으로부터 받은 생일 선물

이었다.

05 (A) '플러그를 뽑다'의 의미로 out (B) 사용하지 않는 충전기가 전기를 낭비하므로 wasting (C) 적은 양을 합했을 때 많은 양이 된다는 의미로 add가 적절하다.

06 주어진 문장은 자신이 꽂아놓은 플러그를 빼라는 말에 대한 반응으로 (B)가 적절한 위치이다.

07 ⓔ "are going to"의 주어인 "an energy-saving conference"가 단수이기 때문에 "is going to"가 되어야 한다.

08 ③ 에너지를 아끼는 다른 방법은 다음주 conference에서 알아볼 내용으로 이 대화에서는 소개되지 않았다.

09 (A) "How much can you spend ~?"는 가격에 관한 질문이므로 "price"가 적절하다. (B) "You might think larger ones are better."는 냉장고의 크기에 대한 언급으로 (B)는 "size"가 적절하다.

10 ⓓ 냉장고의 사이즈가 큰 것이 좋다고 생각할 수 있다는 것과는 대조적인 단점이 언급된 것으로 공간과 에너지를 낭비한다는 의미의 "waste"가 적절하다.

11 "Try to choose the right size for you."라고 했기 때문에 크다고 좋은 냉장고라고 할 수는 없다.

서술형 시험대비   p.75

01 (A) pull   (B) save
02 ⓓ : what → which[that]
03 it is the same as the amount of electricity we normally use for a month
04 I knew that. → I didn't know that.
05 take
06 it's too hard for me to concentrate in class

01 (A) 충전 중이 아닌 충전기이므로 '뽑다'가 되어야 한다. (B) Lina는 전기를 절약하는 방법을 알고 싶어 한다.

02 ⓓ는 things를 선행사로 하는 관계대명사 which[that]가 적절하다.

03 전기의 양과 같은 = the same as the amount of electricity 우리가 보통 한 달 동안 사용하는 전기의 양 = the amount of electricity we normally use for a month

04 집에 사과가 있는 것을 모르고 또 산 것이라고 봐야 하므로 '나는 몰랐다.'가 되어야 한다.

05 식전에 하루 세 번 복용하는 것은 약을 복용하는 방법을 질문한 것에 대한 대답이다.

06 내가 ~하기 너무 어렵다 = it's too hard for me to ~

Grammar

1 (1) less　(2) more　(3) older, wiser

2 (1) The higher you climb, the colder it gets.

(2) The faster the car is, the more dangerous it is to drive.

3 (1) important for Jake to get up early

(2) very kind of you to carry the bag for me

(3) very clever of him to come up with such a good idea

(4) necessary for the cyclists to wear their helmet when riding the bike

시험대비 기본평가
p.78

01 ④　　02 ①　　03 ④　　04 ①

01 'the 비교급, the 비교급'의 구문이다.

02 'the 비교급, the 비교급' 구문으로 '더 많은 책'은 'the more books'라고 해야 한다.

03 주어진 보기의 It은 가주어 It이다 ①, ② 날씨를 나타내는 비인 칭 주어, ③, ⑤의 It은 '그것'을 나타내는 인칭대명사. ④는 가 주어이다.

04 사람의 성향을 나타내는 lazy에 다음에 to부정사의 의미상의 주 어를 <of+목적격>으로 표시해줘야 한다.

시험대비 실력평가
p.79~81

01 ④

02 (1) The harder you study, the better grade you will get.

(2) The more you exercise, the healthier you will become.

(3) The more trees we plant, the more fresh air we will have.

(4) The hotter the weather becomes, the more water you should drink.

03 ④　　04 ⑤　　05 ①　　06 for

07 ③　　08 ④　　09 ①　　10 ⑤

11 (1) It is difficult for him to take care of the cat.

(2) It is necessary for her to buy an umbrella.

(3) It was kind of her to help the old lady.

12 ③　　13 ⑤　　14 ⑤　　15 ①

16 ④　　17 ⑤　　18 ⑤

01 ④ 가주어, 의미상 주어, 진주어 구문에서 사람의 성격 표현이 아닌 경우에는 "for+목적격"이 되어야 한다. of a child → for a child

02 접속사 as를 쓴 구문을 'the 비교급, the 비교급'의 구문으로 전환 한다. <보기> 네가 친절해질수록 더 많은 친구들이 너를 좋아할 것이다. (1) 공부를 열심히 할수록 더 좋은 성적을 받을 것이다. (2) 운동을 많이 할수록 더 건강해질 것이다. (3) 나무를 많이 심 을수록 신선한 공기 많아질 것이다. (4) 날씨가 더워질수록 더 많 은 물을 마셔야 한다.

03 ① to부정사의 의미상의 주어는 'for me' ② 사람의 성격을 나 타내는 형용사 뒤에 'of her' ③ 부사의 의미상의 주어 'for me' ⑤ 의미상 주어 'for Janet'으로 바꿔야 한다.

04 주어진 문장을 영어로 옮기면 "The higher we climb, the colder it gets."이다.

05 ① 사람의 성격 형용사 뒤에서 of+목적격 ② difficult 뒤에는 for us ③ easy 뒤에는 for me ④ nice 뒤에는 of you ⑤ 의 미상 주어는 for+목적격이므로 for him이 되어야 한다.

06 주어진 문장을 영어로 옮기면 "It is natural for your brother to shout out loudly at you."이다. 그 중에서 네 번째 오는 단어 는 for이다.

07 ③: 사람의 성격을 나타내는 silly 뒤에서 의미상 주어의 형태는 'of+목적격' ①, ②, ④, ⑤ dangerous, boring, difficult, easy 는 'for+목적격'의 의미상 주어가 되어야 한다.

08 문법적으로 올바른 문장은 ④이다. ① hoter → hotter ② the much better → much better ③ better its taste is → the better its taste is ⑤ 부사의 비교급(harder) 앞에 the를 쓰지 않는다.

09 ① 'the 비교급+주어+동사' 구문으로 the much는 the more 로 해야 한다.

10 ⑤: '당신이 더 많은 사람들을 만날수록, 더 많은 것들을 배울 수 있다.'라는 뜻이 되도록 답을 고른다.

11 의미상의 주어가 있는 'It ~ for A to ⋯'의 구문으로 완성하고, (3) 사람의 성격을 나타내는 kind 다음에는 'of 목적격'을 쓰도록 한다.

12 ③: 사람의 성격이나 성질을 나타내는 형용사 다음 'of+목적격' ①, ②, ④, ⑤ hard, necessary, safe, okay는 'for+목적격' 의 형태로 의미상 주어를 나타낸다.

13 ① The richer we are, the happier we'll be. ② The older you get, the wiser you will become. ③ The more you smile, the more people will like you. ④ The more you love, the more you will be loved.

14 'the 비교급+주어+동사, the 비교급+주어+동사' 구문이다.

15 ① 'of+목적격' ②~⑤ difficult, okay, impossible, important는 'for+목적격'의 형태로 의미상 주어를 나타낸다.

16 ① tall → taller ② more thick → thicker ③ you want the more → the more you want ⑤ hard의 비교급은 harder이

17 (A) hard (C) easy와 (D) difficult는 사람의 성격, 성질을 나타내는 형용사가 아니므로 의미상의 주어를 for A라고 해야 한다. (B) careless는 사람의 성격, 성질을 나타내므로 of me의 형태로 써야 한다. (E) 문장의 주어는 to부정사로 쓰는 것이 알맞다.

18 ⑤ "the more early"를 "the earlier"로 고쳐야 한다.

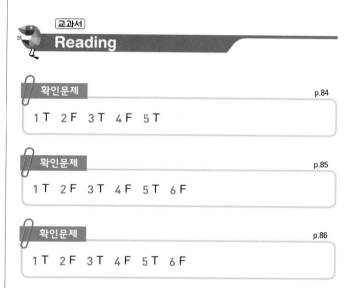

p.82~83

서술형 시험대비

01 (1) It's difficult for us to swim in the river.
   (2) It's kind of you to hold the bag for me.
02 (1) The better the weather is, the more people we can find in the park.
   (2) The fresher the fruit is, the better it tastes.
   (3) The older she grew, the wiser she became.
03 It was strange for her to be late for work.
04 (A) the most → the more
   (B) of him → for him
05 (1) more, better   (2) higher, farther
   (3) more, healthier
06 (1) for us to move this chair
   (2) of you to open the window
07 It was very kind of Tom to help a lost boy to find his mother.
08 (1) The older we get, the wiser we become.
   (2) The more heavily it rains, the faster people walk.
09 was wise of Mary to refuse the suggestion
10 The warmer the weather gets, the better I feel.
11 is hard for them to keep exercising

01 (1) It's difficult for us to swim in the river. to부정사의 의미상의 주어는 "for+목적격"으로 표시한다. (2) It's kind of you to hold the bag for me. 사람의 성격이나 태도를 나타내는 경우 "of+목적격"으로 표시한다.

02 '더 ~할수록, 더 …하다'의 의미로 'the 비교급 S+V, the 비교급 S+V' 구문으로 바꾼다.

03 주어진 문장을 가주어, 진주어의 형태로 쓰고, 부정사의 의미상 주어가 포함되도록 한다.

04 (A) the most → the more 「the 비교급 S+V, the 비교급 S+V」 구문이므로, 최상급 most를 비교급 more로 고쳐 쓴다.
   (B) of → for (to부정사의 의미상 주어로 "for+목적격"으로 쓰는 것이 알맞다.)

05 (1) 네가 더 많이 공부할수록, 더 좋은 성적을 얻는다. (2) 새가 더 높이 날수록, 더 멀리 볼 수 있다. (3) 네가 더 많이 운동할수록, 더 건강해진다.

06 (1) difficult는 사람의 성격을 나타내는 형용사가 아니므로 for us의 형태로 써야 한다. (2) careless는 사람의 성격을 나타내는 형용사이므로 of you의 형태로 써야 한다.

07 사람의 성격을 나타내는 kind가 있으므로, "It was + of 의미상의 주어 + to부정사" 구문을 이용하여 문장을 완성한다.

08 "~하면 할수록, 더 …하게 된다"라는 뜻의 "the 비교급+주어+동사, the 비교급+주어+동사"를 사용하여 영작한다.

09 "현명한(wise)"은 사람의 성격을 나타내므로 "가주어 It + of + 목적격 + to부정사" 구문을 이용하여 문장을 완성한다.

10 "날씨가 따뜻해지다"는 "The weather gets warm."이다. 시제는 현재시제가 적절하다.

11 "그들이 매일 운동을 계속하는 것"은 "for them to keep exercising"이 되도록 한다.

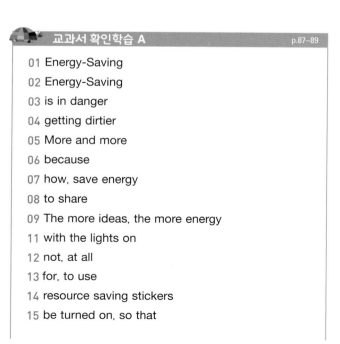

교과서 Reading

확인문제 p.84

1 T 2 F 3 T 4 F 5 T

확인문제 p.85

1 T 2 F 3 T 4 F 5 T 6 F

확인문제 p.86

1 T 2 F 3 T 4 F 5 T 6 F

교과서 확인학습 A p.87~89

01 Energy-Saving
02 Energy-Saving
03 is in danger
04 getting dirtier
05 More and more
06 because
07 how, save energy
08 to share
09 The more ideas, the more energy
11 with the lights on
12 not, at all
13 for, to use
14 resource saving stickers
15 be turned on, so that

16 last, to turn off

17 put some stickers on

18 not to waste

19 The more stickers, the more resources

21 is used

22 It, for, to reduce

23 did an experiment, help to save

24 Look at

25 put, on

26 turned off

27 went down to

28 it

29 escape from

30 putting, on

31 prevent, from getting

32 The more bubble wrap, the cooler

34 to make, on the rooftop

35 Only a few, how it works

36 It's just like

37 prevents, from, in and out of

38 we use to cool

39 helps to cool

40 is, for, to make

41 The more beautiful, the less energy

42 of, come up with

43 worth trying

44 unique

교과서 확인학습 B
p.90~92

1 Energy-Saving Conference

2 Welcome to the Energy-Saving Conference.

3 The Earth is in danger.

4 The air is getting dirtier every day.

5 More and more animals are dying.

6 This is because we are wasting a lot of energy.

7 So how can we save energy?

8 Three different environmental clubs are here to share their activities.

9 The more ideas we share, the more energy we can save!

10 Jimin: Hello, friends.

11 A few months ago, I was surprised to see some empty classrooms with the lights on.

12 That's not right at all.

13 It is essential for all students to use fewer resources at school.

14 So we have designed some resource saving stickers and put them on the switches.

15 They tell us which light should be turned on, so that we can waste less electricity.

16 They also tell the last student who leaves the classroom to turn off the lights.

17 We also put some stickers on the mirrors in the restrooms.

18 They help students not to waste water

19 The more stickers we put up, the more resources we can save at school.

20 Dongsu: Hi, everyone.

21 A lot of energy is used to heat and cool our school.

22 It is important for students to reduce the amount of energy we use.

23 We did an experiment last winter and found that bubble wrap can help to save energy.

24 Look at this chart.

25 In Classroom A we put bubble wrap on the windows and in Classroom B we didn't.

26 When we turned off the heater, the temperature was 16 ℃ in both classrooms.

27 Sixty minutes later, the temperature in Classroom B went down to 7 ℃.

28 But it was 9 ℃ in Classroom A!

29 We learned that bubble wrap only lets a little heat escape from the building.

30 So we started putting bubble wrap on the school windows.

31 This will also prevent heat from getting into the classroom in the summer.

32 The more bubble wrap we put on the windows, the cooler our summer will become!

33 Minwoo: Hello, friends.

34 We decided to make a garden on the rooftop of the school to save energy.

35 Only a few people know how it works.

36 It's just like bubble wrap.

37 It prevents heat from getting in and out of the buildings.

38 So when we have rooftop gardens on our buildings, we can save some of the energy we use to cool the buildings in the summer.

39 Also, the fresh air from the rooftop garden helps to cool the whole city.

40 So it is necessary for us students to make more rooftop gardens at our school!

41 The more beautiful our rooftops become, the less energy our school will use!

42 MC: It's very clever of you to come up with such great ideas!

43 These are all worth trying at school or at home.

44 Thank you for your unique ideas and activities!

시험대비 실력평가

01 in

02 (1) The air is getting dirtier every day.
   (2) More and more animals are dying.

03 ④　　　　04 ④

05 More → The more, cooler → the cooler

06 lower → higher　　　07 much → a little

08 ②　　　　09 ⑤

10 전등이 켜진 몇 개의 빈 교실 또는 몇 개의 빈 교실에 전등이 켜져 있는 것

11 ③　　　　12 ④

13 (A) for us　(B) less　(C) of you

14 to try　　15 ②　　　16 ②

17 in the least

18 The more stickers we put up, the more resources we can save at school.

19 ④

20 ⓐ sixteen degrees Celsius　ⓑ seven degrees Celsius
   ⓒ nine degrees Celsius

21 bubble wrap　　　22 ①

23 These are all worth trying at school or at home.

24 ③　　　　25 ④

01 be in danger 위험에 처하다

02 '공기가 매일 더러워지고 있는 것'과 '점점 더 많은 동물이 죽어 가고 있는 것'이다.

03 '그렇다면 우리는 어떻게 에너지를 절약할 수 있을까요?'라고 물은 다음에, '세 개의 다른 환경 동아리들이 그들의 활동을 공유하기 위해 여기에 있습니다.'라고 했으므로, 뒤에 올 내용으로는 '세 개의 다른 환경 동아리들의 활동에 대한 소개'가 적절하다. ① species: 종, ② endangered: 멸종 위기에 처한, ③ reduce: 줄이다, ⑤ preserve: 보존하다, resource: 자원

04 ⓐ for+목적격: to부정사의 의미상의 주어, ⓑ prevent A from B: A를 B로부터 막다, A가 B하는 것을 막다

05 The 비교급+주어+동사, the 비교급+주어+동사: 더 ~할수록, 더 …하다

06 60분 뒤, 교실 B의 온도는 7℃로 내려갔지만 교실 A는 9℃였

07 뽁뽁이가 오직 '적은 양의' 열만 건물에서 빠져나가게 한다는 것을 알았다고 해야 하므로, much를 a little로 고치는 것이 적절하다.

08 ⓐ와 ②: 가주어, ① 비인칭 주어(시간), ③ 그것(인칭대명사), ④ 가목적어, ⑤ 전치사의 무의미한 형식상 목적어

09 이 글은 '뽁뽁이가 에너지를 절약하는 데에 도움이 된다.'는 내용의 글이므로, 제목으로는 ⑤번 '에너지를 절약하기를 원하나요? 뽁뽁이를 사용하는 것이 어때요?'가 적절하다.

10 'some empty classrooms with the lights on'을 가리킨다.

11 ⓑ와 ③: (돈, 시간 등을) 낭비하다, ① 소용없게 된(형용사), waste products: 노폐물, properly: 제대로, 적절히, ② <사람·체력을> 소모하다; 쇠약[초췌]하게 만들다, ④ 낭비, 허비(명사), ⑤ 경작되지 않은, 황폐한(형용사), cultivate: 경작하다

12 스위치에 붙인 '자원 절약 스티커'가 어떤 전등이 켜질 것인지 알려 줘서, 전기를 덜 낭비할 수 있게 한다.

13 (A) 'it is necessary' 뒤의 의미상의 주어는 'for us'가 적절하다. (B) 우리의 옥상이 더 아름다워질수록, 우리 학교는 에너지를 '덜' 사용하게 될 것이라고 해야 하므로 less가 적절하다. (C) 사람의 성품이나 성질을 나타내는 형용사 'clever'가 있으므로 의미상의 주어는 'of you'가 적절하다.

14 be worth -ing = It is worth while to부정사: ~할 가치가 있다

15 이 글은 '에너지를 절약하기 위해 학교 옥상에 정원을 만드는 것'에 관한 글이므로, 주제로는 ②번 '에너지를 절약하기 위해 학교 옥상에 정원을 만들기'가 적절하다. ① preference: 선호도, ③ mechanism: (목적을 달성하기 위한) 방법, 메커니즘

16 ②번 다음 문장의 They에 주목한다. 주어진 문장의 'some resource saving stickers'를 받고 있으므로 ②번이 적절하다.

17 not ~ at all = not ~ in the least: 조금도 … 아니다

18 The 비교급+주어+동사, the 비교급+주어+동사: 더 ~할수록, 더 …하다

19 두 시간 뒤에 교실 B의 온도가 몇 도일 것으로 예상되는지는 알 수 없다. ① In Classroom A. ② It shows the change of the temperature in Classroom A over time. over time: 시간이 흐름에 따라, ③ It was 16 ℃. ⑤ Yes.

20 Celsius: 섭씨의

21 '뽁뽁이'를 가리킨다. This가 가리키는 것이 'putting bubble wrap on the school windows'라고 하는 것도 가능하지만, 앞부분에서 '뽁뽁이'가 오직 적은 양의 열만 건물에서 빠져나가게 한다고 말한 것과 대비시켜, 'bubble wrap'이라고 하는 것이 더

적절하다.

22 ⓐ와 ①: 작용하다, 작동하다, ② 책; 음악 작품; 그림 등(명사), ③ (시계 따위의) 장치, ④ 일하다, ⑤ (건설•수리) 공사[작업] (명사)

23 be worth -ing: ~할 가치가 있다

24 이 글은 '에너지를 절약하기 위해 학교 옥상에 정원을 만드는 것'에 관한 글이므로, 제목으로는 ③번 '옥상정원, 에너지를 절약하는 아름다운 방법'이 적절하다. ④ efficiency: 효율(성), 능률, landscaping: 조경, ⑤ academic achievement: 학업성취도

25 옥상정원에서 나오는 신선한 공기는 도시 전체를 식히는 것을 도와준다.

01 You are

02 A lot of → Only a few

03 (1) (A) to cool   (2) (B) the fresh air

04 with the lights on

05 (A) less   (B) off   (C) more

06 (A) Classroom A   (B) Classroom B

07 to escape → escape 또는 lets → allows

08 Also, the fresh air from the rooftop garden helps cool the whole city.

09 come up with

01 It ... of ~ to부정사 구문에서는 'of+목적격'을 주어 자리로 옮겨서 문장을 전환하는 것이 가능하다.

02 '오직 몇몇 사람들만이' 학교의 옥상정원이 어떻게 작용하는지 알고 있다.

03 (1) 건물에 옥상정원을 가지고 있으면, 우리는 여름에 건물을 '식히기 위해' 사용하는 에너지 일부를 절약할 수 있기 때문이다.
(2) 옥상정원에서 나오는 '신선한 공기'는 도시 전체를 식히는 것을 도와주기 때문이다.

04 with+목적어+목적격보어: ~을 …한 채로[의]

05 (A) 어떤 전등이 켜질 것인지 알려 줘서, 우리는 전기를 '덜' 낭비할 수 있다고 해야 하므로 less가 적절하다. (B) 마지막 학생이 전등을 '꺼야' 한다고 해야 하므로 off가 적절하다. (C) '더 많은' 자원을 절약할 수 있다고 해야 하므로 more가 적절하다.

06 창문에 뽁뽁이를 붙인 '교실 A'의 온도가 뽁뽁이를 붙이지 않은 '교실 B'의 온도보다 덜 내려갔다는 것을 의미한다.

07 let+목적어+원형부정사, allow+목적어+to부정사

08 helps 다음의 to를 생략할 수 있다.

09 come up with: ~를 생각해 내다, 아이디어나 질문에 대한 답이나 혹은 문제에 대한 해결책을 생각해 내다

01 ⑤   02 ④   03 ④   04 ③

05 If I were you, I'd tell him the truth.

06 do you know how to use this restaurant   07 ④

08 ②   09 ①   10 ④

11 If I were you, I would pull the plug out.

12 ②   13 ⑤   14 ②

15 The more you love, the more you will be loved.

16 ①   17 ④   18 ④   19 ④

20 It was easy for Sam to solve the problem.

21 ②   22 why → because

23 (A) fewer   (B) last   (C) more

24 ⑤

25 We use a lot of energy to heat and cool our school.

26 ④   27 ⑤

28 a simple way to save some of the gas or oil that is used to heat your house   29 ④

01 "이 한자 어떻게 읽는지 아세요?" / 한자 = Chinese character

02 "유용한 토지 또는 석유나 석탄과 같은 광물질과 같은 것"은 "resource 자원"에 대한 설명이다.

03 "나는 불을 켜고 자는 것을 좋아하지 않는다." 불을 켠 채로 = with the lights on / "정말 그것에 대해 생각해 보면 그것에 대한 대답을 찾을 수 있을 거야." 생각해내다 = come up with

04 "이 문은 빗물이 집안으로 흘러드는 것을 막을 수 있다." / A가 ~하지 못하게 하다 = prevent A from –ing, stop A from –ing

05 충고하는 의미로 "내가 너라면 ~할 텐데"에 해당하는 것은 "If I were you, I would ~"이다.

06 방법을 묻는 말로 "어떻게 ~하는지 아니?"에 해당하는 것은 "Do you know how to ~?"이다.

07 ④ 약을 복용하는 방법을 묻는 질문에 대하여 어떻게 약을 복용하는지 대답을 하는 것으로 보아 'Yes, I do'나 'Sure.' 등으로 시작하는 것이 적절하다.

08 ② 주어진 문장은 사과를 구입한 이유를 묻는 것이기 때문에 이유를 설명하는 문장 앞인 ⓑ에 들어가야 한다.

09 목적어 역할을 하는 의문대명사로 사물을 가리키는 경우에 "무엇"이라는 뜻으로 사용하는 what이 적절하다.

10 이 대화에서 지후는 집에 사과가 있는 것을 모르고 또 사과를 사왔다, 그러나 그 사과가 어떤지에 대한 설명은 없다.

11 "만약 내가 너라면 ~할 텐데."는 "If I were you, I would ~." 이다. "~을 뽑다" = pull out

12 리나는 대기 전력으로 낭비되는 전기가 많지 않다고 생각하기 때문에 "약간, 작은"이라는 뜻의 ②가 적절하다.

13 대화의 마지막에 Lina가 "Maybe we should go together!"

라고 하는 것으로 보아 Lina는 conference에 가기를 원한다고 해야 한다.

14 ② 사람의 성격을 나타내는 단어 stupid 뒤에 부정사의 의미상 주어는 "of+목적격"이다. for you → of you

15 주어진 우리말 내용은 "the 비교급+주어+동사, the 비교급+주어+동사" 구문을 이용하여 나타낸다.

16 ① 주어진 문장의 주어 "강에서 수영하는 것"은 to부정사로 나타내고, 가주어와 진주어를 사용하여 영작한다.

17 ④"The+비교급+주어+동사, the+비교급+주어+동사"는 "~하면 할수록 더 …하다"의 의미이다. happy의 비교급은 happier이다.

18 ④ 사람의 성격을 나타내는 형용사 kind 다음에 오는 부정사의 의미상 주어는 "of 목적격"이 되어야 한다. for you → of you

19 ④ "~하면 할수록 더 …하다"는 "The+비교급+주어+동사, the+비교급+주어+동사"의 구문이다.

20 내용상 Sam이 문제를 쉽게 풀었다는 것으로 받아들여서 "It was easy for Sam to ~"가 적절하다.

21 우리가 더 많은 아이디어를 '공유할수록', 우리는 더 많은 에너지를 '절약할 수' 있다고 하는 것이 적절하다. ① waste: 낭비하다, ⑤ refuse: 거절하다

22 '이것은 우리가 많은 에너지를 낭비하고 있기 때문'이라고 해야 하므로, why를 because로 고치는 것이 적절하다. why+결과, because+이유

23 (A) '더 적은' 자원을 사용하는 것이 필수적이라고 해야 하므로 fewer가 적절하다. (B) 교실을 떠나는 '마지막' 학생이라고 해야 하므로 last가 적절하다. (C) '더 많은' 스티커들을 붙일수록, 학교에서 더 많은 자원을 절약할 수 있다고 해야 하므로 more가 적절하다.

24 '지민이의 동아리 회원들이 총 몇 장의 자원 절약 스티커를 붙였는지'는 대답할 수 없다. in all: 총[모두 합쳐], ① Because Jimin saw some empty classrooms with the lights on. ② Because it is essential for all students to use fewer resources at school. ③ They put them on the light switches in the classrooms and on the mirrors in the restrooms. ④ They help students not to waste water.

25 We를 주어로 해서 능동태로 고치는 것이 적절하다.

26 ④번 다음 문장의 This에 주목한다. 주어진 문장의 bubble wrap을 받고 있으므로 ④번이 적절하다.

27 동수의 동아리 회원들은 뽁뽁이가 '겨울에' 오직 적은 양의 열만 건물에서 빠져나가게 한다는 것을 알았다. 뽁뽁이가 여름에는 '열이 교실로 들어오는 것을' 막아준다.

28 '여러분의 집의 난방을 위해 사용되는 가스나 석유의 일부를 절약하는 간단한 방법'을 가리킨다.

29 2 mm가 아니라 '1.5' mm일 때 에너지를 4% 더 많이 낭비하게 될 것이다.

단원별 예상문제
p.106~109

01 concentration	02 ③	03 ②
04 ④	05 ③	06 ③	07 ①
08 ③	09 ③	10 ④	11 ④
12 ④	13 ①		

14 The closer, the warmer   15 ③

16 It is important for students to reduce the amount of energy we use.

17 ①, ③   18 (A) bubble wrap   (B) saving

19 ③   20 ①, ③   21 12

22 No, he isn't. He is not good enough.

23 You should try harder to save resources.

01 주어진 단어는 "동사-명사"의 관계이다. add 더하다, addition 더하기, concentrate 집중하다, concentration 집중

02 그 호텔은 옥상에 있는 야외 식당 때문에 정말로 여름에 인기가 높았다. 옥상 = rooftop

03 그들은 또한 교실에서 마지막으로 나가는 사람에게 등불을 끄라고 말한다. 끄다 = turn off / 에어컨에 있는 검은 네트를 꺼내서 거기 있는 먼지를 털어내라. 털어내다 = brush off

04 ① 집다 = pick up ② heat and cool 냉난방을 하다 ③ prevent 막다 ④ pull out = 뽑다 ⑤ come up with 생각해내다

05 "~하는 것은 너무 …"는 "it is too ~ to 부정사" 구문이다.

06 ⓒ "what ~"은 간접의문문으로 "의문사+주어+동사"의 어순이다.

07 "did you start to learn them?"이라는 질문에 긍정적으로 대답하는 것으로 보아 소녀는 한자를 배우기 시작했다.

08 충고하는 의미로 "내가 너라면 ~"이라고 할 때는 가정법을 사용하여 "If I were you, ~"라고 한다.

09 밑줄 친 (A)는 "다른 화분으로 옮기다"의 의미로 "change its pot"에 해당한다.

10 소녀가 민재에게 어떻게 식물의 화분을 갈아주는지를 가르쳐 주겠다고 했지만 어떤 화분을 사용할지는 언급하지 않았다.

11 주어진 보기의 문장과 ④의 It은 가주어이다. 나머지 문장의 It은 모두 비인칭 주어이다.

12 ④ "The+비교급+주어+동사, the+비교급+주어+동사"의 구문으로 "~하면 할수록 더 …하다"의 의미이다.

13 ①의 for you는 부정사의 의미상 주어이다. 사람의 성격을 나타내는 kind 뒤에서 부정사의 의미사의 주어는 "of+목적격"이 되어야 한다. for you → of you

19

14 "~하면 할수록 …"의 의미로 "the+형용사의 비교급"이 되도록 빈칸을 채운다.

15 각각 다음과 같이 바로잡아야 올바른 문장이다. ① speaking → to speak ② of him → for him ④ for you → of you ⑤ for his → for him

16 It ... for ~ to부정사: It: 가주어, for ~: 의미상의 주어, to부정사: 진주어

17 prevent[keep/stop/hinder/prohibit] A from B: A를 B로부터 막다, A가 B하는 것을 막다, ② 보호하다, ⑤ 줄이다

18 지난겨울 동수의 동아리 회원들에 의해 행해진 실험에서 학교 창문에 '뽁뽁이'를 붙이는 것이 에너지를 '절약하는' 데에 도움이 된다는 것이 발견되었다.

19 주어진 문장의 So에 주목한다. ③번 앞 문장의 내용의 결과를 So 다음에서 설명하고 있으므로 ③번이 적절하다.

20 ⓐ와 ②, ④, ⑤: 부사적 용법, ①: 명사적 용법, ③: 형용사적 용법

21 B: 4개 × 1점 = 4점, C: 4개 × 2점 = 8점, 총합계: 12점

22 13~16점이 "excellent"에 해당하는데, 12점이므로 "excellent"에 해당하지 않는다.

23 민수는 자원 절약을 하려고 더 열심히 노력해야 한다.

서술형 실전문제 · p.110~111

01 (A) of (B) of (C) on
02 check what I have first before I go shopping
03 It is important for you to learn from experience.
04 The more beautiful our rooftops become, the less energy our school will use.
05 (A) reduce (B) escape (C) cooler
06 This will also prevent heat from getting into the classroom in the summer.
07 (A) temperature (B) red (C) blue (D) 16
08 a garden on the rooftop of the school
09 (A) more beautifu (B) less energy

01 (A) ~로 가득 찬 = full of ~ (B) ~의 낭비 = a waste of ~ (C) ~에 바탕을 둔 = based on ~

02 나는 ~을 점검할 것이다 = I'd check ~, 내가 가진 것 = what I have, 쇼핑을 가기 전에 = before I go shopping

03 문장의 주어 "~하는 것"은 부정사를 통해서 나타내고, 가주어, 진주어 구문을 이용한다.

04 "The+비교급+주어+동사, the+비교급+주어+동사"의 구문으로 "~하면 할수록 더 …하다"의 의미를 나타낸다.

05 (A) 사용하는 에너지의 양을 '줄이는 것'이 중요하다고 해야 하

므로 reduce가 적절하다. (B) 뽁뽁이가 오직 적은 양의 열만 건물에서 '빠져나가게' 한다는 것을 알았다고 해야 하므로 escape가 적절하다. (C) 우리의 여름도 '더 시원해질' 것이라고 해야 하므로 cooler가 적절하다.

06 from을 보충하면 된다.

07 이 도표는 시간이 지남에 따라 교실 A와 교실 B의 '온도'가 어떻게 변하는지를 보여준다. '빨간색' 줄은 시간이 흐름에 따른 교실 A의 온도 변화를 보여주고 '파란색' 줄은 교실 B의 그것을 보여준다. 비록 동수의 동아리 회원들이 측정을 시작했을 때 두 교실의 온도는 똑같이 '16'℃였지만, 교실 B의 온도가 교실 A의 그것보다 더 많이 내려갔다. over time: 시간이 흐름에 따라

08 '학교 옥상의 정원'을 가리킨다.

09 As로 시작하여 문장을 전환할 때는 the를 생략하는 것이 적절하다.

창의사고력 서술형 문제 · p.112

|모범답안|

01 (1) waste (2) environmental (3) garden
(4) clever (5) share (6) empty
02 (A) black dust (B) thickness (C) 1
(D) 1.5 (E) 3 (F) 4.5

단원별 모의고사 · p.113~116

01 consideration 　　02 ① 　　03 ②
04 (1) bubble (2) conference (3) resources
(4) experiment
05 ④
06 It helps prevent electricity from being wasted.
07 ⑤ 　　08 ④ 　　09 ② 　　10 ②
11 ② 　　12 ⑤
13 more ideas, more energy
14 helpful for children to read a lot of books
15 ④
16 (some) resource saving stickers
17 (1) (A) which light (2) (B) turn off
18 ①, ②, ⑤
19 (A) escape from (B) getting into
20 Only a few people know how it works.
21 (1) It prevents heat from getting in and out of the buildings.
(2) The fresh air from the rooftop garden helps to cool the whole city. 　22 ④

01 주어진 단어의 관계는 동사-명사이다. pay 지불하다, payment 지불, consider 고려하다, consideration 고려

02 체중을 유지하기 위하여 운동을 하는 것으로 ① "규칙적으로 regularly" 운동하는 것이 적절하다. ② 거의 ~ 아닌 ③ 불안하게 ④ 거의 ~ 아닌 ⑤ 극단적으로

03 "지붕의 위쪽 표면"은 "옥상 = rooftop"이다. ① 뜰 ② 옥상 ③ 실험 ④ 회의 ⑤ 인물, 문자

04 (1) 뽁뽁이 = bubble wrap (2) 에너지 절약 회의 = an energy-saving conference (3) 자원 = resources (4) experiment 실험

05 에어컨을 청소할 때는 전기가 흘러 위험할 수 있기 때문에 안전을 위해서 가장 먼저 플러그를 뽑아야 한다.

06 "~하는 것을 막다"는 "prevent A from –ing"이다.

07 이 대화에서는 에어컨을 청소하는 방법과 청소하는 이유가 소개되어 있지만 얼마나 자주 청소하는지는 언급하지 않았다.

08 "If I were you, I would ~"는 상대에게 충고하는 표현 방법이다.

09 주어진 대화의 (A)which는 관계대명사이다. ① 의문사 ② 관계대명사 ③ 의문사 ④ 의문사 ⑤ 의문사

10 쓰지 않는 플러그를 뽑으라고 할 때 Lina가 "Leave it that way."라고 한 것을 보면 Lina는 처음에는 플러그를 뽑을 생각이 없었다는 것을 알 수 있다.

11 주어진 문장은 "당신이 더 조심스럽게 글을 쓸수록, 실수가 더 적어진다."의 의미로 셀 수 있는 명사 mistake는 the fewer를 사용한다.

12 ⑤ 사람의 성격을 나타내는 표현 다음에 부정사의 의미상의 주어는 "of+목적격"이 되어야 한다. ⑤의 "good"은 사람의 성격을 의미하는 것이 아니어서 의미상의 주어를 "for+목적격"으로 나타내어야 한다.

13 "The+비교급+주어+동사, the+비교급+주어+동사"의 구문으로 "~하면 할수록 더 …하다"의 의미이다.

14 "어린이들이 많은 책을 읽는 것"은 "to read a lot of books"라는 부정사 표현에 의미상 주어 "for children"이 더해진 것이다.

15 이 글은 '자원 절약 스티커를 학교에 붙여서 전기와 물의 낭비를 줄이는' 내용의 글이므로, 주제로는 ④번 '자원 절약 스티커를 붙임으로써 학교에서 자원을 절약하기'가 적절하다.

16 '(몇 장의) 자원 절약 스티커'를 가리킨다.

17 (1) 학생들에게 '어떤 전등'이 켜질 것인지 알려줌으로써. (2) 교실을 떠나는 마지막 학생이 전등을 '꺼야' 한다고 알려줌으로써.

18 ⓐ와 ①, ②, ⑤: 명사적 용법, ③, ④: 형용사적 용법

19 겨울에는 창문에 붙인 뽁뽁이가 오직 적은 양의 열만 건물에서 '빠져나가게' 하고 여름에는 열이 건물로 '들어오는 것' 또한 막아주기 때문에 뽁뽁이가 에너지를 절약하는 데에 도움이 된다고 할 수 있다.

20 how it works: 간접의문문의 어순(의문사+주어+동사)으로 쓰는 것이 적절하다.

21 (1) 그것은 열기가 건물 안팎으로 드나드는 것을 막는다. (2) 옥상정원에서 나오는 신선한 공기는 도시 전체를 식히는 것을 도와준다.

22 민우는 학생들이 학교에 더 많은 '옥상정원'을 만드는 것이 필요하다고 했다.

Lesson
3

All You Need Is Love

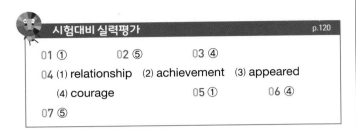

참가자 n. 참가자 (4) research n. 조사

04 주어진 단어는 명사-형용사의 관계이다. meaning 의미, meaningful 의미 있는, excellence 우월함, excellent 탁월한

05 교수님께 추천서를 써 달라고 부탁드렸다. a letter of recommendation = 추천서, recommend 추천하다

06 (1) imagine v. 상상하다 (2) instead ad. 대신에 (3) alive a. 살아 있는 (4) view n. 경관, 전망

07 "참가자가 먼 거리를 달리고, 수영하고, 자전거를 타는 스포츠 대회는 "triathlon 철인 레이스"에 대한 설명이다.

시험대비 실력평가 p.120

01 ① 02 ⑤ 03 ④
04 (1) relationship (2) achievement (3) appeared
(4) courage 05 ① 06 ④
07 ⑤

01 주어진 단어는 유의어 관계이다. blame ~을 탓하다, criticize 비난하다, abroad 해외에, overseas 해외에

02 주어진 단어는 반의어 관계이다. alive 살아 있는, dead 죽은, appear 나타나다, disappear 사라지다

03 "태양이나 다른 별 둘레를 도는 우주에 있는 매우 큰 둥근 물체"는 "planet 행성, 지구"를 나타낸다.

04 (1) relationship n. 관계 (2) achievement n. 성취, 달성 (3) appear v. 나타나다 (4) courage n. 용기

05 길을 잃어버린 소년이 자신의 입장을 설명하자 여자가 길을 알려주는 것으로 보아 빈칸은 도움을 요청하는 "Could you give me a hand?"가 되어야 한다.

06 participate in ~에 참가하다 = take part in

07 ① depressed a. (기분이) 우울한 ② positive. a. 긍정적인 ③ result n. 결과 ④ thanks to ~ 덕분에 ⑤ disability n. (신체적, 정신적) 장애

Conversation

핵심 Check p.122~123

1 ⑤ 2 ④

01 소년이 스마트폰을 분실한 것에 대해서 도움을 제안하는 표현이 적절하다. ⑤는 도움을 요청하는 표현으로 흐름과 어울리지 않는다.

02 빈칸의 말에 대하여 이유를 물었을 때 "I want to see them with my own eyes, not from a book."이라고 대답하는 것으로 보아, 행성을 볼 수 있는 우주 여행을 하고 싶다는 소원을 표현한 것이라고 생각할 수 있다.

교과서 대화문 익히기

Check(√) True or False p.124

1 T 2 F 3 T 4 F

서술형 시험대비 p.121

01 give
02 of
03 (1) factor (2) hardships (3) participants
(4) research
04 excellent
05 recommendation
06 (1) imagine (2) Instead (3) alive (4) view
07 (t)riathlon

01 • 설거지를 도와드리겠습니다. give a hand = 도움을 주다 • 그는 그 계획을 포기하기로 했다. give up = 포기하다

02 • 그녀는 늦게까지 깨 있는 버릇이 있다. be in the habit of ~ = ~하는 습관이 있다 / 그녀는 틀림없이 자신이 아주 자랑스러울 것이다. be proud of = ~을 자랑스러워하다

03 (1) factor n. 요인 (2) hardship n. 어려움, 곤란 (3)

교과서 확인학습 p.126~127

Everday English 1 A-1
Excuse, afraid, Could, give , hand / want, shirt, tell, where / straight, left, next, store / much

Everday English 1 A-2
Excuse, lost / have, give, hand / have, smartphone / Is, smartphone / mine

Everday English 1 B
looking, present / can, hand / son, years, have,

recommendations / about, jacket, popular / fine, colorful / What, green, jacket / pretty, large / one / take

Everday English 1 C

lost, know what / Can, hand / does, look / is, has / wearing / shirt, jeans / see, found

Everday English 2 A-1

space / Why / these amazing, planets, own, from / glad, interested, continue, book

Everday English 2 B

years, hit, while, riding, lost, stayed, for, depressed, find, live, supported, took, with, able, overcome, By, out, meaningful, wheelchair, player, run, in, help, campaign, speech, importance, positive, seem, habit, negative, wish, help, positively

In Real Life

How, give, hand / please, medicine / get, water / get better / hope, way, sorry / mean / sick, looked after, heart, back, say, thanks / okey / want, thank

---

시험대비 기본평가

p.128

01 ④   02 ②   03 ①

01 이어지는 대답에 상점을 찾아가는 길을 알려 주는 것으로 보아 빈칸에는 상점의 위치를 묻는 말이 적절하다.

02 주어진 문장은 아들의 생일을 위한 선물에 대하여 추천을 해달라는 의미이기 때문에 구체적인 상품을 소개하기 전인 (B)가 적절한 위치이다.

03 여자는 아들을 위한 생일 선물을 찾고 있다.

시험대비 실력평가

p.129~130

01 ⑤	02 ②	03 ①	04 ④
05 ②	06 ④	07 ④	08 ②
09 ③	10 ⑤		

01 소원을 나타내는 "I wish I were younger."의 이유가 될 수 있는 ⑤가 적절하다.

02 "~을 알려 주시겠습니까?"는 "Can you tell me ~?", "가장 가까운 상점이 어디에 있는지"는 간접의문문으로 "의문사+주어+동사"의 구조이다.

03 남자가 빈칸 뒤에서 녹색 재킷을 다시 권하는 것으로 보아 빈칸에는 거절하는 내용이 적절하다.

04 "~해 보이다, ~처럼 보이다"에 해당하는 것은 "look+형용사",

"look like+명사"이다. 형용사 fine과 어울리는 것으로 ⓓ는 "looks"가 되어야 한다.

05 대화에 나오는 여자는 아들의 생일을 위한 선물을 찾고 있다고 했으므로 ②는 대화의 내용과 다르다.

06 "~하면 좋겠다."에 해당하는 바람이나 소원을 말하는 표현은 "I wish + 가정법 과거"이다.

07 "I'm so sad that we have to walk down soon."을 보면 산 꼭대기에 선 것이 아니라, 내려가야 한다는 것이 슬프게 만드는 것을 알 수 있다.

08 "~에게 ~을 가져다주다"의 의미를 "get+간접목적어+직접목적어."의 구조로 나타낼 수 있다.

09 "~하고 싶다"에 해당하는 "I wish"는 가정법 과거 표현을 사용하여 "I wish+가정법 과거"가 올바른 표현이다.

10 대화에서 Ryan은 과거에 자신을 돌보아 준 어머니에게 감사표현을 하지 못한 것을 아쉬워하고 있다. 거기에 대하여 어머니가 무슨 말을 할지는 알 수 없다.

서술형 시험대비

p.131

01 I wish I could go to the park and enjoy the picnic.

02 (r)ecommendations

03 ⓔ : them → it

04 Do you have it in a large size?

05 ⓔ : read → reading

06 Let me give you a hand.

07 ⓓ : why don't we ask our friends for help?

01 "~하면 좋겠다."는 "I wish+가정법 과거"이다.

02 (A) 아들의 생일 선물을 사려고 하는데 남자가 재킷을 제안하는 것으로 보아 상대에게 선물에 대한 추천을 요청하는 표현을 했음을 알 수 있다.

03 ⓔ의 인칭대명사 them은 앞에 나온 단수 명사 jacket을 가리키므로 인칭대명사 it이 되어야 한다.

04 상대방에게 묻는 의문문이기 때문에 "Do you have ~?"의 형태가 되어야 한다.

05 ⓔ동사 continue의 목적어는 동명사 또는 to부정사가 되어야 한다. read를 reading으로 고치는 것이 적절하다.

06 "내가 ~하겠다."는 "Let me ~"이고, "도와주다"는 "give a hand"이다.

07 ⓓ는 이유를 물어보는 말이 아니라, 상대방에게는 제안, 권유하는 의미의 표현인 "Why don't you ~?"가 적절하다.

핵심 Check
p.132~133

1 (1) am (2) like (3) on Saturday (4) nor

2 (1) knew (2) were (3) were (4) were

시험대비 기본평가
p.134

01 (1) could (2) as well as (3) not only

02 ④ **03** ③ **04** (1) study (2) playing

01 (1) 콤마 다음 문장이 힌트이다. '나는 (현재) 그럴 수 없다'이므로 현재 사실에 대한 반대이다. 그러므로 'I wish 가정법과거'가 적절하다. (2) 'It 가주어 ~ to 진주어' 구문. 'to wash'와 'to wash'가 상관접속사로 연결되는 문장으로 'as well as'가 적절하다. (3) 'not only A but also B' 구문이다.

02 'not only A but also B = B as well as A' 구문으로 A와 B에 어법상 동일한 것이 나와야 하므로 ④번이 적절하다.

03 보기 문장은 우유를 마시고 싶지만 지금 우유가 없어 못 마시는 것이므로 현재 사실에 대한 부정이므로 'I wish 가정법 과거'가 적절하다.

04 not only A but also B: A 뿐만 아니라 B도 라는 뜻으로 동사는 B에 수를 일치시키며, A와 B에는 어법상 동일한 것이 나와야 한다.

시험대비 실력평가
p.135~137

01 (1) I wish I could swim well.

(2) I wish I could be good at singing.

(3) I wish I could cook well.

(4) I wish I had a sister.

02 ①

03 (1) present (2) present (3) past (4) past

04 ②, ⑤

05 (1) I wish I could go to the park and enjoy the picnic.

(2) I wish I could travel abroad.

(3) I wish I could sing well.

(4) I wish I were tall.

(5) She wished she were[was] a nurse.

06 I wish I were[was] younger.

07 ④ **08** ①

09 (1) Not only you but also she has / She as well as you has

(2) Not the kis but the parents were

(3) Either you or Kim is

(4) Neither my mother nor I am

(5) Both a written test and a practical exam are

10 ④ **11** ② **12** ③, ⑤

13 (1) ⓒ and → but ⓓ can → could

(2) The writer wishes she could spend her time with her grandmother and she could get healthy again.

14 (1) not only, but (2) both, and (3) were[was]

15 ①

16 (1) wish, received 또는 조동사 would[could]

(2) wish, with 또는 run

(3) only 또는 just[merely, simply]

01 I wish 가정법과거 = I wish+주어+과거시제 동사

02 'either A or B'를 묻는 질문이다. 첫 번째 보기는 문장 내 strong과 문법적으로 같은 smart가 적절하다. 두 번째 보기는 or 다음의 주어에 동사의 수가 일치해야 한다.

03 (1), (2)는 'I wish 가정법 과거' 문장으로 현재 사실에 대한 반대를 의미하고 (3), (4)는 'I wished 가정법 과거' 문장으로 과거 사실에 대한 반대를 과거에 희망하는 것이다. (1) 그가 내 충고를 들으면 좋을 텐데. (2) 사람들이 아무 데나 쓰레기를 버리지 않으면 좋을 텐데. (3) 그가 내 충고를 들었다면 좋았을 텐데 (4) 사람들이 아무 데나 쓰레기를 버리지 않으면 좋았을 텐데.

04 ② both A and B가 주어일 때 동사는 항상 복수 취급한다. am → are ⑤ 'B as well as A'에서 동사는 B에 수를 일치시킨다. is → are

05 I wish+주어+과거시제 동사 = I am sorry+주어+주절과 같은 시제의 동사 = It's a pity+주어+주절과 같은 시제의 동사. I wished+주어+과거시제 동사 = I was sorry+주어+과거시제 동사 = It was a pity+주어+주절과 같은 시제의 동사. 'I wish[wished]' 구문에서 were의 경우 구어체에서는 were 대신 was를 쓰기도 한다.

06 현재 사실에 대한 부정. I wish+주어+과거시제 동사

07 I wish+주어+과거시제 동사. can help → could help

08 not only A but also B에서 A와 B는 어법상 같은 것끼리 연결해 줘야 하므로 but women → but from women이 적절하다. ① 그녀는 그녀의 고객들로부터 뿐만 아니라 그녀가 종종 만났던 여자들로부터 정보를 쉽게 얻었다. ② John뿐만 아니라 Donald도 나를 안다. ③ 가르치는 것은, 기계적인 일일 뿐만 아니라 정서적인 일이기도 하다. ④ 선생님뿐만 아니라 학생들도 책 읽기를 원한다.⑤ 그는 스페인어뿐만 아니라 영어도 가르친다.

09 (1) not only A but also B = B as well as A, (2) not A but B, (3) either A or B, (4) neither A nor B 모두 동사의 수는 B에 맞춘다. (5) 'both A and B'는 항상 복수 취급한다.

10 상관접속사 'not only A but also B'에서 A와 B는 문법적으로 같은 것을 연결하므로 not only 뒤에 for being이 나오므로 but also 뒤에도 for teaching이 적절하다.

11 'I wish+주어+과거시제 동사' 구문이므로 am → were 또는 was가 적절하다.

12 그는 전 세계 모든 사람들이 긍정적인 생각의 힘을 알기를 소망한다[소망했다]. 주어+wishes[wished]+주어+가정법 과거형 동사 ~.

13 (1) ⓒ 'not only A but also B'와 ⓓ 'I wish+주어+과거시제 동사'를 묻는 것이다. (2) 글쓴이는 과거에 그랬던 것처럼 할머니와 시간을 보내고 싶다고 하면서 다시 건강해지기를 바라고 있으므로 'I wish+주어+과거시제 동사'를 이용하는 것이 적절하다.

14 (1) not only A but also B: A뿐만 아니라 B도 (2) both A and B: A와 B 둘 다 (3) 'I wish 가정법과거' 문장으로 현재 사실에 대한 반대를 의미한다.

15 ① 너도 비난받아서는 안 되고, 그녀도 비난받아서는 안 된다. / 'neither A nor B'는 B에 수를 일치시킨다.

16 어법에 맞게 영작하면, (1) I wish I received the prize. 또는 I wish I would[could] receive the prize. (2) I wish I ran with you. 또는 I wish I would[could] run with you.이다. (3) This is not only[just] a machine but an artwork.

서술형 시험대비
p.138~139

01 (1) The books as well as all the furniture are for sale.
   (2) The volcano erupted in Japan, not in Korea.
   (3) Neither my father nor my mother is at home.
   (4) I do not like either coffee or tea.
02 (1) not   (2) as well as   (3) not, or
03 (1) ⑤ his → by his   (2) ③ goes → go
   (3) ③ merely → but (also)
04 (1) Throughout history, shoes have been worn not only for protection but also for decoration.
   (2) Not only[just, merely, simply] information but also people may move between societies.
   (3) Economic goods may take the form either of material things or of services.
05 (1) I love dancing as well as singing.
   (2) The teacher asked not only Tom but also Tom's friends to come to the front.
06 (1) to take part in 또는 to participate in
   (2) has
   (3) because you are lazy
   (4) working at the office
   (5) drawing

07 neither by Peter nor by Jane
08 wish I could hang out with my father /
   I can't hang out with my father
09 (1) I wish I could   (2) I wish I had a lot of money.
10 (1) people not merely mentally but also physically
   (2) simply a novel but a literary classic
   (3) not just must be very detailed but must be written

01 (1) not only A but also B = B as well as A (2) not A but B = B, not A (3), (4) either A or B+not = neither A nor B

02 (1) not A but B = B, not A: A가 아니라 B (2) not only A but also B = B as well as A: A뿐만 아니라 B도 (3) neither A nor B = not either A or B: A도 B도 아니다

03 (1) Rachel은 그의 사려깊음 뿐만 아니라 심오한 지식에 감명받았다. 'not only A but also B'에서 어법상 A와 B에 같은 것끼리 연결시켜줘야 하므로 his → by his가 적절하다. (2) 너의 모자와 셔츠 모두 이 청바지와 어울리지 않는다. 'neither A nor B'에서 B에 수를 일치시키므로 goes → go (3) 그녀는 너의 목적을 싫어할 뿐만 아니라 그의 목적도 싫어한다. 'not only[simply, merely, just] A but (also) B: A뿐만 아니라 B도'이므로 merely → but (also)가 적절하다.

04 상관접속사는 어법상 같은 것끼리 연결시켜준다. (1) 역사를 통해서, 신발은 보호를 위해서 뿐만 아니라 장식으로도 착용되어 왔다. (2) 정보뿐만 아니라 사람도 사회 사이를 이동할 수 있다. (3) 경제적 재화는 물질적인 것들이나 서비스의 형태를 취할 수 있다.

05 not only A but also B = B as well as A (1) 나는 노래 부르는 것뿐만 아니라 춤추는 것도 좋아한다. (2) 선생님은 Tom에게 뿐만 아니라 Tom의 친구들에게도 앞으로 나오라고 부탁했다. ask+목적어+to부정사: 목적어에게 to 하라고 부탁하다

06 (1) 올림픽 게임에서 가장 중요한 것은 이기는 것이 아니라 참가하는 것이다. / 'not A but B'에서 A와 B에 문법적으로 같은 것이 나와야 한다. (2) 너뿐만 아니라 그도 거기에 가야만 한다. (3) 너는 무능해서가 아니라 게으르기 때문에 실패할 것이다. / 'not A but B'에서 A와 B에 문법적으로 같은 것이 나와야 한다. (4) 그녀는 사무실에서 일하는 것이나 밖에서 노는 것 둘 중 하나를 즐긴다. / 'either A or B'에서 A와 B는 문법적으로 같은 것끼리 연결된다. (5) 나의 오빠는 걷는 것뿐만 아니라 그리는 것도 즐긴다. / 'not only A but also B'에서 A와 B는 문법적으로 같은 것끼리 연결된다.

07 'neither A nor B'에서 A와 B에 문법적으로 같은 것이 나와야 한다.

08 그림 속의 아들은 소파에서 피곤해 자고 있는 아빠와 나가 놀고 싶어 하는 상황이므로 현재 이룰 수 없는 소망으로 'I wish+주

25

어+과거시제 동사 ~' 구문을 이용한다.

09 (1) A: 이 우유 마시는 게 어때? 신선해. B: 나도 그러고 싶어. 의사가 오늘 나 우유 마시지 말라고 했어. (2) A: 너는 저 옷들을 사길 원하니? B: 응. 그러나 돈이 없어. 내가 돈이 많으면 좋을 텐데.

10 (1) 스트레스는 정신적으로 뿐만 아니라 신체적으로도 사람들에게 영향을 미친다. (2) 그것은 소설일 뿐만 아니라 문학적 고전이다. (3) 그 해결책은 아주 자세해야 할 뿐만 아니라, 컴퓨터가 이해할 수있는 형태로 쓰여져야 한다.

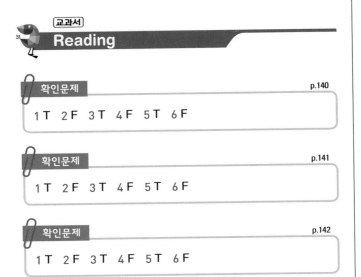

Reading

확인문제 p.140

1 T 2 F 3 T 4 F 5 T 6 F

확인문제 p.141

1 T 2 F 3 T 4 F 5 T 6 F

확인문제 p.142

1 T 2 F 3 T 4 F 5 T 6 F

교과서 확인학습 A p.143~145

01 ALL YOU NEED
02 participated in
03 was held
04 swam, cycled, ran
05 had to push or pull
06 was born with
07 was becoming hard
08 for long
09 is still alive, got first place
11 not only, but also
12 because of
13 felt sad, hide, from
14 with no disabilities
15 blamed herself for
16 smiled at
17 as well as
18 myself, face the world, bright side
19 have begun
20 our first triathlon

21 made way for
22 touched, thankful
23 passed them by
24 cheered for
25 had to endure
26 give you a break
27 I wish I could
28 let you rest
29 ran fast
30 almost, let us go first
31 winner
32 tell, at those races
33 Thanks to
34 all we need
35 had no disabilities
36 Instead
37 other little things
38 face difficulties
39 because, overcome, are together
40 Let's continue
41 stand by you
42 Love

교과서 확인학습 B p.146~148

1 LOVE IS ALL YOU NEED
2 On October 16th, 2010, Eunchong and his dad participated in their first triathlon.
3 It was held in Misari, Hanam.
4 They swam 1.5 km, cycled 40 km, and then ran 10 km.
5 This challenge was especially difficult for Eunchong's dad because he had to push or pull Eunchong during the race.
6 Eunchong couldn't talk or walk because he was born with six different diseases.
7 His skin was dark red and his brain was becoming hard.
8 The doctor said he would not live for long.
9 But Eunchong not only is still alive but also got first place in his first triathlon.
10 Dear Eunchong,
11 I thank you not only for being my son but also for teaching me an important life lesson.
12 When you were a baby, people avoided you

because of your skin color.

13 I felt sad and wanted to hide you from them.

14 Your mom hoped that you would be born with no disabilities.

15 She blamed herself for your sickness.

16 But you always smiled at us and held our hands.

17 You gave us courage as well as hope.

18 So, I promised myself that I would face the world and show you the bright side of things.

19 Since then we have begun our journey.

20 Do you remember our first triathlon?

21 When we began to swim, the other participants made way for us and let us go first.

22 I was very touched and thankful.

23 Some participants even cried when we passed them by.

24 When we started cycling, many people cheered for us.

25 But you had to endure some strong winds and tiredness.

26 So I cycled very fast to give you a break.

27 When we began running, your mom seemed to say, "I wish I could run with you."

28 I wanted to finish the race quickly so I could see her and let you rest.

29 So, I ran fast.

30 When we were almost at the finishing line, the other participants stopped and let us go first.

31 Eunchong, you were the winner!

32 I hope you could tell how much everyone at those races loved you.

33 Thanks to you, your mom and I learned an important lesson.

34 "Love is all we need."

35 We don't ever think, "We wish Eunchong had no disabilities" anymore.

36 Instead, we are just thankful for having you.

37 We are also happy about many other little things.

38 Even when we face difficulties, we are happy.

39 That's because we know that we can overcome any hardships when we are together and love each other.

40 Let's continue to live happily and bravely.

41 We will always love you and stand by you.

42 Love,

43 Dad

01 was held   02 ⑤

03 one point five kilometers   04 ③

05 ②   06 ④   07 ②   08 ④

09 some participants   10 ②

11 (A) made way   (B) go first   (C) go first   12 ③

13 (A) swimming   (B) cycling   (C) running

14 (A) the other participants   (B) letting

15 (A) On   (B) for   (C) alive   16 ④   17 ③

18 ②, ⑤

19 (A) anymore   (B) happily   (C) bravely

20 ④

21 I thank you not only for being my son but also for teaching me an important life lesson.

22 ②, ⑤   23 ⑤   24 ④   25 moved

26 ④   27 ④   28 hardships

29 for → by   30 unhappy → happy

01 be held: 열리다

02 ⑤번 다음 문장의 But에 주목한다. 주어진 문장의 내용과 상반되는 내용을 뒤에 연결하고 있으므로 ⑤번이 적절하다.

03 소수점은 point로 읽고 km는 kilometers로 읽는 것이 적절하다.

04 이 도전은 '은총이 아빠'에게 특히 어려웠다.

05 ⓐ hide A from B: B로부터 A를 숨기다, ⓑ blame A for B: B에 대해 A를 탓하다

06 (A)와 ①, ②, ③, ⑤: 동명사, ③ teach a fish how to swim: 공자 앞에서 문자 쓴다, ④: 현재분사

07 세상을 직면하고 너에게 세상의 밝은 면을 보여주겠다고 자신에게 약속했다고 했으므로, '긍정적인' 성격이라고 하는 것이 적절하다. ① 비관적인, 우울한, ③ 근엄한, 엄숙한, ④ 소심한, ⑤ 부정적인

08 위 글에서 은총이의 피부색은 알 수 없다. ① Eunchong's dad. ② Not only for being his son but also for teaching him an important life lesson. ③ Because of his skin color. ⑤ He always smiled at them and held their hands. He gave them courage as well as hope.

09 '몇몇 참가자들'을 가리킨다.

10 ⓑ와 ②: 휴식 (시간)(명사), ① (법·약속 등을) 어기다, ③ 깨(뜨리)다, 부수다, ④ (식사 등을 위해) 쉬다[휴식하다], ⑤ (~ 사이의) 틈[구멍](명사)

11 은총이 팀의 첫 철인 레이스 동안, 수영을 할 때, 다른 참가자들이 그들이 '먼저 가도록' 길을 만들어 줬다.' 달리기에서 그들이 거의 결승선에 도착했을 때, 다른 참가자들이 멈췄고 그들이 '먼저 가도록' 해줬다. make way for: ~에게 길을 열어 주다, (~

이 지나가도록) 비켜 주다

12 이 글은 '다른 참가자들의 감동적인 배려 덕분에 은총이가 첫 철 인 레이스에서 우승할 수 있게 되었다'는 내용의 글이므로, 주제 로는 ③번 '은총이의 우승 뒤의 감동적인 이야기'가 적절하다.

13 철인 레이스는 수영, 사이클, 달리기의 세 종목을 연이어 겨루는 경기이다.

14 그들이 먼저 '가도록' 길을 양보해 주는 것과 같은 '다른 참가자 들'의 세심한 배려 덕분에 은총이는 첫 철인 레이스에서 우승할 수 있었다. give way to: 양보하다

15 (A) 날짜가 있을 때는 on을 쓰는 것이 적절하다. (B) '오래' 살 지 못할 거라고 해야 하므로 for가 적절하다. for long: 오랫동 안, (C) 명사가 없으므로 alive가 적절하다. alive: 살아 있는 (형용사, 명사 앞에는 안 씀), live: 살아 있는(형용사, 주로 명 사 앞에 씀)

16 participate in = take part in = compete in = enter = partake in: (경기·대회 등에) 참가하다, ④ cooperate: 협력 하다

17 이 글은 '6가지 다른 질병을 갖고 태어난 은총이와 그의 아빠가 그들의 첫 철인 레이스에 참가하여 1등을 한' 것을 소개하는 글 이므로, 제목으로는 ③번 '은총이와 그의 아빠의 첫 철인 레이 스'가 적절하다.

18 thanks to = because of: ~ 덕분에, ~ 때문에 ① ~ 대신에, ③ ~에도 불구하고, ④ ~에 더하여

19 (A) 앞에 부정어 no가 있으므로 anymore가 적절하다. not ~ any more = no more, (B) 동사 live를 수식하므로 부 사 happily가 적절하다. (C) 동사 live를 수식하므로 부사 bravely가 적절하다.

20 이 글은 '은총이네 가족이 서로를 사랑할 때 어떤 어려움도 극복 할 수 있다는 것을 깨닫게 되었다'는 내용의 글이므로, 주제로는 ④번 '가족 간의 사랑으로 어려움을 극복하기'가 적절하다.

21 for를 보충하면 된다.

22 ⓑ와 ①, ③, ④: 계속 용법, ② 경험 용법, ⑤ 완료 용법

23 위 글은 '편지'이다. ① (신문·잡지의) 글, 기사, ② 일기, ③ 전 기, ④ 수필

24 ④번 다음 문장의 So에 주목한다. 주어진 문장 내용의 결과를 설 명하고 있으므로 ④번이 적절하다.

25 touch = move: 마음을 움직이다, 감동시키다

26 은총이의 아빠가 얼마나 빨리 달렸는지는 대답할 수 없다. ① The other participants made way for them and let them go first. ② Because the other participants made way for them and let them go first. ③ He had to endure some strong winds and tiredness. ⑤ The other participants

stopped and let them go first.

27 앞에 나오는 내용과 상반되는 내용이 뒤에 이어지므로 Instead가 가장 적절하다. ①, ⑤: 게다가, ② 게다가, 더욱이

28 hardship: (돈·식품 등의 부족에서 오는) 어려움[곤란], 삶이 어 렵거나 불쾌한 상황들, 종종 충분한 돈을 가지고 있지 않기 때문에

29 '너의 옆을 지킬게'라고 해야 하므로 'stand by'로 고치는 것이 적절하다. stand for: ~을 상징하다, ~을 대표하다, stand by somebody: (어려운 상황에서도) ~의 곁을 지키다[~을 변함없이 지지하다]

30 은총이네 가족은 심지어 어려움에 직면할 때도 '행복하다'고 했다.

01 (A) sad (B) herself (C) myself
02 ⓐ teaching an important life lesson to me
   ⓒ show the bright side of things to you
03 (A) hope, (B) courage
04 their first triathlon
05 Eunchong got first place in his first triathlon as well as is still alive.
06 Because he had to push or pull Eunchong during the race.
07 (A) pushed (B) pulled (C) first
08 I wish
09 rest
10 They ran.
11 of thinking
12 grateful
13 why → because
14 They learned (that) love is all they need.

01 (A) 감각동사 felt의 보어로 형용사를 써야 하므로 sad가 적절 하다. (B) 주어와 목적어가 같으므로 herself가 적절하다. (C) 주어와 목적어가 같으므로 myself가 적절하다.

02 teach와 show는 to를 사용하여 3형식으로 고친다.

03 은총이는 그의 부모님에게 '희망'과 '용기'라는 두 가지 중요한 것을 주었다.

04 '그들의 첫 철인 레이스'를 가리킨다.

05 not only A but also B = B as well as A: A뿐만 아니라 B 도

06 경주 동안 은총이를 밀거나 끌어야 했기 때문이다.

07 은총이의 아빠는 그들의 첫 철인 레이스에서 1.5 km를 수영하 고, 40 km 사이클을 타고, 그런 다음 10 km를 뛰는 동안 은총 이를 '밀거나' '끌었고' '1등'을 했다.

08 I'm sorry는 가정법으로 고칠 때 I wish를 사용하는 것이 적절하다.

09 break = rest: 휴식

10 그들은 사이클링 다음에 '달렸다.'

11 Instead of ~ing: ~하는 대신에

12 thankful = grateful: 고마워하는, 감사하는

13 앞 문장에 대한 이유를 설명하는 문장이므로 because로 고치는 것이 적절하다. 'why+앞에 말한 내용의 결과', 'because+앞에 말한 내용의 이유'

14 그들은 "사랑이 그들이 필요한 전부"라는 것을 배웠다. 교훈의 내용은 현재시제로 쓰는 것이 적절하다.

영역별 핵심문제
p.157~161

| 01 ④ | 02 ① | 03 ⑤ | 04 ⑤ |

05 Let me give you a hand.

06 Standing on the top of this mountain makes me feel good.

07 ⑤	08 ④	09 ①	10 ④
11 ①	12 ②	13 ⑤	14 ①, ⑤
15 ②	16 ③		

17 (1) I as well as you am satisfied with the result.
   (2) My summer vacation plan sounds like both active and dynamic.
   (3) Your decision is fair, not good.　18 ⑤

19 ⑤

20 (1) It's a pity I can't run with you.
   (2) I am sorry I can't vote.
   (3) I am sorry I'm not a teacher.

21 은총이와 그의 아빠가 철인 레이스에 참가하여 1.5 km를 수영하고, 40 km 사이클을 타고, 그런 다음 10 km를 뛰는 것　22 ①　23 ④　24 ②

25 They avoided him.

26 the other participants made way for us and let us go first　27 ⑤

28 Since 2010, you have started the journey with me.　29 ⑤

30 Eunchong's parents' courage (did).

01 철인경기는 자전거 타기, 수영, 달리기로 구성되어 있다. / triathlon 철인경기

02 "삶을 어렵고 불쾌하게 만드는 것"은 "hardship 어려움, 곤란"이다.

03 그녀는 심하게 다쳐서 도움이 필요하다. in need of help = 도움이 필요한 / 나는 나의 연설이 그들이 더 긍정적으로 생각하도록 도움을 주기를 바란다.

04 그 도시에는 식사할 수 있는 훌륭한 데가 많다. excellent =

outstanding(훌륭한, 뛰어난)

05 도움을 제안하는 표현으로 "Let me give you a hand."가 적절하다.

06 "이 산의 정상에 서 있는 것"은 "standing on the top of this mountain"으로 주어가 되는 동명사이다.

07 빈칸에는 도움을 제안하는 표현이 적절하다. ⑤는 도움을 요청하는 표현으로 빈칸에 적절하지 않다.

08 주어진 문장은 사고 싶은 재킷의 사이즈를 묻는 말로, 사이즈에 대한 대답이 나오기 전인 (D)가 적절한 위치이다.

09 빈칸에 들어갈 내용은 종업원이 보여준 옷에 대한 것이므로 "colorful clothes"에 대한 언급이 적절하다.

10 이 대화에서 여자는 아들의 생일 선물을 위하여 옷을 구입하려고 하지만, 그 옷의 가격에 대하여서는 언급한 것이 없다.

11 "Can I give you a hand, Mom?"이라고 한 것으로 보았을 때 두 사람은 모자간이라는 것을 알 수 있다.

12 주어진 대화에서 어머니는 약을 달라고 하는 것으로 보아 몸이 아파 누워 있는 상황에서 빨리 회복되기를 희망하고 있다는 것을 알 수 있다.

13 이 대화에서 몸이 아픈 어머니와 Ryan이 과거에 아팠을 때의 일에 대한 이야기를 나누고 있지만, 나이에 대한 언급은 없다.

14 ② B as well as A: A뿐만 아니라 B도 'as well as'에서 as가 빠져 있다. ③ 주어+wish+(that)+주어+과거시제 동사 has → had ④ not only A but also B: A뿐만 아니라 B도 and → also

15 ② 'not only A but also B' 상관접속사는 A와 B에 어법상 같은 것을 연결해야 한다. not only 뒤에 in China가 있으므로 but also 뒤에도 in Korea가 와야 한다.

16 I wish+주어+과거시제 동사 ~: ~라면 좋을 텐데(현재 사실의 반대로 해석)

17 (1) not only A but also B = B as well as A (2) both A and B = A and B (3) not A but B = B, not A

18 not only A but also B에서 only 대신 merely, just, simply 등이 올 수 있다. / 뇌 정밀검사는 계산하는 동안 단순히 좌뇌에서만 국한된 것이 아니라 뇌의 시각, 청각, 운동 영역에서도 나타난다는 것을 보여준다.

19 'B as well as A'에서 동사의 수는 B에 일치시킨다.

20 I wish+주어+과거시제 동사 = I am sorry (that) I can't ~ / It's a pity (that) I can't ~

21 앞에 나오는 내용들을 가리킨다.

22 win[take, get] first place = finish first = come first: 일등을 하다, ① award: 상을 주다

23 이 글은 '은총이가 그의 부모님께 희망과 용기라는 두 가지 중요한 것을 주었다'는 내용의 글이므로, 주제로는 ④번 '은총이

가 그의 부모님에게 준 두 가지 중요한 것'이 적절하다. ② stare at: ~을 응시하다

24 ⓐ와 ②: (상황에) 직면하다, ① 표면, 겉면(명사), ③ 향하다, ④ 면목(명사), lose one's face: 면목을 잃다, 체면을 잃다, ⑤ (~한) 얼굴[사람](명사)

25 그들은 그를 피했다.

26 사역동사 let+목적어+목적격보어(동사 원형)

27 은총이 아빠가 '네가 그 경기에 있던 모든 사람이 너를 얼마나 사랑했는지 알기를 바란다.'고 했을 뿐이다.

28 '2010년부터 자신과 함께 여정을 시작한 것'을 가리킨다.

29 a great deal of = much

30 '은총이 부모님들의 용기'가 은총이로 하여금 사물의 밝은 면을 보도록 도와주었다.

단원별 예상문제   p.162~165

01 ④	02 ②	03 ②	04 ⑤
05 ③	06 ④		

07 (1) You may find it difficult to both listen to the lecture and to take notes.
(2) We could understand not only his English but also his Korean.
(3) They arrived at the destination not by train but by airplane.
(4) I will either meet my boyfriend or stay home and rest.
(5) Waste neither time nor money.   08 ①

09 ③

10 Not only my students but also I was very shocked to hear the news.   11 ②

12 ④	13 ⑤	14 ③	15 ②

16 Thanks to you, your mom and I learned an important lesson.

17 get over

18 They are (just) thankful for having Eunchong.

19 ②   20 love and care

21 Lily, the younger sister, was so small that she couldn't live.

01 그는 (지금까지) 그 토론의 활발한 참가자였다. 참가자 = participant

02 내 양말 찾는 것 좀 도와줄래? (찾다 = look for) / 우리는 우리 뒤에 오는 사람들을 위해 자리를 내주어야 한다. (자리를 내주다 = make way for)

03 ① wheelchair 휠체어 ② leg 다리 ③ talent 재능 ④ survival 생존 ⑤ road 도로, 길

04 ⓔ 동사 help의 목적격보어는 원형부정사 또는 to부정사이기

때문에 thinking은 (to) think가 되어야 한다.

05 주어진 문장에서 "Thanks to them"은 지지와 보살핌을 준 부모님 덕분이라는 뜻을 나타내기 때문에 주어진 문장은 (C)에 들어가야 한다.

06 이 담화문 속에서 말하는 사람은 교통사고 후에 어려움을 극복한 과정을 소개하고 있다. 사고를 당했을 때 그 차를 운전한 사람에 대한 언급은 없다.

07 모든 상관접속사에서 A와 B에는 문법적으로 같은 것끼리 연결해야 한다. (1) both A and B (2) not only A but also B (3) not A but B (4) either A or B (5) neither A nor B

08 'not A but B'는 B에 동사의 수를 일치시킨다.

09 I wish 가정법과거 = I wish+주어+과거시제 동사(현재 사실에 대한 반대 의미), I wished 가정법과거 = I wished+주어+과거 시제 동사(과거 사실에 대한 반대 의미) ③ can → could

10 'not only A but also B'에서 동사의 수는 B에 일치시킨다.

11 ②번 다음 문장의 She에 주목한다. 주어진 문장의 Your mom 을 받고 있으므로 ②번이 적절하다.

12 ⓐ와 ④: 교훈, ①, ②, ⑤: 수업[교습/교육] (시간), ③ (교과서 중의) 과

13 세상을 직면하겠다고 자신에게 약속한 사람은 '은총이의 아빠'이다.

14 이 글은 '다른 참가자들의 감동적인 배려 덕분에 은총이가 첫 철인 레이스에서 우승할 수 있게 되었다'는 내용의 글이므로, 제목으로는 ③번 '모두 감사드려요! 여러분의 사랑이 우리를 우승으로 이끌어줬어요!'가 적절하다. ① It can't be!: 설마!

15 ⓐ와 ①, ③, ⑤: 부사적 용법, ②: 명사적 용법, ④: 형용사적 용법

16 thanks to: ~ 덕분에

17 overcome = get over: [곤란]을 극복하다

18 그들은 은총이를 가진 것에 그저 감사할 뿐이다.

19 앞에 나오는 내용과 상반되는 내용이 뒤에 이어지므로 However가 가장 적절하다. ① 그러므로, ④ 게다가, ⑤ 즉

20 인간은 '사랑'과 '관심'이 필요하다고 했다.

21 too ~ to ... = so ~ that 주어 can't ...

서술형 실전문제   p.166~167

01 (A) give   (B) pick   (C) why

02 I wish I could drive.

03 call

04 (1) I wish I were[was] tall and strong.
(2) I am sorry (that) I don't have a car.
(3) I wish I could live with my son.

05 (1) Both Chris and Pat were late.
(2) Arriving home, I was both tired and hungry.
(3) Neither Jenny nor Cathy came to the party.

(4) He neither wrote nor phoned.

(5) She's either Spanish or Italian.

06 Your mom hoped that you would be born with no disabilities.

07 hope, courage

08 (A) Eunchong's dad   (B) as well as

(C) bright side

09 made way for 또는 made room for

10 (A) touched   (B) wish   (C) almost

11 In order to give Eunchong a break.

---

01 (A) 도움을 주다 = give a hand (B) ~을 집어들다, 들어올리다 = pick ~ up (C) ~하는 것이 어때? = Why don't you ~?

02 소망을 나타내는 "~하면 좋을 텐데"는 가정법 과거를 사용하여 "I wish I could ~"라고 한다.

03 "Could you please call them for me?"라고 한 것에 대하여 "Sure."라는 대답을 하는 것으로 보아 소녀는 친구들에게 전화를 할 것이다.

04 wish+주어+과거시제 동사 ~: ~라면 좋을 텐데(현재 사실 부정) = I am sorry (that) ~, It's a pity (that) ~. 'I wish' 구문에서 were의 경우 구어체에서는 were 대신 was를 쓰기도 한다.

06 with no disabilities: 장애 없이

07 not only A but also B = B as well as A: A뿐만 아니라 B도

08 이것은 '은총이 아빠'가 은총이에게 보내는 편지이다. 그 안에서 은총이 아빠는 세상을 직면하고 은총이에게 세상의 '밝은 면'을 보여주겠다고 자신에게 약속했다고 덧붙이면서, 은총이가 자신의 아들이어서'뿐만 아니라' 그에게 중요한 인생의 교훈을 가르쳐 주어서 고마워한다.

09 make way for = make room for: ~에게 길을 열어 주다, (~이 지나가도록) 비켜 주다

10 (A) 감정을 나타내는 동사는 수식받는 명사가 감정을 느끼게 되는 경우에 과거분사를 써야 하므로 touched가 적절하다. (B) 실제 일어날 수 없는 것을 바라는 상황이므로 'I wish+가정법 과거'로 쓰는 것이 적절하다. (C) '거의' 결승선에 도착했을 때라고 해야 하므로 almost가 적절하다. almost: 거의, most: 대부분(의)

11 은총이가 쉴 수 있도록 하기 위해서 은총이의 아빠는 아주 빨리 페달을 밟았다.

창의사고력 서술형 문제   p.168

|모범답안|

01 (1) Cheer   (2) rest   (3) dark   (4) especially

(5) Instead   (6) face   (7) touched   (8) bright

02 ((A) wish   (B) could get   (C) not only   (D) wheels

(E) but   (F) make a better world for everyone

03 (A) in Seoul   (B) her hometown   (C) farming

(D) fun   (E) more time

단원별 모의고사   p.169~173

01 participation   **02** ⑤   **03** ②

04 (1) challenge   (2) colorful   (3) courage   (4) excellent

05 ②   **06** ②   **07** ④   **08** ①

09 ①   **10** ②   **11** ③   **12** ②

13 ④

14 (1) I didn't have more money

(2) I don't have more money

(3) he doesn't use the best policy

(4) he didn't use the best policy

15 I wish I spoke English fluently.

16 ③, ③ He enjoyed neither talking with his wife nor listening to his wife.

17 Director Bong Joon-ho won not only the original screenplay award but also the directing award for the movie 'Parasite' at the Oscars.

Director Bong Joon-ho won the directing award as well as the original screenplay award for the movie 'Parasite' at the Oscars.

18 She wishes she were[was] a famous actress.

19 (1) I wish it were[was] the weekend tomorrow.

(2) I wish I were[was] lying on the beach now.

(3) I wish you weren't leaving tomorrow.

20 is not → not only is

21 (A) swimming   (B) running

22 ①, ②, ④, ⑤   **23** people

24 ②, ④   **25** ③   **26** ③   **27** ②

---

01 주어진 단어의 관계는 동사-명사이다. depress 우울하게 하다, depression 우울함, participate 참가하다, participation 참가

02 우리는 여기서 정치적인 운동을 하려고 한다. (run a campaign for ~을 위한 운동을 하다)

03 "사람이 신체의 일부를 제대로 움직이는 것을 어렵게 만드는 신체적 또는 정신적 상태"는 "disability (신체적, 정신적) 장애"에 대한 설명이다. ① 병 ② 장애 ③ 선물 ④ 여행 ⑤ 경관, 장면

04 (1) challenge n. 도전 v. 도전하다 (2) colorful a. 다채로운 (3) courage n. 용기 (4) excellent a. 탁월한

05 산꼭대기에 올라가서 기분 좋게 느낀다고 한 후에 빈칸 뒤에서 다음 주에 또 올 수 있다는 말을 보면 산에서 내려오는 것에 대한 아쉬움을 나타내는 말이 적절하다.

06 "I wish I could live here."는 말하는 사람의 소망을 나타내는 표현이지만 당장의 구체적인 계획을 나타내는 의미는 아니다.

07 교통사고 후에 좌절을 극복하고 삶의 의미를 찾는 상황을 나타내기 때문에 ⓓ는 "meaningful"이 적절하다.

08 자신이 어려움을 극복했던 경험을 소개함으로써 사람들이 긍정

31

적으로 생각하기를 원하는 의미가 되는 것이 자연스럽다.

09 10년 전에 교통사고를 당해서 다리를 잃어버린 경험을 소개하고 있지만 그 당시에 몇 살이었는지는 언급하지 않았다.

10 (가)는 도움을 주겠다고 제안하는 표현으로 "도와드릴까요?"에 해당한다. 도움을 제안하는 표현은 "Can I help you?"이다.

11 주어진 문장은 상품을 소개하고 판매를 권유하는 상점 종업원의 말로 제품을 소개하고 난 뒤 (C)에 들어가는 것이 적절하다.

12 여자는 아들의 생일 선물을 준비하려고 하는데 아들은 15살이라고 했다.

13 'I wish 가정법 과거'의 어순은 'I wish+주어+과거시제 동사'이다.

14 I wish+주어+과거시제 동사 = I am sorry(= It's a pity) (that)+주어+주절과 같은 시제 동사 / I wished+주어+과거시제 동사 = I was sorry(= It was a pity) (that)+주어+주절과 같은 시제 동사

15 I wish+주어+과거시제 동사 = 현재 사실에 대한 반대를 의미하거나 현재 사실을 말하고자 할 때 사용한다.

16 'enjoy neither A nor B'인데 enjoy는 동명사를 목적어로 취하며, 상관접속사 'neither A nor B'로 연결된 문장이므로 listened를 listening으로 고치는 것이 적절하다.

17 not only A but also B = B as well as A

18 그녀가 마치 유명한 여배우인 것처럼 말을 하지만 현실에서는 유명하지 않다는 것이므로 '그녀는 자기가 유명한 여배우이길 바란다'로 생각할 수 있다.

19 세 문장 모두 현재 사실에 대한 반대에 대한 소망을 말하고 있는 문장이므로 'I wish 가정법 과거' 문장을 써야 한다.

20 not A but B: A가 아니라 B, not only A but also B: A뿐만 아니라 B도

21 철인 레이스는 각각의 경쟁자들이 '수영', 자전거 타기, '달리기'의 세 가지 종목에 참가하는 운동경기이다.

22 not only/just/simply/merely A but also B: A뿐만 아니라 B도, ③ nothing but = only

23 '사람들'을 가리킨다.

24 ② to go로 바꿔 쓸 수 없다. ④ giving으로 바꿔 쓸 수 없다.

25 ⓐ와 ③: 마음을 움직이다, 감동시키다, ① (손 등으로) 만지다 [건드리다], ② 관여하다, ④ (먹다, 마시다, 쓰다는 뜻으로) 손을 대다, ⑤ (미소가 얼굴에 잠깐) 스치다

26 주어진 문장의 Instead에 주목한다. ③번 앞 문장의 내용과 상반되는 내용이 뒤에 이어지므로 ③번이 적절하다.

27 은총이의 부모님들은 이제 더는 절대 "은총이가 장애가 없으면 좋겠다."라고 생각하지 않는다.

교과서 파헤치기

1 boring, 지루한   2 alone, 혼자 있는

3 introduce, 소개하다   4 convince, 확신시키다

5 disagree, 반대하다   6 edit, 편집하다

7 concentrate, 집중하다   8 talkative, 말이 많은

9 expert, 전문가   10 strict, 엄격한   11 judge, 판단하다

12 agree, 동의하다   13 interest, 관심

14 cheer, 응원하다, 환호하다   15 career, 직업, 이력

16 advise, 충고하다

---

01 전문가	02 성적	03 조심스럽게
04 반대하다	05 납득시키다, 확신시키다	
06 편집하다	07 어쨌든	08 집중하다
09 표면	10 말이 많은	11 요즘, 책임
12 ~인 것 같다	13 엄격한	14 만족한
15 응원하다	16 무서운	17 혼자 있는
18 내성적인, 수줍어하는		19 관심
20 직업, 이력	21 판단하다	22 지루한
23 두다, 놓다	24 이유	25 축구장
26 충고하다	27 궁금해 하다	28 문화
29 흥미진진한	30 소개하다	31 겉모습
32 같은	33 의미하다	34 계속하다
35 끝나다	36 발표하다	37 검토하다
38 ~하지 않을 수 없다		39 ~할 가치가 있다
40 우연히 마주치다, 우연히 찾아내다		41 ~을 책임지다
42 ~으로 되다	43 ~을 공통으로 가지다	

01 advise	02 carefully	03 strict
04 anyway	05 talkative	06 cover
07 surface	08 disagree	09 edit
10 reason	11 convince	12 same
13 cheer	14 satisfied	15 wonder
16 scary	17 culture	18 interest
19 alone	20 seem	21 concentrate
22 judge	23 look	24 expert
25 grade	26 charge	27 continue
28 mean	29 place	30 boring
31 career	32 shy	33 soccer field
34 lunch break	35 come across	36 used to
37 check out	38 turn into	39 worth -ing
40 have ~ in common		41 after a while
42 cannot help -ing		
43 be in charge of ~		

Everyday English 1 A-2

history, interesting, Don't, agree / afraid, agree with, too hard / Reading, comic books, make, easier / would just, boring

Everyday English 1 A-2

think, the most popular sport, Don't, agree / play soccer during, lunch break / watch, games, too / right

Everyday English 1 B

are, looking at / at, basketball, poster / do you think, best, player / think, the best, Don't, agree / agree, think, best / Why, think so / class won, last year, Don't, remember / because, class, lot, good, players / Anyway, lucky, both of them, this year / class, going to win, this year

Everyday English 2 A-2

satisfied with / What, like about / fun, talkative

Everyday English 2 B

It's / Are, calling from / How, like, life / such a beautiful, miss / happy with / Not so, so different from, so, easy / classmates help / help, really nice / wish, best of luck

In Real Life

who, group members, social studies project / members / satisfied with / Actually, seem, different from, Don't, agree / on, surface, seem different, judge, by, cover / mean by / mean, shouldn't judge, looks, like, get to know / really think, friends with / not, something special, Try to understand

Everyday English 1 A-2

G: I think history is an interesting subject. Don't you agree?

B: I'm afraid I don't agree with you. It's too hard for me.

G: Reading history comic books may make it easier.

B: I think it would just be boring for me.

Everyday English 1 A-2

G: I think soccer is the most popular sport in our class. Don't you agree?

B: I agree. Many students play soccer during the lunch break.

G: And many students watch the soccer games at home, too.

B: You're right.

Everyday English 1 B

G: What are you looking at?

B: I'm looking at the school basketball game poster.

G: Hmm... Who do you think is the best basketball player in our school?

B: I think Jihun is the best. Don't you agree?

G: No, I don't agree. I think Minjae is the best player.

B: Why do you think so?

G: His class won the basketball game last year. Don't you remember?

B: But that was because Minjae's class had a lot of good basketball players.

G: Anyway, we are lucky to have both of them in our class this year.

B: Yes, we are. I think our class is going to win the basketball game this year.

Everyday English 2 A-2

B: Are you satisfied with your new partner?

G: Yes, I am.

B: What do you like about him?

G: He is fun and talkative.

Everyday English 2 B

G: Hello?

B: Hi, Bora! It's me, Minsu!

G: Minsu! Are you calling from France?

B: Yes, I am.

G: How do you like your life in France?

B: France is such a beautiful country, but I miss Korea.

G: Are you happy with your new school?

B: Not so much. Everything is so different from Korea, so it's not easy for me.

G: Do your classmates help you?

B: Some of them do help me. They are really nice.

G: Good for you. I wish you the best of luck.

B: Thanks.

In Real Life

Ryan: Hey Jisu, who are your group members for the social studies project?

Jisu: Hi, Ryan. My group members are Lina, Inho, and Min.

Ryan: Are you satisfied with your group?

Jisu: Actually, I'm not. They seem so different from me. Don't you agree?

Ryan: Well, on the surface they may seem different from you. But don't judge a book by its cover.

Jisu: What do you mean by that?

Ryan: I mean that you shouldn't judge people by their looks. You may like your group members when you get to know them.

Jisu: Do you really think I can be friends with them?

Ryan: Why not? There could be something special about them. Try to understand your group members first.

본문 TEST Step 1   p.09~11

01 How, Met, Best

02 social studies, made, announcement

03 create, in groups

04 Check out, group members

05 calling out, names, each

06 After, while, was called

07 Group 4   08 will be, wondered

09 continued, and

10 couldn't believe, ears

11 didn't know anyone

12 felt like crying, sat

13 have, in common

14 was, drawing, by herself

15 anything, only interest seemed

16 smart, had, nose, book

17 couldn't help thinking

18 convince, should be with

19 Maybe, let me change

20 anything, gently placed, on

21 what, get to like

22 it's worth trying

23 believe, but, walked away

24 easy from, start

25 decide on, topic

26 felt like giving, advice

27 Try to understand, members

28 So, carefully watched

29 came across, amazing facts

30 lot, expert on, culture

31 sounde, bit, because, when
32 a lot, its soccer
33 Vietnamese, used to spend
34 lot, to talk about
35 thought of, perfect topic
36 decided to write
37 had, introduce, culture
38 wrote about, covered, history
39 charge of editing, whole
40 newspaper, a great success
41 received, members became, friends
42 end, with, saying
43 judge, by, cover
44 Read it   45 might turn into

37 had Lina introduce
38 wrote about, covered Vietnamese culture
39 was in charge of editing
40 a great success
41 received an A⁺, became
42 with this saying
43 Don't judge, by its cover
44 Read   45 turn into

01 How, Met, Best
02 social studies, made, announcement
03 will create, in groups
04 Check out, members
05 calling out, in each group
06 After a while, was called   07 Group
08 Who will be, wondered   09 continued
10 couldn't believe
11 didn't know anyone
12 felt like crying, sat with
13 have, in common
14 was always drawing, by herself
15 his only interest seemed to
16 had his nose in a book
17 couldn't help thinking how unlucky
18 to convince, should be with
19 let me change, thought
20 placed, on, shoulder
21 what you want, get to like
22 Don't, it's worth trying
23 believe, walked away
24 from the start 25 couldn't decide on
26 felt like giving, advice
27 Try to understand
28 carefully watched
29 came across, amazing facts
30 so expert on, culture
31 sounded a bit, because   32 a lot
33 Vietnamese, used to spend
34 to talk about, its history   35 thought of
36 decided to write

1 가장 좋은 친구들을 어떻게 만나게 되었나
2 사회 선생님인 최 선생님께서 중요한 발표를 했다.
3 "모둠별로 신문을 만들 겁니다.
4 새 모둠의 구성원을 확인하세요."
5 최 선생님은 각 모둠의 학생들 이름을 부르기 시작했다.
6 잠시 후, 내 이름이 불렸다.
7 "모둠 4, 지수…"
8 "내 모둠의 구성원들은 누굴까?" 나는 궁금했다.
9 최 선생님은 계속 말씀하셨다. "Lina, 인호, 그리고 Min."
10 나는 내 귀를 믿을 수 없었다.
11 나는 그 모둠에 아는 사람이 하나도 없었다.
12 모둠 구성원들과 함께 앉을 때 나는 울고 싶었다.
13 우리는 공통점이 하나도 없었다.
14 Lina는 항상 혼자서 무언가를 그리고 있었다.
15 인호는 아무 말도 하지 않았으며 그의 유일한 관심은 축구 같았다.
16 Min은 영리했지만, 그는 항상 책만 보고 있었다.
17 나는 내가 참으로 불행하다는 생각을 하지 않을 수 없었다.
18 나는 내 친구들과 함께하겠다고 최 선생님을 설득하기로 했다.
19 "어쩌면 내가 모둠을 바꿀 수 있게 허락해 주실지 몰라." 나는 생각했다.
20 하지만 내가 말을 꺼내기도 전에, 선생님은 부드럽게 내 어깨에 손을 얹으셨다.
21 "네가 원하는 것이 뭔지 알아, 지수야." 선생님은 말했다. "하지만 네가 너의 모둠원들을 좋아하게 될 것이라고 확신해.
22 시도할 만한 가치가 있다고 생각하지 않니?"
23 나는 선생님의 말씀을 진짜로 믿진 않았지만, "네."라고 말하고 돌아섰다.
24 프로젝트는 처음부터 쉽지 않았다.
25 우리는 신문의 주제를 결정할 수 없었다.
26 나는 프로젝트를 포기하고 싶었고, 그래서 친구 Ryan에게 조언을 구했다.
27 "먼저 모둠 구성원들을 이해하려고 노력해 봐." 그는 말했다.
28 그래서 나는 모둠의 구성원들을 신중하게 살펴보았다.
29 그리고 그들에 관한 놀라운 사실들을 발견했다.
30 Lina는 일본의 만화책을 많이 읽었고, 그래서 일본 문화에 관해서는 전문가였다.

31 인호의 한국어 발음은 조금 다르게 들렸는데, 그 이유는 어렸을 때 아르헨티나에서 살았기 때문이었다.

32 그는 아르헨티나와 그 나라의 축구에 관해 많은 것을 알고 있었다.

33 Min의 엄마는 베트남 사람이었고, Min은 베트남에서 약간의 시간을 보냈다.

34 그는 많은 역사책을 읽었으며, 베트남과 그 역사에 관해 이야기하는 것을 좋아했다.

35 나는 우리 모둠을 위한 완벽한 주제를 생각해냈다.

36 우리는 세계 문화에 관해 글을 쓰기로 했다.

37 나는 Lina가 일본 문화를 소개하도록 했다.

38 인호는 아르헨티나와 축구에 관해 썼고, Min은 베트남 문화와 역사를 다뤘다.

39 나는 신문 전체를 편집하는 역할을 맡았다.

40 우리의 신문 프로젝트는 대성공이었다.

41 우리는 A⁺를 받았고, 모둠 구성원은 나의 가장 친한 친구가 되었다.

42 나는 이 말로 내 이야기를 끝내려고 한다.

43 책을 표지로 판단하지 마라.

44 그것을 읽어라.

45 그것은 네가 가장 좋아하는 책이 될 수도 있다.

1 How I Met My Best Friends

2 Mrs. Choi, my social studies teacher, made an important announcement.

3 "You will create a newspaper in groups.

4 Check out your new group members."

5 Mrs. Choi started calling out the names of the students in each group.

6 After a while, my name was called.

7 "Group 4, Jisu..."

8 "Who will be in my group?" I wondered.

9 Mrs. Choi continued, "Lina, Inho, and Min."

10 I couldn't believe my ears.

11 I didn't know anyone in that group.

12 I felt like crying when I sat with my group members.

13 We didn't have anything in common.

14 Lina was always drawing something by herself.

15 Inho never said anything, and his only interest seemed to be soccer.

16 Min was smart, but he always had his nose in a book.

17 I couldn't help thinking how unlucky I was.

18 I decided to convince Mrs. Choi that I should be with my friends.

19 "Maybe she would let me change the group," I thought.

20 But before I could say anything, she gently placed her hand on my shoulder.

21 "I know what you want, Jisu," she said, "but I'm sure you will get to like your group members.

22 Don't you think it's worth trying?"

23 I didn't really believe her, but I said, "Okay," and walked away.

24 The project wasn't easy from the start.

25 We couldn't decide on the topic for our newspaper.

26 I felt like giving up on the project, so I asked my friend Ryan for some advice.

27 "Try to understand your group members first," he said.

28 So I carefully watched my group members.

29 And I came across some amazing facts about them.

30 Lina read a lot of Japanese comic books, so she was an expert on Japanese culture.

31 Inho's Korean sounded a bit different, but that was because he lived in Argentina when he was young.

32 He knew a lot about Argentina and its soccer.

33 Min's mom was Vietnamese, and Min used to spend some time in Vietnam.

34 He read a lot of history books and loved to talk about Vietnam and its history.

35 I thought of the perfect topic for our group.

36 We decided to write about world culture.

37 I had Lina introduce Japanese culture.

38 Inho wrote about Argentina and its soccer, and Min covered Vietnamese culture and its history.

39 I was in charge of editing the whole newspaper.

40 Our newspaper project was a great success.

41 We received an A⁺, and my group members became my best friends.

42 I will end my story with this saying.

43 Don't judge a book by its cover.

44 Read it.

45 It might turn into your favorite book.

Reading and Do

1. a bit different, because, lived in

2. a lot, its soccer

3. Vietnamese, used to spend some time

4. a lot of, loved to talk about

1. an expert, because, a lot of Japanese

2. was in charge of writing

3. sound a bit different, when I was young

4. received an A+ on our project

5. have my rose in a histroy book

6. Also, know well about, because, spent, time there

7. covered Vietnamese culture

8. At first, thought, had, in common

9. convince, to let me change

10. edited, whole newspaper

1. Are, satisfied with

2. at the start of this year

3. didn't, anyone, too shy to talk to anyone

4. was always alone

5. everything changed after

6. On, all of, did our best to win

7. not good at, did my best

8. also cheered as, played

9. When, was over, with

10. am very happy with

7. So, I covered Vietnamese culture and its history.

8. Jisu: At first, I thought our group members had nothing in common.

9. But now I'm glad I didn't convince Mrs. Choi to let me change my group.

10. I edited the whole newspaper.

1. Are you satisfied with your school?

2. Well, at the start of this year, I wasn't.

3. I didn't know anyone in my class, and I was too shy to talk to anyone.

4. So I was always alone.

5. But everything changed after sports day.

6. On sports day, all of my class did our best to win the games.

7. I'm not good at sports, but I did my best.

8. I also cheered as my classmates played the games.

9. When the day was over , I was friends with my classmates.

10. Now, I am very happy with my school life.

구석구석지문 TEST Step 2 p.25

1. Inho's Korean sounded a bit different, but that was because he lived in Argentina when he was young.

2. He knew a lot about Argentina and its soccer.

3. Min's mom was Vietnamese, and Min used to spend some time in Vietnam.

4. He read a lot of history books and loved to talk about Vietnam and its history.

1. Lina: I am an expert on Japanese culture because I read a lot of Japanese comic books.

2. I was in charge of writing about Japan.

3. Inho: My Korean may sound a bit different because I lived in Argentina when I was young.

4. I'm so glad our group received an A+ on our project.

5. Min: I always have my rose in a histroy book.

6. Also, I know well about Vietnam because I spent some time there.

13 concentrate, 집중하다   14 information, 정보
15 consider, 고려하다   16 check, 확인하다

단어 TEST Step 1 p.26

01 가로막다, 방해하다	02 충전하다
03 공간, 우주	04 이미, 벌써	05 규칙적으로
06 자원	07 집중하다	08 환경의
09 추가적인	10 벗어나다, 탈출하다
11 식히다	12 혼자 있는	13 필수적인
14 고치다	15 정보	16 지불하다
17 양	18 글자, 성격	19 숲
20 실험	21 식료품	22 불안한
23 절약하다, 아끼다	24 회의, 발표회	25 보통
26 화분	27 가격	28 줄이다
29 독특한	30 사실, 진실	31 낭비
32 옥상	33 고려하다	34 두께
35 혼자서	36 ~하는 편이 낫다	37 털어내다
38 위험에 처하다	39 생각해 내다
40 선택의 여지가 없다	41 ~에 달라붙다
42 ~와 같은	43 ~할 가치가 있다

단어 TEST Step 2 p.27

01 price	02 reduce	03 pay
04 character	05 already	06 forest
07 charge	08 amount	09 conference
10 unique	11 waste	12 rooftop
13 save	14 space	15 alone
16 whole	17 cool	18 grocery
19 heat	20 concentrate	21 consider
22 resource	23 essential	24 nervous
25 spring	26 thickness	27 experiment
28 normally	29 additional	30 escape
31 prevent	32 regularly	33 truth
34 environmental	35 pick up	36 come up with
37 stay up	38 by oneself	39 not ~ at all
40 prevent A from -ing		
41 have no choice		42 stick to ~
43 be in danger		

단어 TEST Step 3 p.28

1 rooftop, 옥상   2 essential, 필수적인   3 leave, 떠나다
4 add, 더하다   5 nervous, 불안한   6 alone, 혼자 있는
7 meal, 식사   8 pay, 지불하다   9 forest, 숲
10 waste, 낭비   11 fix, 고치다   12 resource, 자원

대화문 TEST Step 1 p.29~30

Everday English 1 A-2(1)

look worried, problem / lost, watch, loves, much /
were, tell him, truth / guess, no choice

Everday English 1 A-2(2)

hard, concentrate in class / stay up late / sleep, last
night / If, were, get, fresh, starts

Everday English 1 B

what, holding, looks like, full / went, grocery / Let,
see, buy / bought, because, cheap / already, apples,
such, waste, money / If, were, check, first, go
shopping / right / make, based, information / do

Everday English 2 A-2(1)

getting, kind of message / had, with / how to fix /
beed to download

Everday English 2 B

how, choose, refrigerator, consider, spend, leaves,
think of, larger, too, waste, energy, Try to, right,
consider, how much, look, sticker, uses less

In Real Life

charging, If, were, pull, out / charger, Leave, way /
wasting electricity / a little bit / Actually, add up,
standby, amount, normally use / there are, things,
which, without knowing, daily lives / how, save, ways
/ conference / Maybe, go together

Check Your Progress 1

good at Chinese characters / start to learn / heard,
learning, helpful, too, remember, characters /
understand, character / What, mean / For example,
character, standing / remember, looks

대화문 TEST Step 2 p.31~32

Everday English 1 A-2(1)

B: You look worried. What's the problem?
G: I lost my brother's watch. He loves the watch so
   much.
B: If I were you, I'd tell him the truth.
G: I guess I have no choice.

Everday English 1 A-2(2)

G: Oh, it's too hard for me to concentrate in class.
B: Did you stay up late last night?

G: Yeah, I just couldn't sleep well last night.

B: If I were you, I'd get some fresh air before the next class starts.

W: Jihu, what are you holding? It looks like a bag full of fruit!

B: Yes, I went to a grocery store.

W: Let me see. Why did you buy the apples?

B: I just bought them because they were really cheap.

W: We already have a bag of apples at home! It's such a waste of money!

B: Oh, I didn't know that.

W: If I were you, I'd check what I have first before I go shopping.

B: Yes, you're right.

W: And then I'd make a shopping list based on that information.

B: Okay, I'll do that next time, Mom.

B: I keep getting this kind of message again and again.

G: I had the same problem with my computer.

B: Oh, then, do you know how to fix this?

G: You need to download a program.

M: Do you know how to choose a good refrigerator? First, you should consider the price of a new refrigerator. How much can you spend on your refrigerator? The question leaves a few options for you. Next, you should think of its size. You might think that larger ones are better. But if it's too big, you will waste space and energy. Try to choose the right size for you. The last thing you have to consider is how much energy it uses. When you look at the refrigerator, there is a sticker. Choose a refrigerator with a greener sticker as it uses less energy.

Inho: Lina, you are not charging your phone. If I were you, I'd pull the plug out.

Lina: Why? I'll use the charger later. Leave it that way.

Inho: But you are wasting electricity.

Lina: It's only a little bit.

Inho: Actually, if we add up a year's standby power, it is the same as the amount of electricity we normally use for a month.

Lina: Oh, I didn't know that.

Inho: Yeah, there are a lot of things like that which we waste without knowing in our daily lives.

Lina: Do you know how to save energy in other ways?

Inho: I hear that there's going to be an energy-saving conference at school next week.

Lina: Maybe we should go together!

G: Do you know how to be good at Chinese characters?

B: Oh, did you start to learn them?

G: Yeah, I heard that learning them is really helpful . But it is too hard to remember all the characters.

B: If I were you, I'd try to understand how each character is made first.

G: What do you mean?

B: For example, look at this character. A human is standing next to a tree.

G: Oh, I see. Now I can easily remember what the character looks like.

01 Energy-Saving, Conference

02 Welcome, Energy-Saving Conference

03 is in danger　　04 air, getting dirtier

05 More, are dying

06 because, wasting, lot, energy

07 how, save energy

08 different environmental, share, activities

09 more, share, energy, save　　10 Hello, friends

11 few, empty, with, on

12 not, at all　　13 It, for, to use

14 resource saving stickers, switches

15 turned, so, waste less

16 last, leaves, turn off

17 put, on, mirrors, restrooms　　18 not to waste

19 stickers, put, resources, save　　20 Hi, everyone

21 is used, heat, cool

22 important, reduce, amount, use

23 experiment, wrap, help, save　　24 Look at, chart

25 put, wrap on, didn't

26 turned off, temperature, both

27 later, went down to　　28 it, in

29 lets, little, escape from

30 so, putting bubble, on

31 prevent, from getting into

32 more, put, cooler, become　　33 Hello, friends

34 make, on, rooftop, save

35 Only, few, how, works　　36 just like, wrap

37 prevents, from, in, out
38 rooftop, save, use, cool
39 fresh, rooftop, cool, whole
40 is, for, to make
41 beautiful, become, less energy
42 of, come up with
43 all worth trying, at
44 for, unique, activities

01 Energy-Saving
02 Welcome to, Energy-Saving
03 is in danger   04 getting dirtier every day
05 More and more, are dying
06 because, are wasting
07 how, save energy
08 to share their activities
09 The more ideas, the more energy, save
10 friends   11 A few, with the lights on
12 not, at all   13 for, to use fewer resources
14 resource saving stickers, put, on
15 be turned on, so that, less electricity
16 last, to turn off
17 put some stickers on
18 help, not to waste
19 The more stickers, put up, the more resources
20 everyone   21 is used
22 It, for, to reduce, amount of energy
23 did an experiment, bubble wrap, help to save
24 Look at   25 put, on
26 turned off, temperature, both
27 later, went down to   28 it
29 lets, escape from   30 putting, on
31 prevent, from getting into
32 The more bubble wrap, put on, the cooler
33 friends
34 to make, on the rooftop, to save energy
35 Only a few, how it works
36 It's just like
37 prevents, from, in and out of
38 rooftop gardens, we use to cool
39 helps to cool, whole city
40 is, for, to make
41 The more beautiful, the less energy
42 clever of, to come up with
43 worth trying   44 unique, activities

1 에너지 절약 회의
2 에너지 절약 회의에 오신 것을 환영합니다.
3 지구는 지금 위험에 처해 있습니다.
4 공기는 매일 더러워지고 있습니다.
5 점점 더 많은 동물이 죽어가고 있습니다.
6 이것은 우리가 많은 에너지를 낭비하고 있기 때문입니다.
7 그렇다면 우리는 어떻게 에너지를 절약할 수 있을까요?
8 세 개의 다른 환경 동아리들이 그들의 활동을 공유하기 위해 여기에 있습니다.
9 우리가 더 많은 아이디어를 공유할수록, 우리는 더 많은 에너지를 절약할 수 있습니다!
10 지민: 친구들, 안녕하세요.
11 몇 달 전에, 저는 전등이 켜진 몇 개의 빈 교실을 보고 놀랐습니다.
12 그것은 전혀 옳지 않습니다.
13 모든 학생이 학교에서 더 적은 자원을 사용하는 것이 필수적입니다.
14 그래서 우리는 몇 장의 자원 절약 스티커를 디자인해서 스위치에 붙였습니다.
15 그것들은 어떤 전등이 켜질 것인지 알려 줘서, 우리는 전기를 덜 낭비할 수 있습니다.
16 그것들은 또한 교실을 떠나는 마지막 학생이 전등을 꺼야 한다고 알려 줍니다.
17 우리는 또한 화장실에 있는 거울에도 몇 장의 스티커를 붙였습니다.
18 그것들은 학생들이 물을 낭비하지 않도록 도와줍니다.
19 우리가 더 많은 스티커들을 붙일수록, 학교에서 더 많은 자원을 절약할 수 있습니다.
20 동수: 모두 안녕하세요.
21 많은 에너지가 우리 학교의 난방과 냉방을 위해 사용됩니다.
22 우리가 사용하는 에너지양을 학생들이 줄이는 것이 중요합니다.
23 우리는 지난겨울 실험을 해서 뽁뽁이가 에너지를 절약하는 데에 도움이 된다는 것을 발견했습니다.
24 이 도표를 보세요.
25 우리는 교실 A에는 창문에 뽁뽁이를 붙였고 교실 B에는 붙이지 않았습니다.
26 우리가 히터를 껐을 때, 두 교실 온도는 모두 16℃였습니다.
27 60분 뒤, 교실 B의 온도는 7℃로 내려갔습니다.
28 하지만 교실 A는 9℃였어요!
29 우리는 뽁뽁이가 오직 적은 양의 열만 건물에서 빠져나가게 한다는 것을 알았습니다.
30 그래서 우리는 학교 창문에 뽁뽁이를 붙이기 시작했습니다.
31 이것이 여름에 열이 교실로 들어오는 것 또한 막아 줄 것입니다.
32 우리가 창문에 더 많은 뽁뽁이를 붙일수록, 우리의 여름도 더 시원해질 거예요!
33 민우: 안녕하세요, 친구들.

34 우리는 에너지를 절약하기 위해 학교 옥상에 정원을 만들기로 했습니다.

35 오직 몇몇 사람들만이 그것이 어떻게 작용하는지 알고 있습니다.

36 그것은 마치 뽁뽁이와 같습니다.

37 그것은 열기가 건물 안팎으로 드나드는 것을 막습니다.

38 그래서 건물에 옥상정원을 가지고 있으면, 우리는 여름에 건물을 식히기 위해 사용하는 에너지 일부를 절약 할 수 있습니다.

39 또한, 옥상정원에서 나오는 신선한 공기는 도시 전체를 식히는 것을 도와줍니다.

40 그래서 우리 학생들이 우리 학교에 더 많은 옥상정원을 만드는 것이 필요합니다!

41 우리의 옥상이 더 아름다워질수록, 우리 학교는 에너지를 덜 사용하게 될 겁니다!

42 진행자: 이런 멋진 아이디어를 떠올리다니 여러분은 아주 똑똑하군요!

43 학교나 집에서 모두 해볼 만한 것들입니다.

44 여러분의 고유한 아이디어와 활동에 감사합니다!

본문 TEST Step 4 - Step 5
p.42~47

1 Energy-Saving Conference

2 Welcome to the Energy-Saving Conference.

3 The Earth is in danger.

4 The air is getting dirtier every day.

5 More and more animals are dying.

6 This is because we are wasting a lot of energy.

7 So how can we save energy?

8 Three different environmental clubs are here to share their activities.

9 The more ideas we share, the more energy we can save!

10 Jimin: Hello, friends.

11 A few months ago, I was surprised to see some empty classrooms with the lights on.

12 That's not right at all.

13 It is essential for all students to use fewer resources at school.

14 So we have designed some resource saving stickers and put them on the switches.

15 They tell us which light should be turned on, so that we can waste less electricity.

16 They also tell the last student who leaves the classroom to turn off the lights.

17 We also put some stickers on the mirrors in the restrooms.

18 They help students not to waste water.

19 The more stickers we put up, the more resources we can save at school.

20 Dongsu: Hi, everyone.

21 A lot of energy is used to heat and cool our school.

22 It is important for students to reduce the amount of energy we use.

23 We did an experiment last winter and found that bubble wrap can help to save energy.

24 Look at this chart.

25 In Classroom A we put bubble wrap on the windows and in Classroom B we didn't.

26 When we turned off the heater, the temperature was 16 ℃ in both classrooms.

27 Sixty minutes later, the temperature in Classroom B went down to 7 ℃.

28 But it was 9 ℃ in Classroom A!

29 We learned that bubble wrap only lets a little heat escape from the building.

30 So we started putting bubble wrap on the school windows.

31 This will also prevent heat from getting into the classroom in the summer.

32 The more bubble wrap we put on the windows, the cooler our summer will become!

33 Minwoo: Hello, friends.

34 We decided to make a garden on the rooftop of the school to save energy.

35 Only a few people know how it works.

36 It's just like bubble wrap.

37 It prevents heat from getting in and out of the buildings.

38 So when we have rooftop gardens on our buildings, we can save some of the energy we use to cool the buildings in the summer.

39 Also, the fresh air from the rooftop garden helps to cool the whole city.

40 So it is necessary for us students to make more rooftop gardens at our school!

41 The more beautiful our rooftops become, the less energy our school will use!

42 MC: It's very clever of you to come up with such great ideas!

43 These are all worth trying at school or at home.

44 Thank you for your unique ideas and activities!

Communication Activity

1. how to save water
2. Of course, if, when we brush our teeth, save water
3. How about, how to save oil
4. can save

Before You Read A

1. try to reuse
2. use the stairs, the second floor
3. pull, out when, am not using
4. walk to school, bike to school
5. turn off, when, bright
6. use used paper
7. only when it is necessary
8. try to shorten, taking a shower

After You Read

1. shows how the temperature changed
2. put bubble wrap on the windows
3. When, turn off, the same in both classrooms
4. Sixty minutes later, went down to
5. was higher than that
6. because, lets a little heat escape

3. When the heater was turn off, the temperatures were the same in both classrooms.
4. Sixty minutes later, the temperature in Classroom B went down to 7℃.
5. But the temperature in Classroom A was higher than that in Classroom B. It was 9℃.
6. This is because bubble wrap only lets a little heat escape from the building.

Communication Activity

1. A: Do you know how to save water?
2. B: Of course I do. If we use a cup when we brush our teeth, we can save water.
3. A: That's a great idea. How about oil? Do you know how to save oil?
4. C: We can save oil by ....

Before You Read A

1. I try to reuse glass or plastic bottles.
2. I use the stairs when I go to the second floor.
3. I pull the plug out when I am not using' my computer.
4. I walk to school. (Or I bike to school.)
5. I turn off the light when it is bright.
6. I use used paper when I study.
7. I open the door of the refrigerator only when it is necessary.
8. I try to shorten the time for taking a shower.

After You Read

1. This chart shows how the temperature changed in Classroom A and in Classroom B.
2. In Classroom A the students put bubble wrap on the windows and in Classroom B they didn't.

9 planet, 행성, 지구　10 overcome, 극복하다

11 triathlon, 철인 레이스　12 scenery, 경치

13 present, 선물　14 research 조사

15 endure, 참다, 견디다

16 disability, (신체적, 정신적) 장애

단어 TEST Step 1　　　p.50

01 도전; 도전하다	02 추천	03 경치
04 ~을 탓하다	05 조사	06 100년, 세기
07 경관, 전망	08 결과	09 관계
10 철인 레이스	11 다채로운, 화려한	12 우울함
13 피부	14 응원하다	15 생존
16 질병	17 참다, 견디다	18 용기
19 직면하다	20 (신체적, 정신적) 장애	
21 어려움, 곤란	22 용감하게	23 편안하게
24 밝은, 발랄한	25 성취, 달성	26 지지하다
27 (기분이) 우울한	28 자전거를 타다	29 피곤함
30 여행, 여정	31 감동한	32 극복하다
33 참가자	34 선물	
35 ~을 자랑스러워하다		36 ~ 덕분에
37 B 뿐만 아니라 A도		38 도움을 주다
39 ~을 돌보다	40 진심으로	
41 통과하다, 연락이 닿다		42 ~에 참가하다
43 A 뿐만 아니라 B도		

단어 TEST Step 2　　　p.51

01 present	02 abroad	03 thankful
04 recommendation		05 colorful
06 depressed	07 century	08 achievement
09 cheer	10 tiredness	11 research
12 support	13 cycle	14 disability
15 relationship	16 meaningful	17 disease
18 survival	19 factor	20 bravely
21 endure	22 result	23 scenery
24 bright	25 skin	26 excellent
27 journey	28 hardship	29 overcome
30 participant	31 courage	32 triathlon
33 since	34 face	35 give up
36 look after / take care of		37 by the way
38 be proud of	39 thanks to	40 get through
41 participate in	42 stand by	43 A as well as B

단어 TEST Step 3　　　p.52

1 cycle, 자전거를 타다　2 abroad, 해외에, 해외로

3 alive, 살아 있는　4 century, 100년, 세기

5 participant, 참가자　6 hardship, 어려움, 곤란

7 disease, 질병　8 colorful, 다채로운, 화려한

대화문 TEST Step 1　　　p.53~54

Everday English 1 A-1

Excuse, afraid, Could, give, hand / want, shirt, tell, where the nearest shop is / Go straight, turn left, next to, store / much

Everday English 1 A-2

Excuse, lost / have, lost, give, hand / have lost, smartphone / Is, smartphone yours / mine

Everday English 1 B

looking for, present / can, give you, hand / son, years, have, recommendations / about, colorful jacket, popular / fine, colorful clothes / What, green, jacket / pretty, large / one / take it

Everday English 1 C

lost, know what to do / Can, hand / does, look like / is, has brown hair / is, wearing / white shirt, blue jeans / see, found

Everday English 2 A-1

wish, could, space / Why / these amazing, planets, with, own eyes, from / glad, interested in, continue reading, book

Everday English 2 B

years, hit, while, riding, lost, stayed, for, depressed, find, live, supported, took, with, able, overcome, By, out, meaningful, wheelchair, player, run, in, help, campaign, speech, importance, positive, seem, habit, negative, wish, help, think more positively

In Real Life

How, feel, give, hand / please, medicine / course, get, water / wish, could get better / hope, too, way, sorry / mean / sick, looked after, heart, back, even say, thanks / okay / want, thank, for

대화문 TEST Step 2　　　p.55~56

Everday English 1 A-1

B: Excuse me. I'm afraid I'm lost. Could you give me a hand?

W: Sure.

43

B: I want to buy a shirt. Can you tell me where the nearest shop is?

W: Sure. Go straight and turn left. The shop is next to the fruit store.

B: Thank you very much.

Everday English 1 A-2

B: Excuse me, I have lost something.

W: What have you lost? Let me give you a hand.

B: Thank you. I have lost my smartphone.

W: Is this black smartphone yours?

B: No, mine is red.

Everday English 1 B

W: Excuse me, I'm looking for a birthday present for my son.

M: Oh, can I give you a hand?

W: Yes, please. My son is 15 years old. Do you have any recommendations?

M: What about this colorful jacket? It is very popular.

W: It looks fine, but my son doesn't like colorful clothes.

M: What about this green colored jacket?

W: It is very pretty. Do you have it in a large size?

M: Yes, there is a large one here!

W: Thank you. I'll take it.

Everday English 1 C

A: I have lost my brother. I don't know what to do.

B: Can I give you a hand?

A: Yes, please.

B: What does your brother look like?

A: He is short and has brown hair.

B: What is he wearing?

A: He is wearing a white shirt and blue jeans.

B: Oh, I see. I have found him.

Everday English 2 A-1

G: I wish I could visit space.

M: Why?

G: Look at these amazing pictures of planets. I want to see them with my own eyes, not from a book.

M: I'm glad you are interested in space. Let's continue reading this book.

Everday English 2 B

M: About 10 years ago, I was hit by a car while I was riding a bicycle at night. I lost my left leg and stayed in the hospital for six months. I was depressed and couldn't find a reason to live. However, my parents supported me and took care of me with their love. Thanks to them, I was able to overcome the situation. By doing so, I found out that life can be meaningful to everybody. Now, I'm a wheelchair basketball player and every year I run a campaign for people in need of help. During each campaign, I give a speech about the importance of positive thinking. Some people seem to be in the habit of negative thinking. I wish my speech would help them think more positively.

In Real Life

Ryan: How do you feel? Can I give you a hand, Mom?

Mom: Yes. Can you please get me some medicine?

Ryan: Of course. I will also get you some water to drink.

Mom: Thank you. I wish I could get better faster.

Ryan: I hope you can, too. By the way, I'm sorry Mom.

Mom: What do you mean?

Ryan: When I was sick, you looked after me with all of your heart. But back then I didn't even say a word of thanks.

Mom: Oh, it's okay.

Ryan: I really want to thank you for your love.

---

01 ALL YOU NEED

02 On, participated in, triathlon   03 was held in

04 swam, cycled, ran

05 challenge, difficult, had, push

06 because, born with, diseases

07 skin, brain, becoming hard

08 said, would, for long

09 still alive, got, place

10 Dear Eunchong

11 only, being, also, lesson

12 avoided, because of, skin

13 felt sad, hide, from

14 born with no disabilities

15 blamed herself for, sickness

16 smiled at, held

17 courage, well, hope

18 myself, face, bright side

19 Since, have begun, journey

20 our first triathlon

21 other, made way, let

22 was, touched, thankful

23 cried, passed them by

24 When, cycling, cheered for

25 had to endure, tiredness

26 cycled, give, break

27 running, seemed, wish, could

28 finish, so, let, rest   29 ran fast

30 almost, finishing, participants, let

31 were the winner

32 tell, at those races

33 Thanks to, learned, lesson

34 all we need

35 had no disabilities, anymore

36 Instead, thankful for having

37 many other little things

38 Even, face difficulties

39 because, overcome, hardships, together

40 Let's continue, bravely

41 stand by you

36 Instead, thankful for having

37 other little things

38 Even when, face difficulties

39 because, overcome, are together, each other

40 Let's continue, happily, bravely

41 stand by you 42 Love

본문 TEST Step 2   p.60~62

01 ALL YOU NEED

02 On, participated in, first triathlon

03 was held in   04 swam, cycled, ran

05 had to push or pull, during the race

06 was born with six different diseases

07 was becoming hard

08 said, would, for long

09 is still alive, got first place   10 Dear

11 not only, being, but also, teaching, lesson

12 avoided, because of your skin color

13 felt sad, hide, from

14 be born with no disabilities

15 blamed herself for, sickness

16 smiled at, held   17 as well as

18 myself, face the world, bright side

19 Since, have begun

20 our first triathlon

21 made way for, let, go

22 touched, thankful

23 even cried, passed them by

24 cycling, cheered for

25 had to endure, winds, tiredness

26 give you a break

27 seemed to, I wish I could, with

28 so, let you rest   29 ran fast

30 almost, finishing line, let us go first

31 winner   32 tell how much, at those races

33 Thanks to, learned, lesson   34 all we need

35 had no disabilities, anymore

본문 TEST Step 3   p.63~65

1 당신에게 필요한 건 사랑이 전부다

2 2010년 10월 16일, 은총이와 그의 아빠는 그들의 첫 철인 레이스에 참가했다.

3 그것은 하남의 미사리에서 열렸다.

4 그들은 1.5 km를 수영하고, 40 km 사이클을 타고, 그런 다음 10 km를 뛰었다.

5 이 도전은 은총이 아빠에게 특히 어려웠는데 경주 동안 은총이를 밀거나 끌어야 했기 때문이다.

6 은총이는 6가지 다른 질병을 갖고 태어나서 말할 수도 걸을 수도 없었다.

7 그의 피부는 어두운 붉은색이었고 그의 두뇌는 점점 굳어가고 있었다.

8 의사는 은총이가 오래 살지 못할 거라고 했다.

9 하지만 은총이는 여전히 살아있을 뿐만 아니라 그의 첫 철인 레이스에서 1등을 했다.

10 은총이에게.

11 나는 네가 내 아들이어서뿐만 아니라 나에게 중요한 인생의 교훈을 가르쳐 주어서 고맙구나.

12 네가 아기였을 때, 사람들이 너의 피부색 때문에 너를 피했단다.

13 나는 슬펐고 너를 그들로부터 숨기고 싶었어.

14 네 엄마는 네가 장애 없이 태어나기를 바랐지.

15 네 엄마는 너의 병이 자신 때문이라고 자책도 했어.

16 하지만 너는 우리를 향해 항상 웃어주었고, 우리의 손을 잡아주었어.

17 너는 우리에게 희망뿐만 아니라 용기도 주었지.

18 그래서 나는 세상을 직면하고 너에게 세상의 밝은 면을 보여주겠다고 나 자신에게 약속했어.

19 그때부터 우리는 우리의 여정을 시작했지.

20 우리의 첫 철인 레이스를 기억하니?

21 우리가 수영을 시작했을 때, 다른 참가자들이 우리가 먼저 가도록 길을 만들어 줬어.

22 나는 정말 감동하였고 감사했단다.

23 몇몇 참가자들은 심지어 우리가 지나갈 때 울기도 했어.

24 우리가 사이클링을 시작했을 때, 많은 사람이 우리를 응원했지.

25 하지만 너는 강한 바람과 피곤함을 견뎌야만 했어.

26 그래서 나는 네가 쉴 수 있도록 아주 빨리 페달을 밟았어.

27 우리가 달리기 시작했을 때, 너의 엄마가 "당신과 함께 달릴 수 있으면 참 좋겠다." 라고 말하는 듯했어.

28 빨리 경주를 끝내서 너의 엄마를 보고 네가 쉬도록 하고 싶었어..

29 그래서 나는 빨리 달렸단다.

30 우리가 거의 결승선에 도착했을 때, 다른 참가자들이 멈췄고 우리가 먼저 가도록 해줬어.

31 은총아, 네가 우승자였단다!

32 아빠는 네가 그 경기에 있던 모든 사람이 너를 얼마나 사랑했는지 알았기를 바란다.

33 네 덕분에, 너의 엄마와 나는 중요한 교훈을 배웠단다.

34 "사랑이 우리가 필요한 전부다."

35 우리는 이제 더는 절대 "은총이가 장애가 없으면 좋겠다."라고 생각하지 않아.

36 대신에 우리는 너를 가진 것에 그저 감사할 뿐이야.

37 우리는 또한 많은 다른 작은 것들에 대해서도 행복해.

38 심지어 우리가 어려움에 직면할 때도, 우리는 행복하단다.

39 왜냐하면, 우리는 우리가 함께이고 서로를 사랑할 때 어떤 어려움도 극복할 수 있다는 것을 알기 때문이지.

40 우리 계속해서 행복하고 용감하게 살아가자.

41 우리는 항상 너를 사랑하고 너의 옆을 지킬게.

42 사랑하는

43 아빠가.

---

1 LOVE IS ALL YOU NEED

2 On October 16th, 2010, Eunchong and his dad participated in their first triathlon.

3 It was held in Misari, Hanam.

4 They swam 1.5 km, cycled 40 km, and then ran 10 km.

5 This challenge was especially difficult for Eunchong's dad because he had to push or pull Eunchong during the race.

6 Eunchong couldn't talk or walk because he was born with six different diseases.

7 His skin was dark red and his brain was becoming hard.

8 The doctor said he would not live for long.

9 But Eunchong not only is still alive but also got first place in his first triathlon.

10 Dear Eunchong,

11 I thank you not only for being my son but also for teaching me an important life lesson.

12 When you were a baby, people avoided you because of your skin color.

13 I felt sad and wanted to hide you from them.

14 Your mom hoped that you would be born with no disabilities.

15 She blamed herself for your sickness.

16 But you always smiled at us and held our hands.

17 You gave us courage as well as hope.

18 So, I promised myself that I would face the world and show you the bright side of things.

19 Since then we have begun our journey.

20 Do you remember our first triathlon?

21 When we began to swim, the other participants made way for us and let us go first.

22 I was very touched and thankful.

23 Some participants even cried when we passed them by.

24 When we started cycling, many people cheered for us.

25 But you had to endure some strong winds and tiredness.

26 So I cycled very fast to give you a break.

27 When we began running, your mom seemed to say, "I wish I could run with you."

28 I wanted to finish the race quickly so I could see her and let you rest.

29 So, I ran fast.

30 When we were almost at the finishing line, the other participants stopped and let us go first.

31 Eunchong, you were the winner!

32 I hope you could tell how much everyone at those races loved you.

33 Thanks to you, your mom and I learned an important lesson.

34 "Love is all we need."

35 We don't ever think, "We wish Eunchong had no disabilities" anymore.

36 Instead, we are just thankful for having you.

37 We are also happy about many other little things.

38 Even when we face difficulties, we are happy.

39 That's because we know that we can overcome any hardships when we are together and love each other.

40 Let's continue to live happily and bravely.

41 We will always love you and stand by you.

42 Love,

43 Dad

Communication Activity

1. want to introduce
2. a singer from America
3. Although, couldn't see, became a talented singer
4. are very popular, has received, music prizes
5. wish, could find, become, like him

After You Read B

1. Dear
2. Since, have started, with me
3. thank you
4. participated in, had to endure, difficulties
5. never gave up on
6. helped, see, bright side of things
7. am proud of
8. for being, most wonderful parents
9. so much

Think and Write

1. lives in the southern part of
2. is a farmer
3. went to, showed me around the farm
4. not only, but also, like the most important person
5. is in the hospital
6. wish, could, with, as we did in the past
7. that she gets healthy

8. Thank you for being the most wonderful parents.
9. I love you so much!

Think and Write

1. My grandmother lives in the southern part of Korea.
2. She is a farmer.
3. When I went to her house, she showed me around the farm and told me everything about farming.
4. She not only welcomed me but also treated me like the most important person in the whole world.
5. Now, she is in the hospital.
6. I wish I could spend time with her as we did in the past.
7. I hope that she gets healthy again.

Communication Activity

1. We want to introduce Stevie Wonder.
2. He is a singer from America.
3. Although he couldn't see, his hearing was excellent and he became a talented singer.
4. His songs are very popular and he has received many music prizes.
5. We wish we could find our talent and become a great person like him.

After You Read B

1. Dear Mom and Dad,
2. Since 2010, you have started the journey with me.
3. I thank you for that.
4. When we participated in our first triathlon, we had to endure a lot of difficulties.
5. But you never gave up on me.
6. Your courage helped me see the bright side of things.
7. I am proud of you.

MEMO

적중 100

영어 기출 문제집

정답 및 해설

금성 | 최인철